The Rise and Fall
of Western Colonialism

The Rise and Fall of

*A Historical Survey from the Early
Nineteenth Century to the Present*

Western Colonialism

Stewart C. Easton

FREDERICK A. PRAEGER, *Publisher*
New York · London

FREDERICK A. PRAEGER, PUBLISHER
64 UNIVERSITY PLACE, NEW YORK 3, N.Y., U.S.A.
77–79 CHARLOTTE STREET, LONDON W. 1, ENGLAND

Published in the United States of America in 1964
by Frederick A. Praeger, Inc., Publisher

© 1964 by Frederick A. Praeger, Inc.
Library of Congress Catalog Card Number: 64:15289

Printed in the United States of America

Introduction

By the time of publication of this book (early 1964), it will be almost seven years since the first of the new sub-Saharan African nation-states achieved independence. It was in that year of 1957 that the writer made a tour that took him to almost every remaining colony of any size still in the possession of a European power. Ghana had just gained independence, and the Federation of Malaya expected independence during the course of the year. In some colonies, such as Tanganyika and the Belgian Congo, independence seemed still at least a generation away. The French colonies were still struggling with the reforms granted under the *loi-cadre* of 1956, and French Africans were experiencing their first taste of real power. Kenya was still under emergency regulations, and Jomo Kenyatta was serving his sentence in prison for complicity with the Mau Mau. It is barely credible that now in all Africa only the Portuguese "overseas provinces" remain without at least the promise of early independence, and that the new African nations alone already outnumber the Latin American republics and thus command many more votes in the United Nations.

This extraordinary change—it can only be called "revolutionary" —has caught us almost unawares, and it is still unusual if a college offers a course in either history or government that makes an attempt to explain the colonial antecedents of these new nations. Nineteenth-century imperialism, which brought so many Asian and African territories into the possession of the Western powers, has customarily been treated in a single chapter in the leading European history textbooks, and perhaps another chapter has been devoted to the winning of independence in the postwar period. Occasionally, elective courses on imperialism have been offered, using one of the three or four textbooks in the field, which themselves were usually confined to the British Empire. When the present writer attempted for the first time, in 1959, to give a course treating both the rise and fall of colonialism, he was compelled to use a number of different books and a synthesis of his own covering the most recent period (*The Twilight of European*

Colonialism, still the only book in its field that covers all the remaining colonies of all the European powers).

The present book is the result of the writer's continued efforts to present the whole picture within a manageable compass—not only the postwar developments, but the period of expansion during which the colonies were acquired. Obviously, this is not a book for the specialist. The limitations of space have precluded much explanation, and critical analysis has been kept to a minimum. Little attention is paid to ideology, and the post-independence history of the new nations, important and symptomatic though it is, has been altogether omitted except in the single case of the former Belgian Congo. Economic, social, and cultural factors have had to be excluded, for the most part, in favor of the simple political facts—what happened and when, how and in what circumstances the country was first taken, the impact of the two World Wars on the independence movements, and the rapid progress made since 1945. The book must therefore remain basically an extended outline, to be filled in by teachers, students, and the general reader. To assist them in the task, the bibliography suggests more specialized works which can serve for amplification in whatever area proves to be of interest. The writer hopes that this synthesis and the bibliography will aid those colleges which may wish to include a course in colonialism in their undergraduate curriculum to do so, and that the riches and interest of this new field will in this way be brought to the attention of faculties throughout the country.

For the field itself—whatever the shortcomings of this book— is of enormous interest and of incalculable importance for the understanding of the new world in which we live. The postwar retreat from colonialism and the appearance of the new nations at the United Nations raises many profound questions. What should be the respective roles of the greater and lesser powers in the world of the future? What is the significance of moral protest in a world dominated militarily by two superpowers, and by a few others who are fitted either by their large populations or an advanced technology to challenge their leadership? When a group of small nations unite to cast their votes against a policy pursued by a great power in the United Nations, how effective can their protest be, since it is not backed by comparable armaments? When the chips are down, do the great powers really care how these small nations vote? Did the United States consult Gabon —or give any thought to her—when President Kennedy late in

1962 confronted the Soviet Union over Cuba? Did the signatures of many lesser states to the limited test-ban treaty of 1963 persuade France to append her own?

Leaving aside the international role of these new nations, can one really consider them as nations at all in the sense in which France and Britain are nations? What holds them together? Nationalism, an ideology and emotion, unconsciously acquired by the older nations of Europe, Asia, and America over the course of centuries—of which most of them have been fully conscious only since the age of Napoleon? We glibly call the leaders who brought their countries to independence nationalists, and speak of "nationalist" movements in the colonies. Dr. Hastings Banda of Nyasaland (or Malawi, as he prefers to call it) is one of the most gifted of African nationalists. He is busily engaged in trying to create a Malawi nationalism in Nyasaland, an area carved out of Central Africa by the British after agreement with local tribal chiefs and the Germans and Portuguese, whose interests as neighboring colonial powers conflicted with theirs. Nigeria, the most populous country in Africa, made up of numerous tribes of which three are paramount, is now an uneasy federation, divided by religion, tribal affinities, degree of education, and numerous other factors. Its boundaries were agreed upon by the British and French in the late nineteenth century. Is Nigeria now or can it become a true nation? Even Pan-Africanism, an emotion based in part on a racial stock common to much of the continent, must necessarily have difficulty in accommodating itself to union with an Islamic north, inhabited by a different racial stock from that of sub-Saharan Africa. All that can be said with conviction is that the present "national" entities and boundaries in Africa are unlikely to endure for long, though most of the new nations are now manageable in size and extent, and can be governed with some effectiveness by their present ruling parties.

How useful are the institutions bequeathed to these new nations by their colonial masters? Can the democratic forms and the party system through which these forms have been made to work in the Western nations that developed them survive? Is the ancient African system of government by chiefs and elders relevant to modern democracy? Few African nations have retained the multiparty system with which most of them entered their independence. Opposition is by this time tolerated only in a few, and even in these few it may soon disappear. The governing party will perpetuate itself and rule as it wishes until a revolution or rebellion overthrows it; or perhaps the army will replace it in those countries in which a sizable army exists. Such a revolution has already overthrown in the last months the single-party government of the former French Congo. In the East, ruled by autocracies before the colonial powers took them over, few civilian governments have survived, and few parliaments.

What, in short, did the colonial powers give to the countries they ruled that is likely to prove permanent? They educated a minority in the Western manner, and they founded institutions that could carry on where they left off if the inhabitants of the country so desired. They brought the economies of the colonies within the framework of the world-wide economy dominated by Westerners, even though the colonies were almost exclusively suppliers of raw materials whose prices were and are controlled by Westerners. They introduced the use of money, and gave at least to the educated minority some Western material values. They partly broke down the traditional social structure of some of the colonies.

It is still too early to say how deep this penetration was in the century or less during which most of the colonies were ruled by Westerners. It may be that only the continuing efforts of Westerners to help the former colonies will enable them to survive as nations and to continue the process of Westernization which we, if not always they, consider so desirable. It seems certain that the process has been little more than begun, and that Africa at least could still fall into chaos—a chaos from which the Congo is only with great difficulty being rescued by the devoted efforts of both Westerners and non-Congolese Africans. Beside the gigantic problem of the so-called undeveloped and underdeveloped nations, the Cold War itself recedes into something of the nature of a parochial quarrel, which could sooner or later relapse into a long period of uneasy coexistence which might last for decades (if the armed powers did not release their armaments and put an end to us all).

With the perspective of history, it may be that the retreat from colonialism of the last twenty years will be seen as one of the most fundamental of changes that has ever taken place, for it certainly presents a great challenge to the leaders of mankind. The rulers have granted self-government to those whom they could have continued to subject by force for many more decades, and long before the process they had begun was brought to fulfillment. Will these ex-colonies continue the process on their own by borrowing freely from their former rulers, and will the latter be willing to lend their knowledge and their techniques and whatever else may be needed? These are the great questions, the answers to which may not be known for at least another century, and they are the questions that can and should be raised in any college or university courses intended to deal with this great new phenomenon.

Within our traditional college curriculum, it is difficult to place the particular course for which this book is designed. The present writer has taught such a course, with somewhat different orientation, in both government and history departments. Because it includes all colonies, and not only those in Africa, it cannot be taught by the Far Eastern, Middle Eastern, or African specialists if they confine themselves to their own specialties. The course the writer has in mind is one that introduces undergraduates to the subject of colonialism. The student can then choose some colony or group of colonies on which he may want to acquire a fuller knowledge through his own reading. If he later undertakes graduate work in this field, then he can specialize in the area of his choice. Thus the course can serve as a feeder course leading to area studies, as well as a general course to acquaint the student with the dimensions of the problem.

This was the major purpose in the mind of the writer when he prepared this synthesis, and it is in the hope that it will be used in this manner that he now presents it to our academic institutions and the public.

Granada Hills, Calif.   —S. C. E.
December, 1963

Contents

Part II. The Impetus of Two World Wars

Part III. The Prolonged Struggles for Independence

MAPS

I

THE ACQUISITION
OF COLONIES

1. Rise of the New Imperialism in the Nineteenth Century

Dynamism of Western Civilization

Among all the civilizations known to history, none has been more dynamic than our own, which we call, for want of a better name, Western. Even in its infancy, it prematurely expanded into the Near East at the expense of its religious enemies, the Muslims. After the collapse of the Crusades, the Westerners for a time devoted themselves to their homelands. Then, at the end of the fifteenth century, they began to expand again, this time to the south and west. The Portuguese, having won their own country from the Muslims and still filled with the crusading spirit, conceived the notion of taking the Muslims from the rear, incidentally opening up the Eastern trade with India, hitherto monopolized by their enemies. In this enterprise they were immensely successful, although the cost of maintaining their empire proved to be too great for a small nation. The Spaniards, likewise a crusading people, hired the Genoese Christopher Columbus to sail westward. Columbus was more interested in reaching Jerusalem by this route than in discovering new lands for his masters. But he did discover several of the West Indian islands and the mainland of North America, whereupon Pope Alexander VI, himself a Spaniard, acting in his position as arbiter of Christendom, marked out a boundary line, running from north to south, to divide the newly discovered territories. All that lay west of the line was to be Spanish, all that was east of it Portuguese (Treaty of Tordesillas, 1494). Thereafter, both Spaniards and Portuguese hastened to take effective possession of all they could capture of the immense territories allotted them.

This settlement naturally displeased the latecomers, who had not been in on the division of the spoils. But they were slow to muster their resources, and Spain proved too strong to be dislodged from most of her gains. The English and French, in due course, occupied the territories to the north of the Spanish pos-

3

sessions in America, constantly quarreling among themselves as well as with the Spaniards. At the end of the sixteenth century, the Dutch, who had themselves recently achieved their own independence from the Spaniards, attacked the Portuguese possessions in the Far East. These were poorly defended by the Spanish monarchs, who had inherited the Portuguese Crown and possessions in 1580. The Dutch were thus able to take the lion's share of the former Portuguese empire. The British and French followed the Dutch to the East, the British ultimately winning India, the greatest prize of all. In the eighteenth century, again in competition with the French and the Dutch, the British, whose navy was by now the most powerful in the world, were able to take possession of the last two great undiscovered lands in the Pacific, Australia and New Zealand. The other European powers appropriated most of the remaining smaller islands. Thus, by the end of the eighteenth century, the Westerners had already spread themselves, albeit thinly, over the greater part of the globe.

The major concern of this book is the last century of the colonial system. Some of the colonies acquired by Europeans during earlier centuries became independent during the first half of the nineteenth century—for example, the great bulk of the Spanish possessions in America—and therefore are not discussed here. Canada, Australia, and New Zealand—peopled largely by emigrants from the mother country—achieved their independence without fighting, as soon as the British felt that they could govern themselves. These, too, are not covered in this book, which is confined to those colonies that remained under European control until the present century and have only recently achieved their independence.

European Possessions in the Nineteenth Century

The Americas

The British and French, when they abandoned their North American colonies, retained the West Indian islands. France kept Guadeloupe and Martinique, which were useful to her as sugar producers. Even today they are legally a part of France, having expressed their willingness to retain that status by referendum as recently as 1958. Britain won Jamaica from Spain in 1670 and Trinidad in 1814. Several of the smaller islands were ceded permanently to Britain by France after the Napoleonic Wars. As early as 1815, therefore, the British possessed the majority of the West Indian islands. Spain retained Cuba and Puerto Rico until the end of the nineteenth century. The two colonies on the island of Hispaniola, Haiti and San Domingo, achieved a precarious independence in the nineteenth century. Haiti had formerly been French, and San Domingo Spanish. The Dutch retained a few islands, which now have autonomy under the Dutch Crown. The Danes sold their last possession, the Virgin Islands, to the United States in 1917. The sole territories remaining to European powers on the mainland of South America were the three Guianas, divided among the British, French, and Dutch.

The Far East

During the period that Portugal was under the Spanish Crown (1580–1640), most of her possessions in the East were wrested from her, mainly by the Dutch. In India, she kept the small colony of Goa on the west coast, originally acquired in 1510 (which, together with a few enclaves within Indian territory, was forcibly taken from her by the Republic of India in 1961). The British never considered it worth while to round out their possessions at the cost of a quarrel with the Portuguese, who were their allies in Europe. Macao, on the Chinese mainland, and two offshore islands are retained by Portugal to this day, with the acquiescence of the Chinese, who could take them at any time. These, and half of the island of Timor in the Indonesian archipelago, are the only remaining Portuguese possessions in the Far East.

The Dutch possessions in the Far East were disputed by the British in the Napoleonic Wars. Malacca was captured and held by the British, and Batavia, the Dutch capital of Java, was likewise occupied. In 1824, the British agreed to return Batavia to the Dutch in exchange for recognition by the Dutch of British control of Malacca. Thereafter, the Dutch consolidated their rule of the whole of Indonesia (except for Portuguese Timor) and made it into what was certainly the most profitable empire in the world.

The British were latecomers in the competition for empire in the East, but they had a great advantage in the fact that they were a more populous nation than either Portugal or the Netherlands. Indeed, their major competitors in the eighteenth century, when they first undertook to establish an Asiatic empire, were the French. The conquest of India was not the work of the British as a people or a nation, but was, initially, a private venture of the British East India Company, only intermittently backed by the British Government. The same was partly true of the Dutch East Indies, where the Dutch East India Company for a long time undertook most of the duties of government. Although the French were well established in India before the arrival in force of the British, they received far less support from their own government and eventually had to give way altogether, retaining only a few trading posts until the twentieth century.

The conquest of India by small expeditionary forces, privately recruited and paid by the British East India Company, was the result of an astonishing combination of favorable circumstances. The Mogul empire, ruled from Delhi, had fallen into decay, and the Great Mogul himself was unable to exercise his authority over the outlying provinces of his nominal empire. Moreover, in southern India, the Moguls did not exercise even a nominal rule, since no Mogul had ever been able to conquer this part of the country. The country was parceled out to many Indian potentates who either owed allegiance to the Mogul or were totally independent. Few of them were effective rulers, and interventions by the Company were frequent and, from its point of view, necessary. The total conquest of India was never planned. The British East India Company hired and trained Indian mercenaries, who were always more than a match for the larger Indian native armies they were called upon to meet in battle.

In 1784, the British Government assumed responsibility for general British policy in India and thereafter appointed the governors-general, who were virtually absolute during their period of office, although they were paid by the Company. The policy adopted toward India varied with the government in power at home. Sometimes the governors-general were given strict instructions not to intervene in quarrels between the various Indian rulers, at other times they were told to establish law and order and effective government by whatever means were at hand. In the end, the logic of their position became clear, at least to the man on the spot if not always to the British at home. By the middle of the nineteenth century, the vast subcontinent had been completely subdued. Most of the territory and all the real power and responsibility rested in British hands, even though Indian native rulers in some parts of the country were permitted nominal independence as long as they furthered British policy and made no attempt to interfere with the paramount power.

Ceylon was taken from the Dutch by the British during the Napoleonic Wars, but further expansion to the east, with the addition of Burma and Malaya to the Empire, was postponed to the latter part of the nineteenth century.

Africa

Among the European nations at the beginning of the nineteenth century, only Portugal could lay claim to the possession of a real empire in Africa. The Portuguese had controlled the African slave trade for centuries. When they sold this monopoly to the British, they retained two extensive though ill-defined colonies, Angola in the southwest and Mozambique in the southeast. These colonies had not yet been fully explored, and Portuguese control was largely nominal. In addition to these, Portugal possessed a West African colony known as Portuguese Guinea and a few islands off the coast.

By the beginning of the nineteenth century, Britain had shown little interest in Africa. For more than a century, private merchants under a royal charter had interested themselves in the slave trade and maintained a number of forts to protect their interests—as had other European nations, including the French, Dutch, and Danes. But none showed much initiative in penetrating into the interior. All the companies formed for the purpose of trading in African products other than slaves proved to be financial failures. The first permanent British colony in Africa was the Cape Colony, taken from the Dutch in the Napoleonic Wars. This was an old settlement at the southern tip of Africa, peopled mostly by descendants of French Huguenots and Dutch Calvinists who farmed the land in a patriarchal manner with the aid of slaves. As yet, there were few Bantu Negroes, and the country was populated largely by white men, since most of the Hottentots and the Bushmen, the original inhabitants, had been driven into the interior by the European immigrants.

Attitude of the European Powers

Although since its inception Western civilization has constantly expanded outside the boundaries of Europe, neither peoples nor governments were deeply involved in the empires they won until the late nineteenth century. Private individuals and corporations were responsible for most of the conquests. Governments tended to back them only sporadically; and when they seemed likely to prove unprofitable, they were not loath to abandon them. They wished to limit their commitments and, if possible, their losses. The French might well have won India if they had persevered: France, more populous than England, with a navy frequently as large and efficient as that of her rival and with superior economic resources, seemed destined to empire. But she did not persevere, and when the fortunes of war ran in her favor, she preferred to make European rather than colonial gains from her treaties. Her proconsuls had to make do with less than their British rivals, and they were only too often abandoned by their superiors at home.

Britain, equally doubtful as to the value of her empire, nevertheless increased it after the Napoleonic Wars. In 1815, she restored a few of the territories she had won, but kept most of her recent conquests without any noticeable reluctance. She thus had a head start in the scramble for colonies that marked the last quarter of the nineteenth century, and she never lost her lead in the race. However, it was not until the end of the century that her quest became truly purposeful and she began to invent reasons for continuing the expansion.

This marked the beginning of "imperialism," a disease that affected all the nations of Western civilization and turned what had been a desultory and piecemeal acquisition of colonies into a self-conscious, emotionally motivated demand to be allowed to shoulder what came to be known as the "white man's burden."

The New Imperialism

The characterization of imperialism as a disease is peculiar to the mid-twentieth century and would undoubtedly be accepted today by the vast majority of the world's peoples. Even modern imperialistic nations like the Soviet Union recognize this fact and are careful to define "imperialism" in such a way that their own actions—imperialistic when viewed objectively—can be explained away or even made to appear anti-imperialistic.

Although anti-imperialistic sentiment in the early nineteenth century was common in England—the one country that still possessed an important overseas empire—it took a very different form from modern anti-imperialism and anticolonialism. A number of politically unaffiliated thinkers in England who called themselves Radicals urged, in Parliament and elsewhere, that colonies were both unprofitable to the mother country and oppressive to the natives. These men frequently quoted the opinions of Edmund Burke, the eighteenth-century anticolonialist who, in criticizing the governing of India by the British East India Company, had expressed the opinion that colonies should be held as a trust administered in the interests of the native inhabitants. The balance of trade at the time was actually favorable to Britain; but this fact, even if it had been known, was of little interest to the Radicals, who were more concerned with morality than with economics. Well aware of the fact that the Indian governmental system was paid for from taxes levied in India and that its expenses did not fall upon the British taxpayers, they denounced the system as an extremely heavy burden on the poverty-stricken Indians. And they had little sympathy for the merchants and stockholders of the British East India Company, who alone profited from the Indian trade. When the so-called Opium Wars broke out in China, as the result of the insistence of the merchants on selling the forbidden drug to the Chinese, they were naturally unsparing in their denunciations.

Colonies other than India were much more obviously unprofitable. After the emancipation of the Negro slaves in 1833, the economy of the West Indian islands, which had been based on slave labor, declined rapidly. The plantation owners had to be compensated, if minimally. For decades, disturbances were endemic in the islands; these had to be suppressed, and law and order maintained by British arms. Such enterprises were costly to the British taxpayer and paid him nothing in return.

Against the weight of Radical criticism of the Empire, there was very little pro-imperialist and procolonial sentiment. Not even in the Colonial Office, which administered the colonies, was there much enthusiasm for them. The colonial secretary in the cabinet, constantly under attack from Radicals and the missionary interests in Parliament, could rarely command much support from his fellow cabinet members, who lacked interest in the colonies. The position of colonial secretary was regarded as the graveyard of reputations. The permanent undersecretary in the Colonial Office, who bore the brunt from day to day of colonial business, was the real maker of colonial policy; but not all who held the position during the early nineteenth century had a vital interest in the welfare of the colonists, and several of them were frequently at odds with administrators in the colonies themselves.

The Englishmen who had the greatest personal interest in the colonies were the missionaries. It was they who had agitated the

most for the abolition of the slave trade and the subsequent
emancipation of the slaves. What they desired was the opportunity
to convert the heathen to Christianity. They regarded their converts and potential converts as their own particular charges, whom
they should endeavor to protect from exploitation—and incidentally
protect also from rival missionaries of other branches of Christianity. Naturally, there was little love lost between the missionaries
and the traders. The missionaries did not as a rule desire more
colonies. They could proselytize even in countries under native
rulers, provided they could win their support. But sometimes they
fell foul of these rulers and were killed; then their home government considered that, as a matter of prestige, they should be
avenged. Sometimes missionaries from one country would be
discriminated against in colonies belonging to another. Then their
home government might find it necessary to intervene to protect
them. At all events, pretexts were not lacking for intervention;
and several colonies passed under European rule as an indirect
result of the work of missionaries, who were themselves opposed to
the intervention.

In the first half of the nineteenth century, there was, therefore,
no substantial body of opinion either in Britain or elsewhere that
favored the growth and multiplication of colonies. The Radicals
and free traders were consistently anticolonial, regarding colonies
as a financial liability and totally unnecessary for any legitimate
national interest. Liberals and Conservatives paid little attention
to the colonies, except in the case of those they considered of
strategic importance. But the colonies were there; they had been
acquired by their ancestors and must therefore be administered.
If they could govern themselves, then self-government was a
legitimate aim to be pursued as a matter of policy; if they could
not, then the burden of administration must be accepted, and at
as low a cost to the mother country as possible. There was certainly no reason why their number should be increased.

Effect of the Industrial Revolution

The anticolonialist position began to be eroded seriously in
the latter part of the century, as all European nations were increasingly affected by the Industrial Revolution. The growth of
manufacturing capacity made it desirable for manufacturers and
merchants to find ever more export markets for their products.
It was not possible to sell manufactured products to undeveloped

countries, some of them only recently discovered by the West. It was no accident that China became the primary target for European penetration during the century. Elsewhere, Europeans had to lend money to the foreigners before they could buy. China was highly developed, and she could afford to buy European products. The difficulty in China was the attitude of the Chinese Government, which took the position that all Western goods were inferior and there was no reason why she should trade with Europe. This opposition had to be overcome by force and threats in the early nineteenth century.

There was plenty of money available to be lent to the undeveloped countries. The major problem was how it could ever be repaid at a respectable rate of interest. A few tropical products could be bought, and sold profitably in Europe, as had been done for centuries. But to ensure a large and regular supply of such products, railroads would have to be built and European ideas of organization injected into primitive economies. The Europeans soon found it impossible to do these things without taking over a country and administering it themselves. Then the natives could be compelled by one device or another to work for their new masters, a regular supply of raw material for export could be assured, and sufficient profits could be made to pay interest on the capital invested in improved communications and in the government.

Strategic Motives

Thus, economic motives lay behind the recrudescence of imperialism in the latter part of the century. However, once the process had been set in motion, other considerations became important, and imperialism began to take on a life of its own. Trade routes had to be protected against competitive European nations, and fueling centers had to be provided for shipping. This required the building of fortified posts under European control, and the land for such posts had to be taken from foreigners, by either purchase or military action. When areas close to Europe were involved, the European powers were brought into direct contact with one another, and competition between them became severe, sometimes bringing the various nations close to war as each sought a strategically valuable position for itself. Most important of all, the European nations began gradually to feel that not only their wealth and power but even their national prestige depended on the possession of colonies. Thus an irrational motive entered into what had previously been a simple pursuit of wealth and power; and it was this emotional involvement, on the part not so much of the merchants and statesmen as of the people whom they ruled, that was the most potent factor in the competitive imperialism of the last quarter of the century.

National Prestige

It became no longer enough to possess lands of economic and strategic value. It was important to the national pride of a people for them to possess colonies, whether or not they could pay for their upkeep. It was equally important that no possessions ever be ceded to another power, since this would involve loss of national prestige. Such a loss was felt by the people themselves, spurred on by the popular press, as an unendurable insult to their self-esteem. Thus, late in the race for the partition of Africa, France picked up huge quantities of almost valueless real estate, such as the Sahara Desert, which were not greatly desired by others. Germany under Bismarck for a long time looked upon the pursuit of colonies as a distraction from her real national aim, power and prestige in Europe. Nevertheless, such was the scramble for colonies that even a Bismarck had to give way to public pressure. When Wilhelm II became Kaiser in 1888, he took up the quest with enthusiasm and demanded stridently that Germany be given a "place in the sun." So Germany was permitted to win a few of the less desirable African lands before the continent was entirely divided among her competitors. Italy, the last and least powerful of the European imperialists, had to content herself with a few deserts, which loomed large on the map of Africa but were always heavy liabilities to a poor country with few resources to spare. It was honestly felt by some European statesmen that their countries, as Jules Ferry of France expressed it, would "fall to the rank of second-class powers" if they did not own colonies. Few weighed rationally the question of whether or not the colonies really added anything to national power or wealth, or even contributed to the favorable balance of trade they sought.

Contrast with the Mid-Twentieth Century

Almost all these colonies have now been lost by the European nations that conquered them. To the surprise of many die-hards, it has been discovered that these nations, stripped of their colonies, can survive comfortably without them. This has proved true even of the Netherlands. The Republic of Indonesia not only won its independence from the Dutch but expropriated enormous Dutch investments in the country. Nevertheless, the Dutch economy, aided by the Common Market, has continued to progress.

The possession of colonies is no longer regarded as conducive to national prestige. On the contrary, the colonial powers that gave up their colonies gracefully have probably gained in prestige, whereas the powers that persist in fighting to keep them have been pilloried by world public opinion, especially as expressed in the United Nations. Although Portugal, for example, has as yet lost none of her African colonies, she has few open admirers.

The rise and fall of the colonial system is primarily a phenomenon of the last 100 years. Although it is still too early to view it in perspective, and there are still a few colonies remaining that have not yet been granted their independence, colonialism can now be regarded as an almost completed process. It is the purpose of this book to describe its rise and fall, from the middle of the nineteenth century to the present time: the conquest of colonies by the European powers; the period between the wars, when change was slow and the future of the colonies was still undecided; and the achievement of or progress toward independence of each of the colonies. (Events since the winning of independence are not covered, except in the case of the Congo, where the special circumstances justify a more extended treatment.)

2. *Expansion into the East*

Patterns of Economic Penetration

Although nineteenth-century imperialism was seldom systematic, it is possible to discern certain well-defined patterns of economic penetration. The initial interest of the Europeans was in trade. Most of the Far Eastern countries had goods available for export which could be profitably sold in the West. But this could be done only with the cooperation of Oriental governments capable of maintaining law and order in their countries and willing to allow imports from Western countries to pay for the goods exported.

In the eighteenth century, when the Europeans were opening up their trade, India was in a state of internal disintegration. The British East India Company had no wish to govern the country, but it was gradually drawn into domestic politics and eventually took over the functions ordinarily exercised by the native governments. The British Government could not allow a private company to exercise such responsibilities indefinitely. For a period, it was content to supervise the activities of the Company, which paid for all the expenses of government. After the Sepoy Mutiny, it assumed all the Company's responsibilities and administered the entire country.

In the nineteenth century, the Europeans were hampered in China and Burma by the hostile attitude of the native rulers who would not permit them to trade freely. This led to successive wars in both countries and the gradual undermining of the authority of the local governments. Eventually, the British annexed Burma and converted it into a colony. China was divided into spheres of influence by the various European powers and lost some territory, as well as all its vassal states which owed nominal allegiance to the Chinese Emperor. Hong Kong and Kowloon were ceded to the British during the course of the nineteenth century, and some adjoining lands known as the New Territories were leased to the British for a hundred-year period dating from 1898. But China herself never became a colony, and therefore no detailed consideration of imperialism in China will be undertaken in this book.

Other Far Eastern countries less developed than China and India were conquered by European arms and diplomacy, and were at once subjected to economic exploitation. In the Netherlands East Indies, the main problem faced by the Dutch was how to make the Indonesian people provide them with tropical products for export. In the 1830's, they established the so-called culture (or cultivation) system, under which a fifth of the native land-holdings had to be worked for their benefit. The resulting produce was then collected and exported. Although the system netted tremendous profits for the Dutch Government, it was in many respects inefficient, and prevented the investment of private capital in other enterprises and the growth of efficient European-managed plantations. Beginning in 1877, the system was modified—though by no means completely abolished—by another system which has been widely used by all colonial powers in countries where the natives have been expected to provide agricultural products for export: A poll tax was laid on the Indonesians which could be paid only out of the proceeds of their labor. On land that was not in native hands, the Dutch established plantations, notably rubber, worked by native and imported Chinese labor under European direction and ownership and with European capital. The British did the same in Malaya.

Both the Dutch and the British, with the aid of native and imported labor, exploited the mineral resources of their colonies. All the colonial powers introduced Western techniques into the agricultural system of their colonies. Burma, for example, became one of the world's largest exporters of rice. The export trade was controlled by the colonial powers, in some areas in cooperation with Chinese businessmen. Capital for the vast infrastructure of internal communications necessary to sustain their trade was also supplied by the Europeans.

Few colonies were regarded as good markets for European products, since the natives lacked purchasing power. The great exception was India, which had for centuries exported hand-made textiles. This native textile industry was gradually ruined by the conquerors for the benefit of Lancashire mills, which with their machines could produce immense quantities of cheap cotton goods at prices Indian manufacturers could not meet, but which Indian consumers could afford to pay. For several decades, the British enjoyed a huge market in India, and minor markets in the other colonies. With this exception, resident Europeans imported goods for their own consumption, and heavy industry exported its products to build up the transportation system, paid for by British investors.

None of the Far Eastern countries were regarded as colonies intended for permanent settlement by Europeans. Although there were great numbers of British in India and Dutch in the Netherlands East Indies, almost all were employees of the great companies or of the government and did not look upon the colonies as their permanent homes. They sent their children to be educated in their homelands, and they themselves took periodic leaves abroad. They lived and worked in the colonies because they could enjoy a far better standard of living than at home, and because they made money. In this respect, the Far Eastern colonies differed from such colonies of settlement as Southern Rhodesia, South Africa, and Algeria, which the Europeans regarded as their permanent homes, where they bought land and organized educational institutions for their exclusive use. They bear no resemblance at all to the great British colonies of Canada, Australia, and New Zealand, where the immigrants were in an overwhelming majority and were soon granted complete self-government.

The British Empire in the East

India

By the middle of the nineteenth century, all India south of the Himalayas, except a few outposts of solely commercial importance retained by the French and Portuguese, had come under British rule. Many native princes, both Muslim and Hindu, still exercised authority in their territories; but this authority, as the rulers well knew, always depended on subservience to the British in general policy. There had been several encroachments on these princedoms in mid-century, especially while Lord Dalhousie was Governor-General (1848–56): Dalhousie insisted that, if a prince died without direct heirs, his lands should escheat, as under the feudal system, to the British, even if the prince possessed an adopted son to whom he wished to bequeath his princedom. This doctrine of "lapse" was contested by the affected princes, but they were powerless to prevent its enforcement. Worst of all from their point of view, Dalhousie assumed the right to discipline and depose princes who did not live up to their responsibilities as the British saw them. When Dalhousie annexed the large princedom of Oudh, many of the princes were deeply offended. But the British were too powerful to be withstood.

THE SEPOY MUTINY. The mercenary army that provided the military support for British rule was overwhelmingly Indian; a few British officers commanded the native Hindu and Muslim troops, whom they called sepoys. The army had many grievances against the British, and there was bad feeling between the Hindu and Muslim contingents. But it was a simple mistake made by some Englishman at home that brought on the 1857 mutiny that was to change history. Cartridges sheathed in grease from cows and pigs suddenly arrived in India for the use of the army. The Muslims, who regard the pig as unclean, and the Hindus, to whom the cow is sacred, were equally affronted and believed that the cartridges were intended to be an insult. By no means all the sepoys were involved in the riots that broke out, but for many months British rule in India was gravely endangered. Both sides committed numerous atrocities. Loyal sepoys and the recently conquered Sikhs (neither Hindu nor Muslim) aided the heavily reinforced British to suppress the mutiny; but India was never the same again, nor was there ever any renewal of the unself-conscious camaraderie and fraternization between Indians and British that had been present to some extent before.

After the mutiny, the proportion of British in the Indian Army was far greater than before. The Indian Civil Service, the real ruling power of India, was filled exclusively by competitive examinations administered to graduates of the best English public schools. And the British themselves became the highest caste in a country already caste-ridden, and were accepted as such by Indians. A gulf was established and maintained between the British and Indians, to a large degree by the wills of both.

MODERNIZATION OF INDIA. In 1858, the last remnants of the rule of the British East India Company were swept away, and the British assumed full responsibility for the government and administration throughout what was called British India. Slowly India settled down again, and some reforms were made. A more conciliatory policy was adopted toward the native princes who had remained conspicuously loyal to the British during the mutiny. The doctrine of lapse was no longer enforced, and even Oudh, in due course, was restored to a new native prince. The Great Mogul in Delhi had been forcibly brought out of his retirement for a brief period by some of the mutineers, and restored to his ancient throne. Now the office was completely suppressed and the Mogul sent into exile.

The country was on the whole well administered. There was a tremendous fever of railway and road building, and the population increased beyond the capacity of the land to feed it. The newly built railways were used to lessen the effect of the not infrequent famines, which the British could not prevent. However, very little capital was invested in the improvement of Indian agriculture, except in those sectors where the raw materials for industry and export were produced. Although the Indian middle classes did indeed invest their money in the land, this investment increased the misery of the peasants since it consisted of moneylending, at high rates of interest, on the security of the peasants' crops. As consumer credit, it added nothing to the productive capacity of the agricultural economy.

PLIGHT OF THE EDUCATED CLASSES. The budget of the government of India had to take account of the expenses of the army and the expatriate civil service, which consumed about five-sixths of the entire money available, and there was little left for education and social services, which were consequently neglected. The native teachers were badly paid, and they were seldom efficient, since teaching was not a profession highly regarded by the Indian middle class. Yet high-caste Hindus had always appreciated and valued education and would make a considerable sacrifice to obtain it. This class was able to make its way under the British occupation—at the cost, as a rule, of collaborating with the conquerors. There was no difficulty in obtaining higher education in England, provided the Indian had the money to finance it; and numerous Indians, especially Hindus, took advantage of the opportunity. But when they returned to India, they found all the higher positions in the civil service of their country closed to them. They could fill the lower ranks, but there was a limit beyond which they could not go. What they could do, however, was to practice a profession on their own account. Since the British set up their own system of courts—a system totally incomprehensible to the ordinary Indian who came before them for trial—there was ample opportunity for the lawyer skilled in the niceties of English law. Until the British were compelled to institute censorship, over the opposition of many English liberals in Parliament, there was also opportunity in the field of journalism,—especially anti-British journalism, for which there was a steady demand on the part of the literate Indian public. Nevertheless, there was considerable underemployment among the literate classes; and it is in no way surprising that educated men should have begun to agitate for self-government, or at least increasing responsibility, and for the opening of the higher ranks of the civil service to Indians. This the British were unwilling to concede. By such devices as lowering the maximum age for the civil-service examination and insisting that it be administered only in Britain, they made it almost impossible for an Indian to take the examination, even after formal discrimination against Indians had been abolished.

ADMINISTRATIVE SYSTEM. In the second half of the nineteenth century, the government of India was virtually an autocracy. Beginning in 1877, the government was headed by a viceroy, the personal representative of Queen Victoria, Empress of India. He was assisted by an Executive Council of his own choosing, and later by a Legislative Council, which was made up primarily of officials who were bound to obey the Viceroy and support government policy. There were also unofficial members in the legislature, nominated by the Viceroy as spokesmen for different interests. Initially, these were all Europeans, but in time reliable Indians were also chosen. Although they were given various advisory powers, and the Viceroy listened to any complaints that might be made, the legislature necessarily lacked responsibility. It was the Viceroy and his Executive Council who always made the final decisions. Above the Viceroy was the British Parliament, which advised the Queen; the Secretary of State for India, who was a cabinet member; and his permanent undersecretary, a British civil servant, who occupied his position through various governments and provided the continuity in Indian policy. But the Viceroy in India was the actual ruler of India itself; as long as he kept to his general instructions and consulted with his official superiors in England, his decisions were final.

There was no way the British could be compelled to change this system, or even to take more Indians into consultation, except by agitation and the exercise of moral pressure. This kind of pressure, however, could occasionally be effective, since the British, especially the more liberal members of Parliament, did not like to consider themselves as tyrants ruling an unwilling people. They were confident their rule was beneficent and just and in the interests of the people, who were gradually being brought into the modern world—in which at some distant date they could play a worthy part, aided thereto by the use of British customs and institutions. The Indians had been given a common language, which they had never known before, and for the first time in their history they had an incorruptible government and enjoyed all the benefits of law and order, denied them through centuries of native misrule. What more could they desire?

RISE OF THE CONGRESS PARTY. As it happened, they desired much more—above all, the sense of dignity denied them under foreign rule. They wanted more say in their own government, more jobs in the bureaucracy, and, ultimately, independence. The British themselves had provided the means when they made education in the English language available to the Indians, incidentally providing them with a set of ideas which could later be used to good effect against their masters. Even so, when the Indian National Congress was founded, in 1885, it was not at all revolutionary, and few of its members had any expectation that, in the foreseeable future, the British could be either persuaded or compelled to leave. Indeed, much of the pressure to call the Congress was provided by radical Englishmen who felt that it was time Indians began to assert themselves and demand a "larger share in the management" of their own affairs. These Englishmen consulted the Viceroy, Lord Dufferin, who proved to be quite sympathetic to the project, having no objection to the beginning of serious and moderate political activity in the country. The first members of the Congress, chosen by invitation, were for the most part urban Hindu intellectuals, although there was a sprinkling of Muslim landowners. Their first requests were that up to half of the Legislative Council be elected, and that the Council be allowed to ask questions and discuss the budget. They also indirectly urged the entry of Indians into the higher ranks of the civil service by calling for the simultaneous holding of civil-service examinations in England and India. Some of the requests were soon granted (in 1892): Council members were allowed to discuss the budget and ask questions, and the principle of election was admitted. But the British had no intention of permitting a large body of uninformed voters to foist unwelcome advisers upon the government. They preferred to have various "interests"—for example, chambers of commerce and landholders' associations—suggest names for the Viceroy's consideration. If these interests preferred to choose their representatives by election, that was their business. In practice, at this stage, the Viceroy always agreed with their choices, and they were duly nominated by him to the Council.

The Congress accepted this small dose of reform without enthusiasm and girded itself for the next demands. Obviously, such a group could not be expected to generate any enthusiasm among Indians unless it moved toward a more radical program; nor could it hope to continue to enjoy government approval. The younger members of the Congress, particularly, began to be infected with nationalism; it was a natural step for them to begin to admire their own native institutions and religions, which, in the opinion of many, were superior to those of the West. There was nothing to be ashamed of in being Indian, and there was nothing inherently superior in being English. The English had merely taken advantage of the temporary failure of Indian government in the eighteenth and early nineteenth centuries to fasten their rule upon Indians. And only the continued technical and military superiority of the English prevented the Indians from getting rid of them. Above all, the younger Indians could see no virtue in aping English manners and customs or in adopting their religion, even though it might be temporarily necessary to make use of English education in order to meet Englishmen on an equal footing. Thus the Congress, increasingly influenced by Hindu pressure groups, gradually moved into a position of intransigence. Even so, until after World War I and the ascendancy of Gandhi, it remained a relatively moderate group, pledged to work only by constitutional means.

As it became more representative of Hindu aspirations, the Congress found itself unable to hold its Muslim membership. The leading Muslims recognized clearly that since they were in a permanent minority and were also several decades behind the Hindus in education, if the Congress were to attain its aim and achieve independence, it would be the educated Hindus who would rule. Thus, it seemed clear that it would be better for them to support the British, most of whom were in any case more favorably inclined to themselves than to the upstart Hindu educated classes. In 1906, they formed an All-India Muslim League, which siphoned off the large majority of Muslim Congress members and was able to keep specifically Muslim interests always before the government.

Hindus in later years have tended to claim that the British made use of the age-old principle of divide and rule, a policy that eventually, contrary to later British wishes, resulted in the partition of India. But, in fact, the British did not have much say in the matter at any time. If they had systematically favored the Hindu majority with the intention of bringing them to power in a united India, bloodshed and probably civil war would have resulted. Yet, they did show such tenderness for the Muslim minority and guarded its rights so jealously that they never even gave the other policy a trial, and thus no opportunity to succeed. By granting separate electorates to Muslims in 1909, as soon as elections were permitted under the Morley-Minto Reforms, they unquestionably encouraged them to think in terms of their religion and to regard themselves as Muslims rather than Indians. It may be argued that this step was the crucial mistake that ultimately led to the formation of Pakistan.

MORLEY-MINTO REFORMS. In the last decade of the nineteenth and the first few years of the twentieth centuries, largely under the influence of the extremist Hindu press, sporadic violence began to erupt; and the British decided on a series of reforms called after John Morley, the British Secretary of State for India, and Lord Minto, the Viceroy. But the reforms were hesitating and unimaginative. Apparently afraid of making serious concessions to the Hindus that would antagonize the recently organized Muslims, they offered a bare minimum to the Hindus, hoping that the Congress would be reasonably satisfied and at least refrain from adopting a violently anti-British attitude.

It is clear now that this was the one moment in modern Indian history when a bold step forward might have helped lead the country toward independence as a united nation. India already had far more educated men capable of undertaking the responsibilities of self-government than any of the African states that have so recently won their independence. But, of course, it was too early to perceive this in 1909. The British had not even made up their minds that someday India should be independent and self-governing; still less had they accepted the notion that the British parliamentary system could be transferred to India. So all they did was enlarge the provincial councils, in which the Indians too often showed little interest, then or later. To these councils they granted a majority of unofficial and elected members, chosen by "communal" electorates (Muslims and Hindus voting separately for their members), while they kept the official majority in the central Legislative Council. One nominated Indian, a judge who later became a British peer, was admitted to the sacrosanct Executive Council of the Viceroy.

By the outbreak of World War I, India had achieved no further measure of reform. Congress was still moderate and constitutional in its methods; it had recognized that the place where reforms, if any, would be granted was London, and had set up a number of committees and organizations there, by which the Indian point of view could be put forward, both through the press and directly to the government. When war broke out, India, as a colony, automatically joined, and most Congress leaders backed the war effort. The Indian Army serving overseas distinguished itself in many areas. Although the British ascribed its military achievements to loyalty rather than to the fact that soldiering was a job that paid better than staying at home and provided a change from the monotonous life in India, the very fact of its meritorious service predisposed them to the recognition that Indians, after all, might be capable of fully responsible self-government, even "Dominion status" within the Empire. In 1917, therefore, the government issued the long-awaited statement that Indians could look forward to responsible self-government, and in 1919 introduced a series of new constitutional changes known as the Montagu-Chelmsford Reforms (discussed in Chapter 6).

The Conquest of Burma

In the eighteenth century, the kingdom of Burma, ruled from the city of Ava, on the Irrawaddy river, was the most militarily effective native power among the smaller nations in Southeast Asia. Indeed, it became imperialistic at the same time the British were gradually conquering India; and the Burmese kings were unable to appreciate the fact that Burmese bravery, which was unexcelled in the East, would prove no match for Western technology and military science. When the Burmese conquered Arakan, the western province of modern Burma bordering on British India, and began to interfere in Assam, it was inevitable that the two imperialisms would clash. The British East India Company, which administered India at the end of the eighteenth century, had tried to trade with Burma and often had submitted to humiliations at the hands of the proud and swashbuckling monarchs of the small country. Although conflict between the expanding British Empire and an uncompromising Oriental despotism was probably inevitable, it was the Burmese who were the first to begin hostilities. They invaded British India in 1824, believing they could secure the possession of Assam and perhaps take a part of British Bengal from the Westerners. So firm was this belief that they neglected to protect themselves from invasion by sea. The British took Rangoon without difficulty and sailed up the Irrawaddy toward the capital, compelling the Burmese monarch to recall his troops from the northwest to take care of the threat from the south. But the British, with the aid of their greatly superior artillery, defeated the Burmese troops and dictated a treaty that confirmed their possession of Assam and other disputed areas, and exacted an indemnity, which was paid off by 1832.

The following years were difficult for both the British and the Burmese. The treaty called for the establishment of diplomatic and commercial relations, but the Burmese were still smarting over their defeat and had no intention of observing it if they could help it. They might have avoided further clashes with the British and eventual loss of independence if their monarchs had maintained a fixed policy based upon the realities of the day. But, as it happened, during these crucial years a succession of monarchs won the throne by bloodshed, usually followed by the murder of their competitors; these men had little knowledge of the world outside their borders and of the reality of British power. There were numerous border disputes, with no clear means of settling them, and trade relations were equally uncertain. Eventually, the British, under Indian Governor-General Dalhousie, provoked the second Burmese War in 1852, and again compelled the Burmese to make peace on British terms. This time, the southern province of Pegu, with Rangoon and all other useful ports, was ceded to Britain, which now controlled all the southern and western ports of the country.

Following this war, a palace revolution brought Mindon Min to the throne. The new King was a man of peace who recognized that he must accept annexation and attempt to make the best of what remained. He therefore signed a treaty in 1867 that virtually recognized the truncated kingdom of Ava as a British protectorate. During his reign, the treaty was fairly well observed by the Burmese. But Mindon's successor Thibaw unwisely tried to make capital out of differences between the British and the French, who were engaged, in the 1880's, in building an empire for themselves in Indochina. In 1883, Thibaw sent an embassy to France that signed an agreement by which the French promised to supply him with arms in exchange for extensive trade concessions. This agreement naturally alarmed the British, who feared the arms might be used against them. Although the French, under British pressure, agreed not to implement the agreement, Thibaw had already taken advantage of it to engage in strong action against a British company. This gave the British an opportunity to dispose of the troublesome kingdom once and for all. After presenting an obviously unacceptable ultimatum, they invaded the country in 1885, deposed Thibaw, and annexed his realm, which was ruled by the Viceroy and government of India until 1937.

The various reforms granted to India up to World War I were all made applicable to Burma. These included the Morley-Minto Reforms of 1909. But Burma was not believed to be ready for the application of the Montagu-Chelmsford Reforms of 1919. (Her reaction to this discrimination against her is discussed in Chapter 6.)

Malaya and Indonesia

CONFLICT BETWEEN BRITISH AND DUTCH INTERESTS. British interests in the Malay Peninsula, as elsewhere in the East, were primarily commercial. During the seventeenth and eighteenth centuries, there had been constant rivalry between the British and Dutch East India companies in the Far East, but the British East India Company had, on the whole, found India to be as much as it could profitably handle. The Dutch Company was thus left to rule in Ceylon, Malaya, and Indonesia. However, when the Dutch fought on the opposite side from Britain, during both the American War of Independence and the Napoleonic Wars, the British began to encroach on Dutch positions in the East, taking Ceylon, Malacca, the chief port of Malaya, and even much of Java and Sumatra, including the Javanese capital of Batavia. After the war, a struggle ensued between various British and Dutch interests, with the British East India Company, which had recently lost its trading monopoly in the East, backing the Dutch claims in preference to opening up the Oriental trade to British competitors. On the other side, Sir Stamford Raffles, the Governor of Java during the British occupation, fought against abandoning all his work. He was transferred to a minor post in Sumatra, part of which remained for a short time in British hands. In 1824, a treaty was finally signed between Britain and the new Kingdom of the Netherlands, under which Ceylon and Malacca remained under British control and Sumatra and Java were ceded definitively to the Dutch. The Dutch did not fully subdue the large island of Sumatra until 1904.

THE STRAITS SETTLEMENTS. In 1796, by a combination of shrewd negotiation and occasional force, the British persuaded the Malay Sultan of Kedah to grant them the island of Penang, off the coast of northwest Malaya, together with a bridgehead on the mainland known as Province Wellesley. This acquisition was rapidly built up into a thriving port under a British governor responsible to the British East India Company. In 1819, Sir Stamford Raffles, the Company's agent, was granted by the Sultan of Johore the uninhabited island of Singapore, then largely a mangrove swamp. The Dutch Governor of Java protested. But Raffles was backed by the Governor-General of India, within whose domain Singapore would fall. When Singapore began to prosper as a free port, the British and the Company withdrew their objections, and Singapore was recognized by the Dutch, in the treaty of 1824, as a British possession. Singapore, Penang, and Malacca, all free ports, were given the name of the Straits Settlements. They remained under the British East India Company until its abolition in 1858. They continued to be administered by the government of India until 1867, when they became a crown colony.

FEDERATED MALAY STATES. Once in command of the ports, the British soon began to penetrate the hinterland, aided by dissensions among the Malays, the native people of the peninsula. The Malay sultans in the nineteenth century warred constantly with one another, and disputed successions were numerous. The British were often compelled to interfere, in the interests of law and order and settled trade. In this task they had the support of the Chinese merchants, who became an ever-larger minority on the mainland and from the beginning constituted the largest single ethnic group in Singapore and Penang.

The first British interference was in Perak, the most developed state of the Peninsula, where they backed the legitimate heir against the will of the local chiefs, who had chosen a man who was not a direct heir of the previous sultan. The British deposed this man and pensioned him off. In exchange for this favor, the legitimate heir accepted a resident adviser, whose advice he agreed by treaty to accept. He was the more ready to do this, since it was a Malay custom for the sultan to leave most administrative tasks to a prime minister. Even so, the first Resident accredited to the court of Perak was eventually murdered by the order of the Sultan, who had resented his evident intention to effect a thorough house cleaning in the state. The British thereupon sent a punitive expedition, banished the Sultan, and installed a more subservient monarch and, it should be said, a more tactful Resident. In quick succession, three other sultans accepted residents.

In 1895, the four states with residents (Perak, Selangor, Negri Sembilan, and Pahang) were joined in an administrative federation under a Resident-General (soon to be called Chief Secretary). This official, the chief British officer in the federation, was himself subject to the orders of the Governor-General of the Straits Settlements, who also held the title of High Commissioner for the Federated Malay States. By these means, the façade of independence was maintained, though in fact the British ruled as effectively through their bureaucracy as if the territory had been a colony. The Malay rulers, however, continued to keep their state councils and advisers and retained their positions of honor in their own states. On the whole, they were very well paid for their nominal duties. There was a considerable influx of European and Chinese capital and Chinese and Indian (Tamil) labor into the Federated Malay States, especially for the development of rubber plantations and tin mines.

UNFEDERATED MALAY STATES. In 1909, the British made an amicable agreement with the King of Siam under which, in exchange for the promise to build a railroad from Singapore to Bangkok and various monetary considerations, the monarch relinquished his usually ineffective but legal suzerainty over a number of his southern provinces, all ruled by Malay sultans. These rulers, not relishing the prospect of being reduced to figureheads like their counterparts in the federation, resolutely refused to enter it, though they agreed to accept residents. Thus, the less developed states of Kedah, Kelantan, Trengganu, and Perlis came under British rule as "protected states," although maintaining a considerably greater degree of autonomy in local affairs than the Federated States. Lastly, the Sultan of the large southern state of Johore, bordering on Singapore, decided that he needed capital to develop his relatively rich state and likewise agreed to accept a resident. Thus, by the outbreak of World War I, this small peninsula was a greatly overgoverned state, with three free ports, joined together into a British colony; four states, each with its own residual governmental institutions, and a federal government at the center; and five unfederated, protected states, indirectly ruled through residents but still retaining substantial autonomy in local affairs. The population of the mainland states was still predominantly Malay, though there were considerable minorities of Chinese and Tamils; whereas in the Straits Settlements, the Malays were already a relatively small minority. The British decision not to include Singapore in the Federation of Malaya, which became independent in 1957, was influenced by the reluctance of the ruling Malays to admit a large minority group that would upset the ethnic balance of the new state, and the Federation of Malaysia was sponsored by Malaya because the new territories to be included would tend to redress the balance.

Borneo, Brunei, Sarawak, and Labuan

The large island of Borneo had been very little colonized until the beginning of the nineteenth century. During the century, the Dutch took effective possession of all of the island except the north coast, which, with the neighboring islands, was ruled by the two Malay sultans of Brunei and Sulu. Both were sultanates of considerable antiquity—the former more than 1,300 years old. In 1704, the Sultan of Brunei ceded North Borneo to the Sultan of Sulu, who thereafter ruled a chain of islands for some of which, as well as for North Borneo, he owed allegiance to the Spaniards in the Philippines. In 1846, the British, who were by now interested in the area, compelled the Sultan of Brunei to cede to them the small island of Labuan as a base for operations against pirates. In 1841, in exchange for services rendered and a continued small monetary payment, the Sultan of Brunei granted the mainland territory of Sarawak, not to the British but to an Englishman, James Brooke. Brooke and his descendants ruled Sarawak as "rajahs" for the next century. Although in the 1880's the British extended their formal protection to the territory, they continued to recognize the "white rajahs" as its hereditary rulers.

North Borneo was a different proposition. The Sultan of Brunei seems to have been unwilling to acknowledge that this territory had been ceded to the Sultan of Sulu, and in the late eighteenth century he proceeded to grant trade concessions to various British, European, and American interests. The Sultan of Sulu did the same. The Sultan of Brunei was soon recognized to have exceeded his rights, but in 1878, the Sultan of Sulu entered into an agreement with the Austrian Baron Overbeck, by which a small sum of money was to be paid annually to the Sultan, who was at the time engaged in hostilities with the Spanish rulers of the Philippines. Shortly afterward, the Sultan capitulated to the Spaniards, who then denied his right to cede any territory without their consent. In due course, the Spaniards were pacified by the British and relinquished all their claims to North Borneo in exchange for recognition of their rights to suzerainty over the remaining possessions of the Sultan.

On the strength of the Overbeck treaty, the British North

Borneo Company was formed with a royal charter in 1882, Overbeck himself having been bought out. This Company, unlike the British East India Company, held no monopoly on trade in its area, but was granted the right to develop and rule the territories, and assumed administrative responsibility for them. The British government, for its part, announced a protectorate over North Borneo in 1888, thereby effectively preventing interference by other powers. In 1899, the United States obtained the Sulu islands, together with the Philippines, but not North Borneo, to which she made no claim. The Dutch briefly protested British actions in "their" island of Borneo, but soon dropped all claims. At the end of the century, only Brunei remained independent under a native sultan. In 1906, this sultan, too, was persuaded to accept a British resident. His territory became a protected state, still nominally, and to a considerable extent actually, ruled by the sultan. Brunei, in fact, never became a British colony and to this day remains a "protected state."

French Indochina

In the 1820's, when the Netherlands was engaged in consolidating the empire acquired by the Dutch East India Company, the French had no empire in the Far East. But throughout the eighteenth century, French Catholic missions had been expanding in Indochina (properly called Vietnam) and the neighboring kingdoms, and on occasion French prelates had advised and assisted various Vietnamese monarchs. French governments did not as yet recognize a national obligation to protect missionaries who incurred the displeasure of local monarchs, nor even to avenge their occasional deaths at the hands of natives. In 1839, Pope Gregory XVI recognized the supremacy of French Catholic missions in the East. From this time onward, French Catholic monarchs and the French Navy, whose officers were usually fervently Catholic, frequently intervened on behalf of the 300,000 Vietnamese Christians in the country. When the Vietnamese monarchs attempted to eradicate Christianity as a danger to their country, they incurred further intervention, and traders and concession hunters followed in the wake, eventually costing the Vietnamese their independence.

In the early nineteenth century, the kingdoms of Cochinchina in the south, Annam in the middle, and Tonkin in the north, which together constitute modern Vietnam, were consolidated under one Vietnamese Emperor. He ruled from Hué, in Annam, with the aid of a bureaucracy trained according to Confucian tenets and commonly known as mandarins. The Emperor acknowledged the overlordship of the Emperor of China, who ruled from Peking, and on occasion was able to elicit Chinese military support when in difficulties. This support was of ever less value, as the Chinese empire declined during the century. To the west of the Vietnamese empire were the two small kingdoms of Laos and Cambodia, which intermittently acknowledged the suzerainty of the King of Siam. There were desultory interventions by French forces in the first half of the nineteenth century, and Louis Philippe stationed a naval squadron on a permanent basis in the China seas to protect missionaries and generally keep an eye on growing French interests in China.

However, it was not until the reign of Napoleon III and the establishment of the Second French Empire that serious action was taken against the Vietnamese monarch Tu Duc, who had proscribed all missionary priests and set in motion a severe persecution of all Christians in his realm. This also aroused the Spanish Catholics, who had priests in the country. In 1858, a Franco-Spanish naval squadron attacked the Vietnamese empire, bombarded the port of Tourane in Cochinchina, and soon afterward attacked neighboring Saigon. In 1862, the Emperor came to terms with the French, ceding three provinces of Cochinchina to them and agreeing to pay an indemnity. The next year, he tried to recover his lost provinces by negotiation, but was turned down by the French National Assembly after a treaty had been signed with the French Government. Guerrilla warfare organized from western Cochinchina was no more successful, and in 1867 the French Admiral-Governor de la Grandière annexed the western provinces, thereby bringing the French to the borders of Cambodia. The Cambodian King, Norodom, claimed the support of his Siamese overlord, whom he vainly hoped to play off against the French. After a few futile efforts to exercise his authority in Cambodia, the King of Siam signed a treaty with the French, in 1867, relinquishing his rights and recognizing the French protectorate in that country. King Norodom accepted the inevitable and was glad to keep his crown while accepting a French resident as adviser.

During the next several years, exploratory missions were sent up the Mekong and Red rivers. When the French captured Hanoi, the largest city in Tonkin (North Vietnam), Emperor Tu Duc appealed for help to his Chinese overlords. The aid they sent was ineffectual, but it succeeded in provoking the French into taking stronger measures. In 1883, they compelled the Vietnamese to accept a French protectorate over Annam and Tonkin, an arrangement which the Chinese Emperor accepted two years later. Tu Duc died in 1883, and was succeeded by a number of short-lived, nominal emperors whose regents refused to accept the loss of Vietnamese independence and constantly attempted to disobey the French residents. Desultory guerrilla warfare continued until 1895, by which time the French had fully established their authority.

Meanwhile, local French officials and merchants had designs on the small kingdom of Laos, where Chinese irregulars were operating. In 1883, the Laotian King, Oun Khan, had appealed for help against these irregulars to his suzerain, the King of Siam. The latter had responded to the appeal, but the Siamese showed every intention of keeping the country for themselves. For this reason, Oun Khan agreed, in 1887, to accept the protection of the French, whose representative, Auguste Pavie, won his friendship. But the Siamese did not give up easily. Not until 1893, when the French finally sent a naval expedition directly to Bangkok, did they agree to sign a treaty relinquishing to Laos the left bank of the Mekong. Even so, a part of the former Laotian kingdom, previously independent under the King of Laos, was annexed by Siam, which had never had more than the rights of a suzerain in that country. Thus the King of Laos retained his throne at the cost of some territory lost forever to the Siamese and the acceptance of protection by the French.

The French created an administrative federation of their entire Indochinese domains in 1907. The monarchs of the separate countries, with the exception of Cochinchina, did not actually lose their thrones altogether, but they retained few powers. Nevertheless, the continued acceptance of two kings and an emperor, each retaining some measure of authority derived from his hereditary title, was to prove important after World War II. Although both North and South Vietnam are now republics, the kings of Laos and Cambodia sit on their thrones as constitutional monarchs.

The United States in the Pacific

The Philippine Islands

During the second half of the nineteenth century, the United States gradually emerged as a leading world power. Early in the century, she had expressed in the Monroe Doctrine the intention to take steps to see that Europe kept out of the American continents. Not until after the Civil War, when the western United States was being slowly settled and developed, did her full potentialities for economic growth appear. During the last decades of the century, her leaders became fully aware of what the European imperialists were doing; and although for some time she was content merely to assert her interests and to see that the European powers did not exclude her from their recently acquired spheres of influence (the "open-door" policy), the United States was scarcely less affected than they by the appealing notion of the white man's burden, the duty of the civilized powers to aid in civilizing the rest of the world. Her Protestant missionaries were no less active than those of the European nations, especially in China, and it was the United States that took the initiative in opening up Japan.

Even so, it was the conflict of her interests with those of European powers on her own continent that eventually brought the United States into direct competition with European imperialists. A stern warning from the United States was certainly the crucial factor in persuading Emperor Napoleon III to withdraw his expeditionary force from Mexico, where it had established the Hapsburg Maximilian on the Mexican throne and had kept him there against the wishes of the Mexican people. Despite the United States' pledge in the Monroe Doctrine that she would not interfere with the existing colonies or dependencies of any European power, she was not prepared to tolerate indefinitely the increasingly ineffective rule of Spain in Cuba and Puerto Rico. Similar interests favored intervention in the Hawaiian islands in the Pacific, ruled by a native Polynesian dynasty.

The United States declared war on Spain as a result of events in Cuba, and war with Spain meant that the Spanish possessions in the Pacific might become a prize of the victory. This was well understood by both the British and the Germans, who were themselves engaged in adding to their empires in that area, and who hoped that the United States could be dissuaded, by diplomatic means, from taking the whole of the Philippines for herself. The Americans were well prepared for the eventuality of war with Spain over Cuba, and entirely ready to take over the Philippines for themselves. United States Admiral Dewey, on the outbreak of war, steamed directly to the Philippines and effectively discouraged interference by either the British or the

Germans. Without difficulty, he sank the few feeble warships provided by the Spaniards for the defense of the islands, and landed troops on the mainland. Here they were joined by a Filipino revolutionary army that had taken advantage of the war to capture most of the Spanish garrisons and to proclaim a republic.

Although undoubtedly helped by this Filipino intervention, the Americans were not prepared to lose all the fruits of their own victory, nor were President McKinley and his advisers ready to cede independence to a people they considered unfit for self-government, who would soon have "anarchy and misrule worse than Spain's." The result was that when Spain was compelled to cede the entire archipelago to the United States, the latter found herself engaged in a new war with Filipino insurgents which lasted more than three years.

Nevertheless, it was recognized that the new colony should be granted independence as soon as possible, and there was never any avowed intention on the part of the United States to keep the islands as a permanent imperial possession. A Filipino majority in the legislature was granted even before World War I, and during the course of that war, the Filipino Senate became an elected body. It was stated in the preamble to the law establishing the elected Senate that it was the intention of the United States to grant independence to the Philippines as soon as a "stable government" could be established there. Although the islands entered World War II with a substantially autonomous government, for various reasons Philippine independence was postponed until 1946.

Hawaii

United States commercial interests, especially sugar, were already active in Hawaii during the last years of the native monarchy, and the last queens made no attempt to hamper them or to maintain more than a nominal independence. Yet, this was not enough for the resident merchants and growers, who pretended to believe that Britain or some other power would annex the islands if the United States did not. Their real desire was to share in the tariff advantages which accrued to U.S. nationals. Finding President Harrison agreeable to their designs, a number of eminent citizens of the United States and other nations staged a *coup d'état* which was backed by a force of United States marines. The

monarchy was abolished, and the insurrectionists formed a provisional government until the United States Senate was willing,
after an interval during which Grover Cleveland held the Presidency, to vote for annexation (1898). Hawaii then became a territory, an integral part of the United States, which it remained
until 1960, when it was admitted to the United States as the
fiftieth state.

Other Acquisitions

The picture of United States expansion in the Pacific was completed by the acquisition of several smaller islands. In 1867, she
annexed the island of Midway, without opposition, and Guam was
ceded by the Spanish after the Spanish-American War. Wake
Island, though discovered by the British in the eighteenth century
and claimed by them in 1900, was taken by the United States in
1934, by agreement, as a naval station. The possession of the
Samoan islands was contested for many years by the British, Germans, and the Americans; and since all these powers had strong
naval forces in the area, several threatening situations developed.
After a brief period of joint rule, an agreement was reached
under which Germany took the two larger islands while the
United States took the smallest (Pago Pago), which happened
to possess the best harbor. Britain was compensated by the cession
of German islands elsewhere.

Other Pacific Islands

Competition Between the Powers

Although Germany and Britain were the most active of the
European powers in the Pacific, and both maintained strong naval
forces in the area, the French were not entirely idle. In 1853, they
picked up New Caledonia. In the South Pacific, the French had
some early competition from the British in the Society Islands,
the largest of which is Tahiti; but in the early part of the century, the British Government was not interested in such possessions,
and the French offer of "protection" to the native Queen was
accepted in 1842. When the Queen died, in 1880, France annexed
the territory. In the 1880's, she was also on the point of annexing
New Hebrides, but the British Government, encouraged by the
Australians, who felt the territory was too close to them to be
left in the hands of a foreign power, protested, and the islands
were placed under an Anglo-French condominium.

The struggle for the Pacific islands was not the result of simple imperialistic competition for prestige. Traders were interested in the acquisition of tropical produce, especially copra, which commanded a ready sale in European markets, and the British and German trading companies formed to exploit these products always urged their governments to protect them and give them diplomatic support. Britain had often turned a deaf ear to these requests, at least before international competition became so keen, and the prestige of empire acquired so much support in the popular press. Germany, also at first reluctant, at last decided to support her nationals. Once the imperial nations had acquired interests in the area, their needs multiplied. They needed coaling stations for their ships and cable stations for trans-Pacific communications. Thus, Germany purchased a few islands of the former Spanish Pacific empire, and one (Yap) became the most important single cable station in the entire Pacific; others were used as substations, as well as yielding small supplies of tropical produce and phosphates.

Division of New Guinea

At the end of the century, the largest unclaimed prize in the Pacific was the great island of New Guinea, inhabited by some of the most primitive of the world's peoples—many of them cannibals. German Kaiser Wilhelm II coveted New Guinea; Australia, especially the state of Queensland, not only coveted it but, as its closest neighbor, was most anxious not to see it in the hands of a foreign and potentially hostile power. The Netherlands, too, had an interest in New Guinea, since it might be considered a natural extension of her Indonesian empire. In 1883, Queensland, which as a British colony had no right to do so, annexed eastern New Guinea. Although Britain indignantly disavowed the act, the following year she learned that Bismarck had designs on New Guinea. She thereupon declared a protectorate over southeastern New Guinea, known as Papua. The Germans quickly seized northeastern New Guinea. After protests and diplomatic discussions, an agreement was reached by which the Netherlands was given western New Guinea, Germany the northeastern sector, and Britain southeastern New Guinea. When Germany lost her colonies after World War I, Australia fell heir to the former German sector of New Guinea, which she held as a mandate for the League of Nations. New Zealand inherited German Samoa, also as a mandate.

The Fiji Islands

In 1874, the British annexed their largest possession in the Pacific, the Fiji Islands. Early in the century, a number of Europeans had obtained concessions for sugar and cotton growing, and then found themselves unable to recruit sufficient local labor to work their crops. They resorted to the practice of buying labor from professional "black-birders," who obtained workers by the simple process of kidnapping them from other islands. The Fijian chiefs, including the leading chief, who was accorded the title of King, were unable to put an end to the practice, nor could the King protect his own people against the depredations of the planters. Finally, the King himself was heavily in debt and wanted a solvent power to take over these debts. In 1859, he therefore requested annexation. The request was refused, as was a similar one to the United States. Then the Bishop of Melanesia, a respected missionary, was murdered by the natives of a small island, who had taken him for a "black-birder," and opinion in England began to change. Even so, Gladstone continued to oppose annexation; and it was not until October, 1874, as one of the first acts of the Disraeli administration, that the offer of the Fijians was accepted and the islands became a crown colony. Since it was impossible to keep up the sugar plantations without a sure supply of labor, the government decided to import indentured laborers from India, who today outnumber the native Fijians—a fact that has so far prevented the islands from achieving the independence already enjoyed by much smaller but ethnically homogeneous Samoa.

Japan Enters the Race

Before World War I, Japanese imperialist interests were directed toward the Chinese empire, from which Japan hoped to be able to carve suitable fragments for herself. On the peninsula of Korea, theoretically a vassal state of China under a native king, she backed for many years a modernizing pro-Japanese faction against the royal family. When the dispute turned into open strife, in 1894, both China and Japan sent armed forces to the country. Japan, with more modern military training and equipment, easily conquered the whole of Korea and invaded Manchuria on the mainland, compelling the Chinese to sue for peace. Under the terms of the treaty, Japan was ceded the Liaotung Peninsula, in South Manchuria, and the islands of Formosa and the Pescadores. China also relinquished all her rights in Korea, which became virtually a Japanese protectorate. The European powers, especially Russia, who had her own interests in Korea, were alarmed at the treaty and the annexation of such a large section of the mainland, since they themselves had had to be content with mere "spheres of influence." They therefore compelled Japan to relinquish this territory in exchange for an increased indemnity.

Russia's designs on southern Manchuria and Korea, both of which Japan regarded as in her sphere of influence, resulted in the Russo-Japanese War. Japan won substantially what she had been claiming. Southern Manchuria and Korea were officially declared in her exclusive sphere of influence, and she was conceded the right to "protect" the Korean Government. She also won half the island of Sakhalin, north of Japan. In 1910, Japan completed the process by annexing Korea.

The Three Remaining Independent Nations

By the outbreak of World War I, in the whole of the Far East and the Pacific Ocean there were only three countries that had not come under the rule of either one or another of the European powers or of the United States. Of these, Japan herself had become an imperialist in the Western manner, and by virtue of her quick decision to modernize and her ruthless determination to carry it out, she had made herself the equal of, and respected by, the Western powers. In 1902, Britain signed a naval alliance with Japan as an equal, thus putting the seal of Japan's acceptance as a fellow imperialist.

China had ceded outright a few relatively small territories, including Hong Kong, Wei Hei Wei, and Kiaochow. She had lost all her rights of suzerainty formerly exercised over the neighboring kingdoms, and a considerable part of her territories had been divided into European spheres of influence, in which one power or another had won special privileges. Nevertheless, China remained nominally independent. However, after 1911, her revolutionary government was even less able to make itself respected by foreign powers than the preceding imperial government; it was not as yet secure in its own house.

Siam had lost her vassal states, but the core of the ancient kingdom was still intact. Although Bangkok had once been captured by the French, no European power had been able to make the country into a protectorate or colony, in face of the opposition such an act would undoubtedly have met from its competitors. Much of Siam's success was due to the diplomatic skill of her rulers, who were willing to make concessions while there was yet time, retaining as much as possible in the process. Moreover, she proved herself able to play the European powers successfully one against another without, like Burma, provoking one power to such a degree that it was willing to risk offending its competitors.

Each of these three countries naturally felt compelled to accept some Western advice, and Western influence was still rapidly increasing at the outbreak of World War I. But from the end of the war, and in some part at least as a consequence of the internecine struggles between the European powers, this influence slowly declined, never again reaching the heights of 1914. The Far East had had a long tradition of native self-government, and almost all the countries in this area had been civilized for millenniums. Obviously, it would not be possible for the Western nations to keep these countries in subjection by force indefinitely, since their ascendancy was primarily due to temporary technological superiority. Even though none of the colonies became independent during the "long armistice" from 1918 to 1939, several were close to regaining their independence in 1939. It was the impact of World War II and Japanese imperialism that put an end to Western rule of these ancient civilized nations.

3. Subjection of the Islamic World

During the course of the nineteenth century, the power of the Ottoman Empire, which at its height had extended over large areas of Europe, Asia, and Africa, slowly declined. Turkey was unable to withstand the new spirit of nationalism, and could not prevent her European Christian provinces from being lopped off one by one, beginning with Greece in the 1820's. Outside Europe, she was unable to maintain her possessions against the new imperialists, and by the outbreak of World War I had suffered the loss of all her North African provinces. Egypt, the richest of these, was the first to be lost.

Conflict in North Africa

France and Britain in Egypt

The adventures of Napoleon in Egypt at the turn of the nineteenth century demonstrated to Europe that Turkey was no match for modern, well-armed European troops, as long as they were fully backed by their home governments; nor could the Turks prevent their own governors in Egypt from doing pretty much as they pleased. In 1806, Mehemet Ali, an Albanian officer in Turkish employ, won a few victories over the Europeans on behalf of his employer, and was promoted to be Pasha of Egypt. Before he died, in 1849, he had become virtually an independent potentate. Not only did he consolidate his own rule in Egypt during his reign, but he also conquered the Sudan to the south. For a time, he ruled Syria and much of Arabia, although he was compelled by a British fleet to relinquish these conquests. The Sultan, who had vainly tried to keep control of him, finally conceded to him and his heirs the right to rule Egypt as hereditary pashas, for which privilege they were to pay an annual tribute. In 1867, Ismail, one of Mehemet's descendants, paid an increased tribute in exchange for the more honorable title of Khedive.

In the reign of Khedive Ismail, Egyptian financial troubles came to a head. The Khedive was extraordinarily lavish in all his undertakings, and in the course of his reign the Egyptian national debt increased from a little over £3 million to £68.5 million. European financial interests were always ready to lend him money, at an ever-increasing rate of interest as his credit weakened. The resources of Egypt were totally insufficient to service such loans, most of which had been raised for unproductive purposes.

In 1854, the contract for the Suez Canal was granted to the Frenchman Ferdinand de Lesseps and a predominantly French syndicate; the British did not believe the project would succeed and were not anxious to invest in a project which, in their view, would be a failure. The Canal cost far more than had been expected, and most of the money was raised by Khedive Ismail. By the time of the opening of the Canal, in 1869, the Khedive was rapidly approaching bankruptcy; and his stock in the Canal, although valuable, could not be expected to pay in dividends enough to meet even his annual interest payments.

In 1875, therefore, he decided to sell his Suez Canal shares, his last major asset, to French interests. But before the French could act, the British Prime Minister, Disraeli, hearing they were for sale, raised the money himself and bought them on behalf of the British Government for £3.7 million. This sum was far too small to enable the Khedive to solve his financial problems, and his creditors continued to press him. After several foreign commissions had failed to put his finances in order, the British and French demanded the cession of all the Khedive's personal property to the state, and proposed a series of fundamental budgetary and tax reforms. When these were refused, they persuaded the Sultan in Constantinople to "depose" his spendthrift vassal. The Sultan, surprised at being consulted, readily gave his consent. Ismail, tired of trying to placate his insatiable creditors, accepted his dismissal peaceably and quit the country for a luxurious exile, leaving to his successor Tewfik a government that was in virtual receivership. By this time, the interest due to foreign bondholders represented a full half of the country's revenues.

Tewfik had no option but to allow the British and French to establish a "dual control" over his country. But he also summoned a parliament of Egyptians, including a leading nationalist named Ahmed Arabi, to share the governing of the country with him. These men demanded a voice in the control of expenditure if they were to participate in the government. This "intervention" by Egyptians in their own affairs alarmed the foreign interests, who feared that they would try to bring the dual control to an end or would scale down, even repudiate, the debt. The British and

French, therefore, sent an ultimatum to the Khedive, in 1882, demanding that he dismiss Arabi. To ensure that the Egyptians complied, an Anglo-French fleet was dispatched to Alexandria, whereupon anti-interventionist riots broke out in the city.

The imperialists were now faced with the problem of whether or not to take strong action. The French Government already had its hands full in Tunisia, which France had invaded the year before, and decided to withdraw its part of the fleet. But the British—amid protestations by the Gladstone government that their actions were in the best interests of all, the Sultan, the Khedive, the British people, and the foreign bondholders—persisted. They bombarded Alexandria and landed troops. In a short time, all resistance had been overcome and the country subjugated. Thus the British share of Egyptian debts, amounting to about £30 million, was secured, and the "lifeline to India" through the Suez Canal was taken under British protection.

THE BRITISH PROTECTORATE. Although the British assured the world that their occupation of Egypt would be only temporary, they did not leave for more than sixty years. They did not depose the Khedive, who, like other North African potentates, was permitted to keep his throne, though he exercised no sovereignty, and minor Egyptian officials continued to perform their tasks. The real ruler, however, was the British High Commissioner, who was advised by British officials and supported by a British army. Solvency was quickly restored. The administration was probably the best ever imposed by Britain on any of her colonies, especially under Lord Cromer, High Commissioner from 1883 to 1907. Engineering projects, including the first Aswan dam, were carried out, and there can be little doubt that the peasantry, in particular, benefited from British rule.

But Egyptian nationalism, fortified by Islam, persisted, and British rule was never accepted as legitimate by either the educated classes or the peasantry. When Turkey entered the war on the side of the Central Powers, Britain ceased to pay the annual tribute to the Sultan that she had paid since 1882. The fiction that Egypt was a Turkish province could no longer be maintained, and in 1914, Britain proclaimed a protectorate over the country.

Competition in the Sudan

By conquering Egypt and making herself responsible for Egyptian interests, Britain inherited Egyptian claims to the Sudan, the territory immediately to the south of Egypt that had been conquered by Mehemet Ali. After his death, Egyptian control of the Sudan became increasingly tenuous, and extensive use was made of foreign mercenaries, led by Europeans. Just before the British conquest of Egypt, a religious leader, Mohammed Ahmed, known as the Mahdi, aroused the Sudanese and proclaimed a jehad, or holy war, against both the foreigners and the Egyptians. Gladstone's government at first wished to recognize the Mahdi as an independent sultan of the Sudan, and thus spare Britain the expense of an occupation. Gladstone therefore sent General Charles Gordon, formerly a governor of the Sudan under Khedive Ismail, to negotiate terms.

By the time General Gordon arrived in Khartoum, the Sudanese capital, the Mahdi had already disposed of several small British armies and was in no mood to accept any favors from infidels, or indeed have any dealings with them at all. Moreover, Gordon himself was not the man to negotiate a surrender. Not having been provided with sufficiently explicit instructions, he decided that he was permitted to resist the Mahdi if the negotiations collapsed. But he lacked adequate means for resistance, and he was besieged at Khartoum by the Mahdi's army. The British attempted to rescue him by sending a relief expedition, but by the time it arrived Khartoum had fallen and the defenders had been massacred (January, 1885). The expeditionary force had to retire, and for more than a decade, the Sudan was left to the Mahdi and to his successor Abdullah, the Khalifa.

THE ANGLO-EGYPTIAN CONDOMINIUM. The French, who had only reluctantly accepted the British presence in Egypt, still regarded it as possible to take the Sudan from the south and west, despite British claims on the territory. A small expedition, under Captain Marchand, started eastward from the Congo basin, arriving at Fashoda, on the Nile, on July 10, 1898. There it was to meet two other French parties, which were to converge on Fashoda from different directions; but both had been prevented from making the rendezvous. What Marchand was not prepared for was the arrival of a British general, Lord Kitchener, Commander-in-Chief of the Egyptian Army, who was on his way south from Egypt bent on complete conquest and a thorough pacification of the Sudan—in part as a revenge for Khartoum and for the restoration of British prestige, and in part because of the misgovernment of the Mahdi's successors and their continual wars with the Abyssinians.

Kitchener had begun his slow progress up the Nile in 1896, building a railroad as he went, and defeating those of the Mahdi's followers who resisted his progress. In September, 1898, he won the decisive battle of Omdurman and was ready to deal with the French interlopers at Fashoda, 500 miles to the south. When he arrived, he was greeted by Marchand in the name of France. All the amenities were observed locally, while in England and France the governments, press, and people argued over who had the right to the area—the governments relatively politely, the press and people with a fine patriotic fury. The French, who knew well enough that Marchand would have to give way, nevertheless wished to win some useful concession in exchange. The British, on the other hand, declared that there could be no "compromise with the rights of Egypt." For a time, the two nations appeared to be on the brink of war, for which Britain, although diplomatically isolated at the time, was better prepared than her rival. In November, 1898, France, despairing of a *quid pro quo*, gave way and recalled Marchand. The British then agreed to negotiate, and a general settlement of conflicting claims followed. In 1904, partly as a result of this piece of late-nineteenth-century "brinkmanship" and of a realization by both governments that there were no outstanding problems that could not yield to negotiation, the Entente Cordiale was signed between Britain and France. Thereafter, the British and French supported one another against the rising power of Germany.

Once the Sudan was in British hands, an Anglo-Egyptian condominium was proclaimed over the area, and a remarkable series of reforms was carried out under British auspices. Through various irrigation and other engineering projects, cotton became the leading product of the Sudan. The ravages of the Mahdi and his successors were repaired, and the population grew. British work in the Sudan was perhaps the most successful of all the British colonial enterprises.

France and Italy in Tunisia

The French, edged out of Egypt by the British, turned westward to the North African lands that faced them across the Mediterranean. Algeria was invaded in 1830 and gradually conquered. Tunisia, to the east of Algeria, was eyed covetously by the French settlers in Algeria and by the French Government. As in Egypt, penetration was made easy by the willingness of the

French, as well as other financiers, to subsidize the extravagance of the Bey of Tunis, nominally a vassal of Turkey but in fact independent since the beginning of the eighteenth century. When the Bey found it impossible to meet his interest payments, a French-dominated commission, to which British and Italians were later reluctantly admitted, was appointed for the purpose of supervising his finances. It soon became clear that one or the other of the European powers would establish a protectorate over the country. Germany and Britain had no objection if this task fell to France.

But Italy, which was closer to Tunisia than was France, and which had far more of her nationals in the country ready and willing to be protected, objected strongly. In 1880, she outbid the French to acquire a small British railroad in the country. The Bey himself, if he could not avoid a protectorate, clearly favored the less powerful Italians. In 1881, the French took action. With the ostensible purpose of preventing Tunisian border raids into Algeria and protecting French financial interests, they dispatched a military expedition that the Bey had no means of resisting. The Italians protested vociferously, but they were unable to prevent the accomplished fact. In 1883, a protectorate agreement was signed that retained the Bey; although the administration continued to be partly Tunisian, the real authority in the country was French. Italy did not easily forgive France for her actions. It was in large part her resentment over Tunisia that led her into the Triple Alliance with Germany and Austria, which was in other respects so contrary to her actual interests in Europe (1882). Not until she was permitted to take other Turkish provinces in North Africa did she become reconciled with France.

France and Germany in Morocco

To the west of Algeria lay the large country of Morocco, part of which owed allegiance to the local Sultan of Morocco, a long-established sultanate that had been independent for centuries —it did not even owe nominal allegiance to Turkey. Where the Sultan's writ did not run, various Berber and Moorish tribes lived in sovereign independence. Morocco occupied a more strategic position than the countries to the east that had been taken by the imperialists in the nineteenth century. The country was of interest to Spain, which already ruled the Moroccan city of Ceuta, to Britain, with her fortress of Gibraltar across the Straits, and to the French, her neighbors to the east. Therefore, when France, at the end of the century, showed signs of wishing to extend her empire westward, her intention aroused the other powers. The agreement of at least the most important of these had to be obtained, and she began the necessary diplomatic negotiations.

Italy, which coveted Tripoli (a Turkish province) and was preparing to take it from the Turks, agreed to the French conquest of Morocco, provided the French offered no objection to her proposed conquest of Tripoli. Spain could be allowed to share in the spoils and win some territory to be added to Ceuta. It was a part of the understanding of the Entente Cordiale with Britain, in 1904, that France should be allowed a free hand in Morocco, even though the published details of the Entente made no mention of it. Meanwhile, the Sultan of Morocco had been encouraged to borrow money in France, and the increased taxes he levied on his people to meet the interest payments resulted in a very acceptable series of disorders, from which the Sultan would expect to be protected. By the end of 1904, therefore, all was ripe —except that the French Government had not considered it necessary to consult Germany, whose interests in the area had seemed to be minimal.

This oversight was to cost the French dearly. When they compelled the Sultan to accept what was virtually a French protectorate, Kaiser Wilhelm II, deeply insulted by the offhanded attitude of the French in not consulting and offering him "compensation," appeared in person at Tangier (promised to the Spaniards as part of their share of the spoils) and declared that Morocco should not be the exclusive preserve of any of the European powers. He then demanded an international conference to discuss the whole matter. Germany was too powerful to offend if she seriously meant to support the independence of Morocco, so the French sacrificed the Minister responsible for the declaration of the protectorate and perforce agreed to the conference (Algeciras Conference, 1906). President Theodore Roosevelt, who had been partly responsible for the calling of the conference, exercised considerable influence behind the scenes, or so he claimed, and Germany eventually accepted a compromise. According to this agreement, Morocco was to be under international control. In fact, the French and Spaniards exercised the control, while German financiers were given some voice in financial affairs.

Although the Sultan had agreed to the decisions reached at

Algeciras, since they permitted him to keep his throne, various warlike tribes in the interior resisted French penetration, which was constantly increased in spite of the recent agreements. Germany negotiated a further agreement with France, clearly recognizing French political interests in Morocco in exchange for a more definite recognition of German economic interests, which included the formation of Franco-German syndicates to exploit the country. In 1911, a number of Berber tribesmen attacked Fez, the Moroccan capital, whereupon the French, over German protests, sent an expedition that occupied the city. The Kaiser, incensed at French disregard of German rights and interests, sent a gunboat to Agadir on the Moroccan coast and openly threatened war. After a series of negotiations, he agreed to accept considerable "compensation" in West Africa in exchange for the abandonment of all his claims in Morocco.

All that remained was for the French and Spaniards to take physical possession of Morocco. The French took care of Spanish interests by a treaty giving the Spaniards about one-twelfth of the country, and it was agreed between the powers that Tangier should have an international administration. The Sultan now accepted a formal protectorate that left him his throne but turned over actual control of the country to a French resident-general. The first to hold this office was Louis Hubert Lyautey, later Marshal of France, one of the greatest of all colonial administrators, who devoted most of the rest of his active life to the building up of Morocco. His appointment coincided with the outbreak of a serious rebellion, followed by the abdication of the Sultan in favor of his brother. Lyautey, never content with merely suppressing opposition, founded hospitals wherever the army penetrated and fostered commerce, especially by the building of local markets. His policy won many leading Moroccans to acquiescence in French rule, although rebellions led by the Bedouin tribesmen continued. Lyautey resigned in 1925, but the country was not fully subdued until 1934.

The Spaniards, in their smaller zone, experienced even greater difficulty; however, by the mid-1920's, they had more or less subjected their coastal zone, usually working in full cooperation with the French. When Spain became a republic, in 1931, Spanish Morocco was reorganized under a High Commissioner who held both civil and military authority. It was from Morocco, and with the aid of native Moroccan troops, that General Franco began

his insurrection against the Republican Government in 1936—
which gave him control of Spain by 1939. Tangier was finally
internationalized in 1924, thus fulfilling the agreements of 1912.

Italy's Consolation Prize—Tripoli

Prior to 1870, Italy was fully engaged in the work of unification
at home. Afterward, the same patriotic nationalism that led to
unification persisted in the desire to revive the imperial glories
of Rome. But Italy was economically and militarily weak, and
the European powers with which she had to compete were stronger
than she. After the French conquest of Tunisia, all that was
available of the littoral of North Africa was the huge but barren
Turkish province of Tripoli. Since it was extremely unlikely that
Turkey, always a martial power, would yield Tripoli without a
struggle, it became the task of Italian diplomacy to isolate Turkey
and make sure that Italy herself had the support or neutrality
of every European power. It might then be possible to defeat
the Turks, who were usually fully occupied with either threats
from Russia or wars of independence in the Balkans and might not
be able to spare much military support for their governors in North
Africa.

Patiently, Italy waited for a suitable opportunity, meanwhile in-
vesting heavily in Tripoli and attempting to exercise some economic influence on the country through her banks. When she
signed the Triple Alliance with Germany and Austria, Germany
gave her a free hand, though always making clear that Italy would
be on her own and could not expect active help. Britain was
benevolent, preferring Italy to France as the western neighbor
of Egypt. Even Russia agreed to tolerate an Italian invasion of
Tripoli in exchange for Italian acceptance of Russian designs on
Constantinople, if they ever came to fruition. Russia, in any case,
never opposed the weakening of Turkey. France was the great
stumbling block, since she was Tripoli's neighbor to the west
and at the same time coveted all North Africa for herself. She was
not yet reconciled to the permanent loss of Egypt, from which
the British had, after all, promised to withdraw in due time.
But the Moroccan crisis forced her to abandon her hopes; it had
proved so difficult for her to win the necessary diplomatic support
in Morocco that, after 1906, she could no longer think of expanding eastward from Tunisia. At last she agreed to the proposed
Italian move, and there remained nothing more for Italy to do but
formally to initiate hostilities.

Turkey was not unaware of Italian ambitions, even though the agreements Italy had made with the European powers were secret. But her hands were too full at home for her to resist effectively. She had no fear of Italian military prowess; but if Italy invested enough in the enterprise, the weight of numbers and the ease with which she could supply reinforcements would have their inevitable effect. In fact, Italy had difficulty finding a suitable cause for war. There were no genuine atrocities, no convenient murders of Europeans or missionaries to avenge. Even though the country was corrupt and badly administered, like most Turkish provinces of this period, Italian interests were not threatened. But since the Italian Government, urged on by the press and public patriotic opinion, was quite determined to invade, an ultimatum was composed and dispatched to the Sultan in Constantinople. This naturally painted a horrendous picture of internal conditions in Tripoli and demanded immediate reforms.

Unexpectedly, the Turkish Government replied at once, politely inquiring what kind of reforms the Italians had in mind, since it would be very happy to cooperate with them and even accept Italian advice if it were proffered. But the Italians, thirsting to avenge the battle of Adowa, lost to the Abyssinians fifteen years before, were in no mood to be placated. Since the Abyssinians themselves were not available as targets, at least some military honors could be won and prestige restored by a resounding victory over the Turks. Brushing aside the Turkish response as unsatisfactory, they invaded Tripoli and had little difficulty in subduing the coastal areas (1911–12), though they took many years to win control of the interior. German and Turkish officers aided the tribesmen against the Italians during World War I, confining the occupation to the few coastal towns. After the war, Mussolini was able to settle a number of Italian peasants in the more fertile parts of the country, but the Italians always had to find huge subsidies to balance the colonial budget. Turkey at last recognized the conquest in 1923 at the Treaty of Lausanne. By this time, Italy had renamed her former Turkish province Libya, after the name of the Roman province. It has retained the name to this day, when it is an independent Muslim state.

The Somali Lands—French, British, and Italian

East of Egypt, especially in the area known as the Horn of Africa, lived a Hamitic people called the Somalis, most of them nomads. In earlier centuries, they had driven other tribes out of the area and even occupied a part of the ancient native kingdom of Abyssinia. The Somalis had early been converted to Islam, whereas the Amharic majority in Abyssinia, including its ruling class, belonged to the Christian Coptic Church.

Most of the Somali territories were largely desert, while the inland kingdom of Abyssinia had a more equable climate and rainfall, and there were many fertile areas in the high plateaus. However, it was shut off from the coast by the desert lands, and the terrain between the coast and Addis Ababa, the Abyssinian capital, presented formidable difficulties to the twentieth-century railroad builders. As early as 1862, the French purchased a coastal town on the Red Sea for a small sum, intending to convert it into a major port. Finding it unsuitable, France added the neighboring town of Djibouti. These two, with a small hinterland, comprise French Somaliland, today an "overseas territory" of France. From Djibouti, she was able to build a railroad, finished in 1918, to the Abyssinian capital over an old caravan trail. Even today, when Abyssinia, now Ethiopia, also possesses the former Italian colony of Eritrea, with ports of its own, the only railroad from Addis Ababa to the coast runs through French Somaliland and carries all the heavy traffic. French nineteenth-century empire builders dreamed of driving this railroad through to the other French possessions in North Africa, but the project had to be abandoned in face of British advances and the difficulty of the terrain.

In 1839, the British took the seaport of Aden, across the Red Sea, as a fueling station on the way to India. It was to be administered for nearly a century by the government of India. From Aden, they looked across to the Somali territories, hoping they might provide access to Egypt, which had indeed conquered a small part of the area in the time of Khedive Ismail. The British, as protectors of Egypt, inherited the Egyptian claim, but were compelled to relinquish the territory to the Mahdi. Nevertheless, in the years succeeding the occupation of Egypt, they signed treaties with a number of Somali chiefs and in due course gained possession (in 1884) of a small, and in almost all respects entirely useless, territory, facing north to the Gulf of Aden— thereafter known as British Somaliland or the Somaliland Protectorate. Although the British came to agreements with France and Italy on boundary matters, they were not left in undisturbed possession of their new acquisition. A Muslim leader, always known to the British as the "Mad Mullah"—his real name was Mohammed bin Abdullah Hassan—started a jehad of his own against the European infidels, in which he was quite successful. Indeed, he controlled the Protectorate for more years between 1901 (when the war broke out) and 1920 (when it ended) than did the British. It finally required a considerable expedition in 1920 to defeat him and drive him into exile.

By the 1890's, the British and the French had control of their relatively small and unpopulated areas, and the Italians were hard at work trying to consolidate their two colonies of Eritrea, to the northwest of French Somaliland, and Benadir (later Italian Somaliland), to the south of British Somaliland. Both territories bordered Abyssinia, and both were used for the successful conquest of Ethiopia by Mussolini's armies in 1935. An Italian commercial company purchased the port of Assab on the Eritrean coast in 1869, selling it in 1882 to the Italian Government—largely a book-keeping arrangement, since the original purchase money had been provided from the same source. Three years later, the Italians took possession of a second port, Massawa, and in 1890, they organized the ports and a small and not infertile hinterland as the colony of Eritrea. The Abyssinian monarch, who styled himself "Emperor and King of Kings," finding himself cut off from the sea, decided to drive the Italians out. After defeating them in a minor engagement, he was compelled to withdraw to defend himself against attacks by the Mahdists, by whom he was killed soon afterward. This brought the usurper Menelik to the Abyssinian throne in 1889, supported by the Italians who hoped, with British acquiescence, to establish a protectorate over the country.

Menelik, however, was altogether unwilling to give up his independence, though he needed European armaments. He signed the Treaty of Ucciali with the Italians, by which he was to receive armaments. The Italians regarded this treaty as an instrument granting them the customary rights of a "protecting power," but the Amharic version of the treaty could not bear this interpretation. As soon as Menelik discovered the meaning the Italians attached to it, he denounced the treaty; by this time, he was safely on the throne. Afterward, he turned to France and accepted both military advisers and armaments from them. The French had not yet been checked at Fashoda and were anxious to make sure of at least one ally in the area to the east of the Sudan, through whose country the proposed west-east swath would have to pass before reaching French Somaliland.

The Italians, who with British agreement had just purchased the inhospitable Benadir coast from the Sultan, in 1895 made their supreme effort to join their two Italian coastal colonies by adding Abyssinia. With a great effort, they equipped and transported a considerable expedition of well over 10,000 men and invaded Abyssinia from Eritrea. Menelik waited to encounter the Italians until he could amass an army numerically greatly superior to theirs. In many respects, his French-trained army, accustomed to the country, was the equal in quality to that of the Italians. He also had enough modern French artillery and rifles to match whatever was brought against him. Nevertheless, his total victory at Adowa, in 1896, was a shocking surprise to Europeans, who had been accustomed to winning battles in Asia and Africa against superior numbers without great difficulty. The Italians themselves were stunned. The government that had been responsible for the expedition was driven out of office, and they were glad to be allowed to withdraw from Abyssinia and recognize her "absolute independence." They even paid a considerable indemnity. In 1900, a boundary treaty between Italy and Abyssinia was signed, leaving Italy still in control of her coastal possessions, Eritrea and Italian Somaliland, which she had won at such cost and which, like Libya, were to be a constant drain on her always slender resources.

The Nominally Independent Muslim States

The entire Muslim world outside the remaining provinces of Turkey was now subject to the various infidel powers, with the exception of Afghanistan and Persia (now Iran). The independence of these two Middle Eastern countries was, however, largely nominal, though competition between the Russians and the British was such that neither ever became a colony. It was to the interest of the British to keep Afghanistan, which bordered on their Indian possessions, out of Russian hands. The Russians and the British fought two wars in the nineteenth century to make sure that a friendly ruler occupied the Afghan throne. In 1907, the Russians signed an agreement with the British recognizing that Afghanistan lay outside their sphere of influence. Since neither power itself wished to make unruly Afghanistan into a colony, she was permitted to retain her independence, subject to good behavior.

Whereas Afghanistan was poor and possessed no natural resources, Persia was strategically located and was a country in which profitable concessions might be won by the usual methods. Here Russia and Britain were in direct competition with one another, and the helpless Persian Shah could do little, even though he tried to play off one power against the other. He even went so far as to grant a constitution to his subjects and to hire an American financial adviser, Morgan Shuster, whom he was not allowed to keep. After the Russian Revolution of 1917, the Bolsheviks, preferring to interfere by other methods, abandoned their sphere of influence in the country. The British, after an attempt to restore their prewar position, came to the conclusion that their valuable oil concessions won before the war could be exploited more easily with the cooperation of the Persians, and entered into new mutually profitable agreements with the Shah.

4. The Partition of Sub-Saharan Africa

The continent of Africa is divided by the almost uninhabited Sahara Desert, and it is customary to distinguish between North Africa and sub-Saharan Africa because there are major ethnic and religious differences between the two. Nevertheless, the northern areas of sub-Saharan Africa are inhabited by some peoples racially akin to groups in North Africa, most of whom were long ago converted to Islam. Moreover, the Sahara Desert does not stretch completely across Africa; Sudan and Ethiopia share more in common with North Africans than with the Negroes in Uganda and territories to the south.

Africa in the Nineteenth Century

Abolition of the Slave Trade

At the turn of the nineteenth century, several European powers possessed small coastal settlements in West Africa. The Dutch owned the fortress of Elmina, originally built by the Portuguese; the Danes built the largest of the fortresses, Christianborg Castle (now the residence of the President of independent Ghana); the British owned Cape Coast Castle, originally built by the Dutch and abandoned. Accra, the present capital of Ghana, had been settled by a group of Englishmen in the seventeenth century, and farther north, the British had a settlement at Fort James, an island in the Gambia River, from which they exercised an intermittent control over what is now Gambia. For a period during the eighteenth century, the British also ruled French Senegal, but they restored it to France after the American War of Independence, and virtually abandoned Fort James.

The Portuguese possessed several important coastal settlements in West Africa. During the heyday of Portuguese imperialism, when the Portuguese held a monopoly of African trade, they had been venturesome, and had established relations with Congolese chiefs and kings, and even converted a few to Christianity. But in later years they made little attempt to penetrate inland from the Angolan capital of Luanda, which at the height of Portuguese domination of the slave trade had been a flourishing Europeanized city.

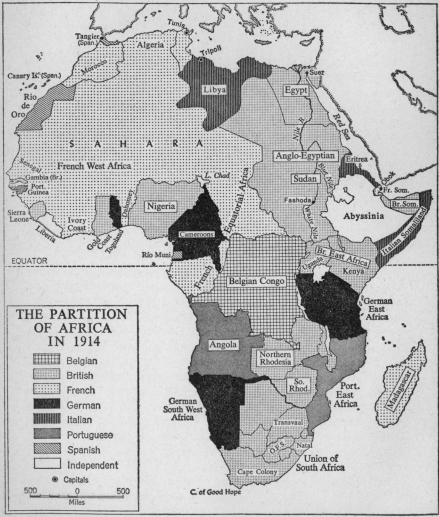

THE PARTITION
OF AFRICA
IN 1914

Belgian
British
French
German
Italian
Portuguese
Spanish
Independent
◉ Capitals

500 0 500
Miles

Map by Vincent Kotschar. From Stewart C. Easton, Western Heritage *(New York: Holt, Rinehart and Winston, Inc., 1961). By permission of the publisher.*

For centuries, the major commercial interest in Africa was in the exporting of slaves. But early in the nineteenth century it became clear that the slave trade was doomed. It had been forbidden by the French Revolutionary Government, in the 1790's; by Britain, in 1807; by the Congress of Vienna, in 1815. In 1833, the British emancipated all slaves in their empire. Although the Arabs were not bound by European laws and regulations, and Portuguese colonists continued to deal in slaves for much of the century, despite formal prohibition by the Portuguese Government, the British, encouraged by missionary and philanthropic interests, assumed responsibility for policing the ban on slavery. It was obvious that if Africa were to continue to be a profitable field for commercial endeavor, new products would have to be exported; for many decades it was not clear what would in fact take the place of slaves as a suitable export commodity, justifying the dangers and risks of exploitation. During this period, several nations abandoned their settlements on the African coast, and those that remained were always starved for funds and, in an era of anti-imperialism, could look for little support from their governments.

Role of the Missionaries

Nevertheless, several groups other than traders were interested in Africa. The rise of science in the eighteenth century had stimulated the growth of numerous scientific societies devoted to the pursuit of knowledge. Among these was the Royal Geographical Society (formerly the African Association), which was especially interested in the exploration of the great African rivers. Many of the mid-century voyages of exploration were sponsored, and to some degree financed, by the Royal Geographical Society. In 1837, an organization known as the Aborigines Protection Society was founded, in part as successor to the Anti-Slavery Society, whose purpose had now been formally fulfilled, though the Society continued to exist. This organization of philanthropists was very influential in Parliament throughout the century. Its prime purpose was to protect the natives from exploitation by ruthless commercial interests, and it took a leading part in exposing the seamier side of the empire-building of, among others, Cecil Rhodes and Leopold II of Belgium. In the process it succeeded in publicizing African exploration.

By far the most influential groups in the pious nineteenth-century atmosphere were the various missionary societies devoted to converting the pagan Africans to one or another of the branches of Protestantism (Britain) or to Catholicism (France and Belgium.) The greatest of all the African explorers was the medical missionary David Livingstone. Both the missionaries and the Aborigines Protection Society, on the whole opposed to the expansion of European empires in Africa, nevertheless favored government intervention to suppress the Arab slave trade.

The Chartered Trading Companies

Ironically, it was the activities of the missionaries and the explorers that drew the attention of commercial interests to the possibilities of new profits and fields of investment in Africa. The memoirs of such explorers as Burton, Livingstone, and Stanley were avidly read by Europeans whose major interests were far from being religious or humanitarian. When Stanley returned from the most difficult of his African voyages, he was met by emissaries of Leopold II, who wished him to make another voyage in the King's interests. Few of the great trading companies organized to do business in various parts of Africa were formed before there was a substantial body of information available from the pens of the early pioneers.

For a brief period in the 1880's, it was official British policy to sponsor the activities of chartered trading companies as a means of developing distant areas. Since the charter had to be granted by the Crown, it became the business of Parliament to discuss each charter before tendering the necessary advice to the Queen. The debates of this period are an indication of how British opinion was moving away from its anti-imperialist bent of the first half of the century, although without committing the government itself to expansion into undeveloped areas.

The great colonies of settlement, Australia, New Zealand, and Canada, had all by this time been granted almost complete self-government. South Africa had a limited self-government, and would have been given more if she had been in a position to accept all its responsibilities. Once the colonies became self-governing, many Englishmen, including Disraeli when in opposition, thought it was silly to consider them as part of an empire. The very idea of an empire seemed an anachronism. If only India, the largest remaining colony, could follow the same path, then the empire could be brought close to liquidation. Only a few small territories would remain, and they would be not much expense.

In the 1870's, Gladstone and Disraeli had alternated as Prime Minister, but their colonial policies had not greatly differed. Disraeli had agreed to the annexation of Fiji, which Gladstone had opposed. But conditions in 1874 impelled Disraeli to this decision, and might well have impelled Gladstone if he had been Prime Minister. Where they differed was in their general attitude toward foreign policy. Disraeli made a positive effort to assert what he regarded as Britain's national interests, whereas Gladstone always appeared to be reluctantly pushed into similar efforts. Gladstone had no sympathy for the concept of the white man's burden. However excellent Britain's administration of Egypt might be, he never regarded British rule there as permanent. He honestly believed that Egypt should be made to honor her debts, since these were an international obligation. But he could not imagine, as later generations did, that it could be any part of Britain's mission to "civilize" the Egyptians. Disraeli, on the other hand, was extremely sensitive to British national honor and prestige, and was willing to take risks, not only to prevent that honor from being sullied, but even to increase the prestige of his country—which he viewed in terms of power and influence, and the respect accorded by foreigners. All this was to change in the last decade of the century. Few Gladstonians remained, and the majority, even in the Liberal party, turned toward its own version of liberal imperialism.

But in the 1870's, not even Disraeli equated national prestige with the possession of colonies. Nor did his Conservative or Liberal successors in the next decade. But by this time the various powers were already scrambling for colonies, and there were good commercial reasons why individual merchants should desire them. There was still very little reliable information on what Africa might provide for the world market. Palm oil, kernels, and copra from the coco palm were in considerable demand in Europe, as was ivory. Diamonds and precious metals were suspected, especially after the rich finds in South Africa. There was plenty of money to spare for colonial investment, and if the new trade did prove profitable, there would be numerous opportunities for sale of heavy equipment to open up the various new colonies.

Nevertheless, very few of the companies organized in these years ever showed a profit. Most of them had to be bought out within twenty years by the government. The Royal Niger Company, formed in 1886 by Sir George Goldie, managed to pay its way until its political rights were bought out by the government, at Joseph Chamberlain's insistence, in 1899. The African Lakes Corporation, founded in 1878, was bought out by Rhodes's South Africa Company in 1893, itself formed in 1889 to exploit mineral concessions granted by King Lo-Bengula of the Matabele. By 1914, the British South Africa Company, which had exploited far more than the original mineral concessions, had nevertheless paid no dividends. It made claims for compensation for its expenses against the British Government and lost. But when it later sold out most of its rights to the British and Southern Rhodesian governments, it received about half of what it had claimed. The Company still exists as an owner and a lessor of valuable mineral rights in Northern Rhodesia and elsewhere. Sir William Mackinnon's British Imperial East Africa Company, founded in 1888, was quite unable to make any money in view of its very considerable expenses. When it was bought out by the government in 1895, its stockholders were left with a deficit of close to £200,000. In the Far East, the British North Borneo Company, founded by Sir Alfred Dent in 1881, retained most of its rights until the Japanese conquest in World War II, but the territory was formally under British governmental protection from 1888. During this long period the Company usually made modest profits, but North Borneo was very little developed. Fortunately, the Company did not have to pay for British military protection. Thus the experiment of trying to administer an empire by private enterprise was scarcely a successful one.

The system was virtually brought to an end by Joseph Chamberlain, who became Colonial Secretary in a Conservative government in 1895. As a former business man, he particularly objected to the untidiness of the system. He was not in the least unwilling to accept full responsibility for the expansion of the colonial system on behalf of his government. But he wished to make the empire pay for itself, which he believed could be done if capital was made available for development. "Our colonies," he stated in an election speech, "are in the condition of undeveloped states," and he proposed to "construct public works such as the Romans left behind." He was as good as his word. Railroads sprouted in Sierra Leone, the Gold Coast, Nigeria, and Uganda. He sponsored attacks on tropical diseases with marked success. He overhauled the antiquated Colonial Office, and much of the modern British interest in the welfare of the colonies stems from his tenure. He also put an end to the surviving trading companies in Africa, with the sole exception of the British South Africa Company, which at the time was busily engaged in organizing Rhodesia, a task which did not seem beyond its powers.

Explorations of Park, Stanley, and Livingstone

There had been little exploration into the interior of Africa until the end of the eighteenth century. Then, in 1795, the Scottish surgeon Mungo Park, under the auspices of the African Association, made an extensive journey inland from Fort James, reaching Bamako on the Niger. Once Park had shown the way and written a classic account of his first voyage, others followed until, by mid-century, the river basins of interior West Africa were fairly well known.

East Africa, on the other hand, had been very little influenced by Europe. The coastal areas were securely in Muslim hands, and the most important city was Zanzibar, the seat of an Arab sultan, noted above all for its flourishing slave market. The Portuguese possessed an ill-defined colony with its capital at the island city of Mozambique, after which the whole colony was later named. This city had been founded in the early sixteenth century; and from it, over the centuries, had been sent several important exploratory expeditions, but little of permanence had been achieved. All the Portuguese in fact owned at the beginning of the nineteenth century were a number of forts and trading posts, including the present capital of Lourenço Marques, then a small fortress. The very fact that these settlements existed, however, was to prove helpful to the exploration of Central Africa. Stanley, for example, would almost certainly never have reached the coast in safety, after crossing the whole of Africa from east to west on his most important journey, if he had not been relieved when at the end of his strength by a Portuguese party sent inland to rescue him.

The exploration of Central Africa from the east and north was greatly hampered by the hostility of Arab slave traders, who were more familiar with the territory, had greater access to local financial resources, and were greatly feared by the native Africans, who had had long experience of them and hesitated to thwart them. Although some explorers, such as Stanley, tried to come to an accommodation with these traders, they proved themselves utterly untrustworthy as allies, no doubt because they were well aware of the hostility of Europeans to their commercial activities. Livingstone, as was natural in a missionary, constantly opposed them and drew the attention of the world to the fact that the local Portuguese had still not abandoned the slave trade. His writings were instrumental in persuading the Europeans to make more serious efforts to stamp out the trade.

In the latter part of the century, African chiefs were usually ready to grant trading concessions to Europeans, and on the whole, the Africans themselves were rarely consistently hostile to European explorers. If they had been, it would have been difficult indeed for any of the explorers to emerge safely from the African interior. As a matter of fact, thousands of Africans endured enormous hardships in the service of Europeans for which they were scantily paid. The African companions of Livingstone were loyal to him to the end without any hope of reward; after the great missionary's death, when they carried his dead body for hundreds of miles to the coast merely because of their love for him, they performed a deed of devotion and loyalty rare in human annals.

South Africa

Conflict Between British and Boers

When the British won the Cape of Good Hope (Cape Colony, later Cape Province) from the Dutch at the end of the Napoleonic Wars, it was inhabited mainly by Dutch farmers, or Boers, who possessed a relatively small number of domestic slaves, but who treated the aboriginal Hottentots as virtual slaves—a policy also followed by the British settlers who migrated to South Africa in the early part of the century. Settler policy toward the Hottentots was regarded as outrageous by the British missionaries scattered throughout the interior. In 1828, the missionary John Philip, who was influential in British political circles, persuaded the government to issue an ordinance (the Fiftieth Ordinance) putting the Hottentots on exactly the same legal footing as Europeans, and instituting procedures under which the Hottentots could obtain legal redress if they were ill-treated. The Boers, who looked upon the Hottentots as racially inferior to themselves, and thus forever doomed to serve the white man, condemned the ordinance as a menace to their way of life, but, being law-abiding people, they accepted it for the moment.

THE GREAT TREK. In 1833, when slavery was abolished throughout the British Empire, the Boers lost their few slaves, but they did not object greatly to emancipation itself. However, many of them were cheated of the money promised to them as compensation, and the terms of compensation were in any case miserly. In 1834, the local Cape Government, dominated by the British governor, attempted to enact vagrancy laws subjecting the Hottentots to so many restrictions that their status would have been little different from what it had been before the Fiftieth Ordinance. When this was disallowed by the British Government, in 1835, large numbers of Boers lost patience, and with their Hottentot servants began a "trek" to the interior where they could be free to do as they wished.

The interior at this time was far from uninhabited. Various Bantu tribesmen, as well as Boers and Englishmen, had been quarreling for years over the limited land available in the semiarid veld, where a Boer family and dependents needed about 6,000 acres for their subsistence. Some of the more warlike Bantu tribes, such as the Zulus and Matabele, had themselves virtually enslaved other Bantu, and on occasion had waged wars of extermination against them. In 1835, the sixth and bloodiest of the "Kaffir wars" had been fought on the eastern frontier of Cape Colony, as a result of which the British governor had annexed a sizable section of Bantu land, and set aside a part of it for European colonization. So it was into a hostile and already overpopulated country that the parties of Boers trekked from 1835 onward.

BRITISH ANNEXATION OF NATAL. The most desirable land outside British jurisdiction lay far to the east, in present-day Natal. This land was not overpopulated at the moment, since a ferocious Zulu chief had recently almost exterminated the peaceful Bantu tribes that had settled there, after which he and his warriors had moved back to the north into their own territory of Zululand. The Boer leader, Piet Retief, was willing to negotiate with the new Zulu chief, Dingaan, and formally requested permission for himself and his trekkers to settle in the territory. This Dingaan granted, but when Retief and other Boer leaders visited him to ratify the arrangements, they were treacherously murdered. The Boers promptly retaliated. They inflicted a decisive defeat on the Zulus, took the disputed land by force, and established a republic of their own (1839). Meanwhile, smaller groups of trekkers had started for the high veld, and their advance guards had penetrated across the Vaal River into present-day Transvaal.

In setting up their republic in Natal, the Boers were determined to keep full control of the land for themselves, using as many Bantu as they needed for servants and laborers, and driving out the remainder. This meant that the latter would be forced over the border into Cape Colony, which the British could not permit. After much discussion with the home government, they finally

sent a considerable expedition by sea to Port Natal, to the east of
the new Boer Republic, where there was already a British settlement. The Boers besieged the port but were severely defeated, and
the British declared the annexation of the territory (1843). Most
of the Boers preferred to leave the new colony of Natal rather than
submit to British rule, and to join their fellow trekkers in the west
and north. In due course, Natal was peopled by British immigrants,
who outnumber the Boers in the province to this day.

INDEPENDENCE OF THE TWO BOER REPUBLICS. In 1848, the British
Governor in Cape Town, Sir Harry Smith, came to the conclusion
that it was necessary to protect the Bantu tribes to the west of
Natal from the Boer trekkers, who had been unable to establish an
effective government and were encroaching on the rights of the
Bantu, many of whose chiefs were under British protection. He
therefore annexed the territory between the Orange and Vaal
rivers, under the name of the Orange River Sovereignty. But most
of the Boers objected, and they were in a strong enough position
to prevent any effective British rule in the territory. They even
showed themselves reluctant to aid in suppressing a new war stirred
up by the Bantu. Meanwhile, the Boers beyond the Vaal, the most
irreconcilable of the trekkers, led by Andrew Pretorius, were
adamant against the extension of British sovereignty into their
own territory. In 1852, the British therefore agreed to the Sand
River Convention, under which the Transvaal was granted its independence as a separate Boer republic, on the condition that
slavery was permanently banned in it. Two years later, by the
Bloemfontein Convention, they granted independence on substantially similar terms to the Orange River Sovereignty, which
then became the Orange Free State. In both Boer republics, the
old Boer laws and native policies were restored.

LIMITED SELF-GOVERNMENT IN CAPE COLONY. In accordance with
the general colonial policy of the time, the British were anxious to
confer self-government on Cape Colony. The colonists, in return,
promised to grant the vote in their proposed lower house to free
Africans and persons of mixed blood who could meet a not very
high property qualification (£25).

In 1853, representative government was granted, under which
there were two legislative houses, the lower with the £25 qualification and the upper with a much higher one. But the executive
remained in British hands. This system, as always, made for constant quarrels between the legislative and executive branches of

government. The next stage should have been fully responsible government. But the legislature could not agree on its terms. Cape Colony was so seriously divided between persons of Dutch and English ancestry, and even geographically between the eastern and western sectors, that each side was afraid the other would dominate it under any system of responsible government. Nevertheless, the Boers and the British, especially in the capital city of Cape Town, were gradually learning to live peaceably with one another. In spite of the failure to agree on the terms of responsible self-government, amicable relations, on the whole, prevailed until the Jameson Raid of 1895. Since there were still more Boers in the Colony than in the two Boer republics, and the Boers elsewhere looked upon it almost as their mother country, agreement might have been reached if there had not been new causes of friction in the north.

ANNEXATION OF THE ORANGE FREE STATE AND TRANSVAAL. The infant Orange Free State, meanwhile, was experiencing difficulties too great for it to overcome. There were too few Boers surrounded by great numbers of hostile Bantu, much of whose land had been seized. Landlocked, like the Transvaal, it depended for most of its imports on the goodwill of the British at the Cape. The local Cape legislature would not even agree to hand over a fair proportion of the customs duties levied upon imports from outside destined for the republics; above all, the Boers lacked arms that they desperately needed for their constant wars with the Bantu. Although the Transvaal was in hardly better condition in the 1850's and 1860's, any suggestion that the two republics unite was promptly vetoed by the British. In despair, therefore, the Free State petitioned the Cape for reunion; but this was turned down by the British in London, who preferred the solution of union with Natal and with the Bantu lands between Cape Colony and that country (Basutoland), whose chiefs had recently requested protection from the British against the Orange Free State. Instead of agreeing to the latter request, the British granted the Free State a part of Basutoland, while they annexed the remainder. In what was left of Basutoland, they promised to protect the Basuto chiefs, whose land today remains an enclave under British protection within the independent Republic of South Africa.

THE DISCOVERY OF DIAMONDS. In 1867, diamonds were discovered in Griqualand West, a territory just to the west of the recognized boundaries of the Orange Free State, north of the Cape Colony, and a little more than 100 miles southwest of Transvaal. While independent miners flocked into the territory and established for themselves a small miner's republic, both of the Boer republics attempted without success to take control, while the Governor of the Cape awaited instructions from England. At last he decided to annex Griqualand West, with the diamond diggings and the city of Kimberley, thereby infuriating both Boer republics. The annexation was also unpopular in England, where Gladstone was Prime Minister. It was believed that federation was the only proper solution for the difficulties of the separate colonies, and that this federation should include both Boer republics. But this solution seemed further away than ever in view of the anger of the republics and the annexation of Griqualand.

Transvaal had the least claim to the mines but the most need of them. Her government in the mid-1870's was totally bankrupt, and she faced an almost certain war with a fierce Zulu warrior named Cetewayo, who for years had been preparing to invade Transvaal and was now ready for the attack. To avoid a war which he did not feel strong enough to win, President Burgers of Transvaal came to an agreement with a British Commissioner named Shepstone under which his republic was to be annexed by Britain. The proclamation of the annexation by Shepstone, with Burger's consent, was welcomed by the Disraeli Government in England but strongly opposed by the Liberal Party of Gladstone, then out of office.

At first Cetewayo restrained his warriors from engaging in the long-planned attack, not wishing to fight the British as well as the Boers. But the British Governor of the Cape forced the issue; whereupon Cetewayo attacked and utterly defeated the British troops sent against him. Although they quickly recovered and were able to defeat and capture the Zulu chief, British prestige was damaged. The defeat was partly responsible for the fall of the Disraeli Government in 1880 and its replacement by a new Gladstone Administration.

THE FIRST BOER WAR. Meanwhile, in Transvaal the Boer nationalists seized the opportunity to try to undo the annexation. With the Zulus no longer a danger, and a government in power in Britain that had opposed it, Vice President Paul Kruger, a strong Boer nationalist, confidently approached the Gladstone Government. But Gladstone objected from humanitarian motives to Boer native policy and hesitated, whereupon the Transvaalers took matters into their own hands. The Transvaal Volksraad (Parliament) decreed a restoration of the republic, and the Boers took to arms, quickly winning the skirmish of the Majuba Hill against the British (1881). Gladstone came to terms at once and recognized the independence of what was from 1884 onward to be called the South African Republic, subject to a number of safeguards that were gradually whittled away by further negotiations during the course of the next few years. In 1883, Paul Kruger became President of the country, and this office he continued to hold until his military defeat by the British in the Boer War. In 1886, gold was discovered in the Witwatersrand, well within the borders of the South African Republic, and it appeared that the financial troubles of the new state would soon be over.

THE UITLANDER PROBLEM. From this time until the outbreak of the (second) Boer War in 1899, gold dominated all South African politics. Miners, mostly from Britain, poured into the country, soon outnumbering the native Boers in Transvaal. British interests, led by Cecil Rhodes, Prime Minister of Cape Colony in the 1890's, won control of the goldfields and later a substantial interest in the diamond industry—to some degree freezing Kruger out of what he considered to be his rightful share in the riches of his country. In spite of this, Kruger determined to maintain Boer predominance in the country by all political means available to him. The foreign miners and other immigrants, known as Uitlanders by the Boers, were refused the franchise in the Republic except under extremely stringent conditions—which were constantly made more onerous as more miners became able to meet them.

On all sides Kruger felt himself hemmed in by the British, unable to move without being checkmated. He had long been trying to win an outlet to the sea by building a railroad with aid of foreign capitalists. First he hoped to reach the west coast via German Southwest Africa, annexed by Bismarck in 1884, then he tried to reach Delagoa Bay in Portuguese Mozambique. But before the discovery of gold in 1886, he could give no security for the capital invested. In 1887, the British annexed Zululand, through which the railroad to Delagoa Bay must pass. Finally in 1895, they closed the last door by annexing Tongaland. Although the railroad was built—since obviously it was likely to prove commercially profitable—it was not under the exclusive control of Portugal and the Republic, since it must now pass through British territory.

Lastly, Kruger and Rhodes both wished to expand to the north into the territory later to be called Rhodesia. But Rhodes had the necessary money and influence to win the contest, and his trading company, the British South Africa Company, effectively shut off Kruger once more from his projected expansion.

Meanwhile, in the Rand, with its new capital of Johannesburg, Kruger continued to refuse concessions to the Uitlanders, who by now outnumbered the Boers not only locally but in the whole Republic. While they continued to pay nine-tenths of the taxes of the country, he imposed ever more restrictions on them. His officials, many of them corrupt and venal, administered the city in their own interests and with the utmost arrogance. Kruger sold monopolies to the Dutch and Germans while refusing similar treatment to the British and British colonial immigrants. At the same time, he tried to fish in the troubled international waters and attempted to enlist the support, in particular, of the German Kaiser Wilhelm II, who did indeed occasionally assist him against the British, thus embittering relations between Britain and Germany. But it was Rhodes and the British, who tried to disown his acts, who eventually put themselves hopelessly in the wrong in international opinion by organizing a conspiracy that, it was hoped, would overthrow the Kruger Government or at the very least would enable the Uitlanders to win redress for their grievances.

THE JAMESON RAID. The existence of the conspiracy was well known to Kruger and even to the Germans; and though its details and timing were kept a secret by Rhodes, the fact that there was such a conspiracy was certainly known to the British Government. At the end of 1895, a small troop of police under the command of Dr. Starr Jameson was poised on the frontiers of the Republic, awaiting a last signal from Rhodes and word from Johannesburg that the time was ripe. The word did not come from Johannesburg, and Rhodes himself countermanded the expedition in a telegram that was never delivered. The result was that Jameson marched, the conspirators in Johannesburg were compelled to declare themselves prematurely, and the expedition was ignominiously defeated by Kruger's troops. Its leaders were captured. The reaction was immediate. Rhodes was compelled to resign his position as Prime Minister of Cape Colony, relations between Boers and British, even in the Cape, were seriously damaged, and the governments of the two Boer republics for the first time in decades established close relations with one another. As a climax, the German Kaiser sent a message of congratulations to President Kruger on his successful defense of his independence—thereby giving the latter the hope that he could expect further support in the event of war.

During the next few years, the situation rapidly deteriorated. No grievances were redressed by Kruger, and no compromises suggested by the new British High Commissioner, Alfred Milner, were accepted. On the other hand, the British recognized that Kruger's independence was of great potential danger to all South Africa. If he appealed for foreign support, it was not at all impossible that Germany might respond. Moreover, the Republic had bound itself solemnly many years before to acknowledge the suzerainty of the British, which, if it meant anything, meant that Kruger was not free to adopt an independent foreign policy against the wishes and contrary to the interests of the British. Thus when Kruger began to import arms, they retaliated by sending troops to Durban. Nevertheless, the Boer President apparently believed to the end that he would be strong enough to drive the British into the sea; and it was he who issued an ultimatum to the British, and he who began the war by sending his army into Natal (1899).

THE SECOND BOER WAR. The British were very indifferently prepared for the war and were locally outnumbered at the beginning. Although the greater part of the world favored the Boers, who were regarded as a tiny brave people fighting for independence against the greatest power on earth, all the major British overseas colonies sent volunteers to aid the mother country; moreover the Germans proved themselves unwilling to go to war with Britain on this issue. So, although the Boers won the initial victory and laid siege to several small British armies, the tide of battle turned very quickly. Ladysmith and Mafeking were relieved, and the Boers driven back into their own territories, which were annexed once more by the British. Kruger went into exile, while guerrilla warfare continued in isolated areas. At last, in 1902, peace was made (Treaty of Vereeniging), and the British, with unexampled generosity, not only did not insist on an indemnity or other war exactions but made a substantial grant of money to the Boers for reconstruction.

As a result of the war, a moderate leadership emerged among the Boers in Transvaal in the persons of two Boer generals, Louis Botha and Jan Smuts, who were instrumental in founding an Afrikaner party (Hetvolk—the people) pledged to conciliation with the British, on condition that self-government be restored to the two former republics and that the Cape Colony Boers (or, more properly, Afrikaners) who had collaborated with the enemy in the war be given back their voting rights, which had been taken from them. This the British agreed to do as a first step toward granting responsible self-government to the whole.

The Union of South Africa

Meanwhile, the British administrators who controlled the government were introducing some efficiency into the chaotic mass of often contradictory laws and regulations of the different colonies in preparation for the necessary customs union. But as soon as each colony again possessed self-government, difficulties arose. The British pressed hard for some form of federation under which internal colonial tariffs would be abandoned and the various railway systems could be in some degree united. The colonists gradually were convinced. However, almost at the last moment the Transvaal Afrikaners proposed a union form of government modified only by a few concessions to the federal principle. Since Afrikaners were in the majority in the Transvaal, Orange River Colony, and the Cape, this suggestion appealed to them—though not at once to Natal, whose white population was almost exclusively British. The leaders of the Natal Government therefore decided to put the issue before the voters in a referendum. It was a difficult choice for the voters. On the one hand, they were afraid that, if they were left out of the union, they would be unable to cope unsupported with the Indians, who had come into the country as indentured laborers and stayed after their contract was fulfilled. Also, the Zulus had not yet been completely pacified, and had recently staged one more rebellion, which had had to be suppressed by troops from the other colonies. On the other hand, if they joined the union, they would be outnumbered in the country as a whole by the Afrikaners. They preferred the latter choice and voted to join the union.

In 1910, the South African colonies thus became the Union of South Africa, with Dominion status. The former colonies under the constitution were reduced to the position of provinces, with only local tasks left to their governments, which were headed by administrators appointed by the central government.

CONTINUING PROBLEMS IN SOUTH AFRICA. The subsequent history of the Union of South Africa has shown that the misgivings of the British in Natal were indeed justified. As long as there was no racial antagonism between the Afrikaners and the descendants of the British, as long as the Afrikaner leadership remained moderate and wished to cooperate with the latter, then both peoples could work together and the great powers of the central government would not be used to coerce the British minority. But with the accession to power of the Nationalist (Afrikaner) Party after World War II, with an over-all majority in the central government, this situation changed. The government successively changed the constitution in its favor, took the Coloured and Negro voters off the electoral roll in Cape Province, where they had retained the vote as a relic of the colonial era; packed the Supreme Court; and ultimately led the nation out of the Commonwealth. This possibility was always present under the union form of government, and no safeguards written into the constitution could prevent it from happening once the Statute of Westminster in 1931 left constitutional changes in the hands of South Africans. The Union of South Africa under moderate Afrikaner leadership joined the British in both world wars, though each time at the cost of a split within the Afrikaner ranks. And each time the dissident group won power soon after the war was over. The dissident element in World War II has held power since 1948, and in view of the recent constitutional changes, it appears unlikely that it will lose power in the near future.

The Europeans—British and Afrikaners together—are in a minority in the country, being outnumbered approximately three to one by the Negroes. The two groups have in many respects the same general attitude toward the nonwhite minority, and neither would approve of any reform designed to give the nonwhites the slightest chance of coming to power in the foreseeable future. But the British element, on the whole, has very little sympathy with the Afrikaner policy of ensuring apartheid, or separateness, forever, nor do they approve of the Nationalist attempt to segregate them in reservations, known as Bantustans. They regard this policy as doomed to failure. The Negro, in the British view, should always be the source of cheap labor; but all hope of bettering themselves should not be taken from them, nor should all their aspirations be rigidly suppressed by the police methods favored by the Nationalists. A very small white minority, made up of both British and Afrikaners, believes in fairly rapid political advancement for the nonwhites, so that they may play their part in a multiracial state. They believe in cooperating with African political leaders to this end.

At present, the problem is insoluble, since the vast majority of whites approves of at least a modified form of apartheid and favors few if any political concessions to the nonwhites—certainly none that would enable them to come to power even in the remote future. In an Africa where Negroes are now in power in all countries except South Africa, the Portuguese territories and, at present, Southern Rhodesia, obviously the rest of the world must look upon the South African Government as an anachronism about which they are yet unable to do anything by peaceful means. If the South African Government is willing to brave the opinion of the rest of the world, as expressed especially in the United Nations, and if it was willing to leave the Commonwealth on this issue, few effective forms of pressure remain, short of at least economic sanctions by its major customers. The world can only hope for some relaxation of the policy of Negro repression through a change in the personnel of the government; but it cannot hope for a total reversal of policy as long as the whites feel themselves endangered by the Negro majority and are not prepared to work with them toward a general multiracial government.

Rhodesia

The winning of Rhodesia by the British was primarily the work of Cecil Rhodes, who used the power and wealth which accrued to him from his control of the Transvaal goldfields and the Kimberley diamond mines to expand to the north of Transvaal. The process was started by the acquisition of a concession to prospect for minerals won from the warrior King of the Matabele, Lo-Bengula, in 1888. It was believed that precious metals would quickly be found there, as they had been in the Rand two years before. On the strength of this concession, the British South Africa Company was founded in London in 1889. As it turned out, little valuable metal was found in Matabeleland or neighboring Mashonaland, a territory recently subdued by the Matabele; and the first agents of the Company turned instead to the land, since Rhodesia was climatically suited for European settlement. Salisbury, the present capital of Southern Rhodesia, was founded, whereupon Europeans began to stake out tracts of land and to compel the local Negroes to work for them. Lo-Bengula, furious at the actions of the Europeans, took to arms against them in 1892. The Company, however, had little difficulty in winning the war and driving Lo-Bengula out of his own country. Rhodesia then became a possession of the British South Africa Company and open to white settlement.

Meanwhile, the Portuguese, who claimed for themselves a wide swath across Africa from Mozambique to Angola, had protested that the territory was legally theirs. The Company brushed this claim aside, its agents ready and anxious, if the Portuguese resisted, to take most of Mozambique too, especially the port of Beira. The matter was settled, not entirely to the Company's satisfaction, by the Anglo-Portuguese treaty of 1891 under which an eastern boundary for Rhodesia was agreed to by both sides. The Company was guaranteed an outlet to the sea at Beira, and permission was granted to build a railroad for the purpose. Even so, it never became a really prosperous concern because of a shortage of valuable minerals and another serious war with the Matabele in 1896.

Meanwhile, in 1891, Lewanika, the paramount chief of Barotseland, requested British protection for his territory, now a part of Northern Rhodesia. The British accepted the offer, but gave the new protectorate to the British South Africa Company to administer until 1924. In that year, the Company's charter expired and it was necessary to make some provision for the future government of both Northern and Southern Rhodesia. By 1923, there were some 35,000 Europeans in the latter, but only about 1,000 in the former. The British therefore decided to bring Northern Rhodesia within the framework of the crown colony system and to administer it directly, though retaining its status as a protectorate. Southern Rhodesia, whose settlers had long been clamoring for self-government—that is to say, rule by themselves over the large African majority—was given the choice by the British of union with South Africa or responsible self-government as a colony, subject to certain limitations. By a majority of 8,744 to 5,989, it chose the latter alternative. Under the new constitution, the British retained the right to disallow Southern Rhodesian legislation that was considered inimical to African interests—and, as always in a colony, the ultimate legal right to change or revoke the constitution.

The third component territory of the present Federation of Rhodesia and Nyasaland is Nyasaland, a territory to the east of Rhodesia which is much less suitable for European settlement. This land was infested throughout the greater part of the nineteenth century by Arab slave traders, against whom various bodies of missionaries indefatigably worked, winning the confidence of many of the natives and their chiefs. In 1891, the chiefs petitioned

Queen Victoria to take the country under her protection, a request which was promptly granted. Thus Nyasaland became and remains to this day a protectorate, in which there have never been many European settlers.

Angola and Mozambique

Portugal, with two ill-defined colonies, one in southeast Africa (Mozambique) and one in southwest Africa (Angola), had long harbored the wish to join the two together by winning the territories in between, by right of discovery. At the same time, she was afraid that, if more powerful nations contested her possession of the two colonies she already had, she might have difficulty in keeping them intact. As early as 1798, Dr. Francisco Lacerda pointed out to the government in Lisbon that the British, who had just taken Cape Town, might well move northward and sever the two colonies forever. The government thereupon entrusted him with the command of an exploratory expedition. But Lacerda died of fever before he had journeyed halfway across the continent, leaving only his diary as evidence of his discoveries. He had in fact passed almost across what was later to become Northern Rhodesia. Two half-caste traders in Portuguese employ succeeded in crossing the continent from Angola eastward in 1806. There are records from this period which show that Portuguese merchants settled in eastern Angola did sometimes export beeswax and rubber through the ports of Mozambique. Silva Porto, the leading Portuguese in eastern Angola, gave valuable geographical information to Livingstone, and the missionary was entertained by the Portuguese Commandant of Tete in northwest Mozambique, an area which was undoubtedly under Portuguese control at this time.

Livingstone's travels spurred the Portuguese to pay serious attention to their African claims before it was too late. A number of treaties had been signed with African chiefs, and some financial grants made for engineering projects. A large expedition of exploration led by Major Serpa Pinto was organized along scientific lines in 1877. Although the expedition itself did not move far out of Angola, Serpa Pinto himself made a remarkable journey across the continent, eventually emerging at Durban. In 1884, an official expedition, organized for the major purpose of bolstering Portuguese claims to the territory between Angola and Mozambique, was successful in making the trans-African crossing and in mapping the lands through which it passed. In the same year, Serpa Pinto was given the task of organizing trade routes from Mozambique to

Lake Nyasa, and Dias de Cavalho entered northern Katanga for the same purpose. The latter signed treaties with a local chief who accepted Portuguese sovereignty.

Although these somewhat belated but nonetheless energetic efforts did not succeed in winning European recognition for all the claims made by Portugal, it is almost certain that without them the present colonies of Angola and Mozambique would have been far smaller in extent than they are. Britain was too powerful, and Portugal too small, for the competition between them to be anything but one-sided. The Portuguese published a map in which the territories they claimed were marked in rose and drew attention to the mute evidence in the form of old forts, churches, and other vestiges of their ancient possession of these lands. They denied the validity of King Lo-Bengula's concessions to Rhodes on the grounds that they had already signed treaties with the Mashona chiefs, who were the real owners of the land, and protested even more strongly the grant of a charter to the British South Africa Company. But Rhodes's men were already occupying the territory granted by Lo-Bengula, and some agreement had to be made. The Portuguese Cortes refused to ratify a fairly generous treaty negotiated in August, 1890. The following year, the British offered them less and refused to sign the treaty themselves until the Cortes had ratified it. In spite of the threat that British insistence would cost the Portuguese King his throne, the Cortes did ratify it, and the treaty came into effect in June, 1891.

Meanwhile, the eastern borders of Angola were also seriously in dispute. The activities of the French under Savorgnan de Brazza and of Stanley in behalf of Leopold II of Belgium had alarmed both Britain and Portugal, whose interests in this area were not in such conflict as on the other side of the continent. Portugal had been accustomed to regarding both banks of the Congo River as her own, for which there was undoubted historical justification. The British Government in 1884 signed a treaty recognizing this particular claim. But public opinion was against granting such a valuable territory to Portugal, which throughout the century had been criticized by humanitarians as unduly dilatory in suppressing the slave trade. While Britain was wavering, Portugal decided that she would gain most from an international conclave; and it was at her suggestion that Bismarck called the great meeting at Berlin in 1884, which took up the whole Congo question. In this atmosphere, the great powers of Germany, France, and Britain, all with interests in the area, and Leopold II, whose International Association of the Congo was most concerned, all had their claims to assert. As a result, Portugal was unable to salvage as much of her colony as she hoped. But in spite of her military weakness, she was aided by the mutual jealousy of the great powers, and lost relatively little. She lost the north bank of the river to Leopold's Association, but was confirmed in the possession of Cabinda, an enclave some miles north of the river, which she holds to this day. She also retained the south bank of the river as far as Noqui. In 1891, the boundaries between Angola and the Congo Independent State were agreed to by the powers.

This, however, was not the last effort on the part of other nations to take the Portuguese colonies. When the Germans took German Southwest Africa and German East Africa (Tanganyika) in the 1880's, they became neighbors of the Portuguese and at once began to covet that part of the Portuguese colonies that lay closest to their own possessions. The British, though willing to accept the existing situation, intended to share in the spoils if Germany were to make any gains at Portuguese expense. An outright grab was not contemplated; but, at the turn of the century, Portugal was in such dire financial straits and had so little to offer as security for any foreign loan that it was widely believed necessity might compel her to sell a part or all of her colonies. The British signed a treaty with Germany in 1898 containing a secret clause to the effect that the contracting powers could partition the Portuguese territories between them—"should it not be possible to maintain their integrity." The secret clause quite certainly was no secret to Portugal. Some apparent diplomatic support recently provided her by Germany in Mozambique had led her to believe that Germany would aid her against Britain. She thereafter decided that Britain would make a more reliable ally than Germany. So she fell in with British wishes during the Boer War, and signed a new treaty with her in 1899.

However, this did not prevent negotiations for a new treaty between Britain and Germany, just before World War I, in which the 1898 agreement was confirmed and made more definite. This treaty remained still unsigned at the outbreak of the war. The fact that these two great colonies remained in the hands of weak and poverty-stricken Portugal proved a blessing to her neighbors in later years. She possessed all the Central African ports on both the east and west coasts; and she was quite willing to allow railroads to be built to them across her territory—either government enterprises, like the railroad from Southern Rhodesia to Beira, or foreign-owned, like the great Benguela Railroad, begun in 1903 and finished in 1929. The capital for the latter railroad, which tapped the mineral wealth of Katanga and later Northern Rhodesia, was largely British (Tanganyika Concessions). It connects directly with the Rhodesian railroad after passing through the (Belgian) Congo. Other railroads connect Nyasaland with Beira and the Republic of South Africa with Lourenço Marques. Lastly, a further accommodation should be noted. Portugal recruits and supplies Negro contract laborers from both Angola and Mozambique for the mines in South Africa, which have always been short of such labor—especially labor as docile as that provided by the Portuguese. Thus, even today, South Africa has some vested interest in the survival of what is called Overseas Portugal.

German Southwest Africa

The German Government did not become greatly interested in colonies until the late 1870's. There were many private organizations in existence that preached the necessity for having colonies, whether for cultural, humanitarian, or commercial purposes. But Bismarck preferred for a long time to allow France to take what she wished in hopes that she would become reconciled to the loss of Alsace and Lorraine. He knew that sooner or later his country would enter into competition with France if Germany sought colonies for herself. But Bismarck could not prevent German traders from becoming interested in colonial trade, nor could he indefinitely turn a deaf ear to their pleas for protection of their trade interests—if not their persons. During the great explorations and partitions of the late 1870's and early 1880's, it became clear even to Bismarck that all Africa might soon be virtually closed to the commerce of those nations that did not have any colonies of their own, since the tariff policies of the colonial powers were now apparently being designed to ensure a monopoly of colonial trade for themselves. Nevertheless, not wishing to become embroiled with any of the colonial powers, he proceeded cautiously, first promising support to a Bremen merchant if he found a suitable port on the west coast of Africa not yet occupied by any European power.

The merchant duly found such a port in Angra Pequeña, far down the coast between Angola and Cape Colony, not far from an isolated British outpost at Walfish Bay. He persuaded a local chief to sell him some land, which was soon extended, also by purchase, farther into the interior. The British in England and at the Cape were caught napping. They had always regarded this part of Africa as their preserve, to be annexed when they were ready.

But so far they had only taken Walfish Bay, which gave them no rights over the rest of southwest Africa. Bismarck, after a few judicious ploys, asked Gladstone's cabinet if it claimed sovereignty over Angra Pequeña, and he received the reply that any German claim to territory between Angola and the Cape would infringe on Britain's "legitimate rights." When Bismarck asked, reasonably enough, what kind of rights these were, the British made no reply, meanwhile feverishly trying to get the Cape Colony, which was by this time self-governing, to annex the territory. But the Cape Government was in the midst of a domestic crisis and could not get around to the annexation until several months had passed. Bismarck had in the meantime announced that he proposed to take his merchant, Luderitz, under his protection. The following year a German warship, with a celebrated explorer named Dr. Nachtigal aboard, sailed down the African coast. Picking up Togoland and Kamerun, the last two West African territories he could find that had not yet been annexed, he finally arrived at Angra Pequeña. The Gladstone Government thereupon decided to welcome the onset of German colonialism with a smile. "God speed her," quoth he, "she becomes our ally and partner in the execution of the great purposes of Providence."

The unfortunate cabinet crisis in Cape Town has had effects to our own day. The Germans made themselves unpopular by expropriating tribal lands for settlement by their own nationals and raised a great rebellion against themselves, which they put down ruthlessly and efficiently with great loss of life—a loss that has even yet not been fully recovered. They left a considerable infrastructure behind them when they were dispossessed of the colony after World War I. But the South Africans received the colony (which they might have annexed in 1883) only as a mandate from the League of Nations—a fact that has prevented them from legally annexing it. Since they never allowed it to become a United Nations trust territory, and the League of Nations is defunct and not necessarily the legal predecessor of United Nations, it remains to this day a knotty question just what is the legal status of the territory and what is to be its future, even while South Africa administers it as if it were one of her own provinces.

French Equatorial Africa

To the north of Angola and Rhodesia stretch the "darkest" areas of "Dark" Africa, the tropical lands of the Congo basin. As early as the 1830's, the French had been ceded some land at the mouth of the Gabon estuary by friendly African chiefs, which they planned to use for naval operations in connection with their intended suppression of the slave trade, as well as for ordinary purposes of commerce. In 1849, they captured a ship with a cargo of slaves whom they proceeded to free, assembling them in a new city to be called Libreville (Freetown). In the next decades, this bridgehead was enlarged by the accession of more chiefs. There was, however, relatively little successful exploration inland until Savorgnan de Brazza, an Italian nobleman naturalized as a Frenchman, began, in 1875, to explore the river Ogooué, which was locally believed to divide Africa in two. His first journey proved his competence as an explorer, and the French now became seriously interested but realized they would have to act quickly before King Leopold II pre-empted both banks of the Congo for himself.

In 1877, Stanley had already reached the wide "pool" in the river, known now as the Stanley Pool, on the south bank of which Léopoldville now stands. Stanley had been unable to descend the Congo to its mouth because of the rapids, but he had managed to make his way to the coast and back to Europe, where Leopold had approached him. Soon, no doubt, he would be back in the Congo. The French therefore fitted out Brazza with a new expedition. He ascended the Ogooué once more, went overland until he reached the Congo, and here persuaded the most important Chief of the region to cede some land for an outpost. Leaving Sergeant Malamine, his second in command, with a few troops to hold the post (now Brazzaville, the capital city of the Republic of Congo [French]), Brazza continued his expedition, ultimately making his way down to the coast and reaching Libreville by sea.

As soon as he was able to get together a new expedition, he set out once more into the interior, signing treaties with ever more chiefs and winning an empire for France estimated to be about one-third the size of his adopted country, and without having to strike a blow. Although the French Government, reacting to losses in the Far East, temporarily lost interest in colonial adventures and did not reappoint him, he was suddenly restored to popular and governmental favor by the news that Sergeant Malamine had been able to stand off all efforts by Stanley, now in Leopold's employ and in charge of a considerable expedition, to wheedle or coerce him out of his post. The French parliament ratified Brazza's treaties and sent him back to the Congo to take official possession on behalf of France of all the territories he had explored. In another expedition, he was able to explore the Upper Congo and sign up the King of Loango, the largest native kingdom in the entire area.

This was the situation when the Berlin Conference met at the end of 1884, at which the French settled for the area explored by Brazza. They conceded to Portugal the north bank of the Congo from a short distance below Brazzaville and did not dispute Leopold's claim to the south bank, which was of no interest to them. They had no desire for the mouth of the Congo, since the rapids have always prevented navigation between Brazzaville and Léopoldville and the mouth. Eventually, a railroad was built (Congo-Ocean Railroad) from Brazzaville to Pointe Noire in Gabon that ensured an outlet to the sea exclusively over French territory. The Belgians had to be content with a railroad from Léopoldville to the port of Matadi just north of the Angolese border.

Like other French empire-builders, Brazza was consumed by the dream of uniting the territories of French West Africa with the Congo basin. To cut such a wide circle inland, it was necessary to explore the river Ubangi, a tributary of the Congo, and eventually reach Lake Chad, south of the Sudan. In 1887, Brazza claimed the area north of the Ubangi for France, and a French expedition in 1889 founded the city of Bangui in the territory later known as Ubangi-Shari (now Central African Republic). The French then pushed on north into the territory of Chad. Here they were faced not only with opposition of local tribes, but also with serious protests from the British and Germans who were now beginning to operate in this area. The British claimed that their colony of Nigeria bordered on the west shore of Lake Chad, while the Germans likewise insisted on Lake Chad as the northeastern boundary of Kamerun. Northwest of Lake Chad, however, stretched the French colony of the Niger, then in the process of being occupied. When, therefore, the French moved north of Lake Chad, they were unable to make the desired connection with French West Africa, even though they had to be content with only the east and southeast shores of the great lake itself.

It was from the Congo that Captain Marchand led his expedition that terminated at Fashoda. With a tiny company of French and African troops, he made his way from Gabon up the Congo and the Ubangi, then struck northeastward across the continent until he reached the Nile in July, 1898. With his puny force, he could not hope to match Kitchener's army, fresh from its victory over the Mahdi. To his chagrin, he was recalled by the French Government, and the French never won their west-east route across Africa.

It took the French many years to subdue the huge territory they had conquered. As a result of their North African policy in the early 1900's, they had to yield some considerable sections of it to Germany in exchange for German concessions elsewhere. This lost territory was returned to them in the form of mandates after World War I. On the whole, French Equatorial Africa retained to the end almost the same boundaries it had at the beginning. The policy adopted by the French toward these colonies was hardly less offensive to world opinion than that of Leopold II, to be described shortly. But in the case of the French colonies, the French press and parliament performed their proper functions. French exploitation of the Africans was unmercifully pilloried in the French press and by critics in the National Assembly, and attempts were made to correct it, though with relatively little success. Brazza himself was sent back late in his life with the mission of putting an end to such unmerciful exploitation. But even he was powerless to achieve much against the opposition of the concessionaires and local officials, who were too often allied with them.

It was widely believed in France that the colonies were full of riches of all kinds waiting to be exploited. The French Government, to avoid having to provide sufficient funds for administration, decided in face of considerable opposition to grant concessions to private companies, which were granted monopolies in the areas assigned to them. These companies were given virtually a free hand in their territories to collect ivory, rubber, and anything else that could be sold, subject only to mild supervision by an inadequate and necessarily corrupt officialdom. The companies engaged in forced labor and any other practices that seemed good to them. Right up until World War II, the government never really succeeded in controlling them, even though the concessionaires were reduced in numbers by bankruptcy and voluntary withdrawal from their nefarious occupation. Although a semblance of order was imposed by the organization of the four colonies into an administrative federation in 1910, the governors and governors-general were rarely accorded enough power to discipline the great private companies; and too many of the poorly paid officials were content to wink at their practices. Even in the 1920's, André Gide, the famous French critic and novelist, and Léon Blum, the Socialist leader, drew public attention to what was going on without being able to force any major changes in the system.

Nevertheless, social relations between the African elite and the French were better than in the colonies of any other power. French Africans, even in the days of the Congo Independent State, were wont to surprise their counterparts in the Belgian territory with the boast that they were French citizens of African birth. For many years, the French adopted the policy of trying to make their African colonial subjects into Frenchmen through the process of assimilation. They taught at least a few among them the French language and culture, welcomed them in their universities, and did not condescend to them. This policy eventually paid off during World War II, when Félix Eboué, a Negro from French Guiana, Governor of Tchad and then Governor-General of French Equatorial Africa, brought the colonies over to the side of De Gaulle in the war and prepared the way for their rapid evolution to independence after the war.

Congo Independent State and the Belgian Congo

The beginning of the colony that was later to become the Belgian Congo was inseparably bound up with Leopold II, King of the Belgians, whose initiative and enterprise were exclusively responsible for its existence. This remarkable monarch felt that his small country, which he ruled constitutionally, provided far too small a field for his energies; and since the Belgians were quite content to be a small nation without external ambitions, there was nothing to be done but engage in colonial enterprise himself as an individual. Although interested at first in the Far East, he soon came to recognize that no easy pickings were to be had by a monarch who possessed a fairly large but far from unlimited private fortune and no governmental backing. Africa, however, was a different matter. In the 1880's, it was still only partially explored, and the European nations were still busily engaged in staking out their particular spheres of influence. If he could hire an explorer who could make treaties with the chiefs and some high-sounding international organization, there was a good chance that the latter might be recognized by the powers as a suitable holding company—provided it offered what most of them wanted, namely a free field for the activities of their own traders. He must not antagonize any power so seriously that it would be willing to defy its competitors and take his possessions from him by force.

In short, a skilled diplomat was needed, and Leopold believed himself to be the man.

Leopold was fortunate in that the most suitable explorer, Stanley, a British subject, had been unable to interest Gladstone in the Congo, and was therefore free to accept other offers. A body known as the Study Group for the Upper Congo, organized by Leopold in 1878, now hired and sent Stanley to the Congo. But no sooner had Stanley left than Leopold bought out the other stockholders; and in fact, Stanley was responsible solely to Leopold when he started into the interior. In 1882, Leopold formed another high-sounding organization, this time the International Congo Association—which was in no sense international since it was Leopold's own creature, nor was it an association since there were no co-owners! It was believed to be a philanthropic organization devoted to suppressing the slave trade and opening up the Congo for free trade among the nations. Leopold was indeed interested in abolishing the remnants of the slave trade, converting the Congolese to Christianity, and other worthy objects—so long as the pursuit of these idealistic ends did not interfere with his making a profit on his investment.

As Leopold was no doubt perfectly aware, the promise of free trade for all in the Congo was one calculated to endear him to traders of every nation and give him a handle to use against any competition from France, Portugal, or Germany—all of which countries by the 1880's had become protectionist. They would have attempted to monopolize the import trade by laying tariffs on foreign imports. Obviously Belgium could not hope to supply the bulk of such imports in a freely competitive market; and Leopold, though King of the Belgians, did not have to support the interests of Belgium against other nations. Leopold also endeared himself to missionaries and humanitarians who, having read Livingstone, Stanley, and others, thoroughly approved of Leopold's humanitarian aims and believed that an "international" organization was just what was needed to achieve them.

When Bismarck called his Berlin Conference in 1884, Leopold had the ground well prepared. Fortified with more than 400 signed treaties, mostly the result of Stanley's work, he was able to present his Association at the Conference as an organization already in possession of what he was claiming and ready to carry out its promises. By an agreement with France, the power most directly concerned, under which she should have the first option to buy out the Association's interest if it found itself financially unable to proceed, Leopold prepared the way for recognition of his Association as a sovereign state with its own flag and its own rights. These rights were duly recognized by Germany—whose government Leopold had approached for diplomatic support—and the United States, and Britain raised no objection. Thus without ever openly discussing the substantial legal question as to whether a single monarch could own a state, actually *be* a state in his own person, the delegates gradually came to accept the idea and treat it as an accomplished fact—even though they were quite well aware of the fact that there was no International Association except Leopold, associating somewhat disingenuously with himself. Once the delegates had given their tacit approval by agreeing on the territory the Association should have, Leopold obtained formal permission from the Belgian Parliament to rule the proposed state. Then, in July, 1885, his representative in the Congo declared Leopold to be the sovereign of the Congo Independent State, and the King was in business.

In the next five years, a great deal was accomplished by a very small number of bold explorers, and effective possession was taken of much of the huge territory marked out for the new state. But Leopold, lacking the necessary resources to take action against the Arab slave traders in the eastern part of the state, preferred to conclude agreements with them under which the settlers were permitted to buy up the slaves, using them thereafter as their own unfree labor supply. In 1889, as the result of an extensive anti-slavery campaign sponsored by a missionary order headed by a Catholic cardinal, a conference was called at Brussels which entrusted Leopold with the task of suppressing the slave trade, and which provided him with the financial means to do so in the form of a loan from the Belgian Government. Leopold's officers then undertook the campaign in earnest and gradually took over the eastern part of the Congo from the Arabs. Meanwhile, a separate expedition led by an Englishman took possession of Katanga with little bloodshed. The King of the area, who had always resisted the blandishments of any white men who brought him treaties to sign, was killed in the process. But, as he was heartily detested by his own chiefs and the chiefs of local tribes whom he had conquered, the white men on the whole were welcomed. Thus the richest territory in this part of Africa passed into European hands.

By the early 1890's, Leopold's position was desperate. His personal fortune was almost gone, and there were still no profits. Nor would the Belgian Government take over his liabilities. The permitted 10 per cent ad valorem import duty, applied without distinction to all imports, provided too little revenue for the extensive expenses involved in the occupation. Profits could be made only if appropriate measures were taken to compel the natives to cut rubber and bring out ivory. Though Leopold may well have known nothing of the details of how the financial miracle was achieved, a system was developed by both state officials and private concessionary companies under which the Africans were compelled to work—by methods which, when they were revealed in the next decade, shocked all Europe. Since state officials received commission on all the ivory and rubber exported, there was no one to protect the Africans; and no one did. From 1895, the Congo paid its way with a good deal to spare, and Leopold ceased to be interested in disposing of his domain.

In the early 1900's, stories began to leak out of the Congo, largely as the result of the work of Edmund Dene Morel, a Liverpool shipping clerk in the employ of the Elder-Dempster Lines. Morel was aroused to action by his examination of Congo trade statistics, which revealed, on the one side, the import of guns and ammunition on a large scale, but few products for African consumption, and on the other, a vast export of ivory and rubber. This led him to dig deeper into the question. Eventually, he became a journalist and founded the Congo Reform Association to publicize conditions in the Congo. The British instructed Roger Casement, their consul at Boma—who was later to be hanged for his part in the Irish Rebellion of 1916—to make enquiries, and he confirmed the revelations of Morel. Indignation grew in the United States and Britain, especially in missionary circles. Leopold appointed a commission, which could not deny the facts, although, since its report was couched in general terms, it did not look quite so black as Casement's. Belgian public opinion, however, was aroused, since most of the responsible officials were Belgian, and not everyone in the world was willing to make fine distinctions between the nation and its monarch. The British took the position that the signatories of the Berlin Agreements of 1885 could call the monarch to account, and were entitled to change the status of the Congo Independent State if they wished. But the general opinion was that a government, rather than a monarch, should accept responsibility for the state. Such a government could be called to account by public opinion. If the Belgian Government were willing, then this would be the best solution. After long hesitation on both sides, Leopold agreed to give his possession to the Belgian people and the latter agreed to accept it. Title passed at the end of 1908, and Leopold died the following year.

It was not found possible to change the system overnight. Under Leopold, power had been delegated by the monarch in Belgium to a governor-general, and so to subordinate governors of provinces and appointed officials. Under the Belgian governmental system, the colonial minister in Belgium, advised by a Colonial Council, appointed the governor-general and his leading officials. Since these men were under tighter control than Leopold's had been, the worst abuses were brought to an end. The Belgians adopted a general policy of paternalism, subjecting the huge concessionary companies to governmental discipline, forcing them to provide amenities for their employees. For many decades the colony was prosperous and solvent, and eventually more primary education and social services were provided for the Congolese than for any other African people, paid for mainly from the profits of the mining industry.

British West Africa

Gambia

After the restoration of Senegal to the French in 1783, the old British colony of Gambia became once more just a fort (Fort James) and the estuary of a river. However, this river, the Gambia, was the most easily navigable river in West Africa, and had been used extensively by slave traders. When, therefore, the British abolished the slave trade in their empire, and undertook to suppress it in Africa, the Gambia settlement took on added importance. From the founding of the British colony of Sierra Leone, in 1808, until 1843, the two colonies were ruled by the same government. Sir Charles Macarthy, Governor from 1814 to 1824, purchased an island in the river, 160 miles upstream, and shortly afterward an agreement was made with a local King, who ceded both banks of the river, thus effectively shutting off the French from the whole river. At the end of the 1880's, the French formally recognized British rule over an enclave on both sides of the river stretching 300 miles upstream (the Gambia Protectorate). The Colony was made up essentially of the capital of Bathurst and Georgetown on the mainland. The Colony and Protectorate received their own government in 1888.

Sierra Leone

Sierra Leone, discovered by the Portuguese and later occupied by British slave traders, began its career as a colony by becoming a haven for liberated slaves. Loyalist Negroes who left the United States after the War of Independence were encouraged by British abolitionists to settle there, as were other slaves who had rebelled against their masters in Jamaica. After several unsuccessful efforts by a company formed for the purpose, a small Negro settlement was finally established by 1798; but since most of the Negroes did not possess either the skill or the initiative for pioneer living in a hostile country, it was far from flourishing. Yet British public opinion would not allow such a promising philanthropic venture to collapse. So the government canceled the company's charter and took it over as a crown colony in 1808, one year after the slave trade had been abolished by law.

Thereafter, the British Government made considerable use of the harbor of Freetown, one of the finest natural harbors in the world, making it the headquarters for the suppression of slavery. When the navy captured slave ships, it freed their human cargoes and settled them (or, more accurately, dumped them) in Freetown to fend for themselves as best they could. These unfortunate Negroes, many of them fairly well educated and all detribalized, found themselves with nothing in common with the still-savage tribes of the hinterland, whom they despised. Yet for many years they themselves lacked the ability to support themselves in Africa. Although British and American Methodist missionaries did their best to help them, these men, though dedicated, likewise lacked experience. Even so, by 1833 there were more than 30,000 Negroes (called Creoles) in the colony, with a different language (a kind of pidgin English) and different customs from their native African fellows. As early as 1827, the British Church Missionary Society founded Fourah Bay College, the first institute for the higher education of Africans to be established in Africa. The college still flourishes under the name of the University College of Sierra Leone.

The entire colony, however, remained an expensive venture for the British Government, which had to keep it alive by annual subsidies. Gradually, the colonial governors began to press inland, making treaties with the upcountry chiefs. This penetration was almost uniformly peaceful, and in 1896 the hinterland was consolidated as a protectorate. Relations between the upcountry tribes and the Creoles never became cordial; and even today when the country has become independent, with an upcountry medical doctor as Prime Minister, the two people are distinct in culture and usually even in appearance. As the Protectorate peoples left their hinterland for the pleasures of urban living, they began to accept the city of Freetown as their capital, and their superior numbers finally enabled them to control the government. The Creoles were unable to halt the process, and their most energetic members in recent years have provided the less educated people of the Protectorate with many of their teachers and some of their technical advisers.

The Gold Coast

The British, Dutch, and Danish settlements in the Gold Coast, established for the purpose of slave trading, ceased to be of much value in the nineteenth century. Throughout most of the century, they were financial liabilities to the three governments that supported them; but for a long time they could not come to the final decision to abandon them, even though trade was now confined to the export of palm kernels and a little gold. In particular, the Danish Government, with the largest and most expensive establishment, supported missionary enterprises and sent regular supplies out at its own expense, receiving very little in return. African traders and rulers constantly tried to play one European nation against another, a task that was easy enough since the Danes, British, and Dutch each had different trading policies. It was the British who eventually prevailed, since it was they who decided that it was necessary to subjugate the Ashanti and were willing to provide the men and resources required for this purpose.

The Ashanti, a strong native people, had begun to expand in the eighteenth century under their king (or Asantahene), who sat on a golden stool supposed to have descended from heaven. They reached the coast in 1803, subjected most of the Fanti, a weaker coastal people, and laid siege to Cape Coast Castle, the British stronghold, from which they were repulsed only with difficulty. In 1821, the British Government assumed full responsibility for the settlements and entrusted Sir Charles Macarthy, Governor of Sierra Leone, with the task of disciplining the Ashanti. Although Sir Charles did his best and won the promise of support from the Danes, he lacked military resources of his own; and the African enemies of the Ashanti were unreliable as allies unless they were sure the British would win. In 1826, Sir Charles was killed in a skirmish after having been deserted by most of his allies.

The British Government, which had always harbored doubts as to whether it was worth while remaining in that part of Africa, was ready to abandon the whole enterprise. But the local merchants were of a different opinion. After persuading the government to hand over control to themselves, they hired an enterprising British Captain, George Maclean, as Governor. During the course of his rule, he signed numerous treaties with various chiefs, including some of the Ashanti, but became involved in a private scandal. Accusations were also made against him that he was abetting the slave trade. The British therefore decided to relieve him of his job as Governor by assuming responsibility once more themselves. By this time, British influence had become paramount in the area. In 1850, the Danes decided that they had had enough and sold Christianborg Castle to the British for £1,000. The Gold Coast was then given a governor and an administration of its own.

This action was displeasing to both the Dutch and the African chiefs. The Danes and Dutch had been accustomed to subsidizing the chiefs, a policy which the British had always refused to follow. Now that the British had taken over the Gold Coast as a colony, they first attempted to impose customs duties to pay for their intended operations against the Ashanti. Foiled in this by the refusal of the Dutch to exact similar duties, they then imposed a poll tax, whereupon a serious rebellion broke out which had to be suppressed by the guns of a warship. In 1863, Ashanti raids began again, subsidized in part by Dutch grants to the Asantahene. Nothing remained to be done but to buy out the Dutch, who in 1872 received concessions in the Far East in exchange for their abandonment of the Gold Coast.

The Ashanti, no longer subsidized by anyone, invaded the colony. A strong expedition dispatched by Gladstone's government defeated them without difficulty, compelling the Asantahene to agree to pay an indemnity. This humiliation caused him to lose face with the other Ashanti chiefs, who now began to dispute his authority, resulting in a series of minor civil wars in the territory. In 1894, a new monarch shocked the feelings of the local British by offering human sacrifices on a grand scale. When they protested this recrudescence of barbarism to the British Government, Joseph Chamberlain, now in control of colonial policy, authorized an expedition that in 1896 captured Kumasi, the Ashanti capital. A protectorate was then proclaimed over the territory.

Soon afterward, the Governor of the colony determined to put an end to Ashanti sovereignty in a spectacular manner by seizing the golden stool, bringing on the last of the Ashanti wars. Although the Governor was at first besieged, he cut his way out and, on the arrival of reinforcements, defeated the Ashanti once again. The golden stool was secreted by its African guardians, but the Ashanti territory was annexed and added to the colony. The territories north of the Ashanti, whose chiefs had requested British protection, were retained as a protectorate under the name of the Northern Territories. The African rulers of these territories were permitted a considerable degree of autonomy until after World War II.

Nigeria

Nigeria, the most populous country in Africa, came into existence with its present boundaries in an almost haphazard manner, mainly through the activities of independent traders interested in the export of palm kernels. Until the 1870's, only Lagos, the island port at the mouth of the river Niger and one of the most unhealthy of all the ports in West Africa, was in British hands. In the 1850's, though the slave trade was largely suppressed, the French began to use Lagos for recruiting indentured African labor for their plantations in Réunion in the Indian Ocean. The British protested at what they regarded as the slave trade under a different name, since most of the laborers, like the slaves, had been prisoners of war. After much hesitation, they sent an expedition to Lagos; and the local Chief, in exchange for a pension, ceded his island to the British, who made it into a colony—the only part of Nigeria that ever was officially ceded, and the only part that became a colony.

The movement that eventually united all of Nigeria under the protection of the British Crown was begun in earnest with the arrival of George Goldie Taubman (later Sir George Taubman Goldie), a British soldier who was a shareholder in an African trading company. All his life he was deeply interested in the final suppression of the slave trade and tried to put an end to the liquor trade among Africans. Showing considerable financial acumen, he succeeded in amalgamating several African trading companies under the name of the National Africa Company, which by 1884 had succeeded in buying up the large French company also doing business in the area. Goldie appeared in person at the Berlin Con-

ference of 1884–85, and was able to show that he and his countrymen were, if not quite in "effective occupation" of the area—a
formula adopted by the Conference—at least the leading power
there and thus entitled to regard western Nigeria as being in their
sphere of influence.

Meanwhile, in southeastern Nigeria an English consul named
Hewett had been actively engaged in obtaining the signatures of
numerous chiefs to treaties requesting British protection. Just before the opening of the Conference, he had been able to declare
the existence of an Oil Rivers Protectorate. This claim also was
accepted by the Conference, so that most of southern Nigeria was
now officially in the British sphere of influence. The Oil Rivers
Protectorate was gradually extended inland by the same process,
becoming the Niger Coast Protectorate in 1893.

In 1886, Goldie was granted a charter for a new major trading
company, the Royal Niger Company, which, unlike most African
trading companies of the period, made money in spite of the
political tasks with which it was entrusted. Although formally
given a trade monopoly and sufficiently powerful to be able to dispose of any commercial competitors, it experienced considerable
difficulty with the French, who, under the guise of scientific expeditions, were engaged in expanding from their own colonies by
means of the same process of signing treaties with African chiefs.
Even Germans were encroaching from the east on what Goldie
regarded as his preserves. In 1890, an agreement was signed with
the French defining the two countries' respective spheres of influence in the north. Another race between the two powers in the
west resulted in the extension of British Nigeria, rather than
French Dahomey.

These activities had brought Goldie and his company into the
ancient Muslim empires of northern Nigeria ruled by native emirs.
There was no alternative to forcing them too to accept British
protection, which most of them were not loath to do, since the
British proposed to leave them with their prerogatives intact as
long as they officially abolished slavery and refrained from breaking
the *Pax Britannica*. A sharp lesson taught them by Sir Frederick
(later Lord) Lugard who stormed several of their fortified cities
in 1903, broke the resistance of those emirs who had not taken
British conditions too seriously.

Meanwhile, in 1900, the British had taken over the political
functions of the Royal Niger Company in exchange for the payment of a considerable sum of money to the Company. They then

established the two separate protectorates of Northern and Southern Nigeria, the latter the successor to the Niger Coast Protectorate of 1893. In 1906, the colony of Lagos was joined to Southern Nigeria as the Colony and Protectorate of Southern Nigeria. In 1914, the two small protectorates were united and the whole of Nigeria administered as the Colony and Protectorate of Nigeria, with its capital at Lagos.

The unification of Nigeria was largely the work of Lugard, who made good use of the existing native institutions, especially the emirates of the most populous northern sector of the country. The policy of using native chiefs, "advised" by British residents, which he called "indirect rule," was extolled by Lugard as the ideal colonial system. In fact, it worked well and was much less costly than centralized administration in territories where there was an accepted traditional African leadership. Nigeria has at least three native ethnic divisions. In the almost totally Islamic north, trade and cultural connections prior to British rule had always been with North Africa. The people are mainly Hausa with an admixture of Fulani (or Peulhs), who conquered the Hausa in recent centuries. Southwestern Nigeria is peopled mainly by Yoruba, of whom almost half are also Muslim. In Yorubaland, the institution of native chiefs was widespread, making indirect rule feasible. But in the southeastern territory, where the non-Muslim Ibos predominate, indirect rule never functioned well. Throughout the twentieth century, the British were sometimes compelled to appoint chiefs of their own choosing in order to carry out the administrative functions required by the system. The African people naturally did not regard these men with the same reverence as they regarded traditional chiefs elsewhere, and indirect rule unquestionably functioned indifferently in Iboland.

In spite of its imperfections, on the whole the system worked fairly well, and it was cheap. In spite of its size and the variety and extent of its population, the country acquired through British institutions a kind of unity that made possible the emergence of a "Nigerian" independent state in 1960.

French West Africa

Until the reign of Napoleon III, the French possessed little in West Africa except some ancient cities in Senegal and a few isolated trading settlements elsewhere. French traders, compelled to look for products to replace the slaves of earlier centuries, could not find much in the hinterland of Senegal other than a few spices, gum arabic, ostrich feathers, and similar exotic products. Not until the peanut, the present staple export from Senegal, was introduced did this area exhibit an economic potential. Although some Frenchmen explored into the interior in the first half of the nineteenth century—especially René Caillié, who penetrated the hidden city of Timbuktu—on the whole French interests remained minimal. Louis Philippe (1830–47) restored some of the old French settlements on the Guinea coast, but it was not yet decided whether systematic penetration should be pursued from French outposts in Guinea, Ivory Coast, or Dahomey in the south, or Senegal.

This was the situation when Faidherbe became Governor of Senegal in 1854, a position he held for eleven years. During this time, he drove inland with African troops, compelling a number of African and Senegalese potentates to accept French protection and opening up the country as far as the river Niger. He also established the system of administration followed by all French colonial governments thereafter.

In the last years of Napoleon and the first years of the Third Republic, colonial expansion again slowed down until France recovered some of the strength she had lost during the Franco-Prussian War. Then she resumed the initiative. Unlike the British, the French self-consciously set themselves to win as much empire as they could, and in French West Africa, their aims were achieved almost exclusively by military means. Although traders were naturally interested in the process and followed where soldiers had blazed the way, the primary purpose appears to have been prestige. The result was that what France took for herself was largely the less desirable and less rich parts of West Africa, although the total area she won was considerably greater than that taken by the British. When the French came into conflict with the British, it was almost invariably the latter who were able to win the diplomatic victories and the territory in dispute, since they were more powerful at the time both in Africa and the world. French governments were hesitant to engage the full resources of the country in distant areas, and public support for an imperialistic policy was intermittent. Except at moments when the national pride was touched, as in the case of Marchand's exploit at Fashoda, most of the French people were indifferent to the needs of their soldier-conquerors and resented the taxes they had to pay for expansion.

The desert areas bordering the Sahara lent themselves to military conquests. Here there were already decaying empires ruled by Negro and Nilotic Muslim kings and emirs. When these were defeated and were forced to accept French overlordship, their subjects followed their leaders. Sometimes, as in Upper Volta, the ruler was a non-Muslim who was quite willing to accept French protection since he was always in danger of attack and forcible conversion by his Muslim neighbors. This potentate, the Moro Naba of the Mossi, was allowed to retain his title and substantial independence. Elsewhere the French found themselves faced with strong opposition from great African warriors, such as Samoury, grandfather of the present President of Guinea, who kept them at bay for years before he was finally captured. In many areas there were rebellions against French rule; since the area had probably been rapidly conquered and never completely reduced to obedience, such rebellions had initial success. Eventually, however, they were all put down and the chiefs reduced to the position of hereditary French civil servants, carrying out the will of their French overlords in exchange for suitable emoluments.

This French variant of Lugard's indirect rule remained the central feature in French colonial policy; it enabled them to run the country through a powerful governor-general, less powerful governors to whom he gave orders, and a relatively small handful of French officials and military officers, whose task it was to train and lead the African troops who were responsible for law and order in the colony.

The northernmost of the territories comprising French West Africa is Mauritania, a Muslim country forming the southwestern sector of the Sahara Desert. The territory, extending as far south as the Senegal River, was taken by the French in the course of the nineteenth and early twentieth centuries, largely as a means of defending Senegal against raids on the Senegalese tribes in the vicinity of the river. The greater part of the country is peopled by Moors, the Negro inhabitants for the most part living in the river area. Mauritania did not become part of French West Africa until 1920, when it was given its own local administration, though even then its capital was Saint-Louis in Senegal.

East of Mauritania is the (French) Soudan, now the Mali Republic, site of the flourishing medieval empire of Mali, whose chief city was Timbuktu. The empire had long been decadent, even before the French began expanding from Senegal, during the regime of Faidherbe. The French were aided by the fact that a Muslim warrior was at the time trying to establish Muslim supremacy over pagan groups in the country. When he was killed in a rebellion, the French were left with relatively little fighting to be done until the rise of Samoury, whom they were compelled to fight for sixteen years and did not capture until 1898.

The country now known as Niger, to the east of Soudan, was explored by Englishmen in the first half of the nineteenth century. But by British consent the territory became a French sphere of influence. The French, as already noted, had hoped to win British Nigeria, but were able to take only the far less desirable Niger which is mostly desert and infertile savannah. Even so, they met strong resistance from the Touaregs, a warlike Berber people who were temporarily subdued in the early nineteen hundreds but rebelled during World War I. This last rebellion was put down only with the aid of the British. In 1922, Niger became a colony. Its eastern boundary borders that of Chad in French Equatorial Africa, thus joining the two French African federations.

South of Mauritania is Senegal, the earliest of the French settlements. Senegal is separated from Guinea, which borders both Senegal and Mali to the northeast, by Portuguese Guinea, which stretches a few hundred miles inland. The French had long owned trading posts in Guinea. When trade began to increase in the mid-nineteenth century, the local chieftains demanded an increase in the customary payments made to them by traders. This led the French to declare a protectorate over a part of the coastal area. But most of Guinea's hinterland was conquered from the interior by the various French expeditions engaged in fighting the Hausa, Peulhs, and other major tribes in the vast area just south of the Sahara. The chieftain Samoury, who was born in Upper Guinea, was eventually captured as far south as the Ivory Coast. In 1884, some German competition appeared in the coastal area of Guinea, compelling the French to assert their historical claims. The Germans accepted these the following year in exchange for the abandonment of French claims in Togoland.

The most economically important of all the states of French West Africa is Ivory Coast, bordering on Mali and Upper Volta, which has its only outlet to the sea through Ivory Coast. The French did not pay much attention to Ivory Coast till late in the century, though they possessed a few trading posts there. In the 1880's, a French trader named Treich-Laplène with governmental backing began signing treaties with the local chiefs, offering French protection. When this was accepted, British expansion was effectively shut off from Ashanti in the Gold Coast to the east of Ivory

Coast. Proceeding northward, Treich-Laplène was able to join one of the most remarkable of French explorers, Louis-Gustave Binger, who had already obtained similar treaties from the chiefs of Upper Volta, especially from the great King of Kong, one of the largest Negro empires in the area. In 1893, the protected territories became the colony of Ivory Coast. In 1896, the Moro Naba, King of the Mossi in Upper Volta, accepted French protection, and the two territories were united in the same colony. Upper Volta was separated in 1919 and made a separate component territory of French West Africa. It was partitioned in 1932 among three of the other territories, only to be separated again after World War II.

Lastly, the farthest east of French territories in West Africa is Dahomey, a narrow strip of land dominated in the nineteenth century by one of the most famous (or infamous) of African kingdoms, that of Abomey, which employed an army of Amazons and was always one of the most bloodthirsty of tyrannies. For this kingdom, severe competition developed among the British, French, and Portuguese. In 1851, the French were allowed by the King of Abomey to establish a port at Cotonou. Porto Novo was disputed between the British and French; and in 1885, the Portuguese, who had undoubtedly built the port in the seventeenth century, claimed it and the rest of Dahomey by virtue of a treaty with the King. The Portuguese were persuaded to withdraw their claim, and the British came to an amicable agreement with the French to take some other settlements farther west, which they abandoned also by agreement a few years later. Meanwhile, the kingdom of Abomey continued to flourish, and the monarch demanded higher duties for permitting trade in his kingdom. The French were preparing to discipline him, but the King attacked first, with his army of several thousand Amazons. It was three years before he could be subdued and sent into exile. His successor, in the French view, mismanaged his kingdom and was deposed in 1900. In the meantime, the French had penetrated the country from the north, where Dahomey bordered on Upper Volta and Niger, and the whole country was consolidated as a colony in 1902.

French West Africa was organized into an administrative federation in 1904. It then comprised those territories that were considered to be fully pacified and held the status of colonies—namely, Senegal, Soudan, Guinea, Ivory Coast, and Dahomey. When Upper Volta was separated from Ivory Coast after World War I, it became a component part of the federation, as did Niger and Mauritania after they had been pacified. Thus by the 1930's, there were eight territories in the federation. The governor-general, who ruled from the federal capital of Dakar, was the chief official, aided by a governor and bureaucracy in each territory. The French, with their preference for a centralized system of government, allowed the governor-general a full measure of power, to such an extent that the territorial governors found themselves reduced to the position of being in almost all respects his subordinates—as, of course, were the various civil service functionaries, including those chiefs who were on the government payroll and performed administrative tasks for the government. French West Africa was therefore in no sense a federation as the word is generally understood. It resembled more the unitary government of the United Kingdom where the central government has substantial powers over the county and other local governments in the country. Details of the policy of assimilation followed by the French in the federation, including French policy toward the intelligentsia that laid the foundations for ultimate independence, will be discussed in Chapter 10.

German West Africa—Togoland and Kamerun

The establishment of a German colony in Togoland in 1885 was the result of an official journey taken by the German explorer Dr. Gustav Nachtigal. The Germans had previously been little interested in colonization, and their trading interests were minimal. But in view of the important position held by Germany in Europe in the 1880's, the other powers did not feel they could prevent her from colonizing in Africa if she wished. Nachtigal's efforts were confined to the making of a treaty with the Chief of Togo, a relatively small town behind the more developed trading center of Porto Segouro—hence the name given to the colony as a whole. The Germans, however, never made Togo their capital but, after two other choices had proved unsuitable, decided upon Lomé, the present capital. By the time agreements were made with the British and French at the end of the century delimiting the boundaries of the colony, the Germans had extended their control northward into the interior and begun to build a railroad. But they were unable to include in their colony all the Ewe, the most important people in the southern area of Togoland. The British had obtained by earlier negotiations a substantial slice of territory to the west of the Volta River (Heligoland Treaty of 1890) that was inhabited by Ewe. Others inhabited French Dahomey, which has no natural boundaries with Togoland. The conversion of Togoland after the war into two League of Nations mandates held by Britain and France joined the Ewe in the British mandated territory with their fellow tribesmen in the Gold Coast, but separated them from the majority of their people in the French mandated territory. They remain separated today, since the non-Ewe majority in British Togoland chose to join independent Ghana in a plebiscite held under United Nations auspices in 1956.

Dr. Nachtigal, after completing his business in Togoland, sailed southward to the Cameroons River. Here German traders had recently become active and signed a number of treaties with local chiefs, no doubt fully aware that an official expedition would soon be on the way. Nachtigal negotiated a treaty with a chief known as King Bell, which the British could not prevent, because their consul Hewett arrived a few days too late. The legal right, therefore, according to the customs of the time, rested with the Germans. Although the coastal area thus won was relatively small, there were no necessary limits to what the Germans could win for themselves in the hinterland, since the entire area northeast to Lake Chad was still in dispute between the European powers. This provided an opportunity for the Germans to compete on more or less equal terms, and for German diplomacy to gain territory in exchange for concessions, not necessarily territorial, elsewhere. In exchange for German acquiescence in their activities in Morocco (as previously noted), the French were compelled to concede to Germany some 100,000 square miles of their Congo possessions. These were incorporated into the colony of Kamerun. By such means the Germans eventually reached Lake Chad, which became the northeastern boundary of Kamerun.

In the brief period they held the almost totally undeveloped and difficult terrain of Kamerun, they began to cultivate large plantations upcountry and started a railroad leading from Douala inland, while Douala itself was made into a considerable port. Kamerun, like Togoland, was divided in two after the war, the smaller sector going to Britain and the larger to France as mandates. The northern sector of the British mandate eventually went by plebiscite to Nigeria, and the southern sector was united with the French mandated territory to become the present independent state of Cameroun. A third sector, the present-day small states of Rwanda and Burundi, were granted to Belgium as mandates.

Portuguese and Spanish Possessions

There remain to note only the territories in West Africa that fell to Portugal and Spain. Portuguese Guinea, just to the south of Senegal, had never been without Catholic missionaries and some traders from the time of its discovery to the present. Since no other power had special interest in this territory, the Portuguese were permitted to keep it. They also possessed the islands of Sao Tomé and Principe in the Gulf of Guinea, the former a very fertile island whose sugar plantations are worked to a large extent by convict labor from the major Portuguese territories in south-central Africa. The Portuguese by a strange anomaly also continued to hold a fortress city in Dahomey named Ouidah, built in 1727 and with a present population of some 15,000, until the independent State of Dahomey reclaimed it in 1961.

Spain continues to rule Fernando Po, an island off the coast of the Cameroons won from the Portuguese in 1778, but ceded to Britain for a few decades in the early nineteenth century, and a few other islands of lesser importance. She was granted by the Berlin Conference of 1885 a territory now known as Rio Muni, formerly Spanish Guinea, bounded by Kamerun in the north and Gabon to the east and south. Her rights were recognized by the Conference because Spaniards had been settling there since the 1840's, and it was then of little potential economic importance. Even today, there are several thousand Spaniards in the territory, giving it a larger percentage of whites in the population than most African territories.

Madagascar

The large island of Madagascar, now the Malagasy Republic, is inhabited by peoples distinct from those of the mainland of Africa. The leading peoples do not come from the mainland but apparently, at some remote period, from Indonesia. Ethnically they are closer to the Malays than to any of the Negro peoples of the mainland. Although the Portuguese discovered the island and founded some settlements there in the sixteenth century, and though the British, Dutch, and French followed, it was primarily the French, among the Europeans, who influenced the Malgache people in the seventeenth century. For some centuries, there were three native kingdoms on the island, each striving for supremacy over the others. At the end of the eighteenth century, the Merina were on the way to establishing themselves as supreme, while the British and French were now contending among themselves for trade and converts on the island. After a joint Anglo-French bombardment of the chief port in 1845, the Malgache Queen was compelled to accept European assistance in the modernization of her kingdom. Thereafter a Merina Prime Minister virtually ruled the country for over thirty years through his influence on successive queens. His policy of playing off the British against the French was successful for a time—he even allowed himself and the Queen to be converted to Protestantism for a while. But the influence of the French was growing. When the Third Republic began to adopt a more active colonial policy, the British felt that they were too deeply engaged elsewhere to wish to take Madagascar, in spite of the fact that there were far more Protestants than Catholics on the island. By this time, about two-thirds of the island was under Merina rule, and most of the remainder, although still administered by local kings, acknowledged the suzerainty of the Merina monarchs. Nevertheless, among the non-Merina peoples there was strong resentment of the ascendancy of the Merina aristocracy and middle class. When the Merina monarchy collapsed, in 1895, many of them took the opportunity to take revenge, even if they had little love for the French.

The refusal of the Merina monarchy and the Prime Minister to recognize the right of Frenchmen to own and inherit property on the island led to a naval expedition during the French Premiership of Jules Ferry. The Malgache were thus forced to accept a loose kind of protectorate that was never properly defined (1885). Negotiations were begun with the British, who agreed to recognize the French protectorate over Madagascar in exchange for French recognition of the British protectorate in Zanzibar. The French, thus given a free hand, presented an ultimatum to the Malgache demanding far stronger powers than they had been accorded in 1885. This the Prime Minister rejected, whereupon the French sent a considerable expedition that met very little resistance and succeeded in taking the capital of Tananarive (in 1895). The Prime Minister went into exile, but for the moment the French maintained the monarchy. In the following year, they annexed the island but without leaving a sufficient body of troops or officials to take over the Merina Administration. Merina authority, thus undermined, collapsed, and a widespread rebellion resulted. In some places, the rebellion was led by former Merina officials against the French; elsewhere it was led by non-Merina peoples against the Merina. At this crisis, the French sent General Galliéni, one of their most capable and experienced officers who had already won praise for his work in the Soudan and Tonkin, to Madagascar as Governor-General with virtually absolute authority and supported by sufficient troops. Galliéni promptly deposed and exiled the Queen, and pacified and reorganized the country. He introduced numerous reforms and continued the modernization that had been begun by the previous regime.

East Africa

Britain and Germany in Zanzibar

The historical background of all East Africa cannot be understood without an appreciation of the part played by the relatively small island of Zanzibar and its sultans and the influence of Arabs and Persians on the entire coast line. The Persians of the Abbasid Caliphate conquered Zanzibar about a thousand years ago and retained it for several centuries. This long occupation has been responsible for the substantial Persian element in the population, so that one of Zanzibar's major political parties today is called the Afro-Shirazi (Persian) Party. Later came the Portuguese, who in turn were ousted by Arabs. In the early 1800's, Zanzibar came under the rule of the Imam of Muscat in the Arabian peninsula. When a later Sultan felt his power to be declining in Muscat, he removed himself and his court to Zanzibar, of which he became undisputed Sultan. For a long time he remained an important potentate in his own right, possessing control over the greatest open slave market in the world.

The Sultan was also the owner of several important coastal areas in East Africa, including the port of Mombasa, for which the British as rulers of Kenya still pay an annual rent, and Dar es Salaam, now capital of independent Tanganyika. The Sultan's writ did not run far inland from the coast, though Arab traders who penetrated regularly into the interior in search of slaves and other trade items usually acknowledged themselves as his subjects. In 1861, Zanzibar became formally independent of the Imamate of Muscat. In 1873, Sir John Kirk, a friend of Livingstone and British consul in Zanzibar, succeeded where his unofficial predecessors as British advisers had failed. With the aid of an ultimatum, he persuaded the new Sultan Barghash to take serious steps to abolish the slave trade and close down the slave market in Zanzibar.

By the 1880's, British and German interests were extremely active throughout East Africa, each working sedulously for its own ends and trying to outwit the other, while each paid formal respects to the Sultan of Zanzibar and his claims to the interior of East Africa. As a result of frequent negotiations between the powers, it was eventually decided that the Germans should have undisputed possession of German East Africa. The Sultan had to be content with about $1 million paid him by the Germans in exchange for the abandonment of his claims in that country, and the retention of substantial powers in his own territories of Zanzibar and Pemba in exchange for allowing himself to be protected and advised by a British resident. He retained nominal sovereignty over his coastal possessions in British East Africa.

German East Africa (Tanganyika)

The Germans succeeded to the Sultan's estate almost entirely through the enterprise of a young free-lance German imperialist and explorer named Karl Peters. Peters raised some money to found a company for German colonization, and betook himself to Zanzibar in 1884 without benefit of Bismarck's blessing. The old Chancellor, indeed, forbade the enterprise. Winning aid from German merchants in Zanzibar, Peters with a few companions proceeded upcountry and succeeded in persuading a number of chiefs to sign treaties with him. When he returned to Germany the next year, he reorganized his company as the German East Africa Company and persuaded Bismarck, who was afraid he would offer his treaties to Leopold II of Belgium, to issue a proclamation taking the territories he had won under German protection. In the same year, a number of British merchants founded an association called the Imperial East Africa Company to exploit concessions just to the north of those of Peters, which had been obtained by one of Britain's most experienced negotiators, Sir Harry Johnston. The conflicting claims of the two companies brought about the negotiations that divided the Sultan of Zanzibar's territories between them. Meanwhile, Peters returned to Africa and obtained treaties from local potentates far up into the well-organized native kingdom of Buganda. He then presented these to his masters in Germany, hoping for the same approval as before.

Although Bismarck had just been dismissed by Kaiser Wilhelm II, even Bismarck could not have given approval to such immense inroads into territories the British regarded as in their sphere. As it

happened, both Bismarck and his successor, Caprivi, desired
Heligoland in the North Sea more than any African lands. They
therefore abandoned most of their African claims by the Heligoland Treaty of 1890. In the next few years, they consolidated their
various African possessions into the colony of German East Africa
(now Tanganyika). The German Government took over the
territory from the German East Africa Company in 1897.

German policy in the new colony was to develop it for the
benefit of European planters and large companies. For this purpose, they proceeded to expropriate lands and to compel the
Negroes to work for their new masters. The result was a large-scale
rebellion in 1905, that was suppressed with ruthless efficiency at
the cost of more than 100,000 lives. Thereafter German capital
and enterprise began to provide an infrastructure of roads and
railways and steamships on Lake Tanganyika. Although German
East Africa was kept virtually intact by the Germans during the
war, they were compelled to cede it by the peace treaties. A German East African mandate was granted by the League of Nations
to Britain, which renamed the territory Tanganyika. At last the
British were able to hold a swath of Africa from south to north,
making possible the fulfillment of the Cape-to-Cairo dream, so
long held by her imperialists.

Uganda

To the south of the (Anglo-Egyptian) Sudan lies the inland
country of Uganda, which contains Lake Albert, to the northwest,
and the northern half of Lake Victoria. In the lakes, the river
Nile rises to flow northward to the Mediterranean. The first penetration of Uganda by Europeans was undertaken from the north
down the Nile and through the Sudan. In the 1870's, several
expeditions reached Uganda under European leaders in the employ
of the khedives of Egypt, who wished to extend their empire
southward. When the Mahdi took Khartoum, the threat to
Uganda from the north ceased. Indeed, the last surviving Egyptian
commander, an Austrian known as Emin Pasha, had to be rescued
by Stanley, and his troops were later enrolled in the British service
by Lugard. Thereafter, explorers and empire-builders—as well as
the Arab slave traders—entered the country from Zanzibar and the
east.

At this time, Uganda was divided into several African kingdoms,
most of them ancient and inefficient except Buganda, which was

the best-organized native kingdom in the whole of Africa. It was ruled by a king known as the Kabaka, under whom was a recognized hierarchy of chiefs, each with a set task to perform (the head of this chiefly bureaucracy under the Crown was an appointed katikkiro, or prime minister). The Kabaka, Mutesa I, who died in 1884, was able to play one European party against another with considerable success. He permitted Islamic, Catholic, and Protestant missionaries into his country, but kept them under strict control. At this time, there was no thought that the country was in any respect in need of European protection.

However, when Mutesa was succeeded by Mwanga, the new monarch began to execute his Christian subjects, who were growing in number, though there were constant quarrels between the Catholics and Protestants and their respective converts. The Muslims, backed by the Arab traders, were also the object of the Kabaka's unfavorable attentions, but they reacted by driving him from his throne—whereupon Mwanga joined forces with the two groups of Christians who restored him. Offices of state were thereafter meticulously shared between Catholics and Protestants, these factions becoming in fact the equivalent of political parties. Meanwhile, the Berlin Conference of 1884–85 had taken place, and the following year, by an agreement with the Germans, the British received Uganda as part of their sphere of influence.

British interests formed a trading company in 1886 that in 1888 was granted a charter under the name of the Imperial British East Africa Company, with the task of governing the lands between Mombasa and Lake Victoria. When an agent went to look over the territory alloted to his company, Kabaka Mwanga, who was again having trouble with a rival sponsored by the Muslims, sent a letter to him asking for his assistance. This letter fell into the hands of the German agent Karl Peters, who promptly rushed to Uganda and persuaded the Kabaka to sign a treaty with him. The Catholic missionaries in the country had no objection to letting Germany have the country (though they themselves were French), and the Protestants, rather than incur the monarch's wrath, signed too. Uganda might well have become a German protectorate had not the Heligoland Treaty of 1890 undone Peters' work and recognized Uganda as a British sphere of influence.

But quarrels between the rival groups of Christians continued in Buganda and frequent Muslim uprisings had to be suppressed in other parts of the country. The Company was so burdened by its governmental expenses that it could make no profits. When it threatened to withdraw in 1892, the Church Missionary Society in England raised enough money for a further year's expenses, but it was clear that the British Government would soon be forced to intervene. A commission sent out to Uganda to investigate came to a provisional agreement with Mwanga, and the next year Uganda was taken under British protection (1893). In the next few years, with the aid of Buganda, the rest of the country was subdued. Buganda herself, with her Kabaka and administrative system, was rewarded with some new provinces, still today a bone of contention with the kingdom of Bunyoro, now that Uganda as a whole has become independent.

The system instituted by the British in Uganda was a variant of indirect rule. In most parts of Uganda, and especially in Buganda, the land that had previously been held in common was now distributed to the various chiefs, who were made responsible for the collection of taxes on behalf of the government—a much more responsible position than they had held hitherto. As in many of the French colonies, the chiefs became the servants of the government, in the process acquiring such a vested interest in the system that they were reluctant to give it up. Thus to the end they objected to the British policy of granting independence to Uganda as a whole under democratic institutions.

Kenya

Kenya, the territory between Uganda and the coast, had also been granted to the Imperial East Africa Company as a field for its activities. The Company planned to build a railroad from Mombasa to Kampala, the capital of Buganda; but after Uganda had become a protectorate, it became necessary for Kenya to enjoy similar protection by Britain, since the railroad would pass through Kenyan territory. In 1895, Britain therefore proclaimed a protectorate over the country, giving it the name of British East Africa. In 1902, the year that the railroad from Mombasa to Kampala was opened, a new and unusual company, the East Africa Syndicate, was formed to settle Europeans in the Kenyan highlands. This land had been vacant at the time of the building of the railroad, since the roaming Masai had made it too dangerous for the more numerous but less warlike Kikuyu to settle there. The following year the first great Kenya pioneer, Lord Delamere, arrived to build his estate. Others followed, mainly from South Africa, all carving out for themselves great estates and eventually closing the "White Highlands" to any Negro settlement. Land tenure was on the basis of perpetual (999-year) leases. In 1907, the customary form of colonial government was instituted, and in 1920, Kenya became officially a colony, to which was added a coastal protectorate made up of the lands still leased from the Sultan of Zanzibar.

The Special Case of Liberia

By the outbreak of World War I, Africa had been thoroughly partitioned by the European powers. Only Abyssinia, which had successfully resisted Italian penetration, and little Liberia on the west coast of Africa, were still independent; even they were subjected to foreign influence. Liberia, founded in 1822 by the American Colonization Society as a haven for freed Negro slaves, had experienced much the same difficulties as Sierra Leone. The freed Negroes, used to the relatively easy living in the United States, found themselves in constant difficulty with the upcountry Africans, who frequently attacked them, and the pioneering work in an Africa that their ancestors had left in some cases several generations previously was extremely difficult. By the end of the American Civil War, there were about 20,000 freed slaves in the country, one-third of whom had been taken directly from slave ships, the other two-thirds sent by the American Colonization Society. The United States aided the settlers only intermittently, even though foreign powers were inclined to look upon the country as a United States protectorate.

In 1847, the Republic of Liberia was constituted, with a form of government closely modeled on that of the United States. United States influence did not prevent Britain and France from seizing the choicest sections of what had previously been recognized as belonging to the little republic and adding them to their own colonies. Some of these sections had been purchased earlier by the Liberian Government with money supplied not only by the United States but by Britain. Throughout the nineteenth century and for much of the twentieth, Liberia's neighbors constantly flouted the authority of her presidents, and it was extremely difficult to obtain any diplomatic help. Few foreign countries even recognized the Liberian Government. Just before World War I, the United States granted a considerable loan to Liberia for development in exchange for her agreement to accept an American adviser. But, although United States economic influence remained strong, and became stronger when after World War I the Firestone Company obtained large concessions in the interior, Liberia never did become an American colony.

Today Liberia is genuinely independent and, by virtue of her independent status, was able to become a charter member of the United Nations twelve years before the first newly independent African state (Ghana) joined her. Thus, in spite of the fact that the economic development of the country has lagged behind that of almost every territory colonized and controlled by Europeans, her long history of at least nominal independence has enabled her to win some acceptance among the new African states as a genuine neutral. In recent times, under President Tubman, who has held his position since 1944, her leadership has been accepted in several important efforts looking toward African unity free from European or Soviet alignments.

Artificial Boundaries of the African States

Attention has been drawn to the manner in which the European imperialists decided among themselves the boundaries of their various colonies without reference to the actual ethnic similarity or difference between the African peoples who make up the population. Even if the Europeans had been aware of the ethnic composition of their new subjects, it is unlikely that the knowledge would have made any difference in their policy. In fact, competition for prestige among the powers took precedence over any humanitarian or ethnic considerations. When the question arose which power should possess which territory, the matter was decided by negotiation. If one power "lost" some territory it claimed, compensation was usually offered elsewhere. In the delimitation of boundaries, little attention was paid even to natural frontiers such as rivers or mountains—and none at all to the wishes of the Africans involved in the transfer of territory. More often the decisions were made on the basis of the relative power wielded by the Europeans in Europe. Behind the policy adopted by Europeans, including most missionaries, lay the assumption that Africans were backward children whose wishes could be neither made known nor consulted. It was up to their new parents and religious advisers to make decisions for them, and *any* European power was so much more civilized than the Africans that its rule could only be of benefit to them.

As a result, the boundaries of the colonies were wholly artificial, and it was largely a matter of chance which European state became responsible for their development, which European language became the language of government and commerce, and which European institutions in a modified form were transferred to the colony. Nevertheless, a kind of unity was imposed on the colonies during the half century or more that the Europeans ruled them; and, except in the case of the United Nations trust territories where plebiscites with limited choice were held, the boundaries of the various colonies became those of the independent nations that have emerged since World War II. It is not surprising that various of the new nations have wished to add to their territories, or that a Pan-African movement should have arisen which tries to unite large numbers of the small nations under one rule. This movement is in its infancy and has as yet no great victories to record, but it may be expected to grow in the future—in spite of having to contend with the vested interest in the existing order that each nation has acquired as a result of its history as a colony.

5. The Caribbean

British Possessions

The British West Indies

ECONOMIC CONSEQUENCES OF ABOLITION. One crucial event dominated the history of the British West Indies in the nineteenth century—the abolition of slavery. Prior to abolition in 1807 and emancipation in 1833, the land in the various islands had been worked by Negro slaves owned by the European planters, many of whom lived in England, leaving their estates to be managed by resident agents. Virtually the only crop raised in most of the islands was sugar, and a preferential tariff for all practical purposes excluded the import of sugar into England from any other part of the world. In accordance with British custom, the islands enjoyed local self-government, though the franchise was limited by a property qualification that no freed Negro could meet. Many of the planters themselves were members of the British Parliament, at least until the First Reform Act of 1832, and thus formed an effective lobby on behalf of West Indian interests.

All this changed after emancipation. Although the planters were financially compensated by the government for the loss of their slaves, it was slavery and the preferential tariff that had enabled them to operate profitably. Most of the Negroes were now content to scratch a bare living for themselves and refused to work for wages. Moreover, *any* wages paid to them, however low, in most cases represented the difference between profit and loss for the planters. To make matters worse, the old English property laws still in effect prevented them from even selling their estates. Under these laws, the buyers had first to clear off the debts of the property before they could receive clear title to it. In almost every case, the estates were so heavily encumbered by debt that they would not have been able to show a profit to the purchaser who proposed to work them with free labor. As a consequence, the only recourse for the owner was simply to abandon his estate. Finally, the last straw to the planters was the enactment by the British Government of free-trade legislation in the 1840's. Without a tariff preference for their sugar, they were inevitably doomed. Thus most of the Europeans by the 1860's had cut their losses and left the islands for good.

POLITICAL CHANGES IN THE NINETEENTH CENTURY. Yet the colonial legislatures continued to function. In some instances, it was not possible to find enough responsible Europeans with the necessary property qualifications to fill the vacant seats. Those who remained were invariably embittered men who felt they had been betrayed by their British kinfolk. Surrounded by a sea of freed hostile slaves, they could not declare their independence; they could not hope for the United States to adopt the colony. All they could do was obstruct. Called upon to vote taxes in their legislatures, they balked, refusing to vote the budget. Some even went on strike and refused to take part in the government. When the Jamaica Negroes in 1865 rioted and captured a local courthouse, the planters suppressed them with such ruthlessness that public opinion in England demanded an end to self-government in the colony. The outgoing Governor, as his last act before leaving for home, persuaded the Jamaican legislature to vote itself out of existence. Quickly, all the other legislatures except Barbados (and Bermuda and the Bahamas, which are not geographically part of the West Indies) followed the Jamaican example.

Thus Britain took over full responsibility for the islands, which became separate crown colonies with British governors and nominated legislative councils. Thereafter, they no longer had to balance their own budgets exclusively from local taxes. In Trinidad, the second largest island, where there were few freed slaves, the importation of indentured laborers from India solved the labor problem. The economy of Jamaica was gradually diversified, and the Negroes, though producing little enough on their own account, contributed at least something to the economy. In the small island of Barbados, where land was scarce, it was very difficult for a freed Negro to make a living for himself without working on the sugar plantations. So he continued to work, for wages, after emancipation. Although the islands remained very poor and few have ever been able to pay their way, there was some economic improvement in the latter part of the century due to improved methods of cultivation and higher prices for sugar. After World War II, a serious effort was made to solve some of the problems through the establishment of a federation, but it proved a failure.

Trinidad and Jamaica are now independent states with a fairly promising future.

British Mainland Territories

BRITISH GUIANA. British Guiana, the only British territory on the South American continent, was taken from the Dutch after the Napoleonic Wars. Originally composed of three small areas on which British planters had settled, it was made into a Crown colony in 1831. British Guiana was afflicted by many of the same problems as the British West Indies, though Indian indentured labor saved the sugar economy after the abolition of slavery. Very little of the extensive hinterland had been explored by the end of the nineteenth century. Indeed, a famous dispute arose between Britain and the United States toward the end of the century. President Cleveland and his Secretary of State Olney insisted that it was a corollary of the Monroe Doctrine that British Guiana not have her boundaries extended at the expense of an independent Latin American state. In spite of the display of considerable truculence by the United States, the British, rather than lose American support needed in more important matters, allowed the dispute to go to arbitration, where it was settled largely in favor of the British point of view.

BRITISH HONDURAS. British Honduras was a small territory, always seriously underpopulated, that had been part of the huge Spanish empire, though never in fact colonized by the Spaniards. British entrepreneurs, mainly exploiting the logwood from which at one time dyes were manufactured, settled there and brought in slaves to cut the wood. The Spaniards permitted this activity with little protest, and the British thus acquired a certain right to stay, though the territory was never legally theirs. When the Spanish colonies became independent, Mexico and the Central American republic of Guatemala put in their claims as legatees of the Spaniards. In 1859, a treaty was signed between Britain and Guatemala recognizing the British rights in the territory on condition that Britain build a road to the Guatemalan border; Mexico relinquished her claim at the same time. Britain made the territory a crown colony in 1862, but did not build the road. In recent times, the Guatemalans have claimed that the treaty has therefore lapsed and that they are entitled to "recover" British Honduras. Needless to say, the British have disputed the claim, and it remains a bone of contention between the two nations. British

Honduras did not suffer from the same permanent depression that afflicted the other British possessions in the area throughout the nineteenth century, since there was a continued demand from Victorian home builders for the mahogany found in the colony. The price obtained for mahogany in export markets was high enough to permit the cutting of the wood by free paid labor.

French and Dutch Possessions

The larger French islands of Guadeloupe and Martinique were slower in abolishing slavery than the British islands, and they continued to enjoy preferential tariffs in France. They are today, like French Guiana (Cayenne), regarded as overseas departments of France and have been tightly administered by France, as if they were metropolitan departments, for more than a century. The much less important Dutch islands have likewise been administered from Holland, as was the mainland territory of Dutch Guiana, or Surinam. Today all these are locally self-governing (since 1954), but remain formally under the Dutch Crown, which appoints the governors of the territories.

The United States in the Caribbean

"Dollar Diplomacy" and "Manifest Destiny"

The British, French, and Dutch islands have been accepted as a fact of life by the United States, incomparably the greatest power in the Caribbean; and since they were acquired prior to 1823, they are tolerated under the Monroe Doctrine. This famous doctrine was enunciated by President Monroe in his annual message to Congress in 1823. It stated, among other things, that the United States would not interfere with any "existing colonies or dependencies of any European power." But "the American continents, by the free and independent condition which they have assumed and maintained, are henceforth not to be considered as subjects for future colonization by any European powers" and European intervention in the American hemisphere could not be viewed in "any other light than as the manifestation of an unfriendly disposition toward the United States." The declaration added, incidentally, that it was not the intention of the United States to take any part in future European wars or in European domestic matters.

Although the latter part of the message has, of course, fallen into desuetude, the main principles of the doctrine have frequently been widened and reinterpreted to take care of new eventualities, especially the revolt of the island of Cuba against the mother country toward the end of the century. In the process of enforcing the Monroe Doctrine, the United States over a period of several decades intervened constantly in Caribbean affairs, acquiring Puerto Rico as an outright possession, leasing the Panama Canal Zone in perpetuity, and treating other areas as virtual protectorates until such time as they possessed governments acceptable to her. Although the United States dominated to a greater or lesser degree the economies of numerous Latin American states and exercised what came to be known as "dollar diplomacy" in all (or, in the parlance of the day, regarded Latin America as her "sphere of influence"), we shall deal only with those territories, either islands in the Caribbean or mainland republics, that were actually occupied for a period by American troops.

Cuba

In the nineteenth century, Cuba was by far the largest sugar grower in the world, supplying, in the 1890's, more than half of the world's crop. In the latter part of the century, the Spaniards, who still ruled the country, were faced with constant revolts, which they attempted to put down by methods that were deeply shocking to Americans. United States corporations had invested heavily in the sugar industry and were rapidly losing patience with the inefficiency of Spanish rule that could not guarantee the stability necessary for the proper functioning of the economy. Lastly, sanitation of the kind known in America was nonexistent, and the island was appallingly unhealthy, presenting a danger to Americans both in Cuba and on the mainland.

During the course of a major rebellion begun in 1895 by the Cubans against the Spaniards, the United States battleship *Maine* was blown up in Havana harbor (February, 1898). Although evidence was lacking as to who was actually responsible for the explosion, the United States Government chose to regard it as the work of the Spaniards, who, too late, attempted to appease the United States with concessions. When President McKinley called upon Congress to authorize the use of force against the Spaniards, Congress agreed, stating in a resolution that Cuba "by right ought to be free and independent."

The one-sided war was quickly over. Spain, as already noted, ceded the Philippines to the United States, but merely abandoned all her claims to Cuba, thus permitting the United States to do with her what seemed fit. American military forces occupied the island for three years, during which a great deal of valuable work was done in promoting better sanitation, educational facilities, and the like. Cuba was then granted formal independence, but agreed to accept a series of limitations on her sovereignty that were incorporated in the Platt Amendment, passed by Congress. The most important proviso of the Amendment was that the United States should have the right to intervene to protect Cuban independence and to maintain "a government adequate for the protection of life, property, and individual liberty." In effect, she was permitted to replace any government considered inimical to American economic interests. A commercial treaty was then negotiated under which Cuban sugar was granted a tariff preference in exchange for a similar preference on American goods entering Cuba. The United States also for a nominal annual sum leased Guantanamo Bay, to be used as a naval base, but with no proviso in the agreement that the base should at any time be returned to Cuba.

In 1902, a President acceptable to the United States was duly installed in Cuba. When he was re-elected to another term of office in 1906, the opposition Liberal Party rose in rebellion, whereupon the United States forces occupied the island and set up a provisional government. In 1908, the Liberal Party was permitted to elect its President. This was followed by a Negro uprising, and again President Taft threatened intervention. In 1913, a thoroughly satisfactory Conservative president, Mario Garcia Menocal, was elected. During his first term of office, United States troops landed to aid in suppressing another Negro uprising; but when Menocal was again elected in 1916, the opposition Liberals refused to accept the verdict and attempted to overthrow him. The United States then declared that she would not accept a government established by force, and marines were sent to restore Menocal.

During the postwar economic depression, the United States intervened in a different manner. After an election widely believed to have been fraudulent, General Enoch Crowder was dispatched to Cuba and he stayed to advise the new government of Alfredo Zayas. But this did not prevent it from becoming increasingly anti-American and demanding the end of the Platt Amendment. From 1930 to 1934, during the worst of the economic depression, disorders were endemic on the island, but the United States intervened as rarely as possible, though she did again send warships in 1933. At last, in 1934, President Carlos Mendieta succeeded in negotiating with President Franklin D. Roosevelt the abrogation of the Platt Amendment; and Cuba was for the first time sovereign in her own domain, except for Guantanamo Bay, which remained in the hands of the United States. During the long personal dictatorship and political ascendancy of Fulgencio Batista, which began in 1936 and did not end until 1959, the United States did not intervene further, though Cuban freedom of action was seriously circumscribed by American domination of the economy of the island.

Haiti

The Republic of Haiti, during the last part of the nineteenth century and the first years of the twentieth, was in an almost constant state of disorder. By 1914, she was also bankrupt and had defaulted on payments, not only to the United States, but to France and Germany. Just before the outbreak of war, both these latter countries had demanded control of the Haitian customs for the purpose of collecting their debts, a practice which had been in use in China in the nineteenth century. Under the Monroe Doctrine, the United States would not permit action by European powers in the Caribbean, and President Wilson attempted to persuade the Haitian President to grant control of his customs to the United States. When he refused, a warship was sent in early 1915, in part on the pretext that the Germans were intending to establish a naval base on the island. In June, 1915, the French sent a small expedition to Haiti. This was followed by numerous disorders and eventually by the murder of the Haitian President. The United States then compelled a new President of her own choosing to sign a ten-year treaty under which she took full control of Haitian finances and promised to supply Haiti with agricultural and other economic aid. She obtained the right to intervene, in the same circumstances as in Cuba, and to organize a police force in the island. In addition, the American marines remained, while United States economic interests entrenched themselves in the island, squeezing out the Europeans who had formerly exercised considerable influence there. When the ten-year treaty expired, it was renewed for another ten years.

At the end of the war, there was a revolt against the American occupation, which was suppressed, though with some difficulty, in view of the formidable terrain of the island. Internal disorders in 1929 led to a renewed outburst of anti-American rioting, followed by the dispatch of a commission that forced through some important administrative reforms. The United States also promised to withdraw her troops at the expiration of the treaty in 1936. The Haitian Congress refused to accept this, insisting on an immediate evacuation. When President Franklin Roosevelt took office in 1933, a number of new agreements were drawn up that were accepted, and U.S. troops finally withdrew in 1934.

The Dominican Republic

Conditions very similar to those in Haiti were prevalent at the beginning of the century in the Dominican Republic, which had achieved its independence from Spain in 1844. The government could not meet its interest payments, and disorders were almost as frequent as in the Haitian half of the island. There was serious danger of intervention by European powers, especially Germany, for the purpose of collecting the debt. Rather than permit any such intervention, President Theodore Roosevelt in 1905 appointed a customs receiver, and a subsequent treaty (1907) granted the United States the right for fifty years to control the Dominican customs. The arrangement was naturally unpopular, even though American guarantees and reforms helped the government attain financial stability. In 1914, there were serious disorders in the Republic, which were partly controlled by U.S. military intervention. In 1916, the United States decided on a military occupation, which now extended over the whole island. The last marine was withdrawn in 1924, when a treaty was signed giving the United States the right to continue her control of Dominican revenues until the balance of Dominican indebtedness was repaid. This customs receivership came to an end in 1941.

Nicaragua

In the early 1900's, Nicaragua was beset, like the Caribbean islands, with financial problems. The area was strategically important to the United States, and there remained the possibility that another canal would be constructed through Nicaragua from the Atlantic to the Pacific. In 1909, President José Zelaya, who had held office for sixteen years, became embroiled with the other Central American states. He also executed two U.S. citizens convicted of sabotage. A revolt was engineered by American and local conservative interests that drove him from office. The following year a treaty was signed under which the United States promised to grant a new loan for reconstruction and to make itself responsible for the collection of customs to service this and previous loans. Indeed, under this agreement the Nicaraguan Government was placed on a stringent allowance for all its expenses. It also agreed to choose a President acceptable to the United States. Although the U.S. Senate did not ratify this particular treaty, it ratified another with similar terms, in 1914, under which Nicaragua accepted American financial control (a commission of three, two from the United States) and granted a ninety-nine-year lease on the strategic Corn Islands, with the right to build a naval base as well as a canal, from the Atlantic to the Pacific.

The Nicaraguans did not take kindly to the rule of a Conservative President approved by the United States. Civil war broke out in 1912, and U.S. marines were sent to the country to restore order. They supervised the election of Adolfo Diaz, another Conservative party candidate, and except for a short break in 1925–26, remained in the country until 1933. In 1936, General Anastasio Somoza became President and established a dictatorship strong enough to run the country for the next twenty years without further intervention.

Puerto Rico

All these countries may be regarded as having been temporary protectorates of the United States. However, there were three smaller territories that became actual colonies: Puerto Rico, ceded by Spain in 1898; the Virgin Islands, purchased from Denmark in 1917; and the Panama Canal Zone, leased from the Republic of Panama in perpetuity. In Puerto Rico, control at first was exercised by a governor-general and executive council appointed by the President, though there was also an advisory House of Delegates elected under universal manhood suffrage. Under the Jones Act of 1917, Puerto Rico became a territory of the United States, and its inhabitants U.S. citizens. Since in the continental United States the status of territory had historically preceded that of state, the Puerto Ricans began to request early statehood, though they did not wish to be represented in the U.S. Congress, preferring local self-government—and be it said, preferring not to pay U.S. income taxes, which could not be collected from them without their having representation in Congress. In the 1930's, a nationalist movement calling for complete independence also made headway in the island. Eventually, in 1947, Congress granted Puerto Rico the right to elect its own governor, and in 1953, after a referendum under universal suffrage, it became a free and self-governing commonwealth, voluntarily associated with the United States.

The Virgin Islands

The Virgin Islands, likewise a possession, were purchased from Denmark largely because of the excellent harbor at Charlotte Amalie on the island of St. Thomas. The islands were under naval administration with a naval governor, until 1931, when they received a civil governor, appointed by the President of the United States. In 1936, a Legislative Assembly was set up whose members were chosen indirectly by the elected municipal councils of the two chief islands. In 1954, the Assembly became directly elected and was permitted to legislate, subject only to veto by the governor, who has continued to be appointed by the President. Obviously, there can be no question of independence for a chronically economically depressed territory of little more than 30,000 inhabitants; but before long at least the governor will probably be elected by popular vote. The U.S. Congress, which at present legislates directly for the territory, may divest itself of this general power, retaining perhaps certain reserve rights for use in special emergencies.

The Panama Canal Zone

Throughout the nineteenth century, the building of a canal connecting the Atlantic and the Pacific oceans had often been discussed. It was rapidly becoming an economic and strategic necessity for the United States, but it was far from decided where it was to be cut or under whose auspices. As early as 1850, Britain, as the leading maritime power, had extracted a treaty from the United States (Clayton-Bulwer Treaty) that bound the United States to construct such a canal only under joint control with herself, and that such a canal should not be fortified. After long and difficult negotiations, this obstacle was overcome in 1901 when the British agreed to permit the Americans to construct the canal and control it with the necessary police power, provided it was always kept open in peace and war to merchants and warships of every nation. It was still not certain, however, whether the canal would pass through Nicaragua or Colombia—there was as yet no Republic of Panama.

As early as 1878, the Colombian Government granted a concession to Ferdinand de Lesseps, builder of the Suez Canal, to construct a sea-level canal through the Isthmus of Panama. But the technical difficulties in building such a canal were formidable. By 1889, the company formed by De Lesseps had failed, and the money contributed, mostly French, was lost. Work on the canal was abandoned, but the concession remained valid. All the rights of the De Lesseps company were transferred to a new organization whose leading light was a French engineer named Philippe Bunau-Varilla, originally an associate of De Lesseps. This man now did his best to interest the United States in constructing the canal across the Isthmus of Panama rather than through Nicaragua, which was generally favored in the United States, at least until 1899. He was successful in converting first President McKinley and then President Theodore Roosevelt to his view; also a U.S. commission that had reported in favor of Nicaragua reversed itself in 1899 and went along with the new plan. A treaty was then negotiated with Colombia (Hay-Herrán Convention) that provided for a ninety-nine-year lease of a strip of territory 6 miles wide across the Isthmus in exchange for an outright payment of $10 million and $250,000 as annual rent.

Here a formidable hitch occurred. The Colombian Senate did not ratify the treaty, preferring to adjourn at the end of October, 1903, without having made a decision. This was not a situation to be accepted with equanimity by Bunau-Varilla, or indeed by President Roosevelt. Bunau-Varilla and a number of Latin American politicians had been preparing for this contingency while the Colombian Senate was procrastinating. Four days after its adjournment, a revolution broke out in the northern part of Colombia, bordering on the site of the proposed canal. President Roosevelt at once sent American forces to prevent Colombia from suppressing it. The revolutionaries then proclaimed the Republic of Panama, and only eleven days later a treaty was signed between it and the United States (Hay–Bunau-Varilla Treaty) granting the United States a perpetual lease of a strip 10 miles wide in exchange for the same payment agreed upon with Colombia. The Canal was then constructed at top speed (a two-level canal, unlike the one started by De Lesseps) and opened to traffic in 1914. In 1921, Colombia was pacified by a payment of $25 million.

To this day, the Panama Canal Zone is U.S. territory under the supervision of the Secretary of the Army. Its governor is almost always a military man, and the U.S. Congress legislates for it. The Panama Canal Company, which operates the Canal, is owned by the U.S. Government. As a footnote to this particular piece of derring-do—for which President Roosevelt took full credit once it had been accomplished—it may be mentioned that in recent years several Latin American nations, including Colombia, have formed an international consortium with the purpose of building another canal, under their own control, that will be able to do without the locks that make the Panama Canal so expensive to operate. If this project, which has the promise of impressive financial support, is ever fulfilled, the Panama Canal could well become an expensive white elephant. Conceivably, then, it might be returned to Panama, as the Suez Canal reverted to Egypt in 1956. Up to this time, the U.S. Government has shown no signs of being willing to restore what it leased in perpetuity in 1903. Unlike Egypt, Panama, having yielded her territory in turn for being assisted to become a nation in her own right, is in no position to nationalize the Canal.

"A Cloud No Bigger Than a Man's Hand"

By 1914, the tide of imperialism had reached its height but had as yet shown few signs of receding. Although in several of the more recently acquired colonies, such as Morocco and Tripoli, the colonial powers had not consolidated their positions, there was no doubt in European minds that this would be accomplished in due course. No ideology had appeared capable of unifying the subjected peoples against their conquerors. Even in India, few recognized the potentialities of the Indian National Congress, the instrument that was to drive the British out of their richest colony.

The United States had taken some steps toward granting independence to the Philippines. Governor Francis Burton Harrison, with the full support of President Wilson and a majority in the Congress, was busily engaged in organizing embryonic political institutions, and in many fields Filipino officials were rapidly taking the place of Americans. The Democratic Party, in particular, was not happy with the role of the United States as a colonial power, and had inserted in its platform of 1912 a hope that the Filipinos could be granted an early independence.

But the European powers had given no thought to such a future for their own colonies. They were powerful, and in their view destined for empire, and they had willingly undertaken the civilization of "the lesser breeds without the law." They little thought that their own nationalism, which had grown so rapidly during the nineteenth century, would prove to be an article for export, and that before another half-century was over it would have become a weapon to be used against them. By 1964, their empires would have disintegrated and their colonies become member states in a United Nations, exercising the right to vote against them in matters they had hitherto regarded as their exclusive prerogative.

II

THE IMPETUS OF
TWO WORLD WARS

6. World War I
and the Long Armistice

World War I in itself had no visible results on the existing colonial system. No nation was made to change its views on the desirability of empire; no nation voluntarily abandoned any colony. President Wilson's principle of self-determination, though it found answering echoes in European breasts, was not thought by any European power to be applicable to the peoples of their colonies, who were not fit for self-government—at least not yet. Such changes as there were in the immediate postwar world came about as a direct result of the loss of the war by the Central Powers. The Austrian empire, all of it in Europe, was divided into several new nations. Germany, while losing little territory in Europe, had to submit to limitations on her sovereignty and the loss of all her overseas territories. The old Ottoman Empire came to an end, to be replaced by a small republic of Turkey; all her former provinces outside this restricted area were taken from her. At the Paris Peace Conference in 1919, therefore, it was at once necessary for the victorious powers to decide what should be done with this pool of former German colonies and Turkish provinces now available for redistribution.

The League of Nations Mandate System

Without the influence of President Wilson as spokesman for the most powerful of the victors, no doubt the colonies and provinces, as after previous wars, would have been simply transferred to one or another of the European powers, who would have negotiated among themselves the details of the settlement. The Arab countries, or those that became Class A mandates, would perhaps have been granted a status similar to what they were granted in the actual peace treaties, but the African and Pacific colonies of Germany would surely have become possessions of the European colonial powers. The League of Nations mandate system was thus in large part a concession to American idealism;

123

it represented the beginning of a concept, accepted also by Europeans, that colonies were a trust rather than simply a property to be exploited and treated as if its peoples had no rights of their own. The fact that none of the former colonies or provinces was annexed outright set an important precedent for the negotiations after World War II, when the United Nations trust territories not only were *not* annexed but were given guarantees of future independence, which with a few minor exceptions have now all been fulfilled.

At the Peace Conference, the Allied Powers established a system of what were called "mandates," divided into three categories—A, B, and C. When they had chosen the type of mandate each territory would become and allocated them among the colonial powers, the Council of the League of Nations, itself established as an integral part of the peace treaties, was required to accept the arrangements and see that the terms of the mandates were fulfilled. This was not at all President Wilson's concept of the mandate system, which, according to his views, should have made the allocations and set the terms. However, President Wilson had to accept the changes insisted upon by the Allies, the more so since his own country refused both to enter the League and to accept any mandates.

The former Turkish provinces, consisting of the predominantly Arab countries of Syria, Mesopotamia, and Palestine, became Class A mandates. In these, the mandatory powers accepted the obligation to prepare their charges for independence after a brief period of tutelage. There was never any question but that, whatever the difficulties, the Class A mandates would in time become independent—though it was not determined after World War I how many new nations would arise. Class B and C mandates did not differ in any major respects from one another. The latter class, which included former German Southwest Africa (conferred by the Supreme Council of the Allied Powers on the Union of South Africa), German New Guinea (conferred on Australia), and a few Pacific islands (which mostly fell to the Japanese), were separated from the B mandates because the mandatory powers did not wish to accept certain provisions that were applied to the latter. In particular, the "open-door" trade policy was not applied to the C mandates, and they could, if desired, be administratively integrated with other territories belonging to the mandatory power. In both B and C mandates, forced labor was forbidden, and a number of other general provisions were made for the well-being of the inhabitants, but no provision was made for ultimate independence. All the former German colonies in Africa except Southwest Africa became B mandates. Kamerun and Togoland were divided into French and British mandates. Most of German East Africa fell to the British, but a small area of just over 20,000 square miles became a Belgian mandate under the name of Ruanda-Urundi. Italy, complaining that she had been excluded unjustly from the mandate system, was granted by the British and French some boundary adjustments in the Horn of Africa and Libya.

Reports on the mandated territories had to be submitted annually to the Permanent Mandates Commission of the League of Nations, made up of experts in colonial administration drawn from different nations, chosen as individuals and not as nominees of their respective governments. The Commission studied and made recommendations to the League Council on the basis of the reports, and questioned the representatives of the mandatory powers on both the reports and the written petitions that were occasionally received from inhabitants of the mandated territories. Since neither the Council nor the Commission was authorized to interfere in any way with the actual administration in the territories, the pressure on the mandatory powers was exclusively moral. But there can be little doubt that the pressure, exercised or implied, had at least some effect on them, as had the system of submitting annual reports. No power liked to be faced with having either to lie or prevaricate, or simply to omit any account of conditions discreditable to themselves.

Politics in the Middle East

The Turkish Provinces

CONTRADICTORY POLICIES OF BRITAIN. During the war, when it was vitally necessary to guard the Suez Canal, since Egypt was close to the theater of hostilities, the British kept Egypt under strict control; at all times there were British and Dominion armies in the country together with their generals, as well as the High Commissioner, who remained the official British representative. There was also an Arab Bureau, made up of experts on Middle Eastern affairs, whose main task was to gather intelligence but which in fact acted as a pressure group for policies not always in accord with those of the British home government. Thus, during the course of the war, three separate policies were decided upon by the

British regarding the future of the Turkish provinces, no one of which could easily be reconciled with the others. Moreover, since only the Balfour Declaration, which embodied the latest of the three policies, was publicly announced, outsiders and even officials who were not kept informed could be forgiven for going ahead with policies that were not in accord with the plans of their own home government. In 1915, Sir Henry McMahon, British High Commissioner in Egypt, came to a secret agreement with representatives of the Arabs, promising that Britain would "recognize and support" the independence of Arabia, Syria, and Mesopotamia, with the exception of Basra and Bagdad where the population was not wholly Arab and where the British had special interests. The coast of Syria, where the population was also not wholly Arab, was vaguely excluded from the agreement; and it was stated that the agreement applied only to those territories where Britain was free to act "without detriment to the interests of her ally, France."

In 1916, acting on the instructions of the British Foreign Office, Sir Mark Sykes, a member of the Arab Bureau, negotiated an agreement with the French (the Sykes-Picot Agreement) under which Syria was to become a French protectorate after the war, southern Mesopotamia was to become a British protectorate, and there was to be an independent Arab country in between that would be partly a British and partly a French "sphere of influence." By this agreement, it is clear, the McMahon promise was considerably modified. Lastly, in 1917, Arthur (later Earl) Balfour, British Foreign Minister, as a gesture to win the support of international Jewry, issued a declaration to the effect that "His Majesty's government views with favor the establishment in Palestine of a National Home for the Jewish people, and will use their best endeavors to facilitate the achievement of this object, it being clearly understood that nothing shall be done which may prejudice the civil and religious rights of existing non-Jewish communities in Palestine." So now the Jews were to be a modifying factor in the independence of Palestine. It was therefore not surprising that the Arabs were to claim that the McMahon promise, on the basis of which they began their revolt against the Turks, had been whittled away to a point where the promised independence was beginning to look like a good deal of a sham.

THE ARAB REVOLT. In 1916, the Arab revolt against the Turks duly broke out, led by the Sherif of Mecca, a descendant of the Prophet, and his sons. A few months later, the legendary Colonel T. E.

Lawrence (Lawrence of Arabia), also a member of the Arab Bureau, joined the rebels and led many of their operations, at the same time giving personal assurances to the Emir Feisal, son of the Sherif, regarding the future independence of Arab lands and the role of Feisal himself in it. Feisal's Arabs for a long time did not advance very far into Turkish-controlled lands, but their guerrilla activities tied down a considerable number of Turkish troops. When General Allenby in Egypt was ready for the big push, the ground had been well prepared; and the Turks were driven back into their own country. In October, 1918, when they sued for peace, Feisal, who like Lawrence had known nothing of the Sykes-Picot Agreement, was already ensconced in Damascus, the capital of Syria, without doubt an Arab city.

The French, at Versailles, stood on the letter of their agreement with the British and insisted on receiving Syria, which had been promised to them, either as a mandate or protectorate. Since this was a formal intergovernmental treaty and had a somewhat higher status in official eyes than promises made to Arab rebels against their own government, the British decided that the Sykes-Picot Agreement must take precedence over the Arab agreement, where the two could not be reconciled. They were thus compelled to back the French, who proceeded to drive Feisal from his capital and take over the country. The British, anxious to redeem themselves in Arab eyes and do the best they could for Feisal and his brother Abdullah, offered the former the throne of a new Mesopotamian kingdom to be called Iraq, with its capital at Bagdad. To the Emir Abdullah, they offered a smaller kingdom to be called Transjordania. Feisal was confirmed in his position by a plebiscite in which he won 96 per cent of the votes.

THE KINGDOM OF IRAQ. Iraq never formally became a mandated territory, since the League of Nations agreed that the new arrangements by which an Arab king had been given the throne fulfilled, in effect, the purpose of the Class A mandates. In 1926, a parliamentary system was established, and the following year a treaty was negotiated to safeguard British interests in the country. Under the treaty, Britain was granted new air bases and was permitted to maintain military forces in the country. Iraq, for her part, undertook not to pursue any policy inconsistent with the alliance or likely to create difficulties for Britain. The treaty was ratified by the Iraqi parliament in 1930, and two years later, she became formally independent and was permitted to enter the League of Nations. Meanwhile, Transjordania, under Abdullah, remained a Class A mandated territory until 1946. It possessed internal autonomy, but was dependent on Britain for defense and enough financial subsidies to keep the feeble economy functioning and balance the budget.

FRANCE IN SYRIA. The French, throughout all of their period as a mandatory power, experienced great difficulties with the Arab nationalists of Syria who had been cheated of their independence. The entire country, however, was not Muslim, and there was a sizable community of Maronite Christians in the area known as Great Lebanon. These Christians alone initially favored French rule; but even they were offended by the highhanded actions of anticlerical French officials. A fierce group of Muslim sectaries called the Druses, whom even the Turks had treated with "kid gloves" during their regime, were bitterly anti-Christian. The French managed to antagonize them to such an extent that a large-scale rebellion broke out in which the Druses were joined by the Arab nationalists. The rebellion lasted for two years and required considerable French forces to suppress. In 1926, Lebanon, which included not only Great Lebanon but other smaller provinces and therefore had a mixed Christian and Muslim population, was separated from the rest of Syria and made into an "independent" republic. In 1936, French Premier Léon Blum attempted to pacify the Syrians by guaranteeing them an early independence, in accordance with the terms of the mandate, but the French parliament refused to ratify the treaty. Most Syrians, therefore, welcomed the intervention during World War II of the British and Free French forces, even though Syrian independence, for military reasons, could not at once be granted. Lebanon and Syria gained substantial independence in 1944, when the Nazi danger had receded; but it was not until 1946 that French troops left the country and France gave up the mandate, which had proved so expensive.

The Importance of Oil

The main reason both the British and French insisted on staying in the Middle East can be summed up in one word—oil. Before World War I, oil was already beginning to be used instead of coal for warships, since it had the great advantage of taking up less space than coal, and this space could be used for armaments. With the ever-increasing use of the internal-combustion engine, access to oil became more necessary, not only for its uses in warfare but for the earning of profits. After World War I, the United States possessed ample oil resources for her own needs, but Britain and France and other European nations did not. Hence the importance of having a sure source of supply available in peace and war. Since the initial capital investment was high, and the pipelines through which the oil flowed to the coast often passed through the territories of several countries, obviously watertight agreements had to be made with each; and the European nations felt they had to have some means at their disposal for policing the agreements and protecting their property. Hence their insistence, in treaties with the newly independent countries, on their right to station troops in the countries. The details of the interlocking arrangements between the various oil corporations, and the manner in which they and their governments were able to compel the countries where oil had been found to keep to the letter of their concession agreements for so long, are often fascinating but lie outside the scope of this book. If it should be wondered why the Western powers took so much trouble to maintain an expensive hegemony over the Middle East in face of the obvious desire of the Arabs to be rid of them, the answer will always be to some degree connected with the presence of oil.

Palestine and the Jewish National Home

This reality underlies, in particular, the readiness of the British to accept and keep the mandate for Palestine, even though one may never find the word "oil" used in any of the open discussions between British, Arabs, and Jews that filled the twenty-six turbulent years of the mandate. It should always be remembered, however, that Haifa in Palestine was the terminus of an important pipeline from the Iraqi oilfields. Moreover, the desire of the British to avoid offending the Arabs too deeply over Palestine was not due to any special tenderness for or sympathy with the Arabs in general as distinct from the Jews, but simply to the fact that the most important oilfields in the Middle East were all in Arab hands except those of Persia (Iran); and Persia was still Muslim, even if most Persians belonged to a different sect from the Arab majority. Although Arabs might quarrel bitterly among themselves on other matters, they never forgot that Islam was a brotherhood as well as a religion. They invariably supported their fellow Arabs and fellow Muslims in Palestine against the Jews; and the British, who might for other reasons have wished to grant concessions to the Jews in Palestine, dared not do so if it meant they would become involved in troubles with the Arabs in countries where they possessed oil interests. British policy in Palestine, therefore, was guided by these extraneous considerations as well as by the needs of the local situation.

The terms of the mandate approved by the Council of the League of Nations in 1922 incorporated the Balfour Declaration in a preamble to the section on the establishment of a Jewish National Home. Like the Declaration, it begged all questions with its statement that it should be "clearly understood that nothing should be done which might prejudice the civil and religious rights of existing non-Jewish communities in Palestine." The leading civil right the Palestinian Arabs claimed was the right to have their own independent state in due course like the other Class A mandates. The mandate then went on to deal with the details of the proposed Jewish National Home in Palestine and laid the responsibility for establishing it clearly on the mandatory power. Great Britain was to "facilitate Jewish immigration under suitable conditions" and "encourage close settlement by Jews on the land, including state lands and waste lands not required for public purposes"; and discrimination on the ground of race, religion, or language was forbidden.

GROWTH OF THE NATIONAL HOME. The history of the years of the mandate may be summarized briefly. The Jewish National Home was duly established, and a Jewish agency (Zionist) was formed for the purpose of facilitating immigration and land settlement. Jews began to purchase land from Arabs who for a long time were willing to sell. Funds were raised by Jews throughout the world; and from a technical and human point of view, the project was immensely successful. It was found that the Jews, whose ancestors had usually been engaged in strictly urban occupations, were quite capable of making good on the land. All kinds of new social institutions were devised that were designed to facilitate the rapid absorption of the immigrants and make room quickly for more. Industries were started, land was reclaimed, and opportunities were offered in the growing economy for Arabs also, had they desired to participate. But the vast majority of Arabs were not in the least interested in altering their ancient way of life, which had remained unchanged for centuries; and the educated Arab leaders resented the Jewish National Home as an obstacle to the achievement of independence. From the beginning, almost none accepted it—though Emir Feisal and other Arabs in earlier years had given their consent to what they had thought of as a small Jewish community in Palestine that would give a few Jews a spiritual and cultural homeland in the country of their remote ancestors and the seat of their religion. No Arabs had bargained for a growing National Home that was gradually becoming a state within a state, more progressive in all respects than their own culture and greatly disturbing to it.

Jewish immigration stayed within bounds until the advent of Hitler to power in Germany. Thereafter, it grew so quickly that the British as well as the Arabs became alarmed. The Arabs, who had never ceased to demand independence for Palestine under their own rule, saw their hopes vanishing. Their opposition to the Jews hardened, giving rise to numerous incidents between the two segments of the population. All the British could do was to enlarge their security forces and attempt to keep the peace. In 1937, the British Peel Commission recommended partition of the country. It was impressed by the fact that the terms of the mandate required the British to promote the establishment of the Jewish National Home; yet, at the same time, it recognized the irreconcilable opposition of the Arabs to continued Jewish immigration. Since the aspirations of the two groups were in direct opposition, there was, in the opinion of the Commission, no alternative but to form separate states, one Jewish and one Arab, with the British holding the balance and maintaining their mandate over such areas as the Holy Places in Jerusalem. Although the Jews were willing to accept partition, since it would give them control over at least their area and permit the immigration of the refugees from Hitler's Germany, the Arabs were completely intransigent and made it impossible for the British to go forward with the scheme. The British took the point of view, until the end of the mandate, that no solution could be adopted unless both sides accepted it. But this was in fact not possible.

THE WHITE PAPER OF 1939. The British Government, which had originally approved the Commission's report and agreed to partition, found itself in 1939 facing the prospect of war with the Axis Powers, while at the same time ships crowded with Jewish refugees were demanding to enter Palestine, and no other country would accept more than a fraction of their number. Britain dared not alienate the other Arab states whose good will would be needed in the event of war. She even consulted the Arab kings but found them at least as uncompromising as the Palestinian Arabs over the question of the Jewish National Home. The government therefore decided to do the only thing that seemed to make political sense. It issued a White Paper in 1939 cutting down Jewish immigration to a maximum quota of 10,000 a year, from which the numerous known illegal immigrants would be subtracted. Meanwhile, to alleviate the existing situation, 25,000 refugees would at once be admitted if the High Commissioner thought they could be absorbed. The total immigration to be permitted in the next five years would be 75,000. The White Paper went on to promise that an independent Palestinian state would be set up in ten years, if by that time it appeared feasible. This would mean that the Arab majority would be maintained, and the new state with its powerful Jewish minority would be ruled by this majority. By this means it was hoped that the Arabs would be appeased. Their future role was guaranteed them, and the restriction of Jewish immigration and land sales would mean that the growth of the Jewish National Home would be stopped at this point while it was still supposedly of manageable size.

This policy, even if it could have been carried out in the existing circumstances, would have solved none of the problems, at least for the Jews—whereas the recommendation of the Peel Commission could have been imposed upon the country if the British had been willing to use force themselves and make use of Jewish troops. Moreover, the Palestinian Arabs would have had a state of their own, however small, instead of themselves becoming homeless refugees, as they did in 1948. In 1939, the Arabs were totally unwilling voluntarily to accept the Jewish National Home of the size that it had by that time become. If they had been given control of the Home, there is no doubt that they would have attempted to destroy it by force, and the Jews would hardly have tamely submitted to their own destruction. A civil war would have been inevitable; the British can scarcely have seriously believed that there could be any other outcome. In the circumstances that prevailed in 1939, the White Paper policy was bound to draw upon them the opprobrium of the world; the Jews could not possibly have done other than refuse all cooperation and by every means in their power attempt to bring their refugees into Palestine in spite of British prohibitions.

The Mandates Commission of the League of Nations considered the policy of the White Paper and found it contrary to the terms of the mandate, since Britain was instructed to facilitate Jewish immigration, not virtually prohibit it. But the League of Nations by that time was itself almost moribund, and it could do little. Even the Arabs, for whose benefit the White Paper had been issued, found it unacceptable since it held out no substantial hope of independence. There was little likelihood that in ten years' time, or even twenty, the situation would have improved in such a way that independence could be granted without involving the new state in a civil war. Other Arab lands were now enjoying independence, and the Palestinian Arabs, led by the exiled Grand Mufti of Jerusalem, believed they could win it quickly by continued pressure on the British. They could be sure of the diplomatic support of the other Arab states, who in 1939 formed themselves into a League of Arab States with the major purpose of combating Jewish aspirations in Palestine. Lastly, if the British were compelled to leave by the exigencies of war, then the Arabs were sure they could take care of the Jews satisfactorily in their own way.

Nevertheless, in spite of opposition from Jews and Arabs, the British put their new policy into effect, with all the suffering that it entailed to the Jews, whose refugee ships were turned back from Palestinian ports, often to sink at sea, while illegal Jewish immigrants who had to be tolerated during the war were deported to concentration camps in Cyprus after the war was over. The policy encouraged also the formation of Jewish groups devoted to direct military and terrorist action against both British and Arabs. These were to play a large part after the war in making the British position untenable. (The last phase of the mandate and the achievement of Jewish independence in the form of the state of Israel are discussed in Chapter 8, which is devoted to the postwar period).

Egypt

EGYPTIAN NATIONALISM AND BRITISH STRATEGIC INTERESTS. When Turkey entered the war on the side of the Central Powers, the British were faced with the necessity of legalizing their position in the country, which had previously been "leased" from the Turkish Sultan. Since the possession of Egypt was vital to her during the war, Britain declared a protectorate over the country—despite the fact that, unlike in other protectorates, no Egyptian had asked her for "protection." During the twenty-four years of Lord Cromer's administration, economic conditions in the country had greatly improved. Egypt now had a valuable export crop, cotton, and her finances were in order. The Suez Canal was paying handsomely for its upkeep, and interest payments were being met. But the nationalism that had sprung to life even before the British occupation had in no way been assuaged. The educated classes to a man were nationalists, and there were far more educated men in the country than in 1882. These men who looked forward to the restoration of Egyptian independence after the war could see no difference between their country and others which were now emerging from a condition of dependence and blossoming forth as independent nations.

But in fact there was a great difference—the strategic position of Egypt and the internationally owned Suez Canal within her borders. Despite the fact that the enemy powers that had threatened the Canal in the recent war had been vanquished, the British did not feel that such an important possession could be relinquished to an Egyptian nationalist government—possibly a hostile and certainly an inexperienced one. For although they may have won the respect of Egyptians during the long occupation, they had done little to earn their friendship.

In the immediate postwar years, counsels in England were bitterly divided over the future of the country. Other newly independent nations had instituted democratic regimes, and the British could hardly give the Egyptians anything less than responsible government as a prelude to outright independence. But they refused to treat Egypt as a nation, and they at first refused permission to let the nationalist leader, Zaghlul Pasha, plead his case at the Peace Conference. When he was at last permitted to see President Wilson, he was coolly informed that the United States recognized Britain's paramount interest in Egypt. As a result of this, serious rioting broke out in Egypt, which had to be suppressed by British troops. A commission of inquiry, led by Lord Milner, of South African fame, went to Egypt to inquire into the causes of the riots. Milner decided that the best policy was to concede independence, and trust to a treaty to take care of Britain's interests. But he could not persuade the government of Lloyd George to agree. Disorders continued in Egypt, martial law was retained, Zaghlul was deported to the Seychelles, and Viscount Allenby, with British troops, continued to rule the country.

NOMINAL INDEPENDENCE UNDER FUAD I. But it was Allenby who, by threatening to resign, compelled the British Government to bring the protectorate to an end. Egypt became nominally independent. However, Britain retained control of Egypt's foreign policy and assumed responsibility for her defense, pending agreement to a treaty that would ensure the security of the British Empire in Egypt, and the protection of all foreign interests and minorities. Such a treaty was also to include a final settlement regarding the Sudan. Egypt became a constitutional monarchy, with a descendant of the House of Mehemet Ali, Fuad I, on the throne. The Egyptians adopted a constitution modeled on that of Belgium, under which the monarch held certain important powers, including the right to dissolve Parliament. Elections were held and Zaghlul Pasha, who had been released after the proclamation of independence, became Prime Minister at the head of his nationalist Wafd Party.

As often happens when a nationalist party assumes power for the first time, the primary interest of the Wafd lay not in improving domestic conditions but in extending Egyptian rule over the Sudan. This the British refused to concede, although the Egyptians supplied most of the minor officials and lower-ranking troops in that country. In 1923, Sir Lee Stack, the British Commander-in-Chief of the Egyptian Army and Governor-General of the Sudan, was murdered, whereupon the British issued an ultimatum to the Wafd Government demanding an end to political demonstrations, the payment of an indemnity, and the withdrawal of all Egyptian forces and officials from the Sudan. Although Zaghlul would not agree to the last condition, and resigned, his successor accepted it. Thereafter, the Sudan went on her separate path, despite constant efforts by the Egyptians after World War II to regain control. She was granted her own independence in 1956, and has never reunited with Egypt.

Meanwhile the Wafd, which was returned to power in several successive elections, continued to refuse all drafts for a treaty with the British. The Egyptians would accept nothing that did not give them complete sovereignty not only over Egypt but over the Sudan. The British would not abandon their position in Egypt, especially to a party that was apparently incapable of governing efficiently and was persistently hostile. Nor would they permit the Egyptians to extend their government to the Sudan, which was prospering under British rule, and was widely regarded as the finest example of British beneficent colonialism.

THE TREATY OF 1936. At last, in 1928, King Fuad appointed a Prime Minister who did not belong to the majority Wafd Party. When the Wafd refused to cooperate and organized numerous demonstrations, the King introduced a new constitution, providing for indirect elections in the lower house of Parliament and an upper house largely appointed by himself. Under this system, the King and his party were able to win control of Parliament. Thereafter, Fuad held virtually absolute power until 1935, when the Italians invaded Ethiopia. British actions during the subsequent crisis brought home to the Egyptians the serious danger of possible war. The British thought it possible that they would now agree to a treaty. Under British pressure, Fuad restored the constitution of 1923, and a new Wafd Government duly ratified a treaty negotiated for the British by Foreign Minister Anthony Eden at the end of 1936.

Under the treaty, the British were permitted to maintain an army of 10,000 men in the Suez Canal Zone, and Britain and Egypt were bound to a military alliance for twenty years, the period of the duration of the treaty. The ultimate status of the Sudan was left unsettled, but it was agreed that Egyptian troops should again be stationed there under the authority of the British Governor-General, and free emigration would be permitted. A year later, its main election issue having disappeared, the Wafd Party split, whereupon the new King, Farouk, dissolved Parliament. Elections were held and an opposition party came to power. During World War II, when Egypt was in serious danger from the Axis Powers, the treaty came into operation, and the British once more used the country as a war base. There was little opportunity for political activity until the war was almost over.

India's Advance Toward Independence

Only India, Burma, Ceylon, and the Philippines made much political progress between the two wars. All were on the threshold of independence at the outbreak of World War II.

DYARCHICAL SYSTEM. In India, the Montagu-Chelmsford Reforms had set up what was called a "dyarchical" system of government. Under this system, provincial legislatures were established with elected majorities in the legislative councils (70 per cent elected, as against 20 per cent British officials and 10 per cent representatives of special interests). In order to give some responsibility to elected ministers, a certain number of departments of government were "transferred" to Indians, that is, Indians were put in charge of them with the title of Minister. Other departments were "reserved" in British hands, notably defense and internal security. The governor also possessed ample powers in reserve and could "certify" a bill as essential and have it passed into law without the assent of the Legislative Council. The franchise remained severely restricted on the basis of property and education, and the communal electorates were retained. To win control of the provincial legislature, a party had to win 51 of 70 elected seats—a virtual impossibility even for the powerful Congress Party as long as an all-Muslim electorate continued to choose some of the representatives.

At the center, there was a two-chamber Central Legislature made up of a Council of State and a Legislative Assembly, again elected by a restricted franchise. This Assembly had certain important tasks to perform, such as passing the national budget. It could and did place tariffs on British cotton goods to protect the Indian textile industry. But the Viceroy's Council remained as the executive; and though three Indian members were appointed to it, these were far from being a majority of the Council, nor were they given charge of specific ministries. The former autocratic powers of the Viceroy were therefore reduced only by the fact that he was now required to consult an Assembly with a majority of elected Indians. Even so, he could, though he rarely did, overrule them when necessary.

The purpose of this constitution was clearly to give Indians a first taste of self-government in the provinces. If they behaved "responsibly," they could expect a further access of power. The wise parent was gradually training his children, rather than giving them more than they could handle at one time, and was carefully watching to see how they behaved. He encouraged them by holding out the promise of ultimate self-government, even (after 1929) Dominion status. But they must first prove themselves. Britain alone would be the judge of progress and bestow the awards. A similar policy was followed in other colonies when they were being prepared for independence. The British have never granted self-government precipitately, as the Belgians granted it in the Congo in 1960 (except in the case of the tiny Somaliland Protectorate, where events moved too fast for them, and even there the Somalis were not expecting to be entirely on their own).

ROLE OF MOHANDAS GANDHI. Although the policy results from their admirable sense of responsibility, the British have never fully realized the insult to human dignity involved in treating as children human beings who do not consider themselves as such—most especially the Indians, who were civilized and self-governing before the time of Queen Boadicea and the Roman conquest of Britain, and whose King Asoka, centuries before Christ, bears comparison as a monarch with any who have lived since his time. In the case of India, Britain regarded her conflict with Indian nationalism (and later, other nationalisms) primarily as a power conflict between a benevolent autocracy, ruling in the interests of all Indians, and an upstart and irresponsible Indian educated class, wishing to sit in the seats of the mighty but not otherwise qualified for rule. Some Indians, indeed, especially among the ranks of the Indian bureaucracy, to some degree shared the British viewpoint, having been trained by the British to despise their own culture. The task was not done consciously but by the simple process of establishing the British legal system and training Indian lawyers in the principles of British justice; by requiring all Indians who wished to rise in the bureaucracy to have themselves educated in English; by organizing all higher instruction according to British methods, with British curricula and examinations given by British universities; and most of all by simply *being* in India as masters, holding themselves aloof from Indians as superior beings and doing precisely as they wished, even though they were a tiny minority in India.

The task of the Indian nationalists was therefore not only to win power, still less merely to win elections, but rather to assert themselves as Indians and by their own methods *compel* the British to give heed to them. Gandhi was not a reasonable man, demanding constitutional reforms. He was a prophet and national leader, demanding independence and nothing less. Never at any time did he *agree* to any of the British plans for reform; he did not accept them as installments, partial advances that would ultimately lead to independence. When the British, at the Round Table Conferences following the publication of the Simon Report in 1930, tried to persuade him to accept Dominion status, with which the British-populated colonies had so long been content, he would not agree to this as a suitable goal for Indians, even though it was pointed out to him that no British Dominion could be kept in the Commonwealth against its will. He insisted that his stand did not mean that after independence he would necessarily take India out of the Commonwealth. This apparent splitting of hairs the British could not understand. Why was he so insistent on the point if he did not mean to do anything about it?

Yet Gandhi's words and actions were in fact always consistent, if it is realized that what he was trying to do was to rebuild the Indian ego, to give his people the sense of being members of a distinctive culture with a long past and a part to play in the future. Fundamentally anti-Western because of his belief in the superiority of his Indian heritage, he opposed the Muslims only in so far as the political and religious teachings of Islam conflicted with his aim of establishing a secular state, in which all religions would be equally protected. He was well aware that the great majority of Muslims in India were converts from Hinduism and ethnically Indian, and he genuinely believed that they too shared the specifically Indian heritage and so could cooperate in the building of a new independent state of all of India. The Muslims, in his view, could be given adequate safeguards for the practice of their religion, but he was unalterably opposed to giving them special *political* privileges; and he was uninterested in the fact that similar privileges were given to Hindus in provinces that were predominantly Hindu in religion.

Therefore, Gandhi never ceased to fight the communal electorates, believing that all Indians—Muslim, Hindu, and Sikh—should unite in demanding independence from the British and play their part in the government afterward. Gandhi and all the Congress leaders believed to the end that the communal electorates were a British device to enable them to postpone the granting of independence, since they wished to claim that Indians could not work together. It is incontestable that the communal electorates did succeed in emphasizing the separateness of the different religious communities. It is also possible that, if there had always been a common roll based on a more liberal franchise and the Muslims had voted simply for candidates, whether they were Muslim or Hindu or Sikh, they would never have expected to receive their own electorates and never have demanded them in later years. At all events, the policy actually followed led inevitably to the formation of Pakistan; and the great all-Indian party, the Indian National Congress, never became truly a national party, but became increasingly the party of the Hindu majority—even though a party of anti-Muslim Hindu nationalists existed also, and it was a member of this party who murdered Gandhi soon after his work had been crowned by the winning of independence.

CIVIL-DISOBEDIENCE CAMPAIGNS. The Montagu-Chelmsford Reforms could hardly have been put into effect at a less opportune moment. The end of the war had been followed by an appallingly lethal influenza epidemic, taking more than 5 million lives in India. Crop failures had resulted in widespread starvation. When there continued to be delay over the promised political reforms and their inadequate nature became known, violence broke out in many parts of India. The government resorted to severe repression and suspension of customary legal rights (Rowlatt Acts, 1919). Worst of all, a British General, determined to teach the Indians a lesson and reassert the will and strength of the British *raj,* ordered the troops to shoot into a threatening but unarmed crowd, killing 379 and wounding more than 1,200 (Amritsar Massacre, April 13, 1919). The reforms were announced at the end of the same year. The Congress, led by Gandhi, refused to permit any party members to run for election in the provinces, and late in 1920, Gandhi launched his first noncooperative civil-disobedience campaign against the British, with the announced aim of compelling the granting of immediate self-government. The campaign involved the boycotting of British textiles and the fostering of Indian cottage industry. Although the campaign was intended to be non-violent, even the authority of Gandhi and Congress leaders could not keep sporadic violence from breaking out. Early in 1922, Gandhi and other Congress leaders were arrested and sentenced to prison.

The absence of Congress candidates in the elections of 1920 did not prevent the dyarchical system from being put into operation. More moderate parties than the Congress fought the provincial elections and were rewarded with positions in the provincial cabinets. In 1923 and 1926, the Congress permitted participation, but the elected Congress members were expected to refuse to cooperate in the resulting governments. Nevertheless, some members did take an active part and passed some useful legislation, while continuing to demand that the "reserved" powers should at once be "transferred" to Indians. Late in 1926, the British Government appointed a commission led by Sir John Simon to examine the working of the constitution in India. Although most Muslims and Hindus boycotted the Simon Commission since it contained no Indians, it was able to collect a vast amount of evidence from other sources. In its report, which was published in June, 1930, the Commission proposed a federal constitution with full and responsible government at the provincial level. When these provincial governments were functioning successfully, a central government could be formed, chosen preferably by the provinces. The Simon Commission also recommended the retention of the communal electorates, which were as always adamantly opposed by the Congress. By this time, the Congress had become a huge mass party with a paid membership of close to 4 million members.

ROUND TABLE CONFERENCES. Meanwhile, in early 1929, civil disobedience had broken out again, marked by symbolic marches to the sea to make salt, thus depriving the government salt monopoly of its revenue. When disorders followed, Gandhi and other leaders were again arrested and imprisoned. A few weeks after their arrest, the long-awaited report by the Simon Commission was published. Its recommendations were at first rejected by all Indian political groups; but after a Round Table Conference held in London, to which the Congress refused to send any delegates as long as its leaders were in prison, the Muslims agreed to accept a federal state as recommended by the Commission. This at least would give them control of a few provinces where they were in a majority. It was at this first Round Table Conference that the Indian native princes first made their views officially heard. Fearing that a Congress government would soon put an end to their anachronistic regimes, they also agreed to enter a federation of which their own states would be recognized as autonomous component parts. All the Indians from the moderate parties were willing to accept communal electorates.

This Conference, of course, was unable to reach any final decisions in the absence of representatives of the Congress, the one party with mass support in India, and the Congress would accept no recommendations unless Gandhi approved them. The Viceroy, Lord Irwin, therefore visited him in prison and agreed to release him to attend a new Round Table Conference on condition that he call off the civil-disobedience campaign. At the Conference, held in the last months of 1931, Gandhi refused to accept communal electorates and insisted that he alone could speak for the Congress, while the Congress, the only "national" party of India, spoke for all Indians. He demanded immediate independence under a Congress Government. Thereafter, the Indian princes ceased to be interested in the proposals for Indian independence and never made any new proposals, though they continued to make polite conversation on the subject with British officials until after the outbreak of World War II. Few troubled even to attend the Third Round Table Conference, held in the fall of 1932. By this time, the British had made what they called a "communal award," which, to no one's surprise, preserved the separate electorates and added another one, that of the untouchables—with the support of

Gandhi, who was now again in prison. He indeed asked for more seats to be reserved for them than the British had awarded. By a "hunger strike to death," he compelled the high-caste leaders of the Congress to accept this concession to the untouchables, with whom he was always in sympathy and for whom he felt a special responsibility.

GOVERNMENT OF INDIA ACT (1935). In August, 1935, the new Government of India Act was passed, putting into effect the recommendations of the Simon Commission as modified by the Round Table Conferences. Full self-government was granted in the provinces, as the Commission had recommended, with only reserve powers retained by the governors especially for the protection of minorities. But according to the Act, the proposed central federal government, which would have been almost completely self-governing, was not to come into operation until a sufficient number of the more populous native princely states had expressed their willingness to participate. The princes in fact never did express willingness, and the British refused to coerce them. It is clear that the princes had not recognized until the Round Table Conferences how much of their prized sovereignty they would have to give up. Now when they were given the chance to sabotage the new constitution, they did so, with the result that the old Viceroy-dominated central government continued to function without change, just as it had since 1919.

For the Congress, the great question was whether or not to co-operate with the new provincial system. It finally decided to fight in the elections and then the elected members would make up their minds whether or not to take office. The candidates agreed to obey the dictates of the Working Committee, the governing body of Congress leaders, rather than act independently, thus using their power to work tactically for early independence. In most of the provinces, the Congress won easily in spite of the communal electorates. But in only one of the provinces where Muslims were in the majority did the Congress win. This was the Northwest Frontier Province, 92 per cent Muslim, where a Congress affiliate, known as the Red Shirt Party, won. In the other Muslim-dominated provinces, all the new governments were coalitions since the chief Muslim group, the Muslim League, was not as yet strong enough as a party to be able to form a government, especially in view of the overrepresentation of the Hindu electorate in the Muslim provinces. In the Congress-dominated states, the

Congress did not at first permit its members to form the government. The British governors therefore chose ministers from minority parties; within a few months the Congress decided to participate, and the minority governments resigned.

HINDU-MUSLIM CONFLICT. But in these provinces, the Congress did not share the ministries with representatives of the minorities. It took them all itself, and the Working Committee of the Congress dictated policy even to responsible ministers. Although the Congress argued that Muslims were free to join the party and thus become provincial ministers and share in the formulation of policy, these tactics infuriated most of the Muslims, whose attitude toward the Hindu majority began to harden. They now came to believe that the Congress intended to dominate the central government after independence, instead of being content with coalition governments run by moderate men belonging to all parties. In particular, they distrusted the control exercised by the Congress over its members, even when they were responsible ministers in different provinces.

The Muslim League, led by Mohammed Ali Jinnah, which had hitherto been only one of several Muslim parties, now became the spearhead for anti-Congress agitation and came to be regarded by most Muslims as the only group that could adequately protect them. All the Muslim ministers in the provincial governments except those in the Northwest Frontier Province joined the League. When the Congress called for the election of a constituent assembly to write a constitution for an independent India, which it believed could not now be far distant, the League refused to participate. Already it was beginning to think in terms of partition as the only real safeguard for Muslim interests. When India was plunged into World War II by the nonrepresentative central government without any consultation of representative Indians, the Congress demanded a promise from Britain of immediate independence as a condition for cooperating in the war. When this was refused, it called on all Congress provincial ministers to resign, leaving the British governors to carry on as best they could. The Muslim League, which supported the war on condition that Muslims be permitted afterward to choose their own future, publicly rejoiced at the departure of the Congress ministers—so far had relations between the two parties degenerated since the years when they had struggled for independence together.

It only remained to play out the last act: the Cripps mission of

1942, the final despairing efforts of Britain and the Congress Party to devise some means of holding together a country which was on the verge of permanent fission, and the actual partition.

Political Progress in Other Eastern Colonies

Burma

RIVALRY WITH INDIA. Burma, before British annexation, had been an empire that embraced several non-Burmese peoples—including the Thai, in the provinces bordering on Siam, and the Karens in the north. After annexation, it was a province of British India. Even though the British were well aware of the antagonism of the Burmese to the ethnically distinct Indians, no restrictions were placed on Indian immigration into Burma. Since the Burmese were a Buddhist people, well educated according to Buddhist principles but lacking interest in Western education and without apparent aptitude for Western financial methods, Indians occupied most of the best positions in the state that were not reserved for the British themselves. Worse still, Indians began to buy up Burmese lands, frequently reducing the Burmese to virtual peonage, and extended credit to the small Burmese farmers at usurious rates. The Burmese, who had previously enjoyed a much higher standard of living than the Indians in their own country, now found themselves constantly in debt to Indian moneylenders; and all too often, even the low-paid coolie jobs were held by immigrant Indians. British and Indian traders, who exported rice and various raw materials, took full advantage of this situation, while the British-dominated government did little to improve it. The ensuing growth of anti-Indian feeling resulted in a serious rebellion against both the British and their Indian collaborators, lasting from 1930 to 1932.

Among the subject peoples, the Thai were Buddhist but resented their domination by the alien Burmese. Many of the war-like Karens had been converted to Christianity but retained their ancient institutions, including their traditional chiefdoms. The British were accused by the Burmese of systematically favoring the Karens, and it is probably true that all the non-Burmese regarded the British as their protectors against the Burmese majority.

Faced by these problems, the British, in 1919, preferred not to grant the Montagu-Chelmsford Reforms to Burma, since the government of the province would certainly be dominated by the Burmese. But their refusal led to such agitation that they bowed to the storm and extended the Indian dyarchical system to Burma in 1921. The Burmese also proved to be divided among themselves. No nationalist party was able to command the adherence of the majority of the Burmese until the Japanese occupation during World War II. Although various nationalist parties won the elections held during the interwar period, few Burmese were willing to become ministers in the government, and most of the available ministries fell to members of the non-Burmese minorities. The Burmese representatives spent most of their energies in demanding that more governmental tasks be transferred to them rather than in trying to cooperate with the British and the minorities in remedying the ills of the country.

GOVERNMENT OF BURMA ACT (1935). When the Simon Commission visited Burma, it took cognizance of the dislike of the Burmese for the Indians and recommended the administrative separation of Burma from India. A special Burmese Round Table Conference, during 1931–32, worked out some of the details of the new responsibilities that would fall to Burma after separation. Yet, curiously enough, the Burmese became suspicious that the reason the British were willing to concede separation was because they planned to keep her as a colony, while India moved forward to independence. They believed it was for this reason that Burma was not to be covered by the proposed Government of India Act, which was to convert British India into a federation. As a result, a large number of Burmese decided that they wished to stay with India and formed an Anti-Separation League, which won the elections of 1932. When these leaders explained to the British that their main reason for wishing to continue with India was that they planned to secede from the federation in due course, the British made it clear that this was not permissible. Thereafter, the Anti-Separation League disintegrated, and the British, by the Government of Burma Act of 1935, conferred on Burma substantially the same powers as they conferred on the Indian provinces.

FIRST COLLABORATION WITH THE JAPANESE. In spite of their increased powers, subsequent Burmese governments were no more stable than before. All were coalitions, and party alignments changed frequently. The new government managed to function, in spite of numerous motions of censure, but was far from satisfactory to the more ardent Burmese nationalists. Some radical students at the University of Rangoon eventually went to Japan after the outbreak of the European war (but before the entry of the Japanese). The Japanese sent them to Formosa for political indoctrination, and they returned to Burma in due course with the invading armies.

Ceylon

The Dutch, who ruled Ceylon prior to the Napoleonic Wars, never fully subjugated the island and preferred to leave the up-country King of Kandy in his position. The British took several decades to bring Ceylon under their undisputed rule. British and Dutch coffee and tea planters and merchants occasionally agitated for some share in the government. But the Ceylonese themselves were not greatly interested during the nineteenth century in the activities of the Legislative and Executive councils, which were dominated by British officials.

The major difficulty involved in bringing Ceylonese into the government, a difficulty which even today remains partly unsolved, is the presence of considerable numbers of Tamil-speaking Indians from southern India in the country, who constitute a fairly large minority. Many of them cannot even be regarded as permanent inhabitants. The Sinhalese majority have always resented the granting of any power to these Indians, whom they regard as having divided loyalties. But when the British decided to devolve some power on the local inhabitants, they felt that all the minorities should be represented, Indian as well as European. They therefore, as in India, provided for communal electorates.

When the Morley-Minto Reforms were granted in India in 1909, some Ceylonese for the first time demanded representation in the British-dominated Legislative Council, but the British paid little attention and instituted no significant reforms. In 1915, there were several disturbances in the colony, partly for political and partly for religious ends, and these were suppressed with considerable severity. Feeling that only an organized political party could put effective pressure on the British, a group of Ceylonese in 1919 organized the Ceylon National Congress, which, like its counterpart in India, was open to all the peoples of the colony. As in India, a number of leading Tamils at first joined the Congress, then retired to form their own communal party. The Congress was quickly successful in obtaining some measure of reform. By 1923, the "unofficials" (this term in British usage refers to all members except civil servants) possessed a considerable majority in the Legislative Council, but only about 48 per cent were elected on a common roll; the remainder were chosen by their communities. The result was that the minorities were seriously overrepresented, whereas the Sinhalese, who formed about two-thirds of the population, had to be content with less than half the elected seats. To make the constitution even more unsatisfactory to the nationalists, the Executive Council retained five British officials as against a mere three elected ministers in charge of departments. Thus the officials really ruled the country, but a number of highly vocal politicians without responsibility for governing were given the chance to criticize to their heart's content in the Legislative Council.

The Donoughmore Commission, which was sent out to the colony in 1927 to advise on changes, severely criticized the existing system and produced a remarkable series of recommendations, which, with a few minor changes, were accepted by the British Government. For the first time in any British non-European colony, universal adult suffrage was granted without any qualifications (previously only 4 per cent of the population had been entitled to vote), and the communal electorates were abolished. In the Commission's view, they tended to foster disunity and increase "communalism"—that is, voting for a candidate on a personal basis without regard to his program, merely because he was the candidate for that particular community. The remainder of the system set up by the Commission was also unique in the British colonies. A State Council was instituted instead of the usual two councils, most of whose members were elected on a territorial basis on a common roll. The minorities were to be represented only by nominees of the governor up to the number of twelve. The State Council was divided into seven committees, each of which chose a chairman; and this chairman would hold the rank of minister and be responsible for the department with whose work the committee was concerned. The seven ministers together with three British officials would make up the governing cabinet. At the same time, since this constitution was highly experimental, the governor's special and reserved powers were considerably extended. What this system lacked, in comparison with the ordinary parliamentary system, was collective responsibility on the part of the ministers; they were responsible, not to the whole Council, but to their own committees, which could depose them if they wished. But Lord Donoughmore had not expected the system to remain static. The British officials could in due course withdraw from the government, and a chief minister could then be appointed who would enforce collective responsibility on his ministers. The committees would then disappear. It was certainly the most advanced colonial constitution of the day, even though the elected ministers were inclined to speak of themselves as "the people's government" and the governor with his three ministers and his special powers as the "governor's government."

The Donoughmore constitution from the beginning was severely criticized by the men who had the task of working it. All demanded the curtailment of the governor's special powers and the replacement of the British ministers by elected officials. But the Ceylonese minorities were not at all sure that they desired the appointment of a chief minister who would naturally allot the governmental portfolios to members of his own party; under the new system, after the first elections some minority members had been chosen as ministers by their committees. To avoid a repetition of this situation, the Sinhalese majority party, after the second election, used its power to pack each committee with a majority of Sinhalese, with instructions that they should vote for only Sinhalese as chairmen. This tactic had the desired effect of demonstrating both to the British and to the minorities that the constitution would not function as planned. The British Governor presented proposals calling for a conventional cabinet and parliamentary system; but by this time, the outbreak of war was imminent, and constitutional reform was shelved for the duration.

The Philippine Islands

When the United States annexed the Philippine Islands in 1898, it was understood that the Filipinos would be granted their own government as soon as feasible. President Wilson, before he left office, declared that they were already fit to govern themselves and should receive their independence. But the Republican Administration which followed disagreed; Americans had invested heavily in the typically colonial economy of the islands, and businessmen feared that an independent government would wish to change the system to the detriment of their profits. The Filipinos produced mostly raw materials and sugar, which entered the United States duty free, as did American manufactured goods into the Philippines. But only a small class of rich Filipinos and United States residents could buy the manufactured goods, so that the tariff arrangements tended to assist U.S. citizens rather than Filipinos, who were discouraged from building a native industry. American complaints that the Filipinos lacked efficiency and were often corrupt were true enough, though Wilson had not supposed that this rendered them unfit for independence. At all events, during the 1920's Filipino efforts to win greater control over their country met with rebuffs, especially from President Coolidge, who informed a Filipino delegation that the very sending of such a delegation against the wishes of the American Governor proved them to be unfit for independence!

Congress, however, did not prove so inattentive to Filipino demands, for there were many complaints from American interests against the sugar preference and the free immigration of Filipino workers. It was also rather obvious that the colony was not really worth what it cost, and that American investment there was small in comparison with other foreign investments. What the United States really needed was the certainty of Filipino naval and military bases, which could be handled by treaty. Congress, therefore, passed a bill in 1932, vetoed by President Hoover and passed over his veto, that provided for Philippine independence after a twelve-year trial period. Meanwhile, a tariff would be placed on sugar imports above a certain quota, restrictions would be placed on Filipino immigration, and the islands would guarantee the required bases. Also the U.S. Supreme Court could review Filipino legislation.

In passing the bill, Congress had provided that the elected Filipino legislature must ratify it within a year. But the Filipino leaders themselves were divided. Some of them, who had worked with Congress in drafting the legislation, were willing to tolerate the bases if it was the only way of winning independence, although they were disturbed by the possibility that the United States, then in a strongly protectionist mood and in the depths of the depression, might place tariffs on Filipino exports. Manuel Quezon, the chief Filipino nationalist, strongly objected to granting any bases, and shared the misgivings of the other negotiators on the tariff. The legislature eventually rejected the bill. The following year, the Democratic-controlled Congress passed a new bill, the Tydings-McDuffie Act (1934), under which the question of the bases was left open for further consideration. Quezon withdrew his opposition to this bill, and the legislature this time ratified it. The islands thus became a commonwealth, with their own President, Quezon, and a constitution written by themselves. Defense and foreign relations remained the responsibility of the

United States, which also retained the right to exercise some supervision over finances.

Agitation for immediate independence, instead of on the promised date of July 4, 1946, continued to be widespread. But it died down when the Japanese began to expand in the Pacific and attacked mainland China, as it was recognized that without the aid of the United States the commonwealth was defenseless. Even so, the islands fell to the Japanese in 1942. The Philippines were recaptured by U.S. forces in 1945, and newly elected President Roxas (Quezon had died during the war) became on the appointed date the first President of the Philippine Republic—the first of the Asian colonies to win this status and enter the newly established United Nations.

Mussolini's Italian Empire

Amid the efforts of colonies to free themselves from European domination, there was one major step taken in the opposite direction. This was the addition of Ethiopia to the Italian empire in northeast Africa. As already noted, the Italians had been badly defeated at the battle of Adowa in 1896, and had thereafter withdrawn from Ethiopia, though maintaining their colonies in Eritrea and Italian Somaliland. From these colonies, Mussolini launched an invasion of Ethiopia in 1935. He hardly bothered to find himself an excuse for the attack, which was intended to be an expression of Italian fascist dynamism as much as an effort to win territory for colonial expansion.

The leading powers were startled by the invasion, which placed squarely on the League of Nations the responsibility for trying to enforce its Covenant. No amount of hedging could possibly conceal the fact that this was just the kind of aggression the League was designed to prevent, or that Italy, which was still not quite a great power, could be stopped if the greater powers desired to do so. If there had been no League and this had been the late nineteenth or early twentieth century, no doubt Britain and France would have made some kind of gentlemanly agreement by which they would have received "compensation" for their neutrality. This was no longer possible in view of the existence of the League and public support for it in the Western democracies, especially Britain. The smaller nations, including wronged Ethiopia herself, took the lead in demanding sanctions against Italy as provided for in the Covenant. Although the British and

French foreign ministers did indeed come to an agreement of the nineteenth-century type, according to which Ethiopia would be dismembered, with Italy winning some 60,000 square miles and Ethiopia in return receiving a guarantee for her remaining territory and an outlet to the sea through Italian territory, the outcry was so great in Britain and elsewhere that the accommodating Foreign Minister, Sir Samuel Hoare, was compelled to resign. Moderate sanctions were then imposed, but they did not include an embargo on oil, the one product that was a strategic necessity for Italy's ships and motorized troops. Italy meanwhile assumed a threatening pose in the Mediterranean, and Hitler's Germany remained an interested spectator.

To both the British and French governments, it did not seem worth while risking a general war on such an issue, so Mussolini went ahead with his invasion and completed the conquest of Ethiopia. King Victor Emmanuel II proclaimed himself Emperor of Ethiopia, and the three Italian colonies, now united, were henceforth known as Italian East Africa. The empire proved to be short-lived, since the Italians were unable to maintain any of their colonial possessions for long during the war. Their German allies had little interest in preventing the British-officered African colonial army from reconquering the country, early in 1941. In January, 1942, Ethiopia was restored to her own Emperor, Haile Selassie. Thus collapsed the last attempt by a European power to acquire new colonies in Africa.

7. World War II and Its Immediate Consequences

It is impossible to overestimate the long-term consequences of World War II for the colonial system. Of primary importance was the establishment of the United Nations, in which former colonies soon came to be well represented and were thus in a position to exercise continuous moral pressure on the colonial powers. Although the loss of so many colonies to the Japanese proved to be only temporary, colonial peoples everywhere now recognized that European powers were no longer invincible. Never again would they feel they were struggling against insuperable odds. Even if they could not defeat the Europeans in open warfare as the Japanese had done, they could at least hope to imitate India, which was on the point of winning her independence as the result of having learned how to exercise pressure most effectively on the British. Several other colonies besides India were near independence at the war's end, in most cases as a direct result of the war. And, as a result of the loss of the war by the Japanese, the Japanese colonies of Formosa and Korea were returned respectively to China and to an independent native government.

The United Nations Trusteeship System

All during the war, the Allied powers had given much thought to the future of colonialism, and to whether the organization that would replace the League of Nations should take a more active part in the supervision of colonies. The mandate system, which had applied only to colonies of the defeated powers, could perhaps be extended, and in any event there would at least be the Italian and Japanese colonies to be disposed of. The United States, which had made her own arrangements for her larger colonies, was particularly interested in seeing other colonial powers follow her example. But the British, under Winston Churchill, showed little interest in extending the mandate system to any other British colonies. The Free French envisaged a plan for French colonies that did not include supervision by any eventual international organization. In the last years of the war, even in the United States opinion was divided. The United States military, determined to fortify the former Japanese Pacific islands, were anxious to be given an entirely free hand in the Pacific. Their influence was

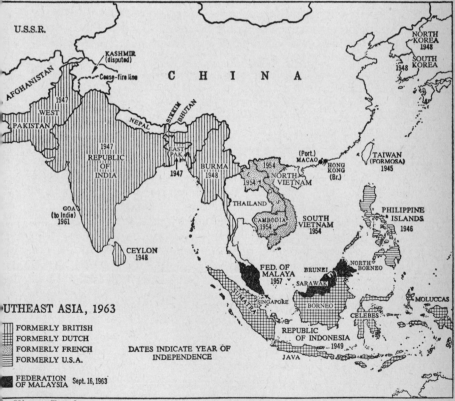

by *Vincent Kotschar.*

therefore thrown into the scales against giving the United Nations any kind of blanket authority over colonies.

Thus, by the time the colonial question came up for discussion between the powers, the early position of the State Department under Cordell Hull—to put pressure on all the colonial powers to give up some of their authority in their colonies and prepare them for independence—had been seriously eroded. At the Yalta Conference, in early 1945, the powers had agreed only to strengthen the mandate system in the existing mandated territories, and in any new territories that would be taken from the enemy at the end of the war. This new trusteeship system, as it was called, could also be applied to a third category of colonies—those voluntarily brought into the system by the colonial powers.

When the San Francisco Conference assembled in April, 1945, the United States was ready with a technical paper, presented by Harold Stassen, which was used as the basis for discussion in a committee convened for the purpose of setting up the trusteeship system; and most of the system finally evolved and accepted by the Conference was the result of the work of Americans. But the system applied only to mandated and ex-enemy territories. No colonial power offered any of its territories to the United Nations, then or later.

Under the new system that came into effect as the result of the San Francisco Conference, all the powers still holding mandates were invited by the United Nations to convert them to trust territories, and to accept a new series of obligations that went beyond those accepted by the mandatory powers. All except the Union of South Africa, which wished to annex former German Southwest Africa outright, agreed. South Africa has to this day refused to transfer Southwest Africa to the United Nations. Southwest Africa therefore exists in a kind of legal no man's land. Even the International Court of Justice, in the opinion of South Africa, cannot make the United Nations the legal successor of the League.

THE TRUSTEESHIP COUNCIL. The powers administering U.N. trust territories have the obligation to prepare them for independence, which was the case only with Class A mandates after World War I. In other respects, the new obligations did not materially differ from those of mandates, but the system for seeing that the obligations were honored did. The United Nations Charter provided for the establishment of a Trusteeship Council, which was to be a "principal organ" of the United Nations, like the

Security Council and the General Assembly. This Council was given the task of exercising a general supervision over the administration of the trust territories. Membership on the Council was limited to the administering powers and an equal number of non-administering powers, thus ensuring that the latter could never outvote the former. All permanent members of the Security Council are entitled to be members of the Trusteeship Council, as either administering or nonadministering powers. If the votes of administering or nonadministering powers are equal, no action can be taken. Without this safeguard, probably none of the former mandatory powers would have converted its mandates into trust territories, and only the former Italian colonies of Somaliland, Eritrea, and Libya would have been available for the new status. Thus the trusteeship system of the United Nations would have collapsed before it had begun.

The designation of the Trusteeship Council as a principal organ of the United Nations was a highly significant distinction for the mandatory powers. In their view, it was *not* to be under the authority of the General Assembly, where there was no veto; and they have always acted in the Trusteeship Council as if the resolutions of the General Assembly on trusteeship matters were to be treated as advisory opinions and not binding on the Council. That this opinion has not usually been shared by the nonadministering powers, or even by the General Assembly, is not relevant, since the General Assembly actually has had no means of coercing the Trusteeship Council. In fact, with the reduction of the number of trust territories to a very few, this has now become virtually a dead issue.*

---

* It is true that Articles 85 and 87 of the Charter seem to imply that the Trusteeship Council operates under the authority of the General Assembly. Indeed, these very words are used in Article 85, paragraph 2: "The Trusteeship Council, operating under the authority of the General Assembly, shall assist the General Assembly in carrying out these functions." But the functions referred to here may well be those which incontestably belong to the General Assembly—namely, the approval of the terms of the original trusteeship agreements, their alteration or amendment, and their ultimate abrogation. It has therefore been argued by the administering powers that it is only when these matters are being considered that the Trusteeship Council operates under the authority of the General Assembly. Similarly, Article 87, which states that "the General Assembly, and, under its authority, the Trusteeship Council, may consider reports . . . accept petitions . . . provide for periodic visits." At all events there is enough ambiguity in the Charter for the lines of authority to have been somewhat blurred, and in fact the Trusteeship Council has not acted as if it were dependent on the authority of the General Assembly

From the beginning, and even before the establishment of the Trusteeship Council, the General Assembly has had a Trusteeship Committee of its own, known as the Fourth Committee, where trust matters are discussed. This Committee, in which all members of the United Nations are represented and which therefore has a permanent anticolonial majority, has always felt it to be a part of its task to offer advice to the Trusteeship Council, which the Council has not considered itself bound to accept. It has also provided a forum for colonial petitioners who have found the Trusteeship Council to be less sympathetic than the Committee. The Committee's unquestioned function has been to recommend action and prepare resolutions for its parent body, the General Assembly, for only the General Assembly could decide when the trusteeship status should be terminated and what final conditions had to be fulfilled before a colony became independent. The Assembly did not have to accept the advice proffered to it by the Trusteeship Council, which the Assembly's majority often regarded as unduly influenced by the administering powers. On several occasions, the General Assembly expressed doubts as to whether genuine independence or a new and disguised version of colonialism was being conferred by an administering power. It could and did call for elections to be held in a territory before agreeing to its independence. It could and did authorize plebiscites and send commissions to observe whether the voters were being given full freedom of choice. Its acceptance or rejection of new members of the United Nations was subject only to veto in the Security Council. These were important functions, and as more and more colonies approached the end of their trusteeship, the General Assembly left the Trusteeship Council with less and less to do.

COMMITTEE ON NON-SELF-GOVERNING TERRITORIES. The Trusteeship Council has had no concern whatever with another feature of the United Nations and one that was not present in the League of Nations. Article 73 of the U.N. Charter deals with non-self-governing territories that are not trust territories. It states that members recognize certain obligations toward these territories, in particular to "ensure just treatment and protection against abuses," to "develop self-government and take due account of the aspirations of the peoples and to assist them in the progressive development

___

and has taken note of, rather than obeyed, the requests of the General Assembly. Most of the administering powers have made it clear that they do not consider themselves bound to heed these requests and have quoted the earlier articles in the Charter to justify their attitude.

of their free political institutions." Paragraph E requires the members "to transmit regularly to the Secretary-General for information purposes . . . statistical and other information of a technical nature relating to economic, social, and educational conditions." The General Assembly, in pursuance of this article, requested all members to state which of the territories they administered were non-self-governing. Then it proceeded to set up a committee on information on non-self-governing territories, which reported to the Fourth Committee after considering the reports. The General Assembly and the Committee also repeatedly asked for political information, which had, at the insistence of the colonial powers, been purposely omitted from paragraph E.

In due course, the original members of the United Nations did provide the names of the territories they administered; some of them also supplied political information, which was of the greatest interest to the Assembly majority. But they never admitted that the Assembly and its committees had the *right* to such information; and when they were questioned on the contents of the reports, several stressed that the Charter had spoken only of reports *for information purposes* and that the information need be only what the administering power wished to supply. Even so, most of the powers usually did answer the questions; but they decided themselves which territories should be designated as non-self-governing. France never admitted that Algeria was anything but an overseas extension of France, and thus she excluded Algeria from United Nations discussion on the grounds that it was purely a domestic issue. Britain never reported on Southern Rhodesia, since the colony was undoubtedly self-governing, even if the rule was in the hands of a tiny minority of Europeans. Portugal, when she at length entered the United Nations, took the same position as France with regard to her overseas provinces. Great pressure was and still is exercised on Portugal to persuade her to submit reports. When disturbances broke out in Portuguese territories and in Southern Rhodesia in 1961, the United Nations set up committees to investigate. Both Portugal and Britain denied that the United Nations had any right even to discuss the territories; but despite their statements for the record, they offered at least some measure of cooperation to the committees once they had been set up. Obviously, through means such as these, the United Nations has succeeded in applying moral pressure on the colonial powers, even though it has, in fact, no legal right to intervene in the internal administration of the colonies.

THE COMMITTEE OF SEVENTEEN. In 1960, the General Assembly also succeeded in passing a resolution calling upon all colonial powers to grant independence to their colonies. It then set up a Committee of Seventeen to take steps to see that the resolution was being complied with. Again, it could not coerce, but it has nevertheless exercised a constant moral pressure in a manner totally foreign to the mild and diplomatic methods of the League of Nations, thus reflecting the far different composition of the United Nations. And this continuing pressure has been a significant factor in the postwar breakup of colonial empires. No nation has wished to be placed in the position of either withholding its cooperation or refusing to answer questions, however loaded and unfair they may have seemed. Nor have these nations wished to undermine the authority and prestige of the United Nations, since they hoped that it would someday prove useful in solving the great problems of war and peace. So, in the matter of colonies, what the United Nations has called for, perhaps prematurely, it has eventually seen put into effect by the colonial power, even though the power would vigorously deny that it was United Nations intervention that brought it about. This is more than could have been predicted for the United Nations when it was first brought into existence, and a good deal more than is ever admitted by its numerous critics.

Fate of the Territories Occupied by Japan

During the war, Britain, France, and the Netherlands were compelled by the Japanese to relinquish their Far Eastern colonies, and the United States temporarily lost the Philippines. The United States, however, had already promised independence to the Philippines. When the forces of General MacArthur recaptured the islands, they ended the "independent" regime under José Laurel that the Japanese had established during their occupation, and on July 4, 1946, the date originally selected many years before, the United States granted independence to a democratically elected government.

It had been thought during the war that the colonial powers would never return to the Far East, so great had been their loss of prestige and the growth of nationalism in the various colonies. But, as it happened, all, with varying degrees of determination, attempted to re-establish their positions. The British were welcomed as liberators in their Malayan territories, in the expectation that they would concede self-government; and Hong Kong businessmen, who profited from the British presence in Hong Kong, had no objection to their return, which ensured them a privileged position denied to their compatriots under the Kuomintang. In Burma, on the other hand, the British were under strong pressure from Burmese nationalists, and after a few feeble efforts to reestablish themselves they decided to withdraw gracefully.

The French and Dutch had been aided in the return to their colonies by British and Australian forces—although the Australians were later to regret this and played a leading part in working for the independence of Indonesia, through the United Nations. They were both unwilling to relinquish their positions to nationalists, and were prepared to concede only a façade of self-government to their colonial subjects. The French in Indochina were faced with a divided nationalist opposition, in view of the attempt of Ho Chi Minh, the leading nationalist, to institute a Communist revolution at the same time as independence. They did not concede until they were militarily defeated in 1954. The Dutch in Indonesia, faced by a far more united opposition than the French, and with far less military and financial resources, gave way in 1949, and granted Indonesia independence, partly as the result of pressure from the United States and the United Nations, but mainly because they recognized that they were too seriously outnumbered by the Indonesians and able to win too few "collaborators" to be able to establish a permanent regime under their control.

Burma

PREWAR ANTI-BRITISH MOVEMENTS. In Burma, a strong anti-British movement had been growing during the last years of the British regime, especially among the youth. This found expression in the nationalist Thakin Party, which later became the Burma Revolutionary Party. When the British arrested and imprisoned some of the Thakins, including U Nu (who was to become the first Prime Minister of independent Burma), others went underground; as noted previously, substantial numbers later went to Japan and were trained as revolutionaries with the avowed purpose of aiding the Japanese on their return to the country with the Japanese armies.

If the British had been prepared to defend Burma effectively and had done so, they might have aroused some loyalty in the Burmese and inspired them to resist. But they preferred to enroll the more "reliable" and warlike Karens and other northern peoples in their army. Indeed, at the outbreak of the war, members of the minority groups outnumbered the Burmese in the army 20 to 1; even the Indians outnumbered them 10 to 1. There were only 4 Burmese officers as against 75 Karens and other northerners, 36 Indians, and 163 British. When Burmese Prime Minister U Saw visited Britain the very month before the Japanese entered the war, to ask for a pledge of Dominion status, he was refused by Winston Churchill. Pearl Harbor was bombed before he could return home, and he attempted to enter into relations with representatives of Japan, for which he was arrested and interned by the U.S. Government.

WARTIME COLLABORATION WITH JAPAN. The Japanese accompanied their drive into Burma with a barrage of propaganda declaring Asia for the Asians. Since their invasion was carrying all before it, large numbers of Burmese were naturally convinced that it represented the "wave of the future." Others, even those jailed by the British, were not so sure. U Nu sent an urgent message to the British (which never arrived) telling them that, if only they would promise independence, the Burmese would help them against the "fascist brigands." But it was already too late. Although the British and their allies made a masterly retreat and carried on the war in the north for as long as they could, the Japanese captured the country, aided by the "Burma Independence Army" (BIA), led by Aung San, which gathered native recruits as it marched. After the conquest, the BIA was entrusted with several important administrative and military tasks by the Japanese, and by various means it managed to retain its cohesion as a unit. Dr. Ba Maw, at one time Prime Minister under the British regime, was released from jail by the Japanese and set up as chief administrator. In as many fields as they could, the Japanese permitted the Burmese to run the internal affairs of the country, but nothing could hide the fact that they were systematically exploiting and despoiling the country or that the vaunted policy of Asia for the Asians was nothing but a propaganda slogan, hardly intended to be put into operation.

In the hopes of winning back some of the popularity they had known at the beginning, the Japanese on August 1, 1943, proclaimed that Burma was now an independent state within the

Greater Asia Co-Prosperity Sphere, with Dr. Ba Maw as *adipadi* (*Führer*). Since internal administration was effectively in Burmese hands as long as Japanese military needs were met, this independence was not quite as illusory as elsewhere. Aung San, as Commander-in-Chief of the Burmese Army and Minister of Defense in Ba Maw's cabinet, enjoyed considerable prestige, since the army was actually independent and the Japanese treated it with respect. But as the fortunes of war changed and it became clear that Japanese days in Burma were numbered and the entry of Allied troops was not far away, Aung San began to build up an anti-Japanese group in the army and organized a party known as the Anti-Fascist People's Freedom League (AFPFL), composed of ten separate political groups, including Communists. When it first became possible to engage in resistance to the Japanese, he undertook secret negotiations with Lord Mountbatten, the British commander on the Burmese front. At the right moment, he led an uprising against the Japanese and thus contributed to their defeat.

THE WINNING OF INDEPENDENCE. Although it was of course true that Aung San had been a "collaborator," his later actions to some degree redeemed him in the eyes of the British. In any case, he was a national hero, and Mountbatten recognized that the British would have to work with him. But the British Governor, Sir Reginald Dorman-Smith, who returned from India where he had been in exile during the war, was still not reconciled to the truth that the Burmese to a man wanted genuine independence and at once. He attempted to set the clock back by appointing an Executive Council with fourteen members, two of them British and five others his nominees. The AFPFL, which as a national Burmese movement could have won all the seats in any election, refused to cooperate, whereupon the Governor appointed an Executive Council with no AFPFL members at all and prevented Aung San from going to England to put the matter before the British. Nevertheless, the Burmese case was argued in Parliament, which now had a Labour majority. A massive strike was organized successfully in Rangoon, and the Governor was recalled, to be replaced by Sir Hubert Rance, a friend of Aung San and former staff officer with Mountbatten.

Aung San, in effect, now became Prime Minister, with an Executive Council dominated by the AFPFL, and he was given full assurance by British Prime Minister Attlee of independence within a year. Elections for a constituent assembly were then held and won overwhelmingly by the AFPFL. While the constitution was being discussed, a number of assassins, hired by former Prime Minister U Saw, who had recently been released from internment, invaded the Executive Council and killed Aung San and five others of the effective AFPFL leadership—a loss that continues to have its effects. Fortunately, U Nu, Deputy President of AFPFL, was not a member of the Executive Council and thus escaped, to be chosen by Sir Hubert Rance as the new Burmese leader of the Council. By agreement with the British, who at Burmese request had left the possibility open, the constituent assembly declared for a republic outside the Commonwealth, and this former Indian province became the sovereign independent republic of the Union of Burma on January 4, 1948.

The Netherlands East Indies

GROWTH OF NATIONALISM. During the course of World War I, the Dutch inaugurated a *Volksraad,* or Legislative Council, which gave the Indonesians their first opportunity to make their voices heard in the affairs of their country. But the Indonesian representatives were carefully handpicked by the Dutch, and the *Volksraad* provided little outlet for their grievances. None of the leading nationalists was a member.

Indonesian grievances, in fact, were many. During and subsequent to the culture system of the nineteenth century, the Dutch instituted a system of indirect rule by local aristocrats and village headmen, who administered the forced cultivation and labor systems. In addition to using these Indonesian leaders, the Dutch also backed the Chinese businessmen, enabling them to take over almost the entire wholesale and retail business of the colony. There was thus only a tiny Indonesian middle class. The total Indonesian high school population at any given time never amounted to more than several hundred. Higher education was simply not available, except to the very few who could surmount all the obstacles and obtain an education in Europe. With the exception of those who belonged to the aristocracy, almost all the intellectuals were anticolonial. The Indonesian student organizations that grew up in Holland in the 1920's were all radical: some Communist-oriented, others simply anti-Dutch. When their members returned to Indonesia, it was with the primary purpose of working for independence. Mohammed Hatta, later to become

Vice-President of independent Indonesia, was at one time a student leader. However, Sukarno, who belonged to an older generation than Hatta's, was never a student leader, but a qualified engineer.

As has been the case in most growing nationalist movements, numerous political parties were formed, often based on little but personalities. The one great exception was the Indonesian Communist Party (Partai Komunis Indonesia, or PKI), which won some support from the Soviet Union after the war but never became a strong organization in the 1920's, although many leaders who did not join it were in sympathy with its Marxist revolutionary ideology and admired its activism. In 1926, the PKI launched an ill-planned rebellion which, because of lack of popular support, never had any chance of success. Very few Indonesians participated in the rebellion, and the Dutch had no difficulty in suppressing it. The Party was outlawed, and most of its leaders were imprisoned. A few top leaders escaped to Moscow, whence they returned after World War II. Communism thus received a setback from which it took a long time to recover, and the leadership of the nationalist movement fell into the hands of the non-Communist nationalists.

During the late 1920's, the Dutch paid little attention to the nationalists and their political maneuverings, and allowed them relative freedom to make speeches, hold meetings, and organize. Then the Great Depression struck Indonesia with fearful severity, and the standard of living of the peasants, many of whom were independent rubber producers, dropped precipitately, as did exports and the prices obtained for them. The Chinese businessmen called in their credit, and peasants became burdened with debt and often lost their land. The nationalists naturally blamed the Dutch, who did little to relieve the situation. A series of Dutch governors, fearing a revolution, changed the previous liberal policy into an oppressive one, and exiled the major nationalist leaders, including Sukarno and Hatta. But despite the outlawing of many political parties, and the work of an efficient secret police, revolutionary activity continued. A few parties that presented no obvious threat to the Dutch were allowed to continue to function.

CONSEQUENCES OF THE WAR. This was the situation when war broke out in Europe. When Holland was overrun by the Germans, in 1940, the Indonesian Dutch Government continued as before. The Indonesian nationalists, feeling they could not overthrow it without outside aid, looked hopefully toward the expected Japanese invasion. At the last moment, the Dutch came to the conclusion that they could not hope to resist the Japanese without some local support. They therefore allowed Hatta and Sutan Sjahrir, another dynamic nationalist leader, who was to become the first Prime Minister after the war, to return to Java just before the invasion; Sukarno, however, had to wait for the arrival of the Japanese before he was freed. The quick collapse of Dutch resistance on Java convinced the Indonesians that their rulers lacked courage—a conviction that helped to give them self-confidence, since it became clear to them that there was nothing especially superior about the Dutch. The Japanese were welcomed as deliverers, and won additional acclamation when they imprisoned every Dutchman they could find. The new conquerors, who themselves lacked manpower for administration, were compelled to employ Indonesians in almost all ranks of the civil service, thus giving them much-needed experience.

But the Japanese soon wore out their welcome. Like the Dutch, they exploited the Indonesians, but their demands on the economy were even more onerous, since they were engaged in an all-out war effort. The brutal behavior of their soldiers outraged Indonesians of every class—even though in some areas of the vast country there were so few Japanese that many Indonesians never saw any. Nevertheless, Sukarno and Hatta kept to their decision to work with the Japanese in exchange for a considerable measure of self-government, while at the same time delegating Sjahrir to organize the underground, with which they kept in touch throughout the war. By the end of the war, this underground was effectively organized and ready to play its part in the establishment of an independent republic.

ATTEMPTED RECONQUEST BY THE DUTCH. Nevertheless, the sudden surrender of the Japanese took the Indonesians by surprise. Some members of the Japanese High Command had been devolving more and more power on the Indonesian leaders, in the expectation that there would be a Communist revolution in Japan that would bring the Russians in on the side of the Japanese. These officers, who evidently hoped for a Communist revolution in Indonesia also, were not, however, backed by their superiors and were disowned by them immediately after the surrender. Official Japanese instructions were that the Indonesians should be kept under control until the Allied commanders arrived to accept the surrender. Thus the Indonesians possessed a strong political organization ready to assume control of an independent government, but lacked enough military power to disarm the Japanese Army except in some of the outlying areas; they were as yet quite incapable of defending themselves against the Allied powers and the Dutch. Although Sukarno was well aware of the dangers of a premature declaration of independence, he was prevailed upon to act rather than leave the initiative in the hands of his opponents. The independent Republic was declared on August 17, 1945, with Sukarno as President and a cabinet and a committee of advisers appointed by himself. The Japanese High Command reacted quickly, jailing Vice-Admiral Mayeda, who had been privy to the Indonesian declaration, and in several parts of the country there was bloodshed as the Japanese tried to suppress the revolution. Nevertheless, the new Republican Government began at once to function and to organize its own army as best it could.

When the Allied troops began to arrive on September 29, the British in Java and Sumatra, Australian in East Indonesia, they found an Indonesian government in operation—a difficult situation for troops whose instructions were to prepare the way for the return of the Dutch, who began to arrive soon afterward. When the British delayed disarming the Japanese and even ordered them to join in maintaining law and order, which involved fighting the Indonesians, the latter resisted fiercely, despite efforts made by the Republican Government to control them. This phase of the reoccupation culminated in the battle of Surabaya, in November, 1945. The British, with Indian contingents, were compelled to fight poorly armed Indonesian bands for ten days before they could subdue the city. The Indian nationalist leaders issued a furious denunciation of the British for using Indian troops in this manner. But by the end of 1945, the British and Dutch were in full control of the coastal cities of northern Java and of East Indonesia, although the Republic controlled the greater part of Java and Sumatra. It was therefore clear that the Dutch, with or without their British allies, would not be able to take control of their former colony without much hard fighting, and the probable intervention of the United Nations.

It was clear to the Dutch that the British could not keep their troops much longer in the colony, in view of public opinion at home and the attitude of India. Australian opinion had also turned in favor of Indonesia—in large measure because of Dutch atrocities in East Indonesia, led by Captain Paul Westerling, a terrorist employed by the Dutch who showed no compunction in using the most ruthless measures against "rebellious" villages and known or suspected nationalists. The only method available to the Dutch, therefore, was to use their armed forces sparingly until their military strength could be built up, and attempt to wear down the Republic, partly by blockade—a feasible policy, since they controlled most of the productive lands of the country. At the same time, they could organize the parts of their former colony that they controlled in such a manner that they could make it appear that the majority of Indonesians were backing them. In the United Nations, they could rely on French, and usually British, support, since both the French and British were engaged in similar actions in their own former colonies and were extremely anxious not to allow the United Nations to interfere in "domestic" disputes. Both of these powers had vetoes which could be cast when absolutely necessary—the French exercised the right once. Even the United States, despite her anticolonial principles, was sensitive on the issue of allowing the United Nations to interfere in matters classified as domestic.

This Dutch policy was in most respects remarkably successful. The territories outside the small area held by the Republic were all carefully organized into states with a façade of independence. Most of the rulers from the colonial period backed the Dutch, and reliable men were appointed as electors, who duly elected majorities of other reliable men. In the disturbed conditions of the time, few knew that the "legislatures" of these states were granted little legislative power, and that the Dutch continued to control the executive. Unless, as sometimes happened, the "reliable" men suddenly turned on the Dutch, the latter experienced no opposition of importance. It was widely believed that the Dutch were in the process of granting independence to these "states," and that the Indonesians were unreasonable in their reluctance to accept a United States of Indonesia. It was even believed to be a kind of "Javanese imperialism" that prevented them from accepting the minor place alloted to the Republic under the Dutch scheme for federation. In the United Nations, the Soviet Union usually, although not always, backed the Republic, whereas the United States, which was naturally inclined to take the opposite side from the Soviet Union, especially after 1947, usually appeared as the opponent of Indonesian nationalism. The compromise solutions advocated by the United States invariably failed to meet

Indonesian wishes, and until 1949 provided Indonesians with an absolute minimum of useful support. The Dutch, perfectly well aware of this, followed their own policy more or less without reference to U.N. wishes, obeying its resolutions only when they coincided with their own intentions. The Indonesians were able to put pressure on the U.S. Government chiefly through the Senate, which had the power to withhold Dutch appropriations under the Marshall Plan.

In November, 1946, when the British were about to withdraw their troops, the Dutch and Indonesians reached an agreement (Linggadjati Agreement, signed March 25, 1947), under which the Republican Government was recognized as the *de facto* government in Java and Sumatra. It also called for cooperation between the Republic and the Netherlands in setting up a United States of Indonesia, composed of three states, East Indonesia, Borneo, and the Republic. The Republic at that time controlled Java, Sumatra, and Madura, which contained about 85 per cent of the whole Indonesian population. These new arrangements were to be put into effect by January 1, 1949, at which time a Netherlands-Indonesian Union would be formed under the Dutch Crown. The two sides interpreted the agreement quite differently, but, although there was a provision for arbitration, the Dutch refused to abide by it and always assumed that their own interpretation was the only possible one. They regarded themselves as having been granted supreme authority in Indonesia until the founding of the U.S.I., whereas the Republic regarded itself as an equal partner to be consulted, with a veto on all arrangements under the agreement.

The Dutch Governor, Hubertus van Mook, proceeded at once, on the basis of his interpretation of the agreement, to form a great many new component states. The Republic, therefore, was soon heavily outnumbered. Only two months after signing of the agreement, the Dutch presented Sjahrir's Indonesian Government with an ultimatum demanding that it agree to full Dutch sovereignty over the whole country until January 1, 1949. The United States adopted the Dutch view of the treaty, thus isolating the Indonesians, who agreed to accept most of the points in the ultimatum. Nevertheless, the Dutch, who had been building up their armed forces, preferred to launch an attack (July 20, 1947). They succeeded in penning the Republican forces within a very small area in southern Java, and were able to gain control of almost all the rest of Indonesia. But they did not destroy either the Republican Army or the Sukarno Government—although they caused deep divisions in the latter, and several changes of cabinet. All that the Indonesians were able to obtain from the United Nations was a Good Offices Committee (GOC), made up of one nominee of the Dutch, one of their own, and a third chosen by the first two. The Republic chose an Australian, the Dutch a Belgian, and the two nominees together decided upon an American, Frank Graham.

The Committee, however, was empowered only to offer its services to bring the sides together, not to mediate. The victorious Dutch Government paid little attention to the Committee's views, since most of its recommendations were favorable to the Indonesian point of view, but busied itself instead with the re-organization of the territories it had won in the recent fighting. The Committee's patience was gradually worn down. In order to save something for the Republic, and in the face of a new Dutch ultimatum with a time limit, it recommended the acceptance of the so-called Renville Agreement, by which the Dutch accepted the principle of free elections for the states under their control and agreed to a cease-fire. The now truncated Republic, as in 1946, was to be only one of the constituent states of the U.S.I., and was outnumbered by the new Dutch puppet states. Graham reminded the Indonesians that if they refused to sign, the U.N. Security Council would probably take no further action, since any serious recommendation would face a French veto. This meant that the Dutch would have a free hand for the renewed military intervention they were threatening. Short of ammunition and unable to resist the pressure, the Republican Government signed (January, 1948), and the Prime Minister resigned soon afterward. Sukarno appointed his Vice President Hatta as Prime Minister, with a presidential cabinet which remained in office until independence—in spite of an attempted Communist *coup*, late in 1948, aided by irregular armed bands, which was suppressed by the regular troops of the government.

Throughout 1948, the Republican position deteriorated. The Good Offices Committee, with different personnel, continued to function, but the Dutch paid increasingly less attention to it, and refused to let it observe their "free elections," or the means by which the country was being organized in their favor. The interim "federal" government set up in Jakarta in accordance with the Renville Agreement was under sole Dutch control, with a few anti-Republican Indonesians added as window dressing. Guerrilla warfare continued, and the truce was frequently broken by both sides. The United States showed no signs of supporting the Indonesian case either in the United Nations or elsewhere, although its members on the GOC were trying hard to get the Dutch to agree to a constitutional convention with delegates chosen in a supervised free election. The Dutch tightened their blockade over the small territory in southern Java still under the Republican Government, and desultory negotiations dragged on until December, 1948.

The Dutch by this time were ready to make their last push to destroy the Republican Government. They now had almost 150,000 troops in the territory, supported by considerable numbers of planes, tanks, and mechanized equipment, as well as unlimited ammunition. The Republican leaders were aware that the Dutch were losing patience, but they did not expect the sudden eighteen-hour ultimatum, accompanied by demands which the Dutch knew must be refused. In a sudden attack launched by paratroopers, the Dutch seized Jogjakarta, the Republican capital, captured Sukarno and Hatta, and thus attempted to present the United Nations and the world with a *fait accompli*. But despite their immediate success, the Republican Government continued to function under new leaders, and its guerrilla warfare was highly effective. Several members of the Security Council tried to pass a resolution demanding, as a minimum, the imposition of a cease-fire and the return by the Dutch to their "Renville" position. But the most for which a majority could be obtained was the call for a cease-fire and a demand for the release of the Republican leaders, who had been exiled to an island off the coast of Sumatra. The Dutch, however, procrastinated in their reply, and continued in their operations. Neither side, in fact, was now willing to cease hostilities, and the Republican troops were counterattacking in several areas and inflicting serious casualties on the Dutch Army. The Republican emergency government functioned effectively, and throughout Java it was recognized that only through their own military efforts were the Indonesians likely to win independence.

ACHIEVEMENT OF INDEPENDENCE. In January, 1949, the U.N. Security Council passed a resolution, sponsored jointly by the United States and several other powers, reconstituting the Good Offices Committee as the United Nations Commission for Indonesia, with the power to recommend action to the Council. The resolution again called upon the Dutch to discontinue military operations, to free the Republican leaders, and to arrange for the transfer of sovereignty to the United States of Indonesia by July 1,

1950, after first holding free elections for a Constituent Assembly to draft a constitution. Although the Dutch did not take the resolution seriously, since it contained no provision for enforcement, their military position was nevertheless weakening rapidly. The Republicans, indeed, had almost recaptured their capital of Jogjakarta. The Dutch therefore felt that their best chance was to use their puppet legislators in the states they controlled to draft a constitution in their favor. For this purpose, they proposed a Round Table Conference in The Hague, on March 12, to which the Republican leaders would be invited. In effect, the Security Council accepted this as a satisfactory solution (March 23). Although the imprisoned Republican leaders refused to have anything to do with the conference, they did interview some of the delegates who were allowed to visit them, impressed them with the successes of the Republican forces, of which most of the delegates were unaware, and succeeded in persuading some of them to put up resistance to Dutch demands. Meanwhile, the U.S. Senate had threatened to cut off funds for the Netherlands under the Marshall Plan if the Dutch did not abide by the Security Council resolution, and the U.N. General Assembly, by an impressive majority, voted to look into the question of Indonesian independence and debate it in May.

The pressure was now on the Dutch. United States officials had gradually come to the conclusion that the Indonesians must be granted independence, and began to express this view forcefully to the Dutch. Perhaps even more important, the delegates of the component states of Indonesia also came to the conclusion that they could win independence, and many preferred this to a continuation of a barely disguised colonial system, however privileged their own personal positions might be. They made this view known to the Dutch, who at last decided to release the imprisoned Indonesian leaders on condition the Republic cease its guerrilla warfare. A cease-fire was arranged for August 1, 1949, and the postponed Round Table Conference began on August 15, 1949. At this conference, the Dutch finally gave way and settled for what they could get in the way of economic protection. A federal government for the United States of Indonesia was agreed to, as well as a Netherlands-Indonesia Union under the Dutch Crown, with both parties as separate independent states. The federal President was to be elected by the Senate and House of Representatives sitting jointly. A few days before the transfer of sovereignty, Sukarno was elected President by this body, despite the fact that most of the electors represented puppet states set up by the Dutch. Everyone recognized that Sukarno was the one indispensable figure with wide appeal to all sections of the population, and the establishment of the independent U.S.I. was regarded as a triumph for his policy.

It was only natural that once sovereignty had been transferred, on December 27, 1949, a strong reaction should have set in against the Dutch-imposed federal system with its fifteen states, each with two senators, who exercised governmental power out of all proportion to the importance of their states. The representatives of these states were also believed to be tainted with collaboration. In the various states, political movements quickly arose demanding closer union with the federal government—a movement naturally encouraged by the federal leaders. The movement was given increased impetus when the Sultan of West Borneo unleashed a rebellion in his area, with the support of dissident Dutch, including the notorious Captain Westerling. The rebellion was put down, and thereafter the movement for unity became irresistible. On August 10, 1950, following fruitful negotiations between the representatives of the states and the Republic, the U.S.I. became the unitary Republic of Indonesia. Sukarno was again elected President, and Hatta, who had been the first federal Prime Minister, became Vice-President. The Senate was abolished and the country was subdivided into ten provinces.

Alone among the former Dutch possessions in Southeast Asia, the western half of the island of New Guinea was retained by the Dutch. West Irian, as it was called by the Indonesians, was reserved for later consideration. Not until 1962 was a solution reached. Indonesia incorporated the territory in 1963, subject to a plebiscite to be held in ten years to determine its permanent status.

Indochina

PREWAR RELATIONS WITH FRANCE. In taking over Indochina, the French did not annex the entire country and make it into a colony. Laos and Cambodia both remained protected kingdoms, while Annam and Tonkin continued under the authority of a legitimate emperor, also protected by the French. Only Cochinchina in the south, with its capital of Saigon, where French commercial interests were strongest, became a colony under direct French administration. The native rulers possessed a certain amount of authority in domestic matters and could never be entirely ignored by the French, since they continued to command the loyalty of the great majority of the people. The French preferred to attempt to persuade the rulers to adopt pro-French policies. Thus the Emperor Bao Dai, who at the age of twelve acceded to the throne of Annam and Tonkin in 1925, had been educated entirely in France by a former French Resident. When he assumed his royal duties in Indochina in 1932, he was thoroughly imbued with French culture, but at the same time was a patriotic Vietnamese ruler who for many years did his best to soften the generally oppressive French regime in his country. The Vietnamese minority in the Colonial Council in Saigon also made similar attempts.

But all efforts came to nothing in view of the opposition of French officials and commercial interests which were strongly entrenched throughout the country. As a result of French obduracy, the only means open to Vietnamese nationalists seemed to rest in conspiratorial efforts to overthrow the regime. The Indochinese Communist Party soon assumed the leadership in these efforts; during the Great Depression, several insurrections in Vietnam partly under Communist leadership had to be put down by force, even though Nguyen Ai Quoc, the exiled Communist leader trained in France, Moscow, and China, attempted to dissuade the revolutionaries from prematurely rising against the French. In Cochinchina, Communists were also engaged in clandestine activity under the leadership of Tran Van Giau. At the outbreak of war, when the Communist Party was dissolved in France, the French rounded up all the Communists they could find in Indochina and were able to suppress most of the clandestine organizations. Nevertheless, the movement persisted and Giau survived to play an important part in the last year of the war. Meanwhile, Laos and Cambodia were comparatively free from such movements under their native rulers.

VICHY COLLABORATION WITH JAPAN. After the fall of France, the Japanese took advantage of French weakness to make increasingly severe demands on both the Vichy Government and the colonial authorities in Saigon, eventually persuading the French to let them have free use of the country for military purposes. After Pearl Harbor, the French Governor was compelled to agree to what amounted to a Japanese protectorate in exchange for the maintenance of his regime in office. During the next years, the Japanese refrained from making excessive demands and left the administrative apparatus of the country in French hands. Not until March, 1945, at a time when they knew the end was not far off, did the

Japanese depose the French Governor and occupy the whole country with their troops. They promptly declared the country independent and confirmed Bao Dai as Emperor of all Vietnam, including the colony of Cochinchina, which he had never ruled. This Japanese gesture, designed to make the return of the French to their colony as difficult as possible, succeeded in this aim, though it was of little help to the Emperor, who could not establish his authority at a time when all Vietnamese groups were jockeying for power themselves.

HO CHI MINH AND THE FRENCH. Several foreign powers were greatly interested in Vietnam. The Chinese Nationalists, who had decided in 1944 that a provisional government should be set up in Tonkin to take over from the Japanese, succeeded in persuading the Allied powers at Potsdam to let them occupy the northern part of the country. Chiang Kai-shek, ignorant of Quoc's true identity since he now called himself Ho Chi Minh, believed he could make use of the League for the Independence of Vietnam (commonly known as the Viet Minh), founded by Ho in 1941, which had been infiltrating into Vietnam even before the overthrow of the French regime by the Japanese. In mid-1945, Ho, now a duly appointed official of the provisional government, moved into Vietnam himself; and after the Japanese surrender, his Viet Minh appeared at Hanoi, the Tonkinese capital, to relieve Bao Dai's viceroy of the authority placed in his hands a few days before by the surrendering Japanese. At the same time, Tran Van Giau in Cochinchina announced himself as the representative of the Viet Minh and for a brief period won the support of the nationalist parties in the south.

Chinese Nationalist troops followed the Viet Minh into the country as soon as they could. Since their main purpose was to put pressure on the French to abandon some of their ancient privileges in China, they had no great objection to the anticolonial Viet Minh, which they regarded as a suitable government to succeed the French. In spite of protests by French representatives who had been airlifted into the north, they acquiesced in the holding of elections in as much of the country as was possible. When these were won easily by the Viet Minh, they permitted Ho to form a government in the area under his control. Bao Dai also yielded his nominal authority to Ho. By the end of 1945, Ho was therefore the legitimate leader of the government in the country, even though he actually controlled only the relatively small area occupied by the Viet Minh.

Meanwhile, in the south the British had arrived to accept the Japanese surrender, as stipulated in the Potsdam agreements. The British force arrived in early September, 1945, to find Giau, the Viet Minh representative, quite incapable of maintaining law and order and unwilling to negotiate with either British or French. The British Commander, therefore, released and armed upward of 1,400 French prisoners of war, thus setting off a series of furious anti-European demonstrations and riots which quickly spread throughout the countryside. When the French arrived shortly afterward, they found themselves faced with a country that was in full revolt and that no nationalist leader was capable of mastering. They proceeded systematically with initial British aid to pacify the countryside. Although the French Commander proclaimed in February, 1946, that in Cochinchina and south Annam peace and order had been "totally re-established," the claim was far from true. In fact, Viet Minh guerrillas were still active, though no longer even nominally under Giau, who had been dismissed by Ho in January, 1946.

At this point Ho, who up to this time had uncompromisingly opposed the French, decided it was time to negotiate in view of the readiness of the Chinese to depart as soon as the French had accepted their demands and of the unquestioned superiority of the French navy, which could send troops by sea to the north whenever it wished. It was clear to him that he must make concessions. He agreed to accept a "federal state" of Indochina within the French Union. Since this involved the relinquishing of Cochinchina altogether to the French, there was a loud outcry, which Ho and his leading Commander Giap were able to quell only by telling their followers frankly enough that it was a tactical move and would last for a definitely limited time. The agreement was duly signed on March 6, 1946. Ho's government for the moment had weathered the storm, but he himself determined to go to France to see if he could win better terms than he had been able to achieve from the colonial authorities on the spot. But the best he could obtain was the recognition of his provisional government as part of the proposed Federal Union. Meanwhile, the French Governor in Indochina had undercut his position by himself setting up a separate government in disputed Cochinchina, which, being the richest part of the territory, was the part that French commercial interests were least willing to abandon.

The position was, indeed, difficult for both Ho and the French. Ho was supported up to a point by the majority of Vietnamese in the north; but since he was engaged in trying to promote a Communist revolution, he could not expect to cooperate for long with the non-Communist Vietnamese, even in the north. It was at least as important for Ho and his followers to create a Communist revolution as it was for them to win independence, and they intended to use the independence movement for the purpose. The French, on the other hand, could not win much support from the non-Communist Vietnamese unless they promised much more than a façade of independence; at the least, they would have to relinquish their hold on Cochinchina. But they could always use their military superiority to subjugate the country, with or without Vietnamese support. Tired of trying to cooperate with the Viet Minh Government, which cooperated only when it seemed to be in its tactical interest to do so, they began to issue ultimatums and use force. Ho struck first on December 19, 1946, with several concerted but unsuccessful raids on French garrisons. But the militia that he and Giap had been organizing were as yet far from capable of making any real dent on the French. All they could do was deny most of the countryside to the French and make use of Mao Tse-tung's techniques for converting the peasants to Communism.

In spite of their lack of support from the Vietnamese, the French realized that some kind of nationalist façade was essential. The obvious choice was to restore the legitimate Emperor Bao Dai, who might command some respect, at least from traditionally minded Vietnamese. But the former Emperor, who was living in exile in Hong Kong, realized quite well how much the French needed him and prolonged the negotiations for many months. At last, he accepted a formula under which Vietnam, including the colony of Cochinchina, was to be independent within the French Union. He also signed a protocol guaranteeing French interests and submitting to some restrictions on independence in the fields of defense and foreign policy. During all this time, the Viet Minh were still battling the French in the north.

CONSEQUENCES OF THE CHINESE COMMUNIST VICTORY. In 1949, the French position was altogether changed by the takeover of the Chinese Government by the Communists, and the arrival of the Chinese at the northern frontier of Vietnam. At once, Ho proclaimed his own Democratic Republic of Vietnam as the only true government of the country, and was recognized by Communist China, the Soviet Union, and most of the Soviet satellites. Although the near presence of the Chinese obviously presented dangers, it also provided a ray of hope to the French in their long war with the Viet Minh. The United States, engaged in "containing" Communism everywhere, might be willing to share in the expenses of the war. But if her help were to be enlisted, then the war must be represented not as an anachronistic attempt by the French to re-establish their colonial empire, but as a genuinely nationalistic venture in which the Vietnamese were merely aided by their former colonial masters. The French National Assembly, which had hitherto refused to ratify the agreement with Bao Dai, now ratified it, thereby making Vietnam at least nominally independent. The Emperor's government and the French Commander decreed full mobilization in Vietnam, creating, at least on paper, a Vietnamese national army for the anti-Communist crusade— even though at this time most Vietnamese harbored a secret admiration for the Viet Minh, which with the most meager resources had for so long succeeded in keeping the flower of the French army at bay.

THE FRENCH VIEW OF THE WAR. As the French had hoped, the United States agreed to grant extensive aid, especially after the outbreak of the Korean War. But she put consistent pressure on them to grant political concessions to the Vietnamese, including full independence as a reward for victory. The French were reluctant to give any such concession. For them, indeed, it remained largely a colonial war. French military and civilian leaders at Saigon were not striking a blow for the "free world" but were simply trying to conquer the Viet Minh, who were disputing their authority and controlled a sizable part of the country. France was pouring out money she could ill afford at a time when she was only just beginning to recover from the war; and Frenchmen and French colonial troops recruited in North Africa and elsewhere were being killed. The only material reason for continuing to do this was to protect French economic interests in Indochina; the major nonmaterial reason was simply pride, the result of a centuries-old military tradition. It was beneath the dignity of a Frenchman to be defeated in a colonial war against non-Europeans. However, metropolitan Frenchmen, though sometimes sensitive to this aspect of the struggle, could not but be aware of the terrible losses in men and the drain on French material resources, which prevented them from carrying out any major social program at home. To many, the worst feature of the war was that France must go constantly, hat in hand, to the United States for money and must listen to American criticism of her colonial and even domestic policies in order to receive subsidies.

It was natural, therefore, that a strong movement should have grown in the early 1950's demanding an end to the war on whatever terms could be negotiated. Once the Viet Minh had developed their guerrilla tactics and had access to Chinese war matériel, it seemed most unlikely that they could be defeated severely enough to knock them out of the war. The only hope was to inflict such heavy casualties on them that negotiations could be carried out on fairly equal terms. After the Viet Minh capture of Dien Bien Phu, a stronghold in the north on which the French had staked their last hope of containing the Viet Minh attack, the French could no longer expect any gain from negotiations. The north was clearly irretrievably lost. Much though they hated to make terms after a defeat, the demand for an end to the war became so overwhelming that some government would be certain to come to power which would take the humiliating step. This task fell to Pierre Mendès-France who, once the negotiations had been completed, fell from office and never became prime minister again.

THE VIETNAMESE VIEW OF THE WAR. The Vietnamese did not trust the French at all. They did not really expect the French to leave if they won the war, or believe that Vietnamese independence would ever be genuine. Moreover, many of them continued to admire the valor of their fellow countrymen in the north, who had learned much from the Chinese but had fought the actual war themselves. A fair number of educated Vietnamese, however, did appreciate the fact that, if the Viet Minh won the war and took over the whole country, their own lives and positions would be grievously endangered and their country would be subjected to a tyranny. They had seen how the Viet Minh had behaved when they actually did control much of the country soon after the war, and they wanted no more of it. These men took over governmental positions in the Bao Dai regime and did their best to impose conscription upon the country. But few of the soldiers they enrolled shared their viewpoint, and desertions were numerous. When the Americans advised the French to train the Vietnamese so that they could bear the main burden of the war, the French agreed, but knew a good deal better than the Americans that such armies, if enrolled and armed, would prove of limited use and almost surely could never hold off the Viet Minh for very long themselves, however well armed and trained they might be. All the Vietnamese would fight for against the Viet Minh was genuine independence and a form of government chosen and supported by themselves, and manifestly superior to that offered by the Viet Minh.

GENEVA AGREEMENTS OF 1954. As the war drew to its close, and Dien Bien Phu, the symbol of French and Vietnamese will to resist, was encircled and subjected to violent attacks from the Viet Minh, the United States tried to win support from Britain and France for an all-out attack by the Western Alliance—even for sending in American troops and trying to win the war by bombing the Chinese as well as the Viet Minh. But neither Britain nor France would agree, preferring to negotiate the best settlement possible with the Viet Minh. At the Geneva Conference of 1954, the decision was made to partition the country temporarily and to hold nationwide elections before the end of 1956, when there would be two separate independent governments functioning and a meaningful choice could be made between them. Although the Viet Minh section of the country would contain 14 million people as against 11 million in South Vietnam, it was believed that in free elections there might be enough opponents of Viet Minh to ensure a victory for the South. Probably, few Westerners believed that the elections would ever be held, but it was the best compromise that could be obtained. At least it provided for a cease-fire, policed by a commission of three neutral countries—Canada, Poland, and India, with an Indian chairman—and it gave a breathing space to bring a truly independent government of Vietnam into operation. The United States was not a party to the agreement, nor were the representatives of South Vietnam consulted. The French signed on their behalf. This permitted the South Vietnamese to refuse to hold the promised elections, and the United States to back them in their refusal.

THE UNITED STATES AND SOUTH VIETNAM. The Geneva Agreements were the signal for the entry on the Vietnamese scene of Ngo Dinh Diem, a highborn former Provincial Governor and Minister of the Interior under the first Bao Dai regime in the 1930's. He had always uncompromisingly opposed both the Viet Minh and the French and, although a man of ability, had refused to hold any office under the French as long as genuine independence was not conceded. Now that South Vietnam was to be truly independent, Diem agreed to accept office, and was appointed Prime Minister with full civil and military powers on June 19, 1954. Unfortunately, he was hardly known in the country, belonged to the unpopular Catholic minority, and had little personal appeal either to the long-time nationalists whom he had consistently cold-shouldered or to the middle class to whose interests he paid little attention. But Diem represented the only type of Vietnamese nationalist who was acceptable to the United States: a man untainted by collaboration with either the Japanese or the Viet Minh and a dedicated anti-Communist. The Americans were unaware of his lack of rapport with his own people, but they did know that he had as little use for French colonialism as they had themselves, and that any independence he accepted would be genuine. Diem at once became embroiled with his own army leaders and his ministers. He dismissed the chief leader and assumed several cabinet portfolios himself, in which acts he was consistently backed by the United States, which, as principal paymaster for the Vietnamese forces, was now in a position to exercise a dominating influence. Without subsidies from the United States, the economy would have completely collapsed, and the army would have disintegrated.

In 1955, the Emperor Bao Dai attempted, with some French support but with very vocal American opposition, to dispose of Diem by summoning him to France, where Bao Dai was living, to give an account of his stewardship. Diem, who was ruling, as he continued to do, with the aid of a cabinet whose leading positions were distributed to members of his family, refused to obey. With the aid of a "revolutionary committee" set up for the purpose, Bao Dai was formally deposed. This result was confirmed in a referendum under the supervision of the Diem government, which to no one's surprise resulted in a huge vote against the monarch. A Republic of Vietnam was then proclaimed on October 26, 1955, and Diem soon afterward was elected President.

CAMBODIA. The two kingdoms of Cambodia and Laos, which had been granted their formal independence by the French in 1949 with limitations similar to those in Vietnam, were granted their complete independence at Geneva in 1954. The French agreed to remain only in an advisory capacity, as requested by the monarchs. In Cambodia, where there had been relatively few Viet Minh troops operating, the withdrawal was quickly accomplished. The monarch, Prince Norodom Sihanouk, gained considerable prestige among his people for his successful fight for genuine independence and took full advantage of it by submitting his deeds to a referendum, asking for his people's approval. When his policy had been overwhelmingly endorsed, he decided that it would be a good idea to use his popularity to govern the country, a task he could not perform while he was a constitutional monarch. He therefore abdicated in favor of his father, who belonged to the senior branch of the royal family, though he had never previously been King, since the French had preferred his young son. Prince Sihanouk then formed a party and won every seat in the Assembly in the ensuing elections, becoming Prime Minister in September, 1955.

LAOS. In Laos, there were far more difficulties to overcome, in view of the existence of an indigenous pro-Communist movement known as the Pathet Lao, which controlled two Laotian provinces and was in constant communication with the Viet Minh. After many efforts to negotiate the departure of Viet Minh troops, who were not easily to be distinguished from those of the Pathet Lao, the royal government in the hands of Prince Souvanna Phouma made an agreement in 1957 with his half-brother Prince Souphanouvong, leader of the Pathet Lao, under which the latter's troops were to acknowledge the royal government and be integrated with the royal army. The Pathet Lao, or, more correctly, its political arm, thereafter would be entitled to take part in the national elections promised for soon afterward. Although for a short time this agreement was kept and the Pathet Lao with its allies showed considerable strength in the elections, the central government, increasingly under American influence, resisted the spread of Communism, and sporadic warfare resumed. This was halted only by an uneasy agreement in 1962 by which Souvanna Phouma was again made Prime Minister, supposedly to hold a balance between his left-wing brother and the right-wing leaders who had with American support been ruling the country for the last few years. This development, whose complexity has only been hinted at here, is not likely to last long in view of the expansionary aims of the Pathet Lao and the Viet Minh.

The Independence of India

CONGRESS LEADERS AND THE WAR. It now remains to discuss two British-controlled countries that were not occupied by the Japanese but succeeded in winning independence soon after, and in part as a result of, the war. When the war broke out, the Congress Party decided not to cooperate with the British war effort until very substantial assurances had been given of formal independence after the war; and it demanded immediate self-government. In 1942, Sir Stafford Cripps was sent out to India to negotiate in the hope of preventing actual damage to the war effort, since Gandhi and other Congress leaders were apparently prepared to go so far as cooperating with the Japanese, who already in possession of a small part of northern India. Cripps assured India that she could become independent after the war and contract out of the Commonwealth if she wished. But in view of the opposition of the Muslims, he promised both them and the native princes that they could decide for themselves whether or not to remain with India or to form separate states of their own. In view of the danger involved and the doubtful attitude of the Congress toward the war effort, he felt unable to offer immediate and complete self-government, though he was willing to concede an all-Indian central government with defense reserved in British hands. The Muslims agreed to the proposals, since they would make the goal of an independent Pakistan possible. The Congress, still hoping to avoid partition, refused and prepared to sabotage the war effort, whereupon the government, with the concurrence of the Indian members of the Viceroy's Council, declared the Congress an unlawful organization. For the last time its leaders were sent to jail.

CONGRESS AND THE MUSLIM LEAGUE. As soon as the war was over, provincial elections were held, which resulted in a greater polarization between the Congress and the Muslim League. The minor parties were almost everywhere defeated. The Congress won the Hindu provinces, the Muslim League the Muslim provinces. In the Northwest Frontier Province, the pro-Congress Red Shirt Party won an absolute majority. The new British Labour government sent Cripps and two other cabinet ministers to India to see what could be done to hasten independence and, if possible, to keep the country together. There was a general recognition, especially among the British and Hindus, that the amputation of India would be likely to lead to extensive communal riots, with possibly a massive exodus from Hindu to Muslim areas and vice versa. This was likely to lead to bloodshed on a scale unknown even in India. In addition, the entire infrastructure had been built on the assumption that India was a single country, and railroads and roads passed through Muslim and Hindu areas without distinction. The country's economic advancement after independence depended on the use of all resources by all sectors of the nation. Moreover, the large province of Bengal as a whole was almost equally divided between Hindus and Muslims. If it were divided so that East Bengal with its Muslim majority fell to Pakistan, there would be no through communication by land between East Bengal and the Muslim areas in western India. Therefore, it was worth a superhuman effort of patient negotiation and concessions, if possible by both sides, to keep the country together and see if the legitimate fears of the different religious communities could be quieted. Obviously, a federal state would have to be envisioned, as the Simon Commission had suggested in 1930. But how could a federal government be strong enough to perform its duties and not too weak to hold the country together? How much regional autonomy would satisfy the minorities?

Communal rioting, which had been sporadic since the end of the war, broke out fiercely in August, 1946, with the "Great Calcutta Killing," which took more than 4,000 lives and wounded another 10,000. It did not cease until the Congress had accepted partition, although there was nothing on a scale similar to the Calcutta riots until the riots in the Punjab in 1947. The British, only too well aware that they were trying to control a human volcano, worked desperately against time to produce a solution that would keep the country together. Their last scheme, though now only a tragic footnote to history, was, for a brief time, accepted by both Muslims and Hindus.

LAST BRITISH PROPOSALS. The proposals called for a central government concerned with what all parts of the country held in common: foreign affairs, defense, communications, fundamental rights, and national finance. This federal government would have its own legislature and executive in which the princely states, if they wished to cooperate, would have their own seats. Secondly, there was to be a "third tier" which would permit the Muslim and Hindu provinces to have their own semifederal government with their own legislature and executive dealing with those subjects not reserved for the central government, which they wished to handle in common. Thirdly, there were to be provincial governments which would have full control of those areas not reserved for the central government and not being dealt with by agreement by the third tier. To bring these governments into being, a constituent assembly was to be chosen by the recently elected provincial legislatures, which would establish the group and provincial governments first before proceeding to the most difficult task of deciding on the federal constitution.

When both sides had given their provisional assent to the proposals, the Viceroy formed a central government made up of Indians from the Congress and the League, with a few from minor parties to hold the balance. The constituent assembly was then chosen. But mutual distrust had grown too great to permit constructive work. The Muslims refused to take their seats in the constituent assembly until a procedure had been worked out that would satisfy them; in the ensuing squabble, they gained the impression that the third tier, on which they counted to keep the Muslim bloc from being dominated by the Hindus, was in reality looked at askance by the Hindus and would never be permitted to come into existence. The Congress continued to work on a constitution in spite of the absence of the Muslims and of the Indian princes, who did not take part on the grounds that it had ceased to be an all-Indian assembly. The British invited the leaders of all groups to London, but nothing was achieved in the face of the demand by the Congress that the Muslim leaders either sit in the constituent assembly or quit the cabinet.

Meanwhile, in February, 1947, the most serious of the prepartition communal disturbances broke out in the Punjab, where Hindus and Muslims were fairly evenly divided and the government was an anti-Pakistan coalition. These disturbances were begun by the Muslim League, which wished to break up the coalition government; but they quickly got out of hand. Flourishing cities were destroyed, and all government for a time broke down. At this, the British at last gave up and declared they would transfer power to Indian hands at the latest by June, 1948, and advised the Indians that they had better solve their own problems and decide for themselves who was to be the British successor.

PARTITION OF INDIA. The Indians of all parties were this time successfully shocked into serious action. While the Muslim League demanded either Pakistan or civil war, Congress leaders sadly and reluctantly came to the conclusion that, if they did not agree to the formation of Pakistan, the India they hoped to inherit would be devastated in a civil war. They conceded the division of Punjab into its Muslim and Hindu sectors; and the Muslims, though they were a majority in Bengal, conceded the division of that province. Communal rioting suddenly stopped, as both parties worked on the necessary details of partition and agreed that plebiscites should be held in the doubtful provinces. The princely rulers were asked to decide which sector they would join or whether they would become independent. Lord Mountbatten, the new Viceroy, helped both sides impartially, and finally the work was done. Britain passed the necessary bills, and both countries became independent in August, 1947. Before the appointed day, enormous numbers of Indians began to leave their homes and move into areas now to be ruled by their own coreligionists, especially in Punjab. Both governments tried to stop the exodus but were powerless. More than 10 million people became refugees, and the loss of life will never be accurately computed.

India, which had already written most of its constitution in the ill-fated constituent assembly, was soon functioning under a parliamentary constitution of its own choosing. Not until 1956 was a new constitution for Pakistan adopted. And only a few years later, it was suspended by Ayub Khan, the present President of the country, who, though approved in a national referendum, rules as a virtual dictator with a constitution of his own choosing.

Of the Indian princely states, all the rulers except the Maharajah of Kashmir and the Nizam of Hyderabad decided to join either India or Pakistan, according to the religious configuration of the majority of their subjects. The Maharajah of Kashmir hesitated, since he was a Hindu ruling a predominantly Muslim people. When his princedom was invaded by Pathans, a group of Muslim tribesmen, he called on India for help, which was duly sent; the Indians still control most of the country. According to the pre-independence agreement, the ruler was permitted to choose, but he was not expected to choose the opposite side from that of the majority of his people. The United Nations has on numerous occasions called for a plebiscite to determine the future of the province, but so far India, standing on her legal right to the territory, has refused. And relations between India and Pakistan have been embittered ever since partition by this long-standing dispute. The Nizam of Hyderabad opted for independence, but India soon invaded his territory and incorporated his state.

Ceylon

As already briefly noted, Ceylon at the outbreak of war was functioning under a constitution that had outlived its usefulness and was on the point of being changed. In 1943, the British promised internal self-government to the Ceylonese, to take effect after the war, though they proposed to retain control of defense and foreign affairs. Asked for their opinion, the Ceylonese ministers proposed fully responsible cabinet government with an enlarged State Council. A British commission was sent to study the matter and decided, in spite of complaints from Tamils about their lack of effective representation, against communal electorates but established a bicameral legislature with the upper chamber having half its membership nominated by the governor, thus taking care of minority representation. The leader of the chief Sinhalese party, D. S. Senenayake, remained dissatisfied and went to London to request full Dominion status from the new Labour Government, which had taken office in Britain after the elections of 1945; then he went home to fight and win the election in his own country under the new constitution.

When Senenayake renewed his demands, the Labour Government was willing to listen. At the end of 1947, it presented his proposals to Parliament, and in February, 1948, Ceylon became independent, and a Dominion within the Commonwealth. To the end, the independence bill was opposed by some of the Ceylonese minorities, especially the Tamils. But until very recently, when the question of the official native language to replace English has caused a revival of dissension, the communal issue has not proved of importance. Although all the Ceylonese governments have been coalitions, the presence in parliament of Marxists and other parties based on ideology, including Trotskyite and Communist parties, has made the communal issue of less importance than party programs and ideas. In this respect, Ceylon resembles India more than she resembles any other newly independent country, though India, with its still-dominant Congress Party, has not had to be governed by strange, ephemeral coalitions and, unlike Ceylon, has enjoyed general governmental stability.

III

THE PROLONGED
STRUGGLES FOR
INDEPENDENCE

8. The Islamic World

The Nationalist Ferment

While Far Eastern colonies were gaining their independence as a direct result of World War II, the nationalist movement and the desire for self-government gained in strength and spread throughout the Middle East, Africa, and Southeast Asia. Among the colonies not yet independent in 1950, a few had formed part of medieval African empires ruled by Africans. But not a single one had ever been a nation-state at any time in its history, nor were its boundaries those of any previously known state. Yet, so powerful was the rising tide of nationalism in the years following the war that politicians in every colony began to organize movements directed toward making their particular colonial territory into a new nation, self-governing, independent, and a member of the United Nations.

True, they would have preferred to form part of larger self-governing states, if that had been feasible. But on the rare occasions they attempted to create larger states, the attempts were abandoned soon after independence. The Federation of Mali split into its two component parts after less than a year of union; the Ghana-Guinea union was never more than a paper one. The so-called United Arab Republic (Egypt-Syria) fissioned, perhaps irreparably. All the new states—in this respect, in no way differing from the old established ones—have been unwilling to relinquish any of their hard-won sovereignty in favor of a larger, and perhaps more viable, state. The new national leaders, well aware of the necessity for larger entities, remain hesitant to yield their exalted status for a possibly inferior one in a larger state. And, as in the case of Kenya, which refuses to permit the secession of the Somali provinces within her borders, they are as militantly determined as any Western state not to yield an inch of territory, even to a dissident minority anxious to form part of another state. It is possible that Kenya, Uganda, and Tanganyika will join in a federal union when Kenya wins her independence. But up to this time only the small British Somaliland Protectorate has freely voted to become part of another independent state.

Thus the Western idea of the nation-state, with its accompanying and sometimes vociferous nationalism, was taken over *in toto* by the former colonies, despite the absence of almost all the elements (a common language, culture, and ethnic stock) that served as cement in the building of the European nations in the last centuries. In their place was only a common struggle for independence against the colonial masters. It is still too early to determine whether strong leadership and the conscious effort to create a nation by all means at the disposal of a modern government will prove effective substitutes, now that independence from the colonial powers has been achieved.

Egypt and the Sudan

THE ARAB LEAGUE. In contrast to the peoples of most of the new nations, the Arabs as a people have a long history. Arab "nationalism" is based on a common language and a common religion, as well as on common memories of the early Middle Ages when the Arabs burst out of the desert as conquerors. However, not all who today claim to be Arabs have an Arab ethnic background, least of all the Egyptians. Nevertheless, it was a significant event in the "Arab" world when an Arab League was founded in Cairo, in 1944. In 1939, a union of Arab rulers had been founded, but it was of little importance since the rulers themselves were on the way out. The Arab League, in spite of numerous differences among its members, has survived to this day. The founding members were Iraq, Egypt, Syria, Lebanon, Transjordan, Saudi Arabia, and Yemen. The Palestinian Arabs were also given a place in the League, though as yet they had no state of their own. The major purpose of the League is to provide a means by which the policies of the different member states, which all have Muslim majorities, can be coordinated, especially in the field of international relations and foreign affairs. Each member has undertaken, among other things, not to go to war with any other member state. Obviously, disagreements were likely to arise and have arisen between the states and also with those Muslim North African states which subsequently joined the League. At the time of writing, Egypt is actively interfering in Yemen and is opposed by the kings of Saudi Arabia and Jordan. But the League may survive this quarrel as it has survived many others.

The unity of the Arab states against threats to Islam has been a primary loyalty. The one policy on which from the beginning all members have agreed is the nonrecognition of Israel, and all League states united to prevent Israel from being established in 1948. At times, some of the states may have wished to come to terms with Israel; but such a policy would unquestionably have involved expulsion or resignation from the League. The sympathy and sometimes active support of the Arab states for the French North African colonies in their efforts to escape from French domination—especially Algeria, whose rebellion was the longest— were of considerable significance in the period of struggles for independence. Nasser's Egypt, which took the lead in demanding Algerian independence and provided a home for its government- in-exile, was strengthened by the existence of the League machinery, which was at the time largely under Egyptian control.

THE WAR YEARS IN EGYPT. Egypt herself, still ruled by Farouk I, was not expected by her protectors to join the war against the Axis powers, nor did she do so until almost the end of the war. But Egypt was used by the Allied Powers throughout the war as a base to protect the Suez Canal. When the Germans and Italians came close to the great Egyptian city of Alexandria and were stopped only at El Alamein, well within the boundaries of the country, perhaps the majority were sympathetic to Allied difficulties. But there was certainly a vocal minority which was stridently pro-Nazi, hoping, somewhat unrealistically, to win the full independence that it seemed the British would never permit. Farouk even appointed a pro-Nazi Prime Minister. This the British would not countenance and compelled him to select the former Wafd Prime Minister instead, since the Wafd, though it had lost most of its influence, was at all events not pro-Nazi and they had grown used to dealing with it. After the war, the British, whose forces in the Canal Zone had risen to more than 80,000 as against the 10,000 permitted by the treaty of 1936, hesitated to withdraw any significant numbers of them. When the Cold War began, they believed their communications to be endangered by the aggressiveness of the Soviet Union, in which point of view they were backed by their NATO allies.

CONFLICT OVER THE SUDAN. Naturally, the Egyptians did not see the matter in the same light. Effective independence seemed as far away as ever, and the Sudan question still rankled. Farouk and his Wafd Prime Minister Mustapha Nahas were determined to "re- store" the Sudan to Egypt, not only for prestige purposes, but be- cause they believed that only by gaining sovereignty over the country could they settle to their own satisfaction the disputed question of their rights to the Nile waters. Unable to persuade the United Nations Security Council to do anything about the troops in the Canal Zone, the Egyptians needled the British in every way they could, sometimes raiding into the British area, to which the British responded with reprisals.

At last, in October, 1951, Farouk and his Prime Minister forced the issue by denouncing the treaty of 1936 and the condominium agreement of 1899. Farouk was proclaimed King of Egypt and the Sudan, and it was proposed to draw up a constitution for the Sudan that would give the Egyptians control of Sudanese defense, finance, and foreign affairs. Even though Egypt was powerless to put these measures into effect, the British were stung to action. A few days after the Egyptian proclamation, they proposed the establishment of a Nile Waters Development Authority to decide the dispute over the Nile waters. But in the British view, only the Sudanese themselves could choose whether or not to join Egypt. To make this choice possible, they proposed to grant self-government to the Sudan as soon as feasible, and were prepared to set up an international commission to "watch over the constitutional development" of the country. Although the Egyptian Government rejected the proposals, the British went ahead with their own plans in the Sudan, hoping sooner or later to win the acquiescence of Egypt.

Events then moved toward a climax in Egypt. A Muslim Brotherhood devoted to driving the British out of Egypt created numerous incidents. The British took reprisals, culminating in a small pitched battle near Ismailia at the beginning of 1952. The Egyptians retaliated with an orgy of pillage and arson in Cairo and elsewhere directed against British and other European property. The famous Shepheard's Hotel in Cairo was burned to the ground on Black Saturday, January 26, 1952. The Wafd Government, impotent and corrupt, was unable to maintain law and order, and the army became restive. Following the exposure of a series of peculiarly scandalous profiteering ventures by government officials, a revolutionary Council made up of nine young and relatively junior army officers overthrew the monarchy in a sudden bloodless coup and drove Farouk into exile. The Council, led by Colonel Gamal Nasser, then set up a respected and incorruptible older general, Mohammed Naguib, as head of state and prime minister.

EGYPTIAN REVOLUTION AND SUDANESE INDEPENDENCE. Order was quickly restored. The new regime and its nominal head were obviously immensely popular, and it now had sufficient authority to reverse the sterile Wafd policy and come to an agreement with Britain. In February, 1953, a new agreement was signed, on substantially the same terms that Britain had put forward at the end of 1951. Naguib accepted the self-government statute the British had prepared for the Sudan, leaving the final decision as to whether to adhere to Egypt or to become independent to a constituent assembly set up by the elected members of a Sudanese parliament. Meanwhile, for the transitional period of three years, the Egyptians would cooperate with the British in preparing the Sudanese for self-determination. The following year, a further treaty was signed under which British military personnel were required to leave the country by June 19, 1956, to be replaced by some 4,000 civilian technicians under Egyptian administrative control to take care of the canal installations.

The Sudanese party opposed to Egypt won the first elections and opted for complete independence. Thus the Sudan became independent in 1956 and, like Burma alone of the former British colonies, chose to remain outside the Commonwealth. The British left the Canal Zone on time in 1956. Thereupon, for various reasons that lie outside the scope of this book, Nasser, who had by this time replaced General Naguib as President of Egypt, "nationalized" the Canal, setting in motion a series of events that culminated in a poorly planned attack on Egypt by British and French forces, and a simultaneous Israeli invasion of Egyptian territory. Despite a serious military defeat at Israeli hands, Nasser's domestic position was strengthened by the support he received during the crisis from the United States and the Soviet Union through the United Nations, which condemned all three aggressors. Britain and France agreed to call off their attack, which had already failed in what seems to have been its primary purpose, the overthrow of the Nasser regime. Israel reluctantly withdrew from her advanced position, but gained a respite from persistent Egyptian violations of her frontier. British and French investments in Egypt were confiscated by Nasser as a reprisal for the attack; only after long negotiations and on Egyptian terms were they partly restored. Thus Egypt concluded the long period of subjection to Britain with a stunning diplomatic victory, and thereafter there could never be any question of her genuine independence from her former "protecting" power.

Libya

The former Italian colony of Libya with its three provinces of Tripolitania, Cyrenaica, and Fezzan had been conquered by the British during the war, as had the other Italian colonies in Africa. They continued to administer all these territories after the war while first the victorious powers, then the United Nations, wrestled with the problem of what to do with them. The position was complicated by the fact that Italy in some measure had redeemed her earlier support of Hitler and by the end of the war had been fighting on the Allied side. Thus she was not necessarily to be excluded from further association with her former colonies.

The Big Four powers first attempted to decide among themselves what was to be done with the colonies. The Soviet Union had first asked for trusteeship over at least Tripolitania, the British for strategic reasons wished to take responsibility for Cyrenaica, and the French requested Fezzan, which had a long border with Algeria. Although the United States was not in 1946 adamantly against the Soviet Union as administrator of a trust territory, the British consistently opposed it. The Soviet Union, believing that Italy might herself soon have a Communist Government, favored Italian trusteeship for all her former colonies—until the Communists failed to win the elections of 1947. Then the Soviet Union tried hard for a four-power trusteeship which would include herself, but was now opposed also by the United States, which strongly objected to Soviet presence in the Mediterranean. Finding themselves unable to agree, the powers were compelled to turn the problem over to the United Nations in 1948.

The First Committee (on political matters) of the United Nations slowly hammered out a solution. This took the best part of two years since the first year's proposals were defeated in the General Assembly. It gradually became clear that certain solutions stood a chance of receiving the necessary two-thirds majority in the Assembly, whereas others did not. No proposal supported by the Soviet bloc alone would win, nor had the Soviet bloc sufficient votes alone to muster the necessary one-third to veto any proposal made by others. On the other hand, at that epoch the Latin American nations together controlled a sizable block of votes—enough, indeed, to be able to veto any proposals not acceptable to them. The states of the Arab League also carried much weight, though not enough to constitute a veto.

Only one of the Black African states, Liberia, had a vote at all in those days. Thus any decision commanding a two-thirds majority would have to offer something satisfactory to both the Latin Americans and the Arabs. A package deal therefore would almost certainly have to be worked out. Since the Latin American states were determined that Italy should not be altogether frozen out, it was necessary to find something for her, in exchange for which the Latin Americans would go along with the arrangements for the other colonies. The inhabitants of Libya were also consulted as far as this was possible; but their views were not decisive, especially since they tended to cancel one another out.

Under the package deal at last agreed upon, Italian Somaliland became a trust territory to be administered by Italy for ten years, with specially rigorous provisions for the protection and advancement of the indigenous inhabitants, and an advisory council of three United Nations members as an extra means of supervision. The question of Eritrea, though not decided at the time, was later solved by allowing her to join Ethiopia in a federal union. At Arab insistence, Libya was to become an independent federal state by January 1, 1952.

Once this decision had been taken, the United Nations was collectively faced with the task of bringing the backward land of Libya up to such a standard of material and educational development that it could thereafter stand on its own feet. Constitutional experts were consulted, and a considerable number of nations, including Britain and the United States, provided technical and financial assistance. On December 24, 1951, a few days early, Libya became an independent state as a constitutional monarchy under the head of the Senussi sect of Islam, who became King as Idris I. The seat of government moves each year between the two capitals of Tripoli and Benghazi (in Cyrenaica), though a new federal capital is in the course of construction. The King has the right to legislate by decree in certain circumstances and has fairly often availed himself of it. Being himself from Cyrenaica, which has seldom enjoyed good relations with the more advanced western province, the King was not popular, especially in the city of Tripoli. When disorders broke out following the first election in 1952, he suppressed all political parties, which still do not exist to this day. In fact, the federal system works somewhat ineffectively, and the provincial governments exercise most of the functions of government. But with the discovery of substantial quantities of oil in recent years, the central government has acquired more power and prestige; and the King himself, who is by far the most outstanding personality in the government, has helped to hold the country together by his ability and his impartiality.

French North Africa

Tunisia

The French were unwilling to concede independence to any of their three North African colonies. The chief reason for this obduracy in face of the obvious fact that they were as capable as most countries of governing themselves was the presence of numerous French settlers (*colons*) who exercised an influence on the governments of the Fourth Republic out of all proportion to their numbers. With monotonous regularity, the French suppressed all political parties who opposed them and imprisoned their leaders. But they were eventually compelled to grant independence to all the colonies, even though in the case of Algeria it was only after a bitter seven-year war.

In 1943, Tunisia, which for a time had been controlled by the Axis Powers, was restored to the Free French. After the war, all political parties, including the Neo-Destour (New Constitution) Party, which had been suppressed in 1938, demanded immediate independence; but for many years the French refused to concede even the possibility. They exiled the Bey, the nominal ruler of the country whom they were supposed to be "protecting," when he gave his support to the nationalists. Not until 1951 did the French Government promise "internal autonomy" at the end of some unspecified period—in this admitting that the existing government council, made up of Tunisian cabinet ministers who were willing to take the advice of French directors, was merely a façade to cover actual French supremacy.

All that was left for the Tunisians was to agitate, dangerous though it was, and if that failed, to take direct "positive action." Not only did the government have its camps for political prisoners; but the *colons*, who as elsewhere in French North Africa filled all the best positions in the civil service and owned the best lands, had a vigilante organization of its own that committed many atrocities, including the murder of the greatest Tunisian labor leader in broad daylight. The government often winked at the activities of this organization, even though it did not openly support it.

The surprising thing about Tunisia to an outsider has always been the fact that few Tunisian leaders were anti-French in the sense that they wished to drive the French from the country. All had been educated in France, often spent considerable periods of their lives there, perhaps married French wives, as did President Habib Bourguiba. They were willing to remain on good terms with the French and protect French interests if only the French would concede self-government and eventual independence. But for years the French relied on simple suppression and exile of Tunisian leaders. While Bourguiba was in jail (1934–36, 1938–42, 1943 until his escape in 1944, 1952–54) or exile (1944–52, 1954–55), he was at least safe from being murdered (or, at least, he was not murdered) and was always a national hero. But with every new suppression, it was more difficult to persuade his party to adopt a policy of conciliation.

From 1952 to 1954, after Bourguiba's last arrest, for making an insurrectionary speech, open terrorism prevailed and was met by counterterrorism on the part of the *colons*. The Tunisian ministers took the case to the United Nations Security Council in 1952 but could not obtain a majority in the Council to have their question discussed. In 1953, the French appointed a moderate Resident-General who put into effect a few new reforms, including some local elections that were boycotted by the nationalists, thus giving the French the opportunity to request the United Nations General Assembly to hold off with any resolutions until the reforms had been tried. The new Resident-General was made the target of the outraged *colons* for his efforts to keep the peace impartially. When Mendès-France came to power in 1954, the situation in Tunisia was such that some definite action had to be taken, even if it cost the Prime Minister his political life. He legalized Bourguiba's Neo-Destour Party, released Bourguiba himself from his French jail, though he was not yet permitted to return to his country, and negotiations were opened. Even though Mendès-France fell from office almost as soon as he had settled the Indochinese war, his successor carried on with the negotiations and reached an agreement under which Tunisia was conceded immediate internal autonomy. French economic and military interests were to be protected, and foreign affairs were to remain a French responsibility.

Agitation for complete independence continued. The French, having at last decided to make their first concessions, discovered they could not stop halfway. They quickly settled for what they could get in the way of protection of their economic interests, and were permitted to keep their great naval base at Bizerte pending further negotiations. In March, 1956, Tunisia became independent with Bourguiba as Prime Minister under the Bey as constitutional monarch. The following year, the Bey was retired, and Bourguiba was elected chief of state of the Tunisian Republic with power to rule by decree. In 1959, under a new constitution, he became President, with substantial powers (somewhat greater than those of the U.S. President), a cabinet of his own choice, and an elected national assembly. The fate of the Bizerte base, whose presence continued to embitter relations with France, was finally decided when the French evacuated it late in 1963.

Morocco

The postwar history and development of Morocco closely resembles that of Tunisia. From a material point of view, the French did much for the country; however, about 300,000 French *colons* owned a sizable proportion of all the cultivable land, and all except the lowest-paid civil servants were Frenchmen. The French Resident-General ruled the country in the name of the Sultan. All political parties were forbidden, though one powerful nationalist party did in fact exist, the Istiqlal, whose known members from time to time were detained.

What distinguishes Morocco from Tunisia was the leadership given to the nationalist movement by Sultan Mohammed V. He was not especially anti-French, nor was he by any standards a radical. But he did demand assurances that the protectorate would not last forever, as it appeared the French intended, and he gave some encouragement to the nationalist Istiqlal. Other more conservative Moroccans from the feudal classes, especially among the Berbers, had little use for the Sultan and liked the French regime, which protected their prerogatives. In particular El Glaoui, Pasha of Marrakesh, the most powerful feudal chief in the country, was the Sultan's bitter enemy and offered his services to the French in driving the Sultan out if they ever wished to have a more pliant ruler on the throne.

The crisis came following the murder of the Tunisian union leader by French vigilantes in 1952. A demonstration and strike in Casablanca was proclaimed by the Istiqlal to protest the murder. The French fired on the crowd, and at once violence erupted throughout the country; then the French Government decided the time had come to exile the man they regarded as the most dangerous Moroccan nationalist, the Sultan himself. After exiling him to Madagascar, they put an elderly puppet (related to El Glaoui) on the throne; few were willing to acknowledge him as Sultan, especially since a sultan in Islam is also head of the religion. From being a more or less respected figurehead, Mohammed V became a hero and a martyr. Terrorism broke out in Morocco on a scale similar to that in Tunisia. Although Mendès-France during his regime (1954) promised reforms, even he dared not restore the Sultan. But once Tunisia was promised independence, there was no alternative, and the Sultan returned in triumph at the end of 1955. El Glaoui publicly made his abject submission, and the country was granted its autonomy, including control of foreign affairs and defense, which had not yet been granted even to Tunisia.

Four months later, France recognized the full independence of the country (March 2, 1956), with Mohammed V as "absolute monarch" and a cabinet which contained several Istiqlal members but all chosen by him. Since that time, he and his successor have made some gestures in the direction of a constitutional government, but the Sultan, now King, remains the sole seat of authority.

Meanwhile, the Spaniards and the Spanish Moroccans always refused to recognize the puppet Sultan who replaced Mohammed V, who was Sultan of the Spanish as well as of the French Moroccans. General Franco won by this refusal more approval from the Arabs, even in Cairo, than he ever enjoyed before. When the Sultan was restored, Franco began negotiations for the return of Spanish Morocco, which was peaceably added to the new state in 1958. Spain retained Ifni over Moroccan protests, but the international city of Tangier became part of the Moroccan state in 1957, though it continued its special privileges until 1960.

Algeria

BACKGROUND OF CONFLICT. The tragedy of Algeria has surely been unequaled among all the lands colonized by the Europeans in the nineteenth century. It has been tragic for everyone concerned, French and Algerians alike; and although the shooting war at last came to an end in 1962, independent Algeria is faced with both internal dissensions and economic dislocations far beyond those of any other colony. Lengthy studies have been written about the complex issues involved in the seven-year Algerian war, and there will be more. All that can be attempted here is a brief outline of the problems and issues involved and a still briefer account of the course of the war and the Evian settlements that brought it to an end.

Algeria, unlike Morocco and Tunisia, was not ruled by native monarchs when the French began their conquest in 1830. It was in fact populated only by a few Arab and Berber tribes, and the city of Algiers was mainly a nest for pirates. From the beginning, the French regarded it as an extension of France, open to French settlement and colonization; many families of *colons* can trace their ownership of land back for almost a century. Although they are French by descent and culture and are French citizens, the large majority of the *colons* have known no other home than Algeria, nor have in many cases their fathers or grandfathers. The only European settlement in a distant land that has any similarity to that in Algeria is South Africa. The Algerian *colons* may thus in some respects be best compared with the Boers and British in South Africa; but the homeland of Boers and British did not lie just across a narrow sea, and there could be no question of regarding it as a detached part of the mother country, as the French regarded Algeria. By the end of World War II, there were more than a million European colonists in Algeria; though not all were of French descent, almost all were French citizens and looked across the Mediterranean to France as a matter of course for their moral and, if necessary, military and material support. Not all the *colons* were wealthy. Many of them had been simple peasant farmers at home before they migrated to Algeria, and they were hardly much more prosperous peasant farmers now. But without exception all regarded themselves as different in all important respects from the Muslim natives whom they employed, and generally superior by virtue of their religion and culture. Moreover, the French Government had systematically withheld equal rights from the Muslims, and any economic improvements had been made for the benefit of the Europeans. The Muslims had perhaps been able to gain some advantages, but if so it had not been because of French interest in them.

As a result of the stable and orderly government provided by the French, the Muslim population had grown until by the end of World War II there were about 9 million. The vast majority were strong, even fanatical adherents of their religion. The French made distinctions between them, granting citizenship to those who were willing to accept the French civil code and live in a European manner. Since this meant that the teachings of Islam had in some degree to be abandoned, these were regarded by other Muslims as virtual infidels. The Muslim majority, however, continued to obey the Koran and be judged by their own Islamic code; if they wished to have more than one wife and could afford it, they were permitted to have them. The French made no effort to interfere with these Muslims, and they lived in their own traditional manner, a separate social community, though necessarily taking their part in the total Algerian economy, which could not have subsisted without their labor. Until very recent times, the French provided them with very little opportunity to win an education. However, if they wished to live in a European manner, all fields were open to them in France. They had the full right to emigrate to France, though on returning to Algeria, they were subjected to discrimination in social and economic matters by the *colons.*

There can be little doubt that at least until World War II the great majority of Muslims accepted French rule as a fact of life and were not unduly disturbed by it. They had no particular desire for the French to leave as they were well aware that the progress of the country was due to them. If they had been asked in a free vote whether or not they wished the French to stay, they would probably have voted for them to stay. Up until the end, it is not at all certain that this would not have been their choice if they had ever been permitted to make it. What De Gaulle tried to do in the period after his return to power in 1958 was to bring the Muslims more closely into the economy, to share with them the governing of the country, to get rid of the numerous disadvantages from which they suffered, and above all to build up the country so that there would be more opportunities available to them.

If this had been done at the end of World War II and had not been delayed until the rebellion was more than four years old, the policy might have had a chance of success. There were at all times large numbers of Muslims—not the usual type of "collaborators," though they were regarded as such by the rebel leaders who did their best to intimidate them—who wished to continue working with the French in a plural society such as the Americans in Hawaii have shown to be possible. The country, in their view, was big enough for both French and Muslims and for a long time to come would need French capital and French industrial and agricultural techniques. It was these men whom De Gaulle tried to bring to the fore and give the opportunity to share in the government of the country. It is part of the tragedy of Algeria that these men, who were among the ablest in the Muslim population, were never permitted this opportunity, and their services are forever lost to independent Algeria. Nor were the Algerian people as a whole ever permitted to express their possible preference for a plural state. For this failure, the die-hard *colons* and the uncompromising nationalists must bear an almost equal share of the blame.

The French Army, which was to play not only a military but a political part in the rebellion, was made up of different parts, each with its own particular ethos. At first, the principal objective of the professional soldiers who had been defeated in Indochina and made to withdraw from Tunisia and Morocco was to recover some prestige in Algeria by defeating the enemy and pacifying the country. But in the course of the war, they began to see their task in a different light. Although naturally sympathetic to the *colons* whom they were defending against an army which used terrorism as its principal weapon, and readily adopting many of their viewpoints, these soldiers came to regard themselves as the sole repository of French honor, of a different class, almost a different race, from the politicians and petty bourgeois in France who understood nothing of such things and were prepared to abandon Algeria and their countrymen simply because the war was expensive and damaging to their world position and for other civilian reasons. The army in time began to develop an ideal and a policy of its own, which were crystallized in the slogan *Algérie Française*. Muslims and French, its leaders believed, should be given absolutely equal rights in the country with a common French citizenship. All would be brothers together. But in return, Algeria should remain as it had always been, a part of France, and it was necessary to fight on until this was assured. The nationalists, who were in their eyes the separatists looking toward a lesser restricted ideal, must be opposed to the end, as must every French leader who even proposed any concession to the nationalists.

How far this exalted ideal appealed to the *colons* is something else again. They had been accustomed to a privileged position, and they were far from willing to abandon it. The majority probably gave support to the ideas of the army leaders simply because it meant the continuation of the war and would prevent a nationalist victory or the withdrawal of French metropolitan aid. But certainly a substantial minority, especially among the young and at the University of Algiers, adopted the military ideal as their own without perhaps fully realizing how much they stood to lose if the privileges they had always known should really come to be shared with the Muslims.

It was impossible for these men to understand the hesitations of the metropolitan French, who had to pay the lion's share of the expenses of the war, had to endure the debates in the United Nations, the opprobrium of much of the world, the constant pressure from allies, the collapse of the political system of the Fourth Republic, the authoritarian rule of De Gaulle, and the abandonment of so much that needed to be done at home. Although they were patriotic Frenchmen, too, and had shared the humiliations of the last twenty years, they could not, like the army and the *colons*, think only of Algeria, even though it came to occupy the almost exclusive attention of their rulers. Especially the conscripts, who in the later years of the war had to fill the vacancies in the army, wanted, like all conscript soldiers, to see the end of the war. When they reached Algeria, some took on the views of their military leaders and fellow soldiers of the professional army, but many did not; at one crucial moment, their views counted and prevented the officers from making a successful *Putsch* against De Gaulle and the metropolitan French.

At the last, it was the metropolitan French whose opinions counted; when they and their leader De Gaulle decided the war had to be brought to an end on whatever terms could be won, the *colons* and dissident army elements were bound to lose. They could resort only to counterterror, which turned what moderate opinion there was in Algeria against them. Without the supply of men and munitions from France, they could no longer hope to hold out indefinitely against the Muslim majority, now backed by metropolitan France. About half the *colons*, perhaps more, departed in a mass exodus, leaving a partly ruined land behind them for the Algerians to restore if they could. Although the purposeful destruction of their work of decades cannot be defended, they were surely right in the belief that, after the years of war and terrorism on both sides, there was little future left for them in the country. There had been too much bitterness, too much distrust engendered for the Muslims to have forgiven and forgotten. This is the legacy of the Algerian war, surely one of the saddest and most tragic in history. In the end, there was nothing to be done except what was done; and both French and Muslim Algerians will continue to pay for it for generations to come.

EARLY NATIONALIST MOVEMENTS. Before the war, an important Muslim independence movement had already started under the leadership of Ben Ahmed Messali, a movement which under different names was to remain in existence until independence. For several years, Messali was the leading Algerian national activist; but after the outbreak of the war of independence of 1954, he steadily lost ground to the fighting organizations, and his followers were mostly in France, where for many years the French compelled Messali himself to live. Since Messali's organizations and newspapers in the end did not play the crucial part that might have been expected in the winning of independence and a good deal of their energies was spent in disputes with those leaders who did by their activities achieve independence, nothing more will be said here of them.

During World War II, when Algiers became the Allied headquarters in North Africa, there was considerable anticolonial sentiment, expressed in large part by an independence party formed under the leadership of Ferhat Abbas. Immediately after V-E Day, a large-scale uprising broke out which was ruthlessly suppressed by French troops and European vigilantes, who killed several thousand Muslims indiscriminately in reprisal. Despite this evidence of emotions seething under the surface, the French went ahead with their constitutional plans. Since Algeria was a part of France, they proposed to incorporate it in the new French Union that was to take the place of the old colonial system.

"FRENCH UNION." A Constituent Assembly, of which Ferhat Abbas, recently amnestied for his part in the rebellion, was a dissenting member, then drew up a constitution for the whole Union, which left the French in substantial control of Algeria as before. The French National Assembly continued to legislate for Algeria. Muslims, who now became French citizens, were allowed to vote for their representatives in the Assembly while retaining their personal Muslim status. But for Algeria there were two electoral colleges, each with different qualifications. The upper college was dominated by Europeans, the lower by Muslims. Only about 12 per cent of the Muslims voted and were eligible for election in the upper college. Any Muslim representatives for this college would have to be acceptable to the *colons*, and therefore moderates, whereas the lower college in free elections always elected nationalists.

A local Algerian assembly was also set up. Although it could not legislate, it was permitted to vote on the Algerian budget. Here, too, the double college ensured the election of a suitable number of *colons*. To prevent the continuous deadlocks that would have resulted from the election of too many nationalists by the lower college, French officials usually interfered in the elections to make sure that enough Muslim moderates would be chosen to pass the budget. In such circumstances, few nationalists thought it worth while to run for election, and the nationalist parties usually chose to ignore the elections altogether.

WAR FOR INDEPENDENCE, 1954–58. Terrorism began on a small scale as early as 1949, but outbreaks were relatively few and uncoordinated until 1954. The French were well aware of the existence of a secret army that was being organized by Messali, but they did not take this too seriously, contenting themselves with occasional arrests of its known leaders. During the years when Morocco and Tunisia were struggling for their independence, there had still been no sign that a concerted uprising in favor of Algerian independence was on the way, in spite of the fact that the "Voice of the Arabs" broadcasting from Cairo had for months been calling on the Algerians to revolt. Probably they had been watching Messali too closely, for the rebellion when it came was led by others.

The next years can be passed over briefly. The Army of National Liberation—its political branch was known as the National Liberation Front (FLN)—would usually advance until French reinforcements arrived, then retreat to its fastnesses in the mountains. The rebels never controlled much of the country, but their army was never destroyed and never stopped fighting, nor did it show any willingness to come to terms except on the basis of surrender by the French and the concession of independence. In the course of the struggle, both sides resorted to terrorism and torture of prisoners to obtain information. Much of the rebel terror was directed against fellow Muslims who cooperated with the French authorities.

Successive French governments, all of them dependent on uncertain majorities in the Assembly, with the largest party, the Communists, in permanent opposition, tried to bring the war to an end. But none dared make any substantial concessions. Public opinion was stirred by revelation of French atrocities and the systematic use of torture by police and military. The French Army in Algeria became increasingly hostile to all French governments, especially those they suspected of being ready to make a deal with the rebels.

The most positive step was urged by Jacques Soustelle, who as Governor-General of Algeria extracted a number of important reforms from a reluctant Assembly and proposed more. In his view, Algeria should be totally integrated with France, but there should be a full equality of treatment in all respects for Muslims and Europeans—a program that was taken up by the army leaders. Many of the reforms were tried in 1956, when sub-Saharan Africa was granted its *loi-cadre* (to be discussed in Chapter 10), but by this time it was almost certainly too late, and the *loi-cadre* itself as applied to Algeria had little meaning in the existing state of the country.

On February 8, 1958, the French Air Force bombed in daylight a Tunisian village in which Algerian rebels were supposed to be harbored. Tunisia, which had at all times given aid to the rebels, complained bitterly to the United Nations Security Council. The United States then attempted to mediate not only the Tunisian dispute but the whole Algerian war, but her proposals were unsatisfactory to the French. Three French governments fell in quick succession. No majority could apparently be found for any policy that could either wage the war more effectively or put an end to it. At this point, the army in Algeria took a hand. To the accompaniment of enthusiastic local demonstrations, a Committee of Public Safety was formed, headed by a parachutist officer, General Massu, and it demanded the formation in Paris of a "government of public safety alone capable of preserving Algeria as an integral part of metropolitan France." When the news came that a new government had been invested with power in France under Pierre Pflimlin, the Committee in Algiers called upon De Gaulle to break his silence, while the civilian head of the government in Algiers publicly refused to accept Pflimlin as Premier. The following day, General de Gaulle stated that he was available for office and "ready to assume the powers of the Republic." The Pflimlin government resisted for a few more days, then resigned, whereupon President Coty, who had used his influence to persuade Pflimlin to resign, sent at once for De Gaulle. The General demanded a free hand to deal with the crisis as he saw fit, a condition accepted by the Assembly, which granted him the power to rule by decree. Algeria was content that its man, the wartime hero who would never countenance the separation of Algeria from France, was now in power and waited hopefully for the steps he would take.

ALGERIAN POLICY OF DE GAULLE. Never were leaders of what amounted to an insurrectionary movement more disillusioned by the results of their handiwork. With very careful timing and precision, De Gaulle gradually released the higher army officers from command, replacing them with nominees he considered safe. At the beginning, he evidently hoped that a program of massive economic reforms, costing $4 billion over a period of five years and known as the Constantine Plan, would save the country for France. Although the plan was put into immediate operation and had already achieved much before independence, it did not contribute to the solution of the political problem. The war continued, and the French even achieved a few successes. In September, 1958, four months after De Gaulle's advent to power, he called upon all French citizens, including the Algerians, to vote on a constitution for the new Fifth Republic. Before the vote could be held, the FLN set up a Provisional Government of the Algerian Republic in Cairo, with Ferhat Abbas as President, and ordered a boycott of the referendum. In spite of this, a large majority of all Algerian Muslims voted to accept the new constitution and stay with France. Shortly afterward, the French abolished the double college, and Algerians and Europeans together voted for their members in the French National Assembly. Since the local assembly had been dissolved in 1956, the Muslims in Algeria voted only for local councils, but for these also the double college was abolished. Local government was thus formally in Muslim hands.

In September, 1959, De Gaulle announced a policy of self-determination for the Algerians, according to which not more than four years after the establishment of peace they could choose either secession, identification with, or association with France. For the *colons* and army officers in Algeria, this promise constituted a flagrant betrayal of their hopes and the trust they had placed in De Gaulle when they brought him to power. In January, 1960, a rebellion broke out in the coastal cities of Algeria against his government, but order was quickly re-established, and the rebel leaders were brought to trial. Some escaped to Spain and elsewhere to organize their forces once more for a last-ditch effort. The top-ranking officers appointed by De Gaulle, backed by the conscript rank and file and loyal elements in the professional army, had proved powerful enough to prevent the success of the rebellion.

EVIAN AGREEMENTS AND INDEPENDENCE. But it remained evident that nothing final could be settled without the agreement of the FLN leaders. Even though they might represent a minority in the country, it was they who controlled the military force with which the French had been contending, and they who were regarded outside France as the only leaders of the independence movement. The FLN alone could guarantee a cease-fire, so that there was no way in which the war could be brought to an end except by negotiations with them, and the FLN was determined to negotiate only on its own terms. Conversations opened at Melun in 1960 quickly collapsed because De Gaulle was still trying to put a real choice before the Algerians and would not concede the position of the FLN that it alone could speak for Algeria. In June, 1961, De Gaulle submitted the policy of granting self-determination to Algeria to a vote in another referendum. When the voters gave him massive approval, he resumed negotiations, which this time were crowned with success. According to the agreements of Evian-les-Bains (March 18, 1962), a cease-fire was to come into effect immediately, and a provisional government was to be set up in Algeria with ministers approved by the FLN. A referendum would then be held in Algeria asking the voters whether or not they approved of independence in cooperation with France. No alternative was offered. If the voters chose independence, then an Algerian National Assembly would be elected within three weeks to which the French would hand over powers as soon as the French people and French overseas departments and territories had signified their approval in a final referendum. The French Army would be reduced to 80,000 men within twelve months, and all would be repatriated within two years. A general amnesty was granted, and Algerian leaders, including Mohammed Ben Bella, who was to become the first President of independent Algeria, held prisoner in France, would be permitted to return and take part in the new government.

De Gaulle had in the end been unable to make his wishes prevail. The referendum, couched in the form demanded by the FLN leaders, was obviously a foregone conclusion. All that he had been able to secure was a paper guarantee for the personal safety and economic interests of those *colons* who wished to stay, and for French national and commercial interests. The great majority of the *colons* placed no belief whatever in its efficacy.

Thus began the last act, the desperate attempt to sabotage the agreement by a terrorist movement known as the Secret Army Organization (OAS), which operated in France and Algeria. In France, assassinations were frequent, and attempts were made on the life of De Gaulle. In the Algerian cities controlled by Europeans, there was a veritable reign of terror, during which the Muslims in a display of extraordinary restraint refrained from taking reprisals, thus robbing the OAS of its last hope that the French would be convinced at the eleventh hour of the danger of their course. The attempt failed, and the OAS called off its campaign—but not until untold damage had been done to property and thousands of lives had been wantonly sacrificed.

Meanwhile, there were numerous quarrels within the FLN leadership over who was to run the independent state. Eventually, Mohammed Ben Bella emerged as the victor. As soon as the results of the French referendum were known (89 per cent Yes), De Gaulle proclaimed the independence of Algeria and formally handed over power to the new republic (July 3, 1962).

The State of Israel

FAILURE OF THE MANDATE SYSTEM. During most of World War II, the Jews in Palestine cooperated with the British. However much they resented British rule, Hitler remained the enemy with whom they could not possibly in any circumstances collaborate. The Palestinian Arab leaders, on the contrary, collaborated with Hitler as much as they were able, and Hitler attempted to take over Iraq through an Arab supporter in 1941. During the whole war period and afterward, the British continued the policy announced in the White Paper of 1939. The moderate Jewish leadership confined its anti-British actions to efforts to circumvent the British immigration regulations, but terrorist movements designed to drive out the British also arose. Irgun Zvai Leumi and the "Stern Gang," the two leading terrorist organizations, took direct action against both British and Arabs, culminating in the bombing of government offices in the King David Hotel in Jerusalem in July, 1946, with the loss of more then 100 lives. The British retaliated with arrests and executions and began to deport illegal immigrants to Cyprus instead of merely diverting immigrant boats to Cyprus as before.

Meanwhile, the conditions in Nazi concentration camps and the pitiful state of the surviving Jews roused the conscience of the world. President Truman sent a personal representative to inquire into these camps and their inhabitants. On the basis of this information and other reports, he called on the British to admit 100,000 refugees into Palestine at once. The British, well aware by now that they could no longer administer the mandate effectively, were convinced that their withdrawal would result in war between the Arabs and the Jews. They therefore held fast to their immigration policy, while submitting the whole problem to the United Nations (February, 1947). A special committee recommended that the country be divided into a Jewish and an Arab state, but with an economic union for the whole country. This proposal was accepted by the Jews subject to the provision of suitable boundaries, but the Arabs remained adamantly opposed. In this opposition, they were stubbornly supported by the British, who had always insisted that any solution must be accepted by both sides, and none could be imposed that did not have British support. The U.N. General Assembly then voted (33 for, 13 against, 10 abstentions) for partition and called upon the Security Council to enforce its decision. But the British still refused to cooperate and would not permit the commission appointed by the General Assembly to enter Palestine until two weeks before the date they had set for their own departure (May 15, 1948).

INDEPENDENCE AND THE ARAB WAR. Meanwhile, armed clashes in Palestine continued, and the British were no longer able to ensure order in the country. Arabs and Jews fought one another openly and seized territory, the Arabs supported by irregulars from neighboring Arab countries. The Security Council, deeply divided, was paralyzed. In April, 1948, the General Assembly met again, and it seemed possible that it would go back on its earlier decision; but the appointed date arrived, and the Jews at once proclaimed their state to be independent and prepared to defend themselves. The United Nations appointed a mediator, Count Folke Bernadotte, while President Truman recognized the independent state of Israel, despite opposition from the career officers in the State Department concerned with the certain Arab enmity that would follow.

In the ensuing war, the Israelis more than held their own against all the Arab states that sent contingents. Although Bernadotte was murdered by Jewish terrorists, his successor, Ralph Bunche, succeeded in negotiating a truce, policed to this day by a U.N. Commission. As a result of the war, the Israeli state acquired more territory than was to have been assigned it under the United Nations partition arrangements and has grimly hung on to it to this day. Large numbers of Palestinian Arabs fled from Israel in spite of all assurances by the Israelis that they could stay and their property would be respected. No Arab state has as yet recognized the state of Israel, and some have boycotted all who have had commercial relations with Israelis. They will not permit anyone to visit both Israel and their states on the same voyage, and there is no entry point into Israel from any Arab state. Against the wishes of the other members of the Arab League, the Kingdom of Jordan (formerly Transjordan), which had become independent in 1946, annexed that part of Palestine which had not been occupied by Israel.

Meanwhile, the state of Israel has survived. Unlike the two Western powers that joined Israel in the attack on Egypt at the end of 1956, Israel was strengthened by her victorious and short-lived war. She was able to bring to an end numerous Egyptian raids into her territory and secure undisputed possession of her southern port of Eilat.

Cyprus and Enosis

CONFLICT BETWEEN GREEKS AND TURKS. The island of Cyprus, which had been ceded by the Turks to Britain in 1878 in exchange for an annual payment, was annexed outright by the British during World War I. The annexation was recognized by both Greece and Turkey in 1923 under the Treaty of Lausanne. Although the island is far closer geographically to Turkey, its population is about 80 per cent Greek, 17 per cent Turkish, and 3 per cent other. Ever since 1821, when the Greeks won their independence from Turkey, the Greek majority in Cyprus has been demanding that the island come under Greek rule. It obtained no satisfaction from either Britain or Turkey. The British have always regarded Cyprus as an important link in their chain of communications and have maintained both military and naval forces there.

The British conferred a constitution on Cyprus after World War I, but the Greeks and Turks showed little interest in it. After numerous disorders, it was suspended in 1931 and not restored until 1948. The leadership of the Greek community in the island has always rested with the Greek Orthodox Church, which has never wavered in its demand for *enosis,* or union with Greece. Greek Cypriots with few exceptions have never regarded themselves as citizens of some entity called Cyprus. They are Greeks living, perhaps only temporarily, in Cyprus The same may be said of the Turks, who likewise belong to a Turkish community in Cyprus. Turkish, unlike Greek, leadership has always been secular. Ever since the rise of Mustapha Kemal to power in Turkey, Islam has taken a second place in the lives of most Turks, and Cypriot Turks have never looked to Islamic organizations such as the Arab League for support.

The demand of the Greek majority for *enosis* has always been unacceptable to the Turks, who have no desire to be ruled by a people who were once their subjects. Since they are close to the mainland of Turkey, they could easily obtain military assistance from their compatriots, whereas the Greeks could not look to similar support from home. The power that ruled the island has been in the middle between the demands of the Greeks and the implied threat of the Turkish Cypriots to appeal for aid to their homeland. As long as the British protected them and permitted their community to live in its own way, the Turks raised no objections. When, however, the Greeks after World War II attempted to oust the British, the Turks in self-defense supported the British until it became clear that they could hold on no longer. Only then did the Turks turn to partition as the sole acceptable alternative.

The British could not grant self-government to the island as long as the Turks were unwilling to submit to majority rule; the Greeks did not even want self-government for the island. They wanted to join it to Greece—a solution all Turks, whether from Cyprus or mainland Turkey, were unwilling to accept. All the British could do was try to hold the balance between the two communities and fill the Legislative Council with reliable nominees who would cooperate with them in this task. As soon as any elected members of the Greek community were on the Council, they began to demand *enosis* and used their position as a sounding board for their views, showing little willingness to cooperate in the processes of government.

BRITISH EFFORTS TO GRANT SELF-GOVERNMENT. After World War II, the British Labour Government proposed almost complete self-government with the British retaining only their bases and some safeguards, but the Greek majority showed no interest in the proposal. A plebiscite was held in 1950 under British supervision, and again the majority was against anything but union with Greece. In 1955, a National Organization of Cypriot Fighters (EOKA) was organized, led by a mainland Greek Colonel named Grivas, pledged to drive the British out and force *enosis* with Greece. Archbishop Makarios, head of the Orthodox Church, founded a youth movement also pledged to *enosis*, which cooperated with the EOKA. When Makarios was found to be personally purchasing arms for the use of the terrorists, he was exiled to the Seychelles Islands (1956), which led to a greatly increased terrorist campaign under Grivas' direction. A Military Governor was able to bring some semblance of law and order into the country, but he could not stop isolated acts of terrorism, nor could he capture Grivas. Although most of the terrorism was directed against the British, from 1957 onward communal riots became ever more frequent. The EOKA turned its attention to those Greeks who were opposed to *enosis*, including even some of the Communists, who in general were opposed to *enosis* under which they could not expect to win power. The Athens radio engaged in incendiary broadcasts, and relations between Turkey and Greece, both NATO allies, became increasingly embittered.

At last, the British put forward the Macmillan Plan, which envisioned a tripartite form of government under which both Greeks and Turks would have their own separate assemblies, to be followed by a central assembly when these seemed to be working satisfactorily. Each assembly would legislate only for its own community. The British would remain for an additional seven years as supervisors, but in the meantime, the British Governor would be advised by representatives of the Greek and Turkish mainland governments. The Turks, who for the last year had been demanding partition as the only solution compatible with their needs, agreed to accept the Macmillan Plan. But the Greeks, suspecting it might prove to be a step in the direction of partition, refused. The worst month of terrorism (October, 1958) followed. The British, stung beyond endurance, retorted with atrocities of their own. NATO attempted to mediate, and the United Nations passed a resolution calling for an immediate end to the fighting. Only then did Makarios, in exile in Britain but not yet permitted to return to Cyprus, conclude that *enosis* was no longer feasible and that some arrangements for the island by itself would have to be agreed to, if only to avoid partition.

ZURICH CONFERENCE AND INDEPENDENCE. Early in 1959, the Turkish and Greek foreign ministers, and later their prime ministers, met secretly in Zurich. From the deliberations emerged a plan for a constitution unique in any country in the world. Once the mainland governments had accepted the solution, the island communities, under extreme pressure, had no option but to accept it, too. Colonel Grivas, who had been fighting only for *enosis*, tried to hold out a little longer but was reluctantly persuaded to return to Greece under an amnesty.

Under the new constitution, Cyprus was to be a republic with two executive officers, a president (Greek) and a vice-president (Turkish). Since there is no significant difference between their functions, they are in effect co-presidents. These two officials preside over a Council of Ministers, containing seven Greek and three Turkish Cypriots, all chosen by their own communities; both president and vice-president have a suspensory veto on legislation. Laws cannot be passed at all if a Supreme Constitutional Court declares them to be against either community. Two communal chambers were set up, each to deal with the affairs of its own community. Each community also elects members of a central House of Representatives, the Turks choosing 30 per cent of its membership and the Greeks 70 per cent, although the Turkish percentage of the population is considerably smaller than 30 per cent. The House of Representatives, the only all-island body, legislates for the whole Republic in fields not reserved for the communal chambers. The civil service was also to be 70 per cent Greek, 30 per cent Turkish, while the 2,000-man army was 60 per cent Greek and 40 per cent Turkish. The British, in exchange for their concession of independence, were promised a base under their exclusive sovereignty. Although differences arose between the British and Cypriots on the size of the base, necessitating the postponement of independence, eventually the island became an independent member of the Commonwealth on August 16, 1960. In spite of many difficulties, especially at budget time, Cyprus has managed to struggle along under its peculiar constitution. But there are few signs pointing toward the emergence of a Cypriot nationalism or indeed any recognition that both Turks and Greeks are irrevocably citizens of a single state. It appears that the Greeks are incurably Greeks, and the Turks incurably Turks.

Somali Territories

ITALIAN SOMALILAND. The former Italian Somaliland, which in 1950 became a United Nations trust territory under Italian administration, was always managed by the Italians with an eye to the independence deadline of 1960 set by the United Nations. For some years, they concentrated on the improvement of the economy. Then, as the deadline approached, they also tried to provide the territory with the nucleus of self-governing institutions that would enable it to undertake its responsibilities as an independent state, including a crash program for training future administrators. The British in the neighboring Somali Protectorate did little until the late 1950's, when it became clear that the Somalis under their control were anxious to join their fellow Somalis in the Italian territory. But this insignificant union was not the limit of Somali ambitions; they desired nothing less than an all-Somali state, made up of five areas inhabited mainly by Somalis. In addition to the Italian trust territory and the British Protectorate, they proposed to incorporate part of Ethiopia, the northern areas of the British colony of Kenya, and French Somaliland. None of the existing governments of these areas showed itself sympathetic to Somali claims.

As early as 1956, the Italians granted semiresponsible government to Somalia, with an elected Legislative Assembly and a Council of Ministers, reserving to themselves only a veto and control of defense and international relations. The Somali Youth League (SYL), hitherto a party devoted to the ideal of Greater Somalia, won the elections and formed the government. Once in office, SYL leaders decided that it was foolish to spend their energies agitating for an obviously unattainable union of Somali peoples. This resulted in an intraparty crisis followed by the formation of a splinter party, the Greater Somali League (GSL), pledged to the old program. But in spite of receiving much material and moral support from Egypt, it never made much headway, and the SYL continued to govern. In elections in 1959, the SYL won 83 of 90 total seats, 60 unopposed, to the accompaniment of choruses of objections from the GSL and other minor parties. Since this was to be the last election before independence, they petitioned the United Nations, claiming there had been wholesale improper disqualifications of candidates by the SYL Government. But the United Nations took no action, and Somalia became independent on July 1, 1960, several months before the due date.

BRITISH SOMALILAND PROTECTORATE. Meanwhile, the British, following a number of disturbances in 1958, at last decided to make some major changes in their Protectorate, which was populated almost exclusively by nomads, lacked educated personnel, and had no large city. In March, 1959, they permitted the first elections to the Legislative Council, which had previously possessed only nominated Somali members. Only five of the thirteen seats on offer were contested, and a moderate party led by a Christian won the majority. By the following year, when the independence of Somalia was imminent, new elections were held for thirty-three seats in a Council that now had a majority of elected members, although the Protectorate was far from self-governing, since the British controlled the Executive Council. By granting a majority in the Legislative Council, the British had made it possible for the Somali elected members to decide on the future of their country without relinquishing British control of the territory in case the members decided they did not wish to join Somalia. As it turned out, an overwhelming majority of the new Council decided for unification, and Britain quickly relinquished the Protectorate, which then became incorporated with the new independent state of Somalia (though retaining some autonomy in local affairs).

Prospects for Greater Somalia

None of the other territories coveted by Somalia is likely to be absorbed in the near future. Ethiopia has adamantly refused even to consider the cession of any territory and, according to the Somalis, is even trying to enlarge her own state at the expense of Somalia. French Somaliland, with a population largely but far from exclusively Somali, has not yet decided to forgo its present status as an overseas territory of France, with all this entails in the way of economic aid. After all, Somalia herself is an unviable territory, hitherto supported by uncertain aid from Italy, Britain, and other nations—although she has recently been able to float a considerable development loan abroad.

The best hope of incorporating any other of the disputed territories is in Kenya, where Somalia has made serious efforts during the past year. Prior to granting full self-government to Kenya, the British, in deference to the views of the minority party in the colony, sent out a commission to redraw the boundaries of the Kenyan districts, to each of which some degree of autonomy was to be granted. A Somali "region" was thus created, containing most of the Somali population of Kenya. Somalia pressed the British to cede this region to her outright before independence. When Britain refused, Somalia broke off diplomatic relations, with the sole apparent result of putting an end to British economic aid. The British held that such a decision had to be made by independent Kenya, whose leaders have so far refused to make any concessions beyond the limited autonomy granted under the pre-independence constitution. Even this may be revoked by the independent government of Kenya, controlled by KANU, the antifederalist party which won the 1963 elections. Nevertheless, Somalia will certainly try to win the region by whatever means she can find. Since a local plebiscite would undoubtedly be in her favor, she and her supporters will press for such a plebiscite in the United Nations. It also remains possible that if an East African Federation, including Kenya, comes into being, Somalia may become a member—in which case the region could be transferred from one component part to another with less loss of face than would be involved by the cession of "an integral part of the national domain" by a newly independent African state.

Aden and the Federation of South Arabia

The Colony and Protectorate of Aden comprise a large and important seaport and airbase, and a hinterland of desert areas ruled by the traditional chiefly system. British possession of the territory has been disputed ever since World War II by the independent Arab imamate of Yemen, which calls it "southern Yemen under British occupation," a claim that won Egyptian support. Individual sultans in the Protectorate have occasionally favored Yemen, preferring to join the main stream of Arab nationalism, represented by Yemen and her ally, Egypt, rather than to continue under the protection of a non-Arab power, Britain. However, the chiefs, who elect the sultans, have been far more interested in retaining their independence, which is almost absolute under the loose British system, particularly in the eastern states. Moreover, the imamate of Yemen has been held for several centuries by a family adhering to the Zeidi sect of Islam, anathema to the orthodox Sunni of the Protectorate.

This situation was changed by the outbreak of a revolution in Yemen, which brought General Sallal, an Arab nationalist supported by Egypt, to the presidency of a Yemeni Republic, and by British efforts to consolidate their position in the peninsula by forming a Federation of South Arabia including the Colony of Aden. At first, only seven western sultanates federated without the Colony (1959). In January, 1963, eleven joined with the Colony, and the Federation, over the protests of Yemen, formally came into being. At present, it seems likely that Sallal's regime will succeed in establishing itself as the government of Yemen, although opposition from the deposed Imam, backed by Saudi Arabia and

Jordan, has not yet ceased. Britain, however, has not yet recognized Sallal's republic.

The Colony of Aden, acquired by the British in 1839, obviously cannot become an independent state. Its one hope for survival, in the British view, was to join the new Federation. Aden has an airbase, probably no longer essential in view of Britain's reduced commitments in the Middle East, and huge British-owned oil refineries. It is also one of the busiest ports in the world. Although neither Britain nor the United States could view with equanimity the loss of this port to hostile nations, this does not mean that Aden must be retained as a British colony. About half the population are Arabs, including many Yemeni, whom the British have hitherto been unwilling to trust with the vote, and elections have been repeatedly postponed. The British control the Executive Council of the Colony, whereas the Legislative Council has an elected majority in which a moderate pro-British party at present predominates. But it holds this position only because the Arab nationalists boycotted the elections held in 1959, and the immigrant Yemeni were at that time disfranchised. A new party, the People's Socialist Party, backed by the labor unions, was recently organized, and is likely to win the next election, for which the British have promised a more liberal franchise. This party has presented its case before the U.N. Special Committee on Colonialism. If it wins the next election, it will almost surely press for union with the Republic of Yemen—if the Republic has survived—and for the dissolution of the Federation imposed upon them by the British and their Legislative Council.

This would leave the sultans isolated, probably unable to subsist as a separate nation, especially in the face of internal opposition from many of their own subjects. Their choice would be limited to union with either Yemen or Saudi Arabia, the latter not immune to the revolutionary virus. The British appear unlikely to be able to maintain their position for very much longer, and the Federation of South Arabia seems to have little chance of survival.

9. The New Africa—British Zone

Anticolonialism and Nationalism in Africa

Although there have been some fairly large native African empires during the last millennium, there was never any political entity comparable to a modern nation-state before 1957. The traditional unit was the tribe, ruled by one or more chiefs or kings. No new African nation is composed of a single tribe, and few tribes are confined within the boundaries of a single modern independent nation.

It was, therefore, the primary task of educated African nationalists who wished to lead their colonies to independence to create a national feeling that transcended tribal loyalties. All the colonial powers made use, in greater or lesser degree, of existing tribal loyalties. It became accepted policy in most colonies to increase the authority of tribal chiefs over their people by granting them salaries or other perquisites of office and delegating authority to them. The system, known as indirect rule, was much less expensive than using expatriate officers who, in any case, could not have commanded an equivalent loyalty from African tribesmen. Ambitious nationalists were seldom tribal leaders. Furthermore, unlike the tribal leaders, they had no vested interest in colonialism. On the contrary, the only way for them to win power was to displace the tribal leaders and divert the loyalty of tribesmen to themselves. They had a weapon for this in the form of anticolonialism. If they could lead the agitation against foreign rule, they could win recognition as the champions of the tribesmen—a role most of the traditional rulers refused to play.

Anticolonialism should be seen as the necessary preliminary to African nationalism, and far more important than nationalism as a means for winning independence. It is the negative side of nationalism. It was too much to expect that nationalist leaders would be able to build up a positive love for and loyalty toward their particular colonies—with their arbitrary boundaries—before they became responsible for their own government; and they seldom did so. Occasional appeals to national feeling were made in the legislative councils of the various colonies—notably in Nigeria, where a federal state had to be granted to offset the separatism of the three major peoples in the country. But, on the whole, nationalism was a very tender plant at the granting of independence, and only in a few of the new nations has it grown appreciably in the years since.

Anticolonialism, however, was an emotion that could be felt by all, and it could be and was exploited to the full to drive out the colonial powers, a definite and attainable end. Anticolonialism's usefulness was not exhausted after independence, either, for colonialism might return in a disguised form, wearing the garments of economic cooperation or foreign aid. Even the last trappings of colonialism—for example, the retention of the British Queen as Head of State—could not be tolerated for long. Only Sierra Leone, the smallest of British African colonies, and Uganda, one of the more recent states to win independence, have retained this symbol. All the others have become republics. Nothing material is gained by removing the symbol, but to Africans a republic is more independent and less connected with the colonial past than a nominal monarchy. It is a step toward nationhood.

Much more potent than Western-style nationalism has been the continuing attempt to exalt the nationalist leader as a charismatic figure to whom all loyalty is due. He is backed, wherever possible, by a single national party whose primary task is to drum up nation-wide support. In this manner, the old tribal loyalty is supplanted without necessarily destroying tribal organization. Only in Ghana has there been a serious attempt to destroy this organization, and this attempt has been the major reason for the unrest in Ghana since independence. Kwame Nkrumah of Ghana, called the "redeemer" by his followers, Sékou Touré of Guinea, Julius Nyerere of Tanganyika, Houphouët-Boigny of the Ivory Coast, Modibo Keita of Mali, Léopold Senghor of Senegal, even William Tubman of Liberia, have been exalted as indispensable leaders by their supporters. In so far as these men succeed in identifying themselves with their "nations," nationalism may grow as a by-product, and it may be that in Africa, where abstractions tend to be personified, this is the form that nationalism will take in the future. But in the struggle for independence, anticolonialism, with its visible target and its practical aims, was clearly the motivating force, just as in the United Nations it is the force behind the drive to help the still remaining colonies achieve their independence.

Constitutional Forms for the Attainment of Independence

When the British subjugated the Africans in the nineteenth century and assumed responsibility for governing colonies, replacing tribal rule with their own, they necessarily transformed tribal organization even while making use of it. When the time came for them to restore power to the Africans, it was not possible for them simply to pack up and go. They would have left behind them a power vacuum resulting in anarchy, not in the restoration of the tribal rule that had preceded their own. Tribal leaders, totally ignorant of the organization of the central government through which the British ruled, could hardly have operated it without preparation or experience.

It was necessary therefore to establish some kind of government to which they could yield their authority. Since the colonies had been living for so many years under British forms of government, it seemed best to accustom the Africans to working with these forms, at least until independence, letting them modify them later in the light of their own experience. Thus the procedure generally followed was to allow the Africans a share in the colonial government by admitting them to the various councils, at first in small numbers, then in ever greater numbers, until they constituted a majority in both the legislative and executive branches. By this time, there would be responsible African ministers, and at last a prime minister with a cabinet of his choice to whom the British could hand over their authority. The details of elected and nominated, official and unofficial members, the composition of executive and legislative councils are important insofar as they reveal the stage of self-government reached at a given time and the means by which ultimate independence was gained.

The British Colonial Office, in which was vested the responsibility for colonial administration, always had in mind the purpose for which the various constitutional changes were designed. It had many methods at its disposal: limiting the franchise to men of education and property, nominating outstanding Africans to the council, keeping a majority of civil servants in each council so that they could outvote the Africans in case of necessity, retaining civil servants at the head of key government departments, and the like. Some of the methods chosen failed to do the job expected; pressures from Africans sometimes prevented adherence to the proposed timetable for advances. But nothing was done without some purpose in view, some desirable objective to be attained—always with the aim of someday being able to hand over authority to a responsible and experienced administration capable of ruling the country after they had gone.

GUBERNATORIAL RULE. The first form of government in British colonies has always been direct rule by the governor, who was chief executive and sole legislator, but responsible to the British secretary of state for the colonies. Since the latter was a cabinet minister who might hope for promotion within the cabinet, he did not usually remain as colonial secretary for more than at most one term of office. Continuity in colonial administration was provided by the permanent undersecretary of state for the colonies, a civil servant who in several instances has been appointed from among former colonial governors.

The governor at all times worked with an executive council made up of his own advisers, which contained at the minimum his own second-in-command, called the chief secretary, who temporarily replaced him when he was on leave; a finance minister; and an attorney-general. It could, at the governor's pleasure, contain other heads of departments, thus making the executive council in effect a cabinet. As soon as the governor felt he could benefit from advice from persons outside the government, he was authorized to set up a legislative council composed of a majority of civil servants and a minority of "unofficials"—professional men, merchants, or others domiciled in the colony. These would always at this stage be Europeans and nominated by the governor. Once nominated to the council, they were expected to give their best advice to the government, but could vote as they wished; however, being in a minority in the council, they could always be outvoted by the "officials"—civil servants bound to obey the government. A major interest of the unofficials in the council usually lay in criticizing the budget presented to them by the governor, to which they could present amendments for his approval. The governor presided over the legislative council and controlled its agenda.

The next stage in the evolution of the colonial government might consist of a number of steps, none of them crucial but all opening up a new area of responsibility to local persons unconnected with the government. The legislative council could be opened to persons who were no longer nominated but elected. This meant that council members were now representatives of their particular electorate. In the early stages of political evolution, these men would still be Europeans, representative of either white settlers or various commercial interests. Sometimes the local chamber of commerce elected representatives. At a later stage, African provincial councils, themselves composed in part of chiefs or notables and in part of the more propertied classes, might indirectly elect members of the council. The British were hesitant to grant universal franchise to Africans until very late in the colony's history for fear that African nationalists would be elected who were professional politicians and not necessarily responsible men of property and who they feared might disrupt the orderly processes of government. For a long time, the civil servants retained a majority in the council, thus enabling legislation desired by the government to be passed over the opposition of the unofficials. The governor himself retained the power to legislate by decree in cases of emergency. If he desired to place a government department in the hands of a member of the legislative council who was not a civil servant, he could nominate to his executive council as many such men as he pleased from the legislative council, as long as he maintained enough civil servants to outvote them.

CONSTITUTIONAL ADVANCES. The crucial step that marked the British intention to grant eventual independence was the granting of what was called "representative government." Under this system, the majority of the members of the legislative council were elected instead of being nominated. There was now an incentive for the Africans to form political parties to contest the elections. If one party won the election by a substantial majority, it was difficult for the executive council to continue to function against the opposition of a powerful party in the legislative council. The governor, therefore, would probably introduce a ministerial system, choosing as minister the leader of the party that had been victorious in the elections and consulting him before appointing other unofficial members to the executive council. These members would be chosen from the ranks of the winning party in the legislative council and granted responsibility for various minor governmental departments, likewise with the rank of minister. As soon as the governor granted the initiative in choosing the agenda for discussion in the executive council to an elected leader, the latter would become the "leader of government business," later premier, chief minister, or prime minister. If no party won a majority in the elections, then the governor, if he wished to institute a ministerial system, was free to choose the most competent members of the legislative council for the cabinet or ministry. However, he would not feel bound to consult any of them before appointing the others. If two parties were fairly equal in numbers, he might create a coalition government and confer the title of chief minister on one of the political leaders.

As soon as there were elected majorities in both executive and legislative councils and a chief minister in charge of governmental business, the governor, usually but not always, would cease to preside at executive council and legislative council meetings. The chief minister would preside over the former and a speaker over the latter. But the three most important civil servants—the chief secretary, finance secretary, and attorney-general—would remain in charge of their departments and would continue to sit in the legislative council. This stage of development is known as semi-responsible government. Fully responsible government was attained only when these three civil servants handed over their portfolios to native ministers.

All that remained to be won was independence itself. During the transition from responsible government to independence, the governor would retain his reserve powers, which included the total suspension of the constitution (a power exercised in Malta as recently as 1958) and the right to take special security measures in case of emergency; the constitution itself could not as yet be amended by unilateral action by the colony. The interval would naturally be occupied by negotiations on the date of independence and its conditions. When these had been agreed to, the British Parliament would pass an enabling act, and the Crown then take the final step, the issuing of an order-in-council granting independence.

Of course, it was hardly to be expected that the Africans and other colonial peoples would simply accept gratefully the successive doses of self-government benevolently conferred upon them by their masters. The African leaders almost always wanted more than they were granted at any given time; and sometimes they refused to use what they were given until they received more. By agitation, by pressure, and sometimes by what the Ghanaians called "positive action," they were often able to persuade the British to speed up their timetable; sometimes a British secretary of state would be more favorable to African aspirations than his predecessor and would willingly grant a more substantial advance than had been intended. But the general procedure has been followed with few deviations ever since it was decided in 1951 that

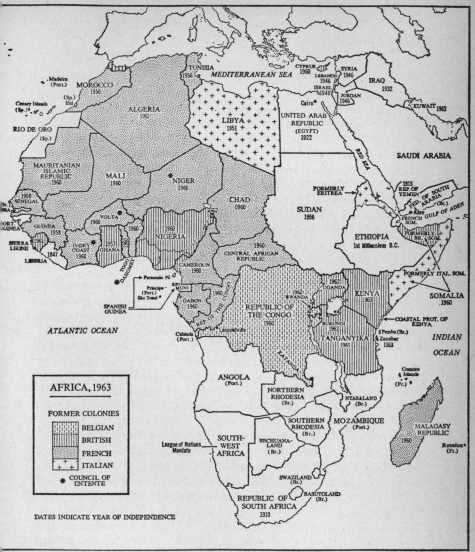

MEDITERRANEAN SEA

Madeira (Port.)

MOROCCO 1956

Canary Islands (Sp.)

(Sp.) Ifni

RIO DE ORO (Sp.)

ALGERIA 1962

TUNISIA 1956

CYPRUS 1960

LEBANON 1946
ISRAEL 1948

SYRIA 1946

IRAQ 1932

JORDAN 1946

KUWAIT 1963

LIBYA 1951

UNITED ARAB REPUBLIC (EGYPT) 1922

Cairo

SAUDI ARABIA

RED SEA

MAURITANIAN ISLAMIC REPUBLIC 1960

MALI 1960

NIGER 1960

CHAD 1960

SUDAN 1956

FORMERLY ERITREA

1918 REP. OF YEMEN

FED. OF SOUTH ARABIA

Aden (Br.)

FRENCH GULF OF ADEN SOM.

SENEGAL 1960

Br. GAM...

...ORT ...UINEA

GUINEA 1958

VOLTA 1960

1960

1960

NIGERIA

CAMEROUN 1960

CENTRAL AFRICAN REPUBLIC

ETHIOPIA 1st Millennium B.C.

FORMERLY BR. SOM.

FORMERLY ITAL. SOM.

SIERRA LEONE

LIBERIA 1847

1957 IVORY COAST 1960

GHANA

TOGO

DAHOMEY

Fernando Pó

Principe (Port.)
São Tomé

RIO MUNI

GABON 1960

1960

REP. OF THE CONGO

UGANDA 1962

RWANDA 1962

REPUBLIC OF THE CONGO 1960

Leopoldville

BURUNDI 1962

KENYA 1963

SOMALIA 1960

COASTAL PROT. OF KENYA

SPANISH GUINEA

ATLANTIC OCEAN

Cabinda (Port.)

KATANGA

TANGANYIKA 1961

Pemba (Br.)
Zanzibar 1963

INDIAN OCEAN

ANGOLA (Port.)

NORTHERN RHODESIA (Br.)

NYASALAND (Br.)

MOZAMBIQUE (Port.)

Comoro Islands (Fr.)

AFRICA, 1963

FORMER COLONIES

BELGIAN

BRITISH

FRENCH

+ ITALIAN

* COUNCIL OF ENTENTE

SOUTHERN RHODESIA (Br.)

SOUTH-WEST AFRICA

League of Nations Mandate

BECHUANA-LAND (Br.)

MALAGASY REPUBLIC 1960

Reunion (Fr.)

SWAZILAND (Br.)

DATES INDICATE YEAR OF INDEPENDENCE

REPUBLIC OF SOUTH AFRICA 1910

BASUTOLAND (Br.)

Map by Vincent Kotschar.

the Gold Coast could follow substantially the same steps to independence that had recently been taken by the major British colonies in Asia.

The New Independent Nations

Ghana

By the end of World War II, the Gold Coast still had an official majority in its Legislative Council, but reform was imminent. Many Gold Coast Africans had studied abroad and were beginning to look forward to greater participation in their own government; the educated classes too often found that there were no positions available for them in the colonial bureaucracy, since the best posts were monopolized by British civil servants. The example of India had shown that the British were susceptible to organized pressure. They had finally granted independence to the Indians, and it was not altogether impossible that they could be persuaded to grant it even to Africans.

The constitution handed down in 1946 was found thoroughly unsatisfactory by the African nationalists. Although an elected majority had been granted in the Legislative Council, most of the seats were filled by indirect election. The chiefs and traditional authorities, who seldom looked with favor on the young intelligentsia, dominated the small electorate; and only five seats were chosen directly by ballot. Nevertheless, it was an older man of a chiefly family, a respected and ordinarily conservative lawyer, Dr. J. B. Danquah, who gave the first impetus in the postwar period to the nationalist movement. Although he had at first accepted the new constitution as satisfactory, he later quarreled with the government and decided that it was simply "window dressing." In order to press for more reforms, he organized a political party called the United Gold Coast Convention (UGCC) and invited a young nationalist named Kwame Nkrumah to return from England and become its secretary. Nkrumah proved to be too dynamic a personality to be confined within the leading strings of the conservative UGCC. After his arrival, he virtually took over the party, converting it into an organization capable of active agitation and with a strong appeal to the masses. In 1948, under the influence of the rhetoric of Nkrumah and some of the more active of the UGCC leaders, a serviceman's demonstration was turned into a minor riot which the British were compelled to suppress by force. Danquah, Nkrumah, and other leaders were arrested and briefly imprisoned.

Nevertheless, the British decided that the time was ripe for a new constitution, and they set up a commission headed by an African judge to listen to evidence and make proposals. Danquah sat on the commission and joined in most of its proposals, whereas Nkrumah, deciding in advance that the conservative composition of the commission would prevent it from making any radical suggestions, boycotted it. Before it had made its report, Nkrumah founded his own party, the Convention People's Party (CPP), and engaged in a program of direct political agitation, not excluding violence, which he called "positive action." This landed him in prison once more, where he remained until after the first election was held under the new constitution.

Under this constitution, a large number of seats were filled by indirect election, but it was still possible for an elected majority to come to power. To do this, a party needed to win almost all the seats available for direct election. The CPP succeeded in doing this, making it virtually impossible to carry on the government without its consent. Nkrumah was triumphantly taken from jail and made "leader of government business." The following year, he was granted the title of Prime Minister, but for the time being the three leading British civil servants remained in the Executive Council (semiresponsible government).

In April, 1953, Nkrumah decided it was time to put pressure on the British for another installment of self-government. He introduced a bill into the Legislative Council calling for fully responsible self-government and direct elections based on universal suffrage and demanding a declaration from the British that independence would follow soon afterward. The bill was passed unanimously, whereupon the British appointed another commission whose recommendations were substantially accepted. The Executive Council became a cabinet, the Legislative Council became a Legislative Assembly, and universal suffrage and direct elections were granted. The British civil servants were not to be part of the new cabinet or Legislative Assembly.

By this time, however, opposition to Nkrumah had developed, especially in Ashanti territory, whose still-powerful chiefs resented the ascendancy of the upstart Prime Minister. But the opposition had been unable to form any effective political party of its own, and was badly defeated in the elections of 1954. His position thus strengthened, Nkrumah proceeded to move as rapidly as possible toward independence—in the process exciting stronger opposition from his opponents, both in Ashanti territory and in the less developed Northern Territories, where chiefly influence was still strong. The opposition was two-pronged. On the one hand, it tried to persuade the British to provide the country with a federal rather than a unitary constitution, hoping to retain some power in the hands of traditional authorities in Ashanti, where there was some possibility that opponents of the Prime Minister and his CPP would win the next elections. On the other hand, the opposition tried to make sure there would be another general election before independence. Throughout the colony, but especially in Ashanti, the opposition had been able to foment such disturbances that the British called upon Nkrumah to hold an election—after which, if the new Assembly asked for it, they would grant independence. However, they were not prepared to insist on a federal constitution, preferring to set up Regional Assemblies and incorporate in the constitution some clauses which proved useless after independence.

The opposition had still not organized an effective political party by the time of the pre-independence election. The CPP lost the majority of seats in Ashanti but increased its representation elsewhere, thus getting an effective over-all majority in the new Assembly. When the motion calling for immediate independence was put to the Assembly, it was passed unanimously, the opposition members refusing to take part in the vote. On March 6, 1957, the Gold Coast became independent under the name of Ghana, with the Queen of England as its titular head. On June 30, 1960, Ghana became a republic under a new constitution which permitted Nkrumah to hold the offices of President and Prime Minister at the same time.

The United Nations trust territory of Togoland, under British administration, which had always been administered as an integral part of the Gold Coast, was given the opportunity in May, 1956, of choosing between continued existence as a trust territory or union with Ghana when the latter became independent. The vote was 3 to 2 in favor of union, the Ewes voting heavily for continuation of their status as a trust territory in hopes of being able to join their compatriots in French Togoland at a later date. The U.N. General Assembly accepted the majority vote, and western Togo became an integral part of Ghana at independence.

The Federation of Nigeria

REGIONAL CONFLICT. Nigeria was the second British colony in sub-Saharan Africa to win independence—more than three years after Ghana had reached the same goal. The Nigerians might well have been the first, since the British had long agreed in principle to Nigerian independence, and Nigeria was rich in political leaders of acumen and experience. But for years the Nigerians were unable to agree among themselves. There was no national party that could have unified the country, as the CPP had unified Ghana. Instead, there were three major parties, each dominant in its own region and among its own people, and none had much support in the other regions. Thus it gradually became evident that the government would have to be of a federal type and that the resulting central government would be a coalition of two major parties, with the third in opposition. It says much for the political maturity of the Nigerian leaders that they did not press for independence before a formula for representation had been accepted that promised a modicum of political peace in the future. Not until 1959 did the backward but populous Northern Region accept regional autonomy for itself, the last step before federation. It then remained only to organize a fully responsible federal government and hold new elections. Independence followed on October 1, 1960.

For a long time, the British refused to accept the idea of a federal government for Nigeria, since they recognized the difficulty of such a form and knew that it would prove to be more expensive than a unitary state. But it was necessary because of the marked differences in all essential respects between the two southern regions and the Northern Region. The Northern Region, which holds the majority of the population, mostly Fulani and Hausa, was governed entirely by its predominantly Muslim chiefs until 1946; and the British Resident gave his advice unobtrusively. This advice was almost invariably followed without dispute, since the Muslim emirs valued their privileges, which they were likely to lose if the British ceased to support them. These emirs realized also that, in a unitary state under a democratic form of government, with a merit system for appointments, the better-educated Yoruba and Ibo from the south would hold most of the governmental and administrative posts in their region. Thus the traditional rulers in the north held tightly to what they had and fought a skillful rear-guard action against encroachment by the nationalists from the south.

CONSTITUTIONAL DEVELOPMENT. The first nationalist movement of importance was sparked by Dr. Nnamdi Azikiwe, who, after returning from the United States with a doctorate in 1934, founded a number of newspapers that crusaded for political and social reforms. He organized a political party in 1944 known as the National Council of Nigeria and the Cameroons (NCNC), the British-mandated Cameroons being at the time administered from Nigeria. As long ago as 1923, the electoral principle had been introduced in Nigeria. The capital city of Lagos elected three members and the city of Calabar one member to the Legislative Council. Despite the general expectation that the elected seats would be increased, a new constitution handed down in 1946 set up regional assemblies, dominated by chiefs, and made these the electoral body for the central Legislative Council, leaving only the same four seats as before to be chosen by direct election.

The NCNC, which at that time was the only nationalist party and commanded some support in every region of the country, fought hard against the constitution even after it had been proclaimed by the governor. But all the party was able to win were some concessions in such matters as the Africanization of the civil service and a promise from the British to consult the Africans the next time a constitution was under consideration. Even so, the Macpherson Constitution of 1951 was scarcely more to the liking of the nationalists. This time the four directly elected seats were abolished. All members of the central House of Representatives were to be chosen by the regional houses of assembly, whose members were themselves chosen by electoral colleges in which chiefs exercised a strong influence. A Council of Ministers replaced the old Executive Council; but the ministers also were chosen by regional assemblies, four to each region, and they were not given full charge of their departments. There was no chief minister, the British governor exercising his functions by presiding over the Council of Ministers and preparing its agenda. Nevertheless, the central government was far stronger than the regional governments. The regional houses were granted a number of relatively unimportant local matters on which to legislate, leaving the bulk of subjects within the jurisdiction of the central House of Representatives. The Council of Ministers also had a veto on all laws passed by the regions.

This constitution seems to have been clearly designed to check, or at least had the effect of checking, the growth of parties with a national appeal, since no Yoruba or Ibo could hope to be chosen by the Northern Regional Assembly, acting as a whole, even though they might hope to be elected in individual electoral districts where opposition to the rule of the emirs was strong. Although the form of government was obviously capable of being converted into the federal system, the powers granted to the central government made it clear that such a system was not expected to evolve from it. In other words, the constitution was leading nowhere; nor did eventual independence seem much nearer. But it was possible for political parties, especially if organized on a tribal basis, to fight in the elections for the regional assemblies with some hope of success, in spite of the indirect method of election. Two major parties were therefore founded in time to fight in the election—the Action Party in the Western Region and the Northern People's Congress (NPC) in the Northern Region. Both won in their regions, while the older NCNC won in the Eastern Region. Few seats outside their own region were won by any of the parties.

The major issues in the House of Representatives elected under the Macpherson Constitution were the form of government under which Nigeria should gain her independence and whether it should come as early as 1956, as urged by the Eastern and Western regions, or be postponed for many years, as insisted on by the Northerners. Since the Northern Region possessed half the total membership of the House, deadlock resulted. Frustration was such that all parties finally decided to press for a federal government that would permit the Northerners to do more or less as they wished in their region while not hindering the march of Nigeria as a whole toward independence. Faced with this united demand, Britain accepted the inevitable and thereafter assisted the Nigerians toward the kind of government they desired, ready to grant independence as soon as the Nigerian domestic differences should be sufficiently resolved.

In 1954, in the Eastern and Western regions, the regional assemblies were given greater powers and were organized to permit direct election by an electorate composed of all taxpayers. The members of the central House of Representatives were elected directly. In the Northern Region, where the chiefs were strongest, indirect election was maintained for both federal and regional elections, with the vote confined to men. The number of elected ministers was reduced to ten—three from each region, and one from the Cameroons. Before making his appointment, the

Governor-General was now required to consult the leaders of those parties that had won a majority in each region in the last federal elections. By a curious and unexpected quirk, the Ibo Party (NCNC) won the federal election not only in the Eastern (Ibo) Region but in the Western (Yoruba) Region also, whereas the native Yoruba Party (Action) won the regional elections. So the NCNC obtained six ministers, while the Action Party had none. But the leaders of each party preferred to sit in their regional assemblies rather than in the weaker federal House of Representatives.

THE WINNING OF INDEPENDENCE. In 1957, the House of Representatives passed a unanimous resolution calling on the British to set a date for independence. At the conference that followed, it was decided that all the regions could have fully responsible self-government as soon as they requested it. Once the regional governments were functioning effectively, a date for independence could be set. A federal election would be held prior to independence, in which the Northern Region would for the first time elect its representatives directly. Lastly, it was agreed that a federal prime minister should be appointed, though the Governor-General would continue to preside over the Council of Ministers. Alhaji Abubakar Balewa, leader of the party (NPC) with the most seats in the House of Representatives, was chosen to be Prime Minister, though he was not the national leader of his party, which was headed by the Sardauna of Sokoto, Premier of the Northern Region. The majority of his ministers were not even members of his party, since six ministers were members of the NCNC.

As permitted under the new arrangements, the Eastern and Western regions at once claimed and were granted full responsibility in their regions. The Northern Region did not follow their example until 1959. The last British civil servants then retired from the Council of Ministers, the Governor-General ceased to preside, and the Prime Minister became at last master of his own house. The pre-independence federal election campaign was marked by some disorders resulting from efforts by the Action Party to electioneer in the Northern Region, hitherto forbidden to it. Chief Awolowo, leader of the party, complaining of the large size of the Northern Region, vainly agitated for the formation of a new region peopled mostly by non-Muslims. In this election, the two party leaders of the Eastern and Western regions left their regional assemblies and stood for federal office, though the Sardauna of Sokoto stayed at home and continued as Premier of the Northern Region. The NPC won the largest block of seats, as was inevitable in view of the greater population of the Northern Region. The NCNC, after winning the second largest bloc, allied itself with the NPC, leaving the Action Party, with 73 seats of 320, as the official opposition. As soon as the British withdrew, Dr. Azikiwe, of the NCNC, became Governor-General of the new state (November 16, 1960). Balewa remained Prime Minister, presiding over a coalition government, and was knighted, though his position continued to depend on the support of the NPC. However, the Sardauna, as leader of the largest party, remained the most powerful man in the country. Nigeria remained a British Dominion until October, 1963, when she became a republic.

THE CAMEROONS. When the Federation of Nigeria became independent, in October, 1960, the trust territory of the Cameroons under British administration was separated from the new state pending the determination of its fate by the United Nations. In September, 1959, a plebiscite had been held in Northern Cameroons, which for forty years had been administered in the hope that its people would make a choice that could be implemented as soon as Nigeria became independent. It had been widely believed that the inhabitants of this territory would opt for union with Nigeria, with whom it had many cultural, religious, and racial ties. But when the territory was given the choice of either joining Nigeria when the latter attained independence or continuing its trust status, the vote went in favor of the latter alternative—an impossible arrangement for Britain unless Southern Cameroons made the same decision, which did not seem probable. Nevertheless, for a brief period Northern Cameroons reverted to trust status until both Nigeria and the Cameroons under French administration had become independent, when a meaningful choice was possible.

The plebiscite in both territories was held in February, 1961, the choice now being limited to union with independent Nigeria or with independent Cameroun. The Northern Cameroons voted for union with Nigeria, and Southern Cameroons for union with Cameroun. Cameroun has been trying ever since with somewhat indifferent success to integrate two very different types of administration, complicated by differences of language as well as totally different governmental traditions.

Sierra Leone

Sierra Leone was first settled by freed Negro slaves called Creoles. Later Britain expanded into the hinterland and established a protectorate there. The more primitive peoples of the Protectorate, ruled by their chiefs, greatly outnumbered the Creoles, who were much better educated but were not allowed to play a political part in the state commensurate with their education. When an elected unofficial majority was granted in the Legislative Council in 1951, the Creoles received only half of the seats alloted to the Protectorate, whose council members, chosen indirectly, were responsive to the wishes of traditional authorities. In the Colony, the Creoles, themselves divided, won only four of the seven members alloted to the colony. Two of the remainder fell to the Sierra Leone People's Party (SLPP), a party primarily strong in the Protectorate. Seeing that this party commanded some support in the whole country, the paramount chiefs in the Protectorate decided to back it, thus providing the SLPP with a comfortable working majority in the Legislative Council. The governor's own nominees made up the remainder of the council. The Executive Council was enlarged to include four civil servants and four elected members, making possible a ministerial system, which was duly created in 1953. In 1954, the leader of the SLPP, Dr. (now Sir) Milton Margai, a non-Creole medical doctor from the Protectorate who commanded wide support in the country, was accorded the title of Chief Minister, though he did not preside over either council. His government devoted itself largely to social and economic reforms.

Thus far, all had proceeded fairly smoothly. There were some riots in Freetown in 1955 and some minor disturbances in the Protectorate that were settled by the deposition of paramount chiefs accused of extortion. Under a new constitution that took effect in 1957, the chiefs lost some of their power. The majority of the members of the Legislative Council, renamed the House of Representatives, were to be directly elected, which left only 12 paramount chiefs to be chosen by district councils in the protectorate. Four British civil servants continued to sit in the Executive Council until 1958.

After the ensuing election, which the SLPP won handily, fission occurred in the ranks of the ruling party. A group led by the Chief Minister's brother, Arthur, believing that Sierra Leone was at least as well prepared for independence as her neighbor, the former French Guinea (which had just achieved it), broke away to form the People's National Party (PNP). The family quarrel, however, did not last long. A new constitutional conference was held in London in April and May, 1960, and independence was promised for April 27, 1961. Sir Milton thereupon formed a coalition government in which his brother held a portfolio—leaving another former minister and leader of the PNP, Siaka Stevens, outside the government. Stevens proceeded to form a new opposition party known as the All People's Conference (APC), which demanded elections before independence as had been required in Ghana and Nigeria, threatening disturbances if the request were not heeded. According to Stevens, Sir Milton's government, elected in 1957, had long outlived its mandate. But the British, with a moderate Prime Minister in office who was quite satisfactory to them, made no attempt to put pressure on him. The last two months were indeed marred by sporadic disturbances, and the government detained Siaka Stevens and others, in the interest of national security, until after the date of independence. They were released soon afterward, and the state of emergency under which the opposition leaders had been "detained" was brought to an end. Stevens and the secretary of the APC were then convicted and sentenced under the regular laws to six months in prison for conspiracy and libel against the Prime Minister and his Finance Minister. Although the secretary's conviction for conspiracy was quashed on appeal, his sentence for libel was served.

Elections were finally held in May, 1962, a year after independence. Sir Milton's party won only twenty-eight seats against twenty won by the APC in alliance with another local party. Margai continued to hold office only with the aid of twelve independents. If Gambia, not yet independent, is excepted, in Sierra Leone alone, among British African countries, is there evidently an opposition of substance capable of providing an alternative government.

Tanganyika

The former League of Nations mandate and United Nations trust territory of Tanganyika, a large but still mostly undeveloped country, obtained independence on December 9, 1961. The ruling party, Tanganyika African National Union (TANU), during the years prior to independence, had succeeded in taking under its wing almost all the politically active persons in the country, including Europeans; and one European, elected by a largely African constituency, had held office in the government from the beginning of the ministerial system. Although until a few years earlier Tanganyika had made almost no progress toward independence, in spite of criticism of the slow pace of progress from the United Nations, the end when it came was swift. Almost the entire credit for this rests with Julius Nyerere, the Prime Minister at independence and leader of the TANU, whose moderate and nonracial policies were designed to attract the support of a considerable white settler population, which elsewhere had consistently opposed the granting of responsible self-government to an African majority.

As late as 1955, all the British felt able to offer to Tanganyika was a Legislative Council made up of thirty-one persons (fourteen unofficial) pledged to support the policy of the government and thirty nominated by the governor, in the proportion of ten from each of the three peoples in the territory—Europeans, Asians, and Africans. These representatives were not required to support the government, but since they were nominated and not elected, there was clearly little scope for an African nationalist party. All it could do was agitate for further political reform and organize the party in preparation for the day when reform would be granted. It is true that the proportion of educated Africans was very small for the population, and it would have been extremely difficult to form an all-African government with an Africanized civil service; but it is not necessarily true that the best British policy was to try to build safeguards into the constitution that would ensure equal representation of all the races. When they tried to do this, Nyerere outsmarted them in a most disconcerting manner.

In 1958, the British devised an electoral scheme designed to ensure the election of equal numbers of each race to all the 30 seats formerly filled by nomination. The entire electorate, which under the severe property and educational qualifications in the territory amounted to only 61,000 persons, was given three votes each, all of which had to be cast, for members of different races, if the vote was to be valid. Nyerere thereupon invited members of all races to support TANU in exchange for its votes in the elections. Such was the discipline of the party and so successful was this maneuver that the African vote was sufficient to turn the tide for all Europeans and Asians who solicited its support.

Of the thirty elected members, ten from each race, twenty-eight were supporters of the TANU. The thirty-one members of the Legislative Council pledged to support the government would have been quite adequate if the elected members had belonged to different parties. But such a solid bloc of opposition votes, all promised to the same party, could not be ignored by the British, especially when Nyerere refused to enter the Executive Council and kept his party in opposition.

In December, 1959, the British enlarged the Legislative Council by providing fifty seats to be elected on a common roll—that is to say, by a predominantly African electorate—while reserving only twenty-one seats for Europeans, Asians, and one Arab. Africans for the first time constituted a majority on the Council. A few months later the Executive Council was converted into a Council of Ministers, including the usual three British civil servants (semi-responsible government). Provision was also made for a chief minister, though he would not preside over the Council. Nyerere, the obvious choice for the position, protested, but agreed to take it when his party won seventy of seventy-one seats in the elections of August 30, 1960. Meanwhile, Nyerere, with British support, requested the United Nations Trusteeship Council and the General Assembly to approve in advance the 1960 elections as indicative of public opinion in the territory and to waive the usual requirement of an election immediately prior to independence. This was granted, and there were no further electoral formalities before independence.

Since it was obvious that the TANU Government was as responsible as any government was likely to be in the territory, there was no evident reason why independence should be postponed. The new nation's economic and educational problems would remain, but would be best handled by a native independent government. In March, 1961, discussions were opened, and the British Colonial Secretary, Iain Macleod, announced at their close that the country would have full internal responsible self-government by May 1, with Julius Nyerere as Prime Minister presiding over a cabinet containing one Asian and two European ministers. All the British civil servants would leave the government unless the Prime Minister wished to retain them. Independence was promised for December 9, 1961, and came into effect on that date.

On January 22, 1962, Nyerere unexpectedly announced his resignation from his position as Prime Minister in favor of

Rashidj Kawawa, Minister Without Portfolio, to devote his full
time to the work of the TANU, of which he would remain
President. His departure from office proved to be only temporary,
since it was soon decided that Tanganyika would become a republic within the Commonwealth, with a president as head of
state. Against token opposition, Nyerere was elected to this
position and was given considerable discretionary powers, including the right to veto legislation. Kawawa was appointed Vice-
President and leader of government business in the National
Assembly when Tanganyika became a republic, on December 9,
1962.

Uganda

BUGANDA—A STATE WITHIN A STATE. The former British African
protectorate of Uganda became independent in October, 1962.
At least seven years before, the British had decided that the country should be prepared for independence as rapidly as possible.
They had always hoped that the three East African colonies of
Uganda, Kenya, and Tanganyika, which possess a considerable
number of common services, would find it possible to unite in a
confederation or even a federation; but they did not propose to
delay the independence of the individual segments until this union
could be arranged. Above all they wished to grant independence
to Uganda, which had few settlers, a viable and comparatively
prosperous economy, a fairly high proportion of educated persons,
for Africa, and strong traditional authorities who were still listened
to with respect. But the Africans presented obstacle after obstacle
to the organization of the artificial state of Uganda as an independent nation, and the British reacted more stubbornly and un-
imaginatively than elsewhere in Africa. More persons have been
jailed, detained, fined, and had their freedom of movement restricted in Uganda than in any other country in Africa except
Kenya and the Rhodesias, where European settlers have complicated the problem of granting independence.

The constitution finally agreed to, on the basis of which the
British granted independence, is full of pitfalls; and difficulties
cannot fail to rise in its operation. However, Uganda did become
an independent state, at least in form, and inherited the usual ap-
purtenances of sovereignty as a nation. But it has as yet in no way
become a nation, and few of its inhabitants have even begun to
acquire a sense of separate nationality. The National Assembly is

led by a prime minister, kept in office by the votes of the delegates from the kingdom of Buganda, whose first loyalty is to their own kingdom and its Kabaka. These delegates are not elected, but nominated by the Lukiko (parliament) of Buganda. They belong to a political party called the Kabaka Yekka (Kabaka Only).

The historical background of this strange situation was touched on in Chapter 4. All the explorers who visited the kingdom of Buganda in the nineteenth century remarked that it was a well-administered country and that the people had the greatest loyalty to their Kabaka. Most of these visitors treated the monarch with considerable deference, and Mutesa I was able by skillful diplomacy to keep his kingdom intact all his reign. His successor, Mwanga, was not so fortunate and was eventually left with no choice but to accept the "protection" of the British. The agreement of 1900 between the Kabaka of Buganda and the British left the Kabaka considerable powers, even though ultimate authority rested in the hands of the British.

Buganda, the largest and most powerful as well as the best organized of the kingdoms of Uganda, was only one of several kingdoms, including Bunyoro, which until the mid-eighteenth century had been larger than Buganda; and each of the kings signed a separate agreement with the British. Other areas in the country owed allegiance to lesser chiefs, who could not command the kind of devotion the kings could. The British ruled these areas more directly; and in them won some support for their policy of independence—Milton Obote, later Prime Minister, was from one of these areas.

Within Buganda, there had always been a few educated men who resented the strong influence exercised by the great chiefs in their kingdom. Although they had not wavered in their loyalty to the Kabaka himself, they objected to the fact that it was the chiefs who formed the overwhelming majority of the members of the Lukiko, which was thus in essence an advisory council of chiefs rather than a true parliament. If they themselves were unacceptable to the chiefs and the Kabaka, there was no political future for them in Buganda. For this reason, disturbances had been endemic in Buganda, since the chiefs were anxious to hold on to power as long as they could. Even so, few of these educated Baganda (the name for the people of Buganda) were ready to support a national administration over the Kabaka and to defy the latter's wishes, and it was very difficult for them to form a political party that acted against the wishes of the Kabaka and the chiefs.

Moreover, it was difficult indeed for a national party whose base was elsewhere than in Buganda to obtain members in Buganda unless the Kabaka approved their efforts. Thus at all times, Buganda was a state within a state and expected to do as it wished without interference from the Protectorate Government controlled by a distant and, from the Baganda point of view, ignorant, governor. If the Protectorate Government insisted on some action being taken by Buganda, the Kabaka usually agreed for the sake of maintaining amicable relations with the governor; but even so, many of his chiefs probably resented his apparent subservience, not recognizing the real power of the governor as well as did their master.

From the British point of view, relations with the independent-minded Baganda were not too unsatisfactory as long as they had no special policy of their own to pursue. The country was reasonably quiet, except for some local disturbances in Buganda in 1945 over wages and the insistence of the Protectorate Government on instituting a land policy suspected by the Baganda. Relatively few British officials were needed in Buganda, which was therefore comfortably able to pay its way. Indirect rule was justifying itself in providing an inexpensive administration largely in the hands of Africans, but in no way detrimental to British economic interests.

OPPOSITION AND EXILE OF THE KABAKA. But the trend in the British colonial empire was toward centralization, and without doubt the governmental system in Uganda was untidy. Membership in the usual Legislative and Executive councils was of interest only to Asians, who outnumbered the British, and to British unofficials. When the British after World War II wished to add Africans to the Legislative Council, they met with unexpected opposition from Buganda, whose leaders regarded the British-dominated Council as an exotic institution of no conceivable interest to themselves. The young Kabaka, Mutesa II, not wishing to offend either the British or his own people, neatly evaded the issue by appointing to the Council his own Katikkiro (Prime Minister), whose loyalty to Buganda was unquestioned. However, when more African members were added to the Legislative Council in 1949 and 1950, and he was asked for nominees, his Lukiko refused to make any appointments, claiming that it had never been contemplated in the protectorate agreement of 1900 that Buganda was to be part of some entity called Uganda. It was a nation in itself and sent no representatives anywhere but to its own parliament. The Kabaka, on this occasion, overruled the Lukiko and appointed another member, while a small group of dissident Baganda joined with members from other tribes to form a would-be national party called Uganda National Congress (UNC).

This was the situation when Sir Andrew Cohen became Governor of Uganda in 1952, pledged to put into effect a reorganization of the Protectorate Government that would set the country firmly on the road to independence. Such a reorganization was bound to consist in part of bringing Buganda more closely into the work of the central government; and though individual Baganda might be willing and anxious to take part in eventual national government, neither the Kabaka nor his chiefs in the Lukiko were interested. In order to oppose it by methods that the British could be expected to understand, yet that were peaceful and did not lay them open to reprisals, the Baganda leaders fell back on the law as represented in the original protectorate agreement of 1900. They claimed that Buganda had been an independent kingdom in 1900 and that its affairs were therefore the concern not of the Colonial Office, but of the Foreign Office, which dealt with independent nations. Moreover, it had never been contemplated in 1900 that the British would set up a government in Uganda in which the Baganda would be expected to play a part. It was therefore the decision of the Kabaka and his Lukiko that they would not prejudice their position further by choosing any Baganda members of the enlarged Legislative Council proposed by the Governor. They would also, it was implied, frown upon any attempt by the Governor to nominate Baganda members, who would be unrepresentative of the views of the kingdom. The most the Kabaka was willing to do was to democratize to some degree the electoral system for the election of the Lukiko and to accept some more British advisers whose work would be confined to Buganda.

Sir Andrew, after doing his best to persuade the Kabaka to modify his position, took the only course permitted him under the agreement. He withdrew recognition from the Kabaka, who was exiled to England. This action infuriated the entire Baganda people, including the politicians in the Uganda National Congress, whose leaders resented the domination of the chiefs in their own kingdom but were nevertheless loyal to the Kabaka. It was their hope that in due course the latter would consent to become a constitutional monarch, perhaps as head of the independent state of Uganda.

In the absence of the Kabaka, and without any representatives from Buganda or from two of the smaller kingdoms in Uganda, which also refused to send representatives, it was impossible to implement any further changes or to make the new Legislative Council function effectively. The Lukiko of Buganda, though continuing to govern Buganda as before, adopted an attitude of stubborn opposition to any cooperation with the central government until the return of the Kabaka. The British finally found they had no other recourse; however, they won the reluctant consent of the monarch to a change in the agreement of 1900, to which the Lukiko gave its consent—though, as later events proved, with reservations. The major changes accepted by the Kabaka were that in the future he would nominate the Baganda members of the Legislative Council and would rule constitutionally in his own kingdom through the medium of an indirectly elected Lukiko and regularly appointed ministers, chosen from the Lukiko.

The second promise was easy to carry out, since the chiefs still controlled the electorate and the Kabaka had never acted within Buganda as an absolute monarch. But the Kabaka appointed only UNC members as his representatives to the Legislative Council, thus effectively tying them to himself, not to the general policies of the party, which looked toward the independence of a self-governing, unitary Uganda. Once they were in the Legislative Council, they gave no further support to the idea of a unitary nation, thereby splitting the party down the middle. The non-Baganda members of the UNC, unable to win support in Buganda, experienced great difficulty in organizing themselves as an effective party, since there were no cities of substance and even few important villages outside Buganda. The work of organizing these areas was ultimately done by Prime Minister Milton Obote in 1959 through the medium of a new party, the Uganda People's Congress.

DEBATE OVER A FEDERAL GOVERNMENT. In 1959, a new Governor decided that all eighteen African members of the Legislative Council should be directly elected, in Buganda as elsewhere, and a Speaker should be chosen to preside over the Council. From the Baganda point of view, this meant that the British had determined to have an African-controlled central government which would eventually control all affairs of the country, including those of Buganda. The Lukiko therefore proclaimed that the new agreement of 1955 had been broken and unsuccessfully took the matter to court, demanding that the British grant Buganda independence as a separate state. When the British refused even to consider the petition seriously, the Lukiko passed a resolution calling upon the Kabaka to dissociate himself from all proposals for a self-governing Uganda. The other kingdoms, which had previously refused their cooperation, called upon their monarchs to do the same.

The action of the Lukiko stirred up opposition on all sides. The non-Baganda peoples who were anxious to play their part in a self-governing Uganda, objecting to its obstructionism, criticized quite justly the unrepresentative composition of the Lukiko, which though elected was still dominated by the chiefs. But they were powerless to take action in Buganda, where the government did not recognize political parties and refused to authorize elections. Since the British did not attempt to compel the acquiescence of either Buganda or the two other dissident kingdoms, only ten seats were contested, half of them falling to the UNC.

The new Legislative Council then set itself to decide, without the benefit of Baganda advice, how the state was to go forward to independence, while in Buganda itself, various disturbances and boycotts led the central government to declare Buganda a disturbed area. By no means all the Baganda agreed with the policy of the Lukiko, but very few would have settled for a strong influence in the policies of the central government in preference to the separate independence of Buganda. Underneath the whole controversy lay the undoubted fear of the Baganda that, in a unitary state in which they would not be in a majority, they would be dominated by persons they believed to be in all respects their inferiors. Moreover, they were seriously worried lest the solution be left to a national government of Africans after the state had already been granted independence. This fear was intensified after July, 1960, when chaos resulted in the Congo because the Belgians had postponed their decision on the crucial matter of the kind of state the Congo was to become until after independence. The idea of a federal state, which seemed to outsiders so obviously the only possible solution, was still not seriously contemplated in either Britain or Uganda.

In December, 1959, a committee of the new unrepresentative Legislative Council recommended a change in the constitution permitting an elected majority chosen by universal suffrage. To this the Lukiko adopted an attitude of uncompromising opposition. The British accepted the major part of the proposals, but had begun to doubt whether the unitary state so long desired by them could be imposed over the opposition of Buganda. They therefore established a Relationships Commission, headed by the Earl of Munster, to make recommendations on the future relation between the various kingdoms of Uganda and the central government. This did not prevent the Lukiko from taking the bull by the horns on December 31, 1960, and declaring Buganda an independent state, or from calling on all those who were loyal to the Kabaka to boycott the elections under the new constitution. However, it did not propose to prevent the elections from being held in Buganda if anyone wished to brave the displeasure of the Kabaka and his chiefs.

The declaration of independence was of course declared by the British to be illegal, and was obviously merely a gesture of defiance. But the election boycott was more than 90 per cent effective. The few who dared to cast their votes expressed their preference for a small, hitherto little-noticed, largely Catholic party known as the Democratic Party. The altogether nonsensical result was that the Democratic Party, which had some scattered support elsewhere, won the most seats in the Assembly by virtue of the fact that it won twenty of the twenty-one available in Buganda, and its leader became Chief Minister. The other parties, which won far more votes in the country as a whole, were forced to go into opposition.

The new central government, headed by its Democratic Chief Minister, who was himself from Buganda and a member of the Lukiko, began its term of office in April, 1961; but it was only a caretaker government until the Munster Commission could report. The report itself was a masterpiece of constitutional virtuosity. It recommended that Buganda enjoy a federal relationship with Uganda, while the other three kingdoms should have a semifederal relationship. The other districts in the country, not having traditional rulers, were not to be permitted either a "federal" or "semifederal" relationship, but if they wished they might institute a "ceremonial head of state." Buganda was "required" to be represented in the National Assembly, either by direct or indirect election at its option. In return, the National Assembly should have no power to make laws concerning the traditional structure of Buganda except by consent of the latter, but in exchange for these concessions, Buganda must hold direct elections for its own assembly (the Lukiko).

At the new constitutional conference held in October, 1961, agreement was at last reached. Uganda was to become internally self-governing (responsible government) in March, 1962, and independent on October 9, 1962. Buganda agreed to accept the federal relationship with the central government, and the Lukiko was granted the right to choose all members of the Buganda delegation to the central House of Assembly. Buganda also agreed to the direct election of 68 members of the 100-member Lukiko, the remainder being chiefs or the Kabaka's nominees. As usual under British federal governments in the colonies, a list was drawn up distinguishing between the areas in which the central and regional governments were both permitted to legislate, and those in which one or the other held the exclusive right to legislate. Buganda, but not the other kingdoms, was treated in exactly the same manner as the component parts of other federations, the unique feature of Uganda being that Buganda alone enjoys the advantage of a federal status and is thus a state within a state, rather than a province in a federation.

FINAL ELECTIONS AND INDEPENDENCE. Continuing to display their unmatched appreciation of political realities, the Baganda leaders now formed a party in Buganda that was certain to be unbeatable in the elections for the Lukiko under the new democratic system. This party took the name of the Kabaka Yekka (Kabaka only), and its sole aim was to defeat all candidates who did not believe in the Kabakaship. This move at once deprived the Democratic Party of the opportunity of winning a single seat in Buganda at the next general elections, since the Lukiko had the right to nominate all Baganda members of the National Assembly, and it was certain to be dominated by the Kabaka Yekka Party. All other minor parties in Buganda, whose members wished to have a chance of being chosen for the National Assembly, at once agreed to merge with Kabaka Yekka.

In February, 1962, sixty-five of the sixty-eight elected seats in the Lukiko fell to the Kabaka Yekka. The remaining three, all in counties claimed by the Bunyoro kingdom, went to Democratic candidates. At the ensuing general election for the National Assembly, the Democratic Party won only twenty-four seats, and the Uganda People's Congress led by Obote won thirty-eight. The Lukiko chose as representatives of Buganda only members of the Kabaka Yekka, who thereupon joined the UPC in a coalition government in which they held the balance of power. The former Chief Minister and leader of the Democratic Party was completely frozen out of the election. As a Muganda (name for individual Baganda), he could win a seat only by choice of the Lukiko and its Kabaka

Yekka majority. Fortunately for Obote, he was a Lango, not a Muganda, and could become the new Prime Minister and co-operate freely with his Kabaka Yekka colleagues, never having been in the position of being compelled to make a choice such as had fallen to his unhappy predecessor. Under this new government, Uganda became independent on the promised date of October 9, 1962. Late in 1963, it was announced that the Kabaka of Buganda had agreed to fill the purely ceremonial office of President of the Republic of Uganda, thereby signifying his personal acceptance of the existence of the new state against which he had fought so long.

It should be added that a special commission of the Privy Council recommended the cession of two of Bunyoro's lost provinces by Buganda, while allowing the latter to keep the remaining four. This settlement was accepted by Bunyoro but adamantly refused by Buganda. The British Colonial Secretary was forced to hand down a decision under which the central government would administer the provinces for two years, after which a referendum would be held to determine whether they would belong to Bunyoro, Buganda, or the central government. Both kingdoms protested, and the quarrel added a sour note to the otherwise joyful independence celebrations.

Zanzibar

The two tiny states of Zanzibar and Gambia each have populations of about 300,000. Until recently, Britain would never have even contemplated full independence for either, though she was prepared to grant complete internal self-government to each. But she could not hold on to the territories indefinitely. Arrangements were made to grant both states independence, in the hope that Zanzibar will join in a proposed East African Federation, and that Gambia will be able after independence to find her suitable place within a French-speaking Greater Senegal.

The protected state of Zanzibar, consisting of the two islands of Zanzibar and Pemba, had been ruled by a Sultan who accepted the advice of a British Resident. Until 1957, there was little constitutional advance. The Sultan presided over the Executive Council, while the British Resident presided over the Legislative Council. British officials comprised the majority in each council, and no members of either were elected. In that year, the British decided some elements of democracy should be introduced into Zanzibar by having some members elected to the councils. Two parties formed to fight in the elections, one dominated by Africans (called the Afro-Shirazi Party, or ASP), the other by Arabs (the Nationalist Party). Within the Afro-Shirazi Party, there is a strong minority of Shirazis claiming descent from the original Persian settlers in the island who, in spite of the intermarriage of their ancestors with the Africans, regard themselves as a distinct people with interests often differing from those of the pure Africans. Since the Africans and Shirazis numbered some 200,000 and the Arabs only 44,000 in 1957, the Afro-Shirazi Party won most of the seats available for election. There was as yet no sense of urgency, and few had any thought that the British were contemplating democratic self-government for the near future.

The Arabs constitute a powerful minority in the country and own close to 90 per cent of the usable land. They have always regarded the Africans as inferior, the descendants of men and women who less than a century ago were their slaves. As long as there was a high qualification for voters, their own privileged position was secure, but the British elsewhere had extended the franchise and would surely do so some day in Zanzibar. A number of Arabs concluded that their best hope was to give political leadership to the Africans. These men believed that it might be possible to persuade the electorate to vote along other than racial lines and insisted that all the people of Zanzibar were Zanzibaris first and Africans and Arabs second.

In 1959, when the British proposed new elections under a wider franchise, the question became urgent. The Nationalist Party had succeeded in enrolling a number of non-Arabs, but it was faced by a strongly racialist African Party from which many of those who claimed Shirazi ancestry were in the process of separating. Both parties were dissatisfied with the proposed constitutional changes; and when their representatives in the council demanded more drastic reforms, the British, after sending out a commission, agreed to increase the Legislative Council to twenty-one elected members and to institute a ministerial system under a chief minister (semi-responsible government).

Elections under the new system were held in January, 1961. By this time the Afro-Shirazi Party had split, and many of the Shirazis had formed their own party, though the earlier party continued to keep the name of Shirazi in its title. The election resulted—by a single vote in a single constituency—in a plurality for the Afro-Shirazi Party, which held ten seats to the nine won by the Nationalist Party. The breakaway party, the Zanzibar and Pemba People's

Party (ZPPP), won three, and with them the balance of power. It proved extremely difficult for the Resident to form even a coalition government, since the three representatives of the ZPPP divided once more as soon as the four ministries were to be allocated. In the end, the two major parties had one ministry each, and two of the three members of the ZPPP held the other two. Obviously, a new election must be held as quickly as possible; a constitutional change was made—the addition of one seat to the Legislative Council—in hopes of resolving the deadlock. For this election, the ZPPP formed a definite electoral alliance with the Nationalist Party.

The elections held in June, 1961, were marked by widespread fighting between Africans and Arabs resulting in sixty-eight dead, mostly Arabs. The ZPPP won the same three seats as before. The Afro-Shirazi and Nationalist parties each won ten, but the Afro-Shirazi Party's vote exceeded by more than 1,000 the votes of the other two parties combined—a result, so the Afro-Shirazi leaders claimed, of gerrymandering in the island of Pemba. The Nationalist leader, on being invited to become Chief Minister, deferred to the ZPPP leader, who thus became Chief Minister, presiding over a coalition from which almost all Zanzibaris of pure African ancestry were excluded.

During the course of 1962 and 1963, the British took important steps to remedy the grievances of the Afro-Shirazi Party by granting virtual universal suffrage and compiling new voters' rolls, at the same time instituting precautions against fraud. Despite continued disagreement between the parties on the timing of further constitutional advances, the British granted responsible government in June, 1963, and held elections the following month. During the election campaign it became clear that the ZNP-ZPPP alliance, after two years' experience in governing, was in better shape to fight the election, and that racial considerations were no longer as important as hitherto. It was therefore not surprising when the coalition won by a comfortable majority, thus earning the right to carry the small state forward to independence (December 10, 1963). The question of the projected East African Federation—more favored by the opposition ASP than by the government parties— was still undecided at the time of writing.

There have been sporadic demands by all parties in Zanzibar for the return of the Coastal Strip (now part of Kenya), for which the British, under an agreement of 1895, still pay the Sultan of Zanzibar an annual rental. With Kenya's independence, it is

hoped that Zanzibar will be willing to cede the territory outright
to Kenya in exchange for a monetary payment—of which she is
greatly in need. Kenya obviously cannot return the Strip to
Zanzibar, since it contains Mombasa, her only seaport, and the
terminus of the railroad through Kenya to Uganda—though if
Zanzibar entered the proposed Federation some compromise could
probably be arranged without difficulty on the question of sovereignty over the Strip. In previous years, Egyptians and other
foreign Muslims, as well as the Communist powers, backed the
demands of Zanzibar against the British. But with Kenya an independent state, the problem has resolved itself into a purely
financial one, and is no longer likely to cause any trouble or offer
scope for Cold War political propaganda.

Gambia

There are no racial or settler problems in the small colony and
protectorate of Gambia; if she were not so small and her economy
were not so unviable, Gambia would surely be independent by
now. Her constitutional advance moved at the same pace as that
of Sierra Leone, and she obtained representative government by
1954. But when it came to granting a full ministerial system with a
chief minister and other expensive luxuries, the British balked,
since the total revenue of the territory was less than £1.5 million.
The Governor's frequent lectures to the Legislative Council on
the subject of fiscal responsibility in no way lessened the Gambians' sense of grievance at the fact that they were not even granted
semiresponsible government while the rest of Africa was winning
independence. When the British Colonial Secretary visited the
country in June, 1959, some stones were thrown in the hope of
speeding reform. In the end, the British permitted a ministerial
system; but ministers, for the sake of fiscal rectitude, would have
to be content with "generous" allowances and not salaries. There
would be only ordinary ministers, not a chief minister. The
Legislative Council was then renamed the House of Representatives, and its membership increased from twenty-one to thirty-four,
twenty-seven being elected under universal franchise and three
nominated. The Executive Council was enlarged to permit six
elected or nominated ministers plus four British civil servants.
This at last was semiresponsible government (September, 1959).

In the subsequent election, the People's Progressive Party won
all twelve seats allotted to the Protectorate, while another party

won five of seven seats allotted to the more advanced colony—a situation not unlike that of Sierra Leone. But when the British decided the following year to appoint a Chief Minister, the Governor chose P. S. N'Jie, the leader of the opposition United Party, believing that he would be able to command greater support in the House of Representatives, since party discipline was still very weak among the House members. Later in the same year (1961), it was decided that by May, 1962, the country should have full responsible internal self-government, though independence was still not promised. It was evident that revenue would continue indefinitely to fall short of expenditure by more than £.5 million. Again the question of union with Senegal was ventilated, but the Gambian ministers desired independence first so as to be able to talk with the Senegalese as "equals." The election was duly fought, with the PPP obtaining eighteen of thirty-two seats. This meant that David Jawara, a former veterinary officer, could not again be passed over in favor of the leader of the opposition. He therefore became Premier.

Soon after taking office, Jawara began discussions with Senegal, resulting in an agreement in principle for a union between the two countries, under which Senegal would assume the burden of meeting the budgetary deficits of the colony. But this merger, which might appear to be the obvious solution to the problem of an unviable colony, and which would give Senegal the use of a navigable river and valuable port facilities, would give rise to numerous short-run difficulties. Few Gambians speak French, the administrative and legal systems are British, and large numbers of Gambians, quite possibly a majority, are reluctant to see themselves swallowed up by a neighbor, in spite of African tribal affinities with many Senegalese. Jawara's conversations with the Senegalese were severely criticized by the opposition, and his own party split into two over the question.

Following further discussions with the British, it was decided to grant Gambia her independence in the near future, thus giving her a chance to get along on her own. The opportunity to win economic help from other countries, which is often forthcoming for independent states but not for colonies, may save her from having to unite with Senegal. But the inescapable fact remains that with what is virtually a one-crop economy, peanuts (also the major crop of Senegal), she can never become a viable state, and the administrative expenses of running an independent state will eat up all available revenue. Although attempts at diversification have been made in the past, they have either been hamstrung by local conservatism, or proved impossible in the climate and soil of Gambia. Gambia seems to be an example of a country whose outright independence should not be encouraged—as Britain, indeed, always discouraged it. But Britain was not prepared to resist the demand for independence indefinitely when it had the immense advantage of allowing her to divest herself of a financial burden, as well as of her last—and quite useless—colony in West Africa.

Kenya

THE SETTLER PROBLEM. Before it is possible to understand the slow pace of constitutional advance in Kenya, it is necessary to add some further details to the material in Chapter 4. Kenya is a country whose economic development has depended to a very large degree upon the capital and initiative of Europeans, and to a lesser degree on Asians. From the early years of the century, Europeans began to enter Kenya as permanent immigrants, intending to live on the land, not in the cities, as was the custom elsewhere. By the 1930's, there were approximately 10,000 living on about 10,000 of a total of some 70,000 square miles of cultivable land, mostly in the "White Highlands," from which Africans were excluded unless they were employed by Europeans. As a rule, they held their estates on 999-year leases, and grew such crops as coffee, tobacco, and pyrethrum, which were sold in foreign markets and were the basis for what prosperity the country has known. Not all of them succeeded, and many in the course of the years lost their capital investment; the successful ones had not only invested their capital, but exercised unremitting care and experimented persistently under conditions they had never experienced before. Thus they came to feel that it was they, and they alone, who had developed the country, neglecting altogether the role played by the Africans whom they employed to do the actual manual work. It was unthinkable that an African-dominated government should ever be permitted to impose crippling taxes on them, much less dispossess them.

Nevertheless, the Europeans owned far more land than they profitably used. Their great estates were run in a manner not unlike European medieval baronies, and they were able to enjoy a style of living impossible elsewhere in the world. It was this aspect of their presence in Kenya that most offended the Africans, especially the perennially land-hungry Kikuyu, by far the largest single tribe in the country. They could not see why they could not follow the European example of growing money-making crops for export, if they had the land and could acquire the capital. Yet the Kenyan Government prohibited them from growing certain crops for export, even on their own lands, on the grounds that Africans would not grade them properly and would thus damage the reputation of Kenyan export crops in the world market.

At the time of European entry into the country, the Highlands were not occupied by the Kikuyu—perhaps only temporarily as Kikuyu spokesmen have urged in recent years. It is indeed possible that they had fled before the raids of warlike Masai tribesmen, some of whom were found in the Highlands by the entering Europeans, and that someday they would have returned had not the Europeans pre-empted the land. However this may be, it is undoubtedly true that European medicine, sanitation, and stable government have succeeded in lowering the Kikuyu death rate to such an extent that the land shortage is now very severe. Even if the entire White Highlands were added to the Kikuyu area, there would still not be enough to satisfy African land hunger. Some of the land not in actual use by Europeans was recently opened for African settlement. Although it was only a small percentage, the process was bitterly opposed by most of the Europeans in Kenya, since it appeared to them to open the way toward the total loss of their properties. It was, they claimed, only on the strength of a British guarantee of permanent possession that they sank their capital and energies into its development.

The British Government, with the whole of its colonial system to consider, had interests in the colony different from those of the settlers. Before World War II, it usually allowed the settlers to determine policy, even though they were never granted a majority in either the Legislative or Executive councils. But it soon ceased to be politically possible to neglect African grievances altogether. When a widespread terrorist movement known as Mau Mau began to take direct action against the settlers and moderate Africans, they were compelled to take a long, hard look at the colony and its future. Obviously, the Africans outnumbered the Europeans and Asians so overwhelmingly that they could not be kept indefinitely from the majority rule they were already winning elsewhere in Africa. The notion that Africans were forever doomed to be in a subordinate position in their own country because they were inferior was belied by the fact that the British elsewhere were giving increasing governmental responsibilities, and even independence, to other Africans of the same Bantu people. The British Government could not indefinitely refuse to heed world opinion, which approved the African independence movements so overwhelmingly; and it was difficult to counter the argument that the Africans were being kept from advancement simply because the economic interests of the settlers so dictated.

Thus in recent years, there has been a bitter quarrel in both Kenya and Rhodesia between the settlers, who think they are being betrayed, and successive British governments, which have felt it necessary to give concessions to the Africans, bring them into the government, and promise ultimate independence. Although Africans are divided among themselves, mainly along tribal lines, all Africans are agreed that the British pace has never been fast enough; and very few indeed have much use for the settlers, except for those few who are willing to be ruled by Africans and to continue to contribute their services to the economy after independence. The British wished to see Kenya with a multiracial government similar to that of Tanganyika prior to independence. They tried with a great deal of ingenuity to tie African hands in such a way that certain rights would be guaranteed to Europeans under the constitution, and that they would be represented in government councils. But most settlers felt bitterly sure that the Africans, by one means or another, would free themselves from such restrictions once they were independent and that paper safeguards would prove valueless. They believed that expropriation was virtually certain in the long run. Having never placed any trust in the Africans when they themselves were supreme in the country, it is virtually impossible for them now to learn to entrust themselves to their tender mercies. For this reason, they are now trying to persuade the British Government to compensate them for their losses if they sell, or guarantee them financially against expropriation.

The African nationalists are naturally unwilling to saddle themselves with an immense debt and will not speak of any specific sum that they will give as compensation. Meanwhile, many of the settlers have already left, taking as many of their assets with them as possible. Others have even threatened to "scorch" their earth before leaving, if they are compelled to go. The spectacle of two major African parties quarreling among themselves, each unable to form a government without the other—a situation that lasted for more than a year—did not reassure them. When the elections held in May, 1963, brought to power a responsible government led by Jomo Kenyatta, whom almost all settlers regarded as the inspiration, if not the actual leader, of Mau Mau, they knew their long battle was lost, and that they either had to leave the country or readjust themselves to living in a world different from what they had hitherto known. Faced with this decision, and Kenyatta's obvious desire to be conciliatory, considerable numbers of European farmers decided to take their chances and stay. Even some of those who had already sold their land made application to buy it back. Since the prosperity of the country in large measure depends on the continued presence of Europeans, there are far more grounds for optimism than could have been imagined less than a year ago.

STAGES OF CONSTITUTIONAL ADVANCE. The advance of Kenya toward independence has progressed through three well-defined stages since World War II. During the first period, lasting until the outbreak of the Mau Mau rebellion, in late 1952, the white settlers were able to maintain their privileged position virtually intact. The second stage saw a number of efforts by the British to draw some "reliable" Africans into the government, while at the same time discouraging the growth of African nationalist political parties, which, they feared, might incite the revival of Mau Mau terrorism. The third stage was marked by the final recognition that independence under African rule was inevitable, and by successive doses of constitutional reform, combined with an effort to persuade the Africans to take the Europeans into some form of partnership.

The leader of the first stage of African agitation was a Kikuyu named Jomo Kenyatta, an educated African who had written a widely admired anthropological book on his own people. Returning to Africa after World War II, he founded a party known as the Kenya African Union (KAU). There was as yet little that such a party could achieve, since as late as 1952, the six Africans in the Legislative Council were all nominated. The Europeans (ten), Asians (six), and Arab (one) were all elected by their own communities. Some of these were allowed to run various government departments, but the most important portfolios were still held by British civil servants, and there was an official majority in both Executive and Legislative councils. Some KAU members, frustrated by their impotence, became involved in oath-taking ceremonies of a peculiarly revolting kind, designed to maintain unity in a conspiracy that was hatched by extremist elements in the country. It has never been proved that the KAU as an organization was directly involved, and numerous Africans refused to take the oath or join the conspiracy. Once the rebellion had broken out, these were the most frequent victims, since they prevented the terrorist leaders from making it a mass movement to drive out or kill all the Europeans in the colony.

The Mau Mau rebellion erupted late in 1952. Settlers were murdered, usually under atrocious circumstances, a state of emergency was proclaimed, and British troops were brought in from abroad. The state of emergency in a British colony suspends for the period of its duration any constitutional guarantees that may exist, as for example, habeas corpus. The governor may issue decrees for the purpose of maintaining law and order; suspected terrorists and other possibly dangerous persons may be held in detention indefinitely without trial. Freedom of speech and assembly is likewise suspended, and political parties function only at the discretion of the governor. The state of emergency in Kenya lasted until January, 1960. For a period of more than seven years, the government had an absolutely free hand to deal as it wished with African nationalists and other potential troublemakers. Jomo Kenyatta himself was convicted of complicity in the Mau Mau murders. Since actual murder could not be traced to him, he was condemned to only seven years imprisonment. The KAU was proscribed and dissolved.

There are many views on the question of how far Kenyatta himself, apparently a highly civilized as well as educated man, was involved, since the circumstances of the trial hardly favored the rendering of an impartial verdict. But the two most important single results of Mau Mau were undoubtedly the elevation of Kenyatta himself to the rank of a martyr, and a change in the British attitude toward African aspirations. Many Africans had allowed themselves to be tortured and killed rather than join in the Mau Mau atrocities, and most Africans condemned its violent methods. Although it was no longer possible to ignore the fact that the Africans had genuine grievances, it was still difficult to know just what could be done, beyond getting rid of some minor irritants. In the inflamed state of public opinion both in Britain and Kenya, it was close to a political impossibility to make any concessions that gave anything of real substance to the Africans; all concessions had to be tentative, hedged around with safeguards against their misuse, and thus were little calculated to win African approval. Indeed, in the years since Mau Mau, many Africans who did not support the movement at the time have come not only to condone it but regard it as a great attempt at self-assertion on the part of the African majority without which there would never have been any reforms at all.

The first advance was the Lyttleton Constitution of 1954, which set up a Council of Ministers, including one of the nominated Africans, while keeping the composition of the Legislative Council as before the rebellion. The Africans regarded this change with apprehension rather than gratitude. With three European and two Asian ministers chosen from among the elected members of the Legislative Council, it seemed to them to be a step toward a settler government. Few were pacified by the promise of a commission to look into the matter of how Africans could be elected at some future date. But the commission set to work, and under a complex electoral formula, a relatively small number of Africans were given in 1957 the opportunity to chose eight members of the Legislative Council. In spite of the fact that no political parties were yet permitted to function, all eight members who were elected pledged themselves to oppose the constitution; all those Africans who had previously allowed themselves to be nominated, including the one minister, were defeated. The new members at once called for further constitutional advance and refused to accept any position in the government. Thus the Council of Ministers now had no Africans in it, and it was clear that a multiracial government could not be wished upon the country by such means as had hitherto been tried.

For a time the Council of Ministers attempted to operate without any Africans, while the elected members sometimes boycotted the Legislative Council and sometimes used it as a forum for their political views. At last, the European and Asian ministers resigned, making a new constitution necessary. A. T. Lennox-Boyd, the Colonial Secretary, then tried a different method of obtaining his multiracial government. Fourteen Africans were now to be elected, giving them parity with the Europeans, while the Asians retained the same number as before. But all the elected members and the British civil servants, sitting as an electoral college, were given the opportunity to choose a further twelve "specially elected" members, four from each community. This meant that there would now be four new African members, who would have been chosen by a predominantly non-African electorate. Such men would be moderates and could, if necessary, hold the position of ministers in case the elected Africans refused to serve.

Whereas most of the Europeans accepted the new constitution

as a means by which a façade of African participation was assured, the African nationalists objected, since they were to be robbed of their most potent weapon, refusal to serve in the Council of Ministers. The directly elected African members, including the new ones, refused their cooperation in advance, and took no part in the election of the "special members," who were thus chosen entirely by non-Africans and represented no one in the African community. Only one African, a "special member," became a minister. He obtained the full cooperation of the Europeans and was notably successful in his task as Minister of Housing, though it blighted his future political career. The other position intended to be filled by an African was temporarily left vacant.

The new constitution produced two apparent victories for the cause of racial cooperation. A new multiracial party, the New Kenya Party (NKP), was organized by Michael Blundell, pledged to work with Africans. The party accepted the fact that independence could not be far off, but was anxious to prevent the nationalists (often spoken of by the settlers as African racialists) from winning a monopoly of the independence movement. The other result was the splitting of the hitherto monolithic group of the directly elected members. Eight of these men revolted against their leadership and decided to give a limited cooperation to the government in the hopes of winning some immediate reforms, such as integrated schools and equality of economic opportunity. The elected members pledged to noncooperation formed the nearest to a political party permitted under the continuing state of emergency. They fought hard for a further measure of constitutional advance and the abolition of the "specially elected" members. In due course, under a new Colonial Secretary in England, their pleas were heard, and what was to prove the most crucial of Kenyan constitutional conferences was held in January and February, 1960.

At this conference, the British, still believing that the only hope for the future lay in multiracialism, systematically favored Blundell's NKP, although it had little support among either Africans or Europeans. The resulting constitution was written in such a manner that he and his party would have every chance of making a good showing at the polls. At the conference, the African elected members worked together, even choosing Ronald Ngala, one of the dissident minority, as their spokesman. Tom Mboya, the leading politician from the majority, accepted the compromise with many reservations and on his return to Africa stated publicly that his group would continue to press for early independence. Under the new constitution, twenty seats would be reserved for members of the European and Asian community, but they would be elected on a common roll, that is, by a predominantly African electorate except in one or two constituencies. To ensure that no member was elected without some support from his own community, all candidates must first receive 25 per cent of the vote in a primary election of their own community. If this percentage were attained, then both candidates in the primary would go forward to the general election, where the huge African vote would be the deciding factor. Blundell himself received just over 26 per cent of the vote in his own primary, whereas his opponent, the leader of the major European party, received about 76 per cent. Evidently a few electors voted for both! In the general election, as expected, the European primary winners were overwhelmingly defeated by the African vote, and Blundell and most of his NKP colleagues were therefore declared elected. Three of the Europeans in the NKP could not win even the necessary 25 per cent in their primary, thereby giving their seats automatically to the right-wing settlers' party.

THE KANU-KADU STRUGGLE. The lifting of the state of emergency in January, 1960, enabled the Africans at last to form political parties on a countrywide basis. At once, the tribal antagonism that underlay the ephemeral façade of African unity burst into the open. Two major African political parties were soon formed—Kenya African National Union (KANU), and Kenya African Democratic Union (KADU). The KANU was largely made up of Kikuyu and Luo (Mboya, its General Secretary, is a Luo), while the KADU, led by Ngala, took in most of the other tribes, including a majority of the Masai leaders who had hitherto played no part in Kenya politics. For a time, both parties united in demanding the release of Kenyatta, who had served his sentence but was still held in detention in the north, claiming him as the one national leader who could lead the people to independence. But the Governor refused to release him before the election. When this resulted in a plurality for the KANU with eighteen seats against twelve held by the KADU, the KANU decided to press harder for Kenyatta's release and made it a condition of taking office in the Council of Ministers, which under the new constitution was required to contain four African, one Asian, and three European elected members in addition to the usual British civil servants. The KADU, after sending delegations to visit Kenyatta, continued to call for his release, but soon declared itself willing to participate in the new government, recognizing that the twelve seats it had won had resulted from gerrymandered electoral districts rather than popular approval (550,000 votes for KANU, 150,000 for KADU). It might be the last chance for a minority party to take over the reins of government and show the British that there was an African party willing to work both with them and with the moderate Europeans.

Both the two moderate parties, the KADU and the NKP, were strengthened when the Legislative Council voted for the dozen specially elected (renamed "national") members, who were retained under the new constitution; but, even so, the KADU still held far fewer seats than the KANU. The NKP was more successful, ending up with seven members as against three members of Kenya Coalition, the right-wing settlers' party. Soon afterward, Ngala became leader of government business, and three of his colleagues were given ministries. NKP members were given the ministries reserved for Europeans.

Although the Governor continued to resist pressure to release Kenyatta, this step was finally taken in August, 1961. For a brief honeymoon period, Kenyatta did his best to bring the two African parties together, but the differences between them proved too great to bridge. Despairing of becoming national leader of both parties, he finally accepted the presidency of the KANU. Shortly afterward, he was elected to the Legislative Council to replace a KANU member, who had resigned to give him the vacancy.

Meanwhile, the government under Ronald Ngala, who now had the title of Chief Minister, had been trying to function; but for various reasons he had lost most of his Asian support, and some Europeans deserted the government on specific issues. Several times government policy was pushed through only with the aid of a group of ministers nominated by the Governor who had to vote as he wished. Clearly, in spite of the experience some Africans were gaining in the role of ministers, this was no preparation for independence. Therefore, a new constitutional conference was held in February, 1962, to determine what further steps could be taken that might lead to the election of a government of national unity and, as the Africans hoped, to the setting of a definite date for independence.

At this conference, the KADU put forward the idea of a semi-federal state with strong powers in the regions, whereas the KANU offered a strong bill of rights which would guarantee their rights to all minorities. When no agreement could be reached between the two parties, the Colonial Secretary, Reginald Maudling, suggested a combination of the two proposals, including six regional authorities with strong powers in local matters and an upper house of parliament with representatives from all tribes and each of the thirty-eight existing administrative districts. This upper house would have powers strong enough to prevent the violation of any constitutional safeguards, including the disposition of land in the White Highlands (now called Scheduled Areas). A true coalition government with both KADU and KANU members was to be formed at once.

When the conferees returned to Kenya, having agreed in principle to Mr. Maudling's solution, a new ministry was formed without a chief minister, both Kenyatta and Ngala as party leaders holding identical positions as Ministers of State with responsibility for constitutional affairs. All the portfolios in the ministry were then divided equally between the two parties, even to the extent that the parliamentary secretaries of each minister belonged to the other party.

INDEPENDENCE AND PROSPECTS FOR THE FUTURE. This coalition, under the supervision of Governor Sir Patrick Renison, governed the country until a semifederal constitution was written, the longest constitution (223 pages) ever granted to any British colony. The constitution included a number of safeguards for the rights of minorities. However, procedures for amending the constitution were agreed to only verbally by the leaders of the two major parties. Much depends on whether these verbal agreements are adhered to, since the party that won the elections of May, 1953, is the antifederal party, and agreed to the federal clauses only under protest. The constitution established seven regional governments with Regional Assemblies, and a federal Senate to which forty districts and the city of Nairobi send one member each. The establishment of these regions was the price that had to be paid by the predominantly Kikuyu KANU to win agreement to the constitution as a whole from KADU and the British. But the regions will be very expensive to maintain as separate governmental units, and the shortage of educated Africans and their limited administrative experience may make them unworkable. In this event, KANU, which can muster a majority of approximately two to one in the central House of Representatives, will be under considerable pressure to amend the constitution. KANU, however, with nineteen of forty-one members, does not have an over-all majority in the Senate. Under the verbal accord achieved with KADU before the elections, its present majority is far from enough to enable it to amend the constitution.

Constitutional talks to give a final form to the pre-independence constitution took place in September, 1963, and independence was scheduled for December 12, 1963. A new British Governor, Malcolm MacDonald, son of the former British Prime Minister Ramsay MacDonald, the most famous of British colonial trouble shooters, was sent to ease the transition. It should be noted that the Somali region boycotted the election altogether. It elected no Regional Assembly, and no members in the federal House of Representatives or the Senate. However, not all the Somalis, who number about 200,000 in Kenya, are included in the northern region. The other Somalis are therefore "represented" by candidates from other races in other regions.

The decisive victory of Kenyatta and KANU at the polls had a calming effect on all classes in the country. Although KANU was expected to win, the decisive nature of the victory, demonstrating support for Kenyatta as the charismatic leader in so many non-Kikuyu areas of the country, was a surprise. But it was almost certainly a salutary victory, since the opposition can no longer claim with confidence to be the spokesman for the rights of minor tribes, fearful of being intimidated by the Kikuyu. Nor can the Europeans deny the appeal of Kenyatta and say that he speaks only for his tribe. The elections, held in a calm atmosphere under universal adult suffrage, demonstrated that he had respectable country-wide support. Yet, the victory was not so overwhelming that he can afford to neglect altogether the wishes of the opposition, which controls three of the Regional Assemblies as well as having forty-one members in the central House of Representatives.

The long struggle for independence and the persistent opposition of the settlers to each African advance have in the process provided the Kenyan Africans with far more experience in working together than most African nationalists enjoyed prior to their independence. It may even be that the condescension of the settlers and their frequently voiced contempt for African efforts have put Africans on their mettle. It is a fact, for instance, that African-grown tea and coffee from small peasant holdings have commanded prices on the world market higher than the Europeans have been able to win for the produce grown on their estates. If enough Europeans accept African rule, and remain in the country to prevent the collapse of their sector of the economy, it is not impossible that a truly multiracial state will come into being. The British hoped to achieve this by political manipulation, but failed in the face of African intelligence and intransigence. But if the multiracial nation comes into being as part of a normal evolutionary process, it can yet provide a lesson for Southern Rhodesia and the Portuguese overseas provinces, where Europeans have continued to resist the process by all means at their disposal.

The British Problem Child—The Federation of Rhodesia and Nyasaland

Formation of the Federation

The Federation of Rhodesia and Nyasaland presents to the British and the world an even more intractable problem than did Kenya. The reason for this is the unfortunate fact that, unlike in Kenya, the settlers were permitted by the British to govern Southern Rhodesia as a "self-governing colony." The settlers have run the government since 1923, and have no intention of voluntarily relinquishing their power. In Southern Rhodesia, in 1923, Europeans alone were given the vote, sat in the Assembly, and filled all the places in the government. By granting self-government at that epoch when no one as yet had given any serious thought to the possibility that Africans would some day be able to govern themselves, the British effectively cut themselves off from the opportunity to exercise the power and influence they have always wielded in their other colonies. They retained only two safeguards of significance: the right to disallow legislation which they considered discriminatory toward Africans, which was abandoned late in 1962, and the right to change the constitution, a power which they retain in every colony until independence. On several occasions since 1923, they might legally have disallowed legislation, since it has sometimes obviously been discriminatory, especially in the field of land tenure. But they refrained from doing so, and in fact left the whole field of legislation to the colonists.

The constitution of the Federation formed in 1953 granted to the central government almost the same powers as those granted to Southern Rhodesia in 1923; and it was almost as difficult for the Africans to exercise any moderating influence on federal policies as it was in Southern Rhodesia. In exchange for their participation in the Federation, the "protected persons" of the two protectorates of Nyasaland and Northern Rhodesia were given an African Affairs Board which was permitted the right to scrutinize legislation introduced by the federal government and, if it were discriminatory, "reserve" it until Her Majesty's pleasure had been determined; that is, until the British Parliament voted on it. In 1957, Parliament, led by a Conservative majority, passed a crucial measure involving the federal franchise which had been reserved by the Board. The Africans thereafter regarded the Board as a piece of window dressing with no effective powers; from that time onward, few placed any further trust in safeguards, preferring to fight for a franchise which will enable them to control the government. The settlers drew the same conclusions. They, too, were not prepared to accept paper safeguards if the Africans should ever be in a position to dominate them.

Until after World War II, Northern Rhodesia and Nyasaland were ruled as protectorates by British officials, and there was little demand by Africans for any change. They felt sympathy for their fellow Africans in Southern Rhodesia, subjected to settler rule with its accompanying pass laws, discrimination, racial segregation, restrictions on native landholding, and other features not greatly different from conditions in the Union of South Africa. They tended to avoid going to Southern Rhodesia unless economic reasons made it imperative, and they returned as soon as they could. They regarded themselves as in all respects much better off under British colonial rule, even though Africans were discriminated against by their white fellow workers and white employers.

But Southern Rhodesia, which lacked any major sources of wealth outside agriculture, looked covetously upon the mineral resources of Northern Rhodesia; and its leaders searched for means by which these could be brought under their control. Obviously, this could best be achieved by incorporating Northern Rhodesia into the colony and keeping the government of both territories securely in the hands of the whites—few as the whites were in Northern Rhodesia. Even before World War II, two British commissions had considered a federation between Southern Rhodesia, Northern Rhodesia, and the populous but small and poor protectorate of Nyasaland. But the commissions, fully aware of the hostility of the Africans to any such union, rejected the idea, at least for the near future.

After the war, the question was again raised. This time the plan for a federation was pushed through by a Conservative Government over the objections of the Labour and Liberal parties, and in September, 1953, the Federation of Rhodesia and Nyasaland came into being. The Southern Rhodesians had been required to agree to the inclusion of Nyasaland, which had the sole advantage to them of assuring them of cheap African labor from the protectorate. In exchange, some of the revenues of the Federation would have to be expended in less developed Nyasaland. But since the Northern Rhodesian mines would provide the necessary revenue, there was not any great objection to the scheme. In their preamble to the federal constitution, the British had attempted to reassure the people of the protectorates by stating clearly that they "should continue under the special protection of Her Majesty to enjoy separate government, as long as their respective people so desire." But a preamble expresses only an intention and is not a legally binding declaration capable of being enforced in the courts.

AFRICAN OPPOSITION. Those Africans who were consulted on the Federation, and they were few, almost to a man refused assent to it. When they found themselves overwhelmingly outnumbered by the European proponents of Federation, they boycotted the talks that preceded it, meanwhile trying unsuccessfully to arouse British public opinion against it. The Africans in the protectorates and all but a tiny minority in Southern Rhodesia have never wavered in their opposition to the Federation. This minority, accepting the federal government as a fact of life for the foreseeable future and unwilling to become part of a permanent opposition, has been welcomed by the settler government. The more moderate of the federal parties in recent years has even given its members some positions in the government. But these men, elected by European and not by African votes, are widely regarded by the African majority as collaborators with the enemy and stand no chance whatever of ever being elected in any African constituency.

Under the constitution of the Federation, Africans were not disfranchised, but voting qualifications were too difficult for any substantial number to meet. The settlers claimed that, if the Africans would only wait and earn for themselves the right to vote, in time as a matter of course they would share in the government. Meanwhile, the settlers insisted that, unlike in South Africa, they and the Africans were "partners," to which the Africans liked to cite the famous remark of the first Prime Minister of the Federation, Lord Malvern, who once spoke of the partnership as one between "the horse and his rider." They also, with justice, pointed to the famous Franchise Bill of 1957, under which the settlers had devised a safeguard for themselves against the time when Africans might be able to elect a few members of their own. The bill included the provision that for every African elected, a new constituency would be created, with a new member, presumably a European elected by a permanently white electorate, thus keeping the white majority in the Assembly intact.

Some population statistics (in round figures) offer a perspective on the racial problem. Southern Rhodesia in 1959 had 215,000 Europeans and 2.63 million Africans. In Northern Rhodesia, there were 73,000 Europeans to 2.28 million Africans, and in Nyasaland 9,000 Europeans to 2.75 million Africans. Each territory had a small minority of Asians, who outnumbered the Europeans only in Nyasaland. Since the Federation in the years of its existence always encouraged white immigration, in 1953 the African proportion of the population was even larger. By way of comparison, the European population in Kenya was about 50,000 in the same year, and there were approximately three times as many Asians as Europeans in Kenya. In the Union of South Africa in 1958, there were slightly more than 3 million Europeans, 1.3 million persons of mixed blood, and 9.25 million Negroes. These figures account for the fact that it may well be possible for the Europeans in South Africa to maintain their ascendancy by force without yielding to African demands, whereas in Kenya, such an eventuality was clearly impossible. In Southern Rhodesia, the proportion of 1 to 12 makes it still not quite impossible for the Europeans to keep the Africans in subjection by force, if the latter do not obtain reinforcements from outside.

THE FEDERAL CONSTITUTION. In Southern Rhodesia, the Europeans until Federation had a constitution entirely to their liking. There was a common roll, but income qualifications for the franchise were set so high that only 380 Africans could meet them, as against 45,000 Europeans. All 30 seats in the Legislative Assembly were thus held by Europeans, and all ministers were Europeans. After Federation, changes were made under which more Africans could vote, but there was a built-in safeguard to enable the Europeans to maintain their supremacy. Two different electoral rolls were created, known as the ordinary and special rolls. The latter had franchise qualifications less difficult for the Africans to meet, but the number of Africans registered on the special roll must never reach more than one-sixth of those registered on the ordinary roll, which retained its high-income qualifications. Electors on the two rolls voted together without distinction for the same candidates, in effect confining the African vote to little more than one-sixth of the total. This constitution was not changed until 1961, as will be considered in more detail later in this chapter. In the elections of 1958, following an intraparty crisis in the United Federal Party (UFP), the Southern Rhodesian branch of the ruling Federal Party, the UFP just scraped a victory over the Dominion Party, which was further to the right than itself. Few Africans troubled to register and vote in this election, since they felt that no significant difference existed between the two European parties, and their quarrel was of no particular concern to them. Few voted even in 1962, but this time the successor to the Dominion Party won.

In Nyasaland after the war, there were ten officials and ten unofficials in the Legislative Council, with the governor having the casting vote in the event of a tie. The Executive Council had seven members, of whom two were unofficials, neither of them Africans. Of the unofficials in the Legislative Council, three were Africans, indirectly elected, mainly by traditional authorities and therefore not strongly representative of the people. The Europeans and the one Asian in the Council were likewise indirectly elected, by public bodies representing European and Asian interests in the protectorate. There were not enough of these minority groups in the territory to make direct election feasible.

In Northern Rhodesia, the constitution at the time of federation provided for a Legislative Council made up of twelve elected European members and eight British civil servants. In addition to these, there were two European unofficials, nominated by the governor to look after African interests, and four indirectly elected Africans, chosen as in Nyasaland. The Executive Council was made up of five officials and four European unofficials, one of whom was the member in charge of African interests. This constitution, like that of Nyasaland, left power securely in the hands of British officials but not in the hands of the settlers, who were strongly represented and held governmental ministries but did not possess a majority in either Council. The Africans had no say in the government of either protectorate except in the choice, largely by traditional authorities, of the outnumbered Africans in the legislative councils.

Under the federal constitution, provision was at first made for the election of six Africans, increased in 1957 to twelve. But the African representatives for the two protectorates continued to be elected indirectly as before, while the Southern Rhodesian representatives were chosen by the overwhelmingly European vote of the Southern Rhodesian common roll electorate. One European member from each territory was also chosen to represent African interests. In Southern Rhodesia, he was elected by the usual electorate and could therefore be expected to have one eye on African interests and the other on his European electors. The other two members were nominated by the British governors of the two protectorates. Since there were thirty-five members in the Assembly in 1953 and fifty-nine under the changes of 1957, it is clear that the Europeans were still quite safe from any inroads by Africans into their position of supremacy. To make matters still more difficult for African nationalists, the method of election was designed so that all elected Africans would be acceptable to traditional authorities, who might be expected to resent the competition offered to their authority by Africans qualified by their education rather than by their heredity.

CONSTITUTIONAL ADVANCES. The first concessions to African nationalism appeared in 1958, in the crucial territory of Northern Rhodesia. In that year, the British decided to permit the direct election of a limited number of Africans. But they introduced such a complicated system of voting, designed to prevent Africans from attaining majority rule while encouraging them to believe that better things were to follow, that no one was satisfied—least of all Sir Roy Welensky, Prime Minister of the Federation, who exercised so much pressure that the British, not for the last time, modified the proposals to meet some of his objections. Without attempting to enter into the details of this new constitution, it can be said that, as in Southern Rhodesia, two different electoral rolls were created with different property and educational qualifications. By an ingenious series of devices, two Africans would be elected who would have to be acceptable to Europeans and two Europeans acceptable to Africans. Two Africans, possibly those acceptable to Europeans, had to be included in the Executive Council and thus became ministers. But the British Governor was permitted a good deal of discretion in the choice of his ministers, unless one party were able to win an absolute majority in the Legislative Council. The Northern Rhodesian branch of Welensky's United Federal Party made an all-out effort to win this majority, but fell short by three seats. The Governor was therefore able to form an Executive Council dominated, not by the UFP, but by himself and his British officials, though the UFP was granted several ministries. For the first time, a genuinely multiracial party appeared in these elections and won those seats in which the European candidates had to be acceptable to the predominantly African electorate. Both the multiracial and the African parties at once began to press for further constitutional advances, which were eventually granted in 1961—though the elections under the new constitution were not held until October, 1962.

VIOLENCE IN NYASALAND. Nyasaland made no constitutional advances at all until 1959. A few minor changes were contemplated after the disturbances in Nyasaland in the early part of 1959, and some of these were brought into effect, including the entry of two reliable African ministers into the Executive Council. Then the pace of events caught up with the British, and they were compelled to make such extensive changes that Nyasaland rapidly became self-governing, in spite of the fact that Nyasaland had hitherto been regarded as the most backward of the three territories in the Federation. These changes, in turn, made it impossible to keep Nyasaland in the Federation against her will, and led inexorably to the Federation's final dissolution.

In mid-1958, Dr. Hastings Banda, a doctor who had formerly practiced medicine in London and Ghana, returned to the country of his birth with a reputation as an African nationalist earned by his writings and speeches over many years. He was at once elected President of the Nyasaland African National Congress (NANC), and proceeded to fan the flames of nationalism in his territory. Nyasaland had been waiting for just such a leader to give direction to the many separate efforts of others and especially to give voice to the strong opposition to the Federation that was smoldering in the territory. Although he preached non-violence, a number of sporadic outbreaks of violence occurred, which appeared to the government to be increasing in intensity. Promptly, the federal government moved troops and riot squads into the territory, which incensed but did not overawe the Africans. The Governor suddenly declared a state of emergency, explaining afterward—though not at the time—that a murder plot against all Europeans was being planned. Under the emergency regulations, the NANC was banned, and Dr. Banda and others of its leaders were detained without trial.

The rioting then became more serious. The riot squads, mostly made up of Southern Rhodesian settlers, did their job with a hearty good will, paying particular attention to African political meetings, which had become illegal under the emergency regulations. More than fifty Africans were killed after the proclamation of the emergency and several hundreds wounded. No member of the security forces was killed.

With the perspective of subsequent events, it is clear that the Nyasaland disturbances of 1959 were the turning point in the Federation. On the one hand, the British Conservative Government refused to accept many of the findings of the Devlin Commission, which reported to the government on the disturbances, preferring to emphasize those points which supported the Governor's version of events. This led many Africans to believe that, as long as the Conservative Government remained in office, little could be won from the British except by pressure. At the same time, the British Government and people, suddenly made aware of the serious opposition to Federation in Nyasaland and presumably elsewhere, realized that the problem sooner or later would have to be faced. Lastly, those Africans who had previously been willing to tolerate the Federation for the sake of its apparent economic advantages were convinced by the brutality of the settlers and the role of the federal government in the suppression of the disturbances that the Federation must be broken up as soon as possible, whatever the cost.

Dr. Banda himself, ironically, was dealt a full hand of trumps by the government. His detention in Southern Rhodesia for more than a year raised him to the rank of a martyr in much the same manner as the Kabaka of Buganda and Jomo Kenyatta. Since almost every Nyasa African remained loyal to him, it became impossible for the British to make any progress in Nyasaland without him. His conditions must be met, however difficult they might be. So, while he sat peaceably in detention, all the British could do was to try to save face and to extract a few concessions, which Banda was in any case willing to grant and would have granted before the disturbances.

When it became clear that he would soon have to be released, Sir Roy Welensky thundered against appeasing a disturber of the peace. But all moderate opinion in England insisted that every day he was kept in jail, the more difficult the situation would become. Negotiations must be opened with him, and this could not be done while he was still in jail. So on April 1, 1960, he was released and returned to Nyasaland to find Iain Macleod, the British Colonial Secretary, waiting for him, and he was invited to London for a conference. Installed as President of the

Malawi Congress (MCP), which had replaced the old, illegal NANC, he exhorted his followers to have confidence that he would achieve his aims, and the disorders, endemic since his arrest, died down at once. In June, the emergency regulations were lifted; and in July a constitutional conference was held in London.

As a result of the conference, virtual semiresponsible government was granted without any further transitional stages. When the elections under the new constitution were held in August, 1961, the victory of Dr. Banda and his Malawi Congress was so one-sided that there was no longer any point in delaying full semiresponsible government. Not only did the MCP win every seat on the lower roll (with 99 per cent of the votes cast), but it also won three seats on the upper roll, where the number of European voters was not enough to offset the votes of the Africans with the necessary qualifications. It was therefore only a logical step when two British officials in February and March, 1962, gave up their portfolios to Africans, thus giving the latter control of the Executive Council and with it the government of Nyasaland —subject only to the presence of a minority of British officials in Executive Council and the final safeguards reserved to the governor. The "dangerous agitators" of 1959 have "suddenly" become responsible and hard-working ministers, and the African-controlled government has proved to be an effective and conscientious body of administrators. Dr. Banda invited all Europeans who wished to stay and work in the country to do so, but he continued to insist that his territory must leave the Federation and refused even financial help from it. A further constitutional conference was held in November, 1962, at which, to the fury of Sir Roy Welensky, the British conceded to Nyasaland the right to secede from the Federation and promised full responsible government to the protectorate to take effect early in 1963, with the governor retaining his usual reserve powers until independence. On February 1, 1963, Dr. Banda became Prime Minister with his own cabinet. Late in 1963, the British announced that Nyasaland would become an independent state on July 6, 1964.

Self-Government for Northern Rhodesia

While these steps to self-government were being taken in Nyasaland, Northern Rhodesia was still in the throes of the struggle, and the Africans have had to fight not only the local opposition but all the resources that could be brought against them by the Federal Prime Minister. Sir Roy Welensky was fully aware that, if Northern Rhodesia, the richest member of the Federation, were to follow in the footsteps of Nyasaland, there might soon be no Federation and no Federal Prime Minister. He was fighting not only for the survival of the Federation but for his own political life.

The 1959 election in Northern Rhodesia resulted, as we have seen, in the election of a thoroughly unrepresentative government in which some Africans held responsible positions. But the nationalist party, the Zambia National Congress (ZNC), led by Kenneth Kaunda, was banned before the elections and so had none of its members in the new Legislative Council. Kaunda's movements were restricted during the election, and soon afterward he was sentenced to nine months' imprisonment for "convening an unlawful assembly and conspiracy to effect an unlawful purpose." In fact, the nationalists who, like the Nyasaland detainees, were branded by the settlers and government as "dangerous agitators" and "extremists," had little choice. They could either hold meetings illegally or resign themselves to political impotence. The members of the ZNC who remained at large after the elections formed a new party called the United National Independence Party (UNIP), pledged to work for an early African majority in the Legislative Council, followed by secession from the Federation. The program appealed to nationalists in the older party, the African National Congress (ANC), led by Harry Nkumbula, which had not been outlawed and had therefore been permitted to contest the election. This party also favored secession but was in other aspects regarded as more moderate. Many of its members, having come to the conclusion that moderation was winning no victories, left the ANC to join the UNIP, which rapidly became the most militant of the African political organizations in the protectorate, even though Kaunda himself was a staunch advocate of nonviolence. After serving his sentence, Kaunda was chosen as head of the UNIP and went to London to plead his cause before public opinion. The UNIP was banned in part of Northern Rhodesia under the security ordinances.

At last, the British began to recognize that some opportunity for legitimate activity must be given to African political leaders, and some hope of serious participation in the government. Secretary Macleod, after much hesitation, agreed to new talks in December, 1960, at which both African parties suggested considerable advances, including universal suffrage, African majorities in both councils, and reserved seats for minorities, to which the European representatives strenuously objected. Indeed, as soon as the Europeans saw that Macleod seriously intended to make an African-controlled government possible, they boycotted the talks.

Eventually Secretary Macleod handed down a constitution of unexampled complexity whose manifest intention, as in Kenya, was to ensure the election of a multiracial government. Welensky, recognizing at once that his United Federal Party would almost certainly be defeated under the new constitution, stormed over to England to make his views heard. In an acrimonious debate in the House of Lords, the Marquess of Salisbury, an influential right-wing Conservative, made a personal attack on Secretary Macleod, and the Archbishop of Canterbury tried to pour Christian oil on the troubled waters. A few more ingenious amendments were then made to enable the UFP to have a fighting chance to win control of the government, in the process complicating the system to such a degree that, as some opponents insisted, a slide rule became a necessity for determining who had been elected. In Sir Roy's words, the new constitution was a "reasonably workable instrument which has a fair chance of providing for the continuation of responsible government in Northern Rhodesia."

The Africans, irrespective of party, were deeply shocked. The Monckton Commission only a few weeks before had recommended to the British Government that both Nyasaland and Northern Rhodesia be granted majority (African) rule, and they had believed that the British Government would heed the advice. Yet the Commission's advice, at Sir Roy's behest, was now being blithely disregarded. The Africans had expected so much and received so little that neither party, even if they buried their own differences and united, could hope to win enough seats to form a government.

The UNIP at first decided to boycott the elections altogether. Tension in the territory increased so alarmingly that both Catholic and Protestant Church leaders urged further talks to prevent the outbreak of violence. Government security forces were accused of beating up Africans and setting in motion a reign of intimidation and summary punishment far greater than any intimidations of which the frustrated Africans might have been guilty. British liberals and the multiracial Liberal Party in the territory supported the churchmen. Several pointed out that Kenneth Kaunda was a moderate and peaceable man. What kind of a leader, they asked, would the British and settlers prefer? If he always returned from conferences empty-handed, the Africans without doubt would replace him with one of their advocates of all-out violence, who were not lacking in the party.

Faced with this kind of pressure, the British infuriated Welensky and his supporters by agreeing to more discussions. In the course of the long dispute that followed, Secretary Macleod gave way to a new Secretary, Reginald Maudling, but the sole result was the removal of the most obviously discriminatory provision in the constitution. From having been discriminatory in favor of the UFP, it now became even more hopelessly complex than before and could hardly fail to result in a deadlock.

The two ordinary upper and lower rolls with different qualifications were retained. The complication arose with the fifteen "national" seats, which were the heart of the constitution and were expected to provide a number of members, acceptable to both Africans and Europeans, who would hold the balance of power between Welensky's United Federal Party (Northern Rhodesian affiliate) and Kaunda's UNIP. One of these seats was reserved for the Asian community, leaving fourteen to be chosen by the voters on both upper and lower rolls voting together, with the lower roll votes depreciated by a stated percentage. Each national candidate had to receive 10 per cent of the vote of one roll and 20 per cent of the vote of the other, and the candidate winning the combined highest percentage would be declared the winner. The British constitution-makers, unaware of the feeling in the territory, had hoped that the multiracial Liberal Party would win most of the national seats and that the remainder would go to the African National Congress, supposedly the more moderate of the two African parties. But Kaunda preferred to run his own white candidates as members of his own party and was not prepared to give the Liberal Party a free run for the national seats, whereupon the party turned against him, thereby annihilating itself in the elections and failing to win a seat.

The election campaign was fought with the utmost violence, especially by the UFP, which dropped leaflets accusing Kaunda of being a Communist, black racialist, Pan-Africanist, terrorist, or anything else that might discredit him. The Africans fought among themselves, but did not retaliate against the UFP campaign in kind. Kaunda remained the moderate, nonviolent leader he had always been and tried to stick to the issues. The UFP, by its display of spleen, so far alienated the African voters that it could pick up only two national seats, though it was able to prevent the UNIP from winning any. In the first election, the UNIP smothered the ANC, collecting 80 per cent of the votes on the lower roll, though the ANC succeeded in winning three seats to the UNIP's twelve. On the upper roll, the UNIP won a single seat in a constituency where there were too few whites to beat the few qualified Africans. The remainder fell to the UFP. The ANC, which had won two of the national seats in the first election, picked up another two in the runoff. But the remaining eight national seats remained vacant, reducing the membership in the Council to thirty-seven instead of the intended forty-five.

Following the election, Harry Nkumbula, leader of the ANC, who now held the balance of power, decided to join his fellow Africans in the government in exchange for 3 of the 6 ministries for members of his party—in spite of the fact that he had accepted considerable help from the UFP in the campaign. Since he had, like the UNIP, always opposed Federation, he thus joined the UNIP in demanding secession, to which the British were compelled to agree. As the new Prime Minister of Southern Rhodesia put it in the Southern Rhodesian Assembly: "The question of Southern Rhodesian secession will not arise. We shall have been seceded from."

Deadlock in Southern Rhodesia

FAILURE OF PARTNERSHIP. Until the last election in Southern Rhodesia, held in December, 1962, the situation was so serious that the United Nations, over the objections of the British, took it into consideration and debated it as a matter of urgency. But when the election had been won by the Rhodesian Front, the party of the right-wing settlers, most curiously the tension eased. The settlers had at last shown their true colors and demonstrated in an unmistakable manner that they did not believe in partnership, but rather in what has been widely described as "polite apartheid." Africans could now hope that the British would someday intervene and use their remaining power of suspending the constitution if the Rhodesian Front attempted to put its declared policy into operation. Moreover, since the Rhodesian Front has no desire to keep the Federation together, when the time comes to dissolve it and both Nyasaland and Northern

Rhodesia attain their independence, some new status will have to be devised for Southern Rhodesia, to which the British will have to give their assent. The Africans do not believe that Britain can concede independence to Southern Rhodesia under a government controlled by the Rhodesian Front. Britain has indeed temporized, and Southern Rhodesia still does not know her future.

During the Nyasaland disturbances of 1959, the Whitehead government in Southern Rhodesia at once declared a state of emergency in the colony as a preventive measure, fearing that they would spread to Southern Rhodesia, where anti-Europeanism was strongest. Although the disturbances did not spread, a series of security measures comparable only to those in South Africa were enacted. When the state of emergency was finally lifted, the majority of these ordinances became a part of the ordinary law. Southern Rhodesia is often described, even in England, as a police state, and tensions have grown so rapidly that it is regarded as nothing extraordinary when settler members of the Assembly publicly demand that the death penalty be imposed on the nationalists. Sir Robert Treadgold, Chief Justice of the Federation, in November, 1960, resigned his position rather than enforce the security laws.

Such repression has in turn led to movements of desperation on the part of the Africans, even though they have not been countenanced by the major African political party. "Liberation Armies" have been reported, and rumors of national uprisings have been frequent. But the responsible African leaders have no illusions as to the possible success of any such efforts as long as the settlers control the government and have continued to hope that the British will come to their aid. In fact, the British have apparently not yet made up their minds. Meanwhile, the major African party has fissioned, perhaps because it scents victory in the near future—a not infrequent feature of African politics when independence is in sight and the leader who emerges from the competition can expect to become the prime minister who leads the country to independence.

WHITEHEAD CONSTITUTION AND REFERENDUM. At the end of 1960, constitutional changes were discussed in London, attended by a delegation of Africans as well as Sir Edgar Whitehead's government. Sir Edgar had decided that the time had come to get rid of as many legitimate African grievances as possible. The hated pass laws were to be repealed, social discrimination was to be abolished as far as possible, and ultimately something might even be done about the inequitable land-apportionment laws under which the best land was still reserved for Europeans. But he was adamantly opposed to any constitutional advances which would give the Africans any chance of coming to power in the foreseeable future.

Under the proposed new constitution, there were to be sixty-five seats in the Assembly, of which fifty were to be A seats and fifteen B seats. For all seats, the electorate would consist of all registered voters, whether they belonged to the upper (high qualification) roll or the lower roll. But for the fifty A seats, lower-roll votes would count only until they reached 25 per cent of the upper-roll votes. For the B seats, all upper-roll votes were to be similarly devalued. The result of this arrangement would be that fifty seats would be chosen by the predominantly European vote and fifteen by the predominantly African vote. Thus the African nationalists could look forward to a maximum of fifteen seats. Although some other Africans might be elected, they would necessarily be members of a European-dominated party, such as Sir Edgar's UFP.

Under this constitution, there would be a Declaration of Rights for the protection of all the peoples of the colony, and a Constitutional Council to which appeals could be taken against discriminatory laws and practices, in exchange for which the British would drop their own right to disallow legislation. But existing laws that contravened the Declaration, including the recently passed security regulations, would remain on the statute book. Moreover, since it was possible to amend the constitution and override the Constitutional Council by a vote of two-thirds of the members of the Assembly, the 23 per cent of African nationalists in the Assembly would be insufficient to prevent changes.

Although the African delegates suspected that Sir Edgar's concessions were primarily designed to persuade the British to abandon the right of disallowance, they at first agreed to cooperate, even while they protested against the continued discriminatory franchise. After they had had time to digest the full implications, they declared unreservedly against the new constitution and decided to boycott both the referendum on it that Sir Edgar proposed to hold and the subsequent elections.

The die was now cast. Joshua Nkomo's National Democratic Party (NDP) organized its own referendum among the Africans, announcing in due course that there had been 467,189 votes against and 584 votes for. But Sir Edgar won his official referendum by a considerable majority—41,949 to 21,846—and the constitution was therefore adopted. But the cost had been heavy. Sir Edgar, courting the votes of the right-wing settlers, had assured them that the new constitution was a "final concession" to the Africans, which they had long suspected, and confirmed the Africans in their belief that there was little difference between the two settler parties. Even the London *Times* called the campaign "squalid," and it was accompanied by such severe repression of the African nationalists, who had done their utmost to enforce their boycott, that little chance remained of winning their cooperation afterward.

The referendum had two immediate consequences. Nkomo now announced his party's boycott of the forthcoming elections, thereby preventing the constitution from working as had been hoped. If the boycott of the lower roll proved to be effective, it might well be that the A votes, devalued as they were, could decide the election, and no Africans would after all be chosen. The second consequence was the formation of a new liberal European party (New Africa Party), organized by Garfield Todd, a former Prime Minister of Southern Rhodesia who had been ousted by his party because he was considered too friendly to African aspirations. Although his program, which called for an immediate Afro-European multiracial government, was unlikely to win many votes among the settlers, at least its formation was a demonstration to the world that the settlers were not all of one mind. Todd insisted that the present policy would lead inevitably to violence, held in check now only by the moderation of the Africans. Todd also was later to do yeoman service for the Africans in his appearance before the United Nations.

UNITED NATIONS INTERVENTION. During the next months, strikes, demonstrations, and violence continued, which were repressed with the usual police efficiency. Sir Edgar postponed the elections originally intended for October, 1961, and in December of that year he outlawed NDP but did not arrest Nkomo, who was one of the few nationalist leaders still at large. Nkomo two weeks later formed another party, the Zimbabwe Africa People's Union (ZAPU), and then left the country, supported by Todd, to take his case to the Special Committee on Colonialism of the United Nations.

The committee visited London to urge the British to call a

new constitutional conference. Receiving no satisfaction, it referred the question to the General Assembly, which, over the opposition of Britain and other countries who were not willing to agree that the situation was of great urgency, passed a resolution calling for a new constitution to be drawn up by representatives of all political parties. Furthermore, it called for immediate steps to be taken to restore the rights of the non-Europeans in Southern Rhodesia and to remove all restraints and restrictions on political activity. The British delegate denied the authority of the United Nations to intervene in the affairs of Southern Rhodesia and explained why Britain herself for legal reasons could not interfere directly. Nevertheless, the resolution was passed by seventy-three votes to one (South Africa), with twenty-seven abstentions. Britain and Portugal refused to take part in what they considered an illegal vote. The United States was one of the abstainers.

BELATED EFFORTS AT SOCIAL REFORM. In May, 1962, the Southern Rhodesian Government, in the hope of putting an end to some of the ugliest demonstrations, decided to ban all political meetings. Twenty-four–hour strikes were then called by the nationalists, to which employers responded by dismissal of all who took part in them and their eviction from dormitories owned by the companies. In August, the Southern Rhodesian Assembly passed the most drastic of all its laws directed against the African nationalists, defining intimidation in such an inclusive manner that hardly any active nationalist could avoid being convicted under it, and imposing a penalty of up to ten years. The law also defined a prohibited meeting as any assembly of more than 12 persons in a public place or 100 in a private home. Moreover, it declared as unlawful any organization derived from a "parent" unlawful organization, thus striking at the recently organized ZAPU and its leaders.

Although the bill when presented caused an outcry from all liberal white opinion, from every Church organization, and several members of the bar, as well of course as from the Africans, it was duly passed. Even in England, back-bench Conservatives began to suggest that Britain ought to use her remaining reserve powers. The Vice-President of the ZAPU, a highly respected African medical officer, was found dead in suspicious circumstances. The driver of the automobile in which he was supposed to have been killed in an accident at a railroad crossing insisted that he had been lynched by eight Europeans. True or not, the Africans to a man believed the driver and not the official explanation. When leaflets were distributed in September calling for the formation of a Liberation Army, Sir Edgar Whitehead took the final step and banned the ZAPU, banishing its remaining leaders to remote parts of the territory.

During all this period, while action was being taken against the African political leaders, Sir Edgar's Government had been pushing through the Assembly his bills designed to improve the social and economic position of the Africans, though he was unable or unwilling to repeal the Land Improvement Act, which reserved the best lands in the territory for Europeans. The new measures might have borne some fruits if they had been applied earlier and in different circumstances. But by now the Africans had ceased to be interested. In no mood to accept less than had been conceded to their fellow Africans in Northern Rhodesia and Nyasaland merely because there were 100,000 more Europeans in Southern Rhodesia, they were fighting now for self-government, not legal equality in a society dominated by Europeans. Although Sir Edgar Whitehead bravely defended his policies before the Fourth Committee of the United Nations, he lost the election in Southern Rhodesia. The majority of the white electorate proved to have as little interest in racial partnership as the Africans; they wished to retain the supremacy they had enjoyed for forty years, and as far as votes could assure it, they cast them.

FALL OF THE WHITEHEAD GOVERNMENT. Now the battle lines are tightly drawn. On the one side are the Africans, aided by such influence as the United Nations can bring to bear on their behalf. On the other side, the Rhodesian Front, to which will be added most of those whites who reluctantly gave Sir Edgar's policy a trial until it was proved a failure. Caught in the middle are the British, with their world prestige at stake, led by a Conservative Government that needs desperately any prestige it can win to compensate for failures elsewhere and faced by an opposition at home that has little sympathy with the settlers. Britain cannot permit independence to a Southern Rhodesian Government of white supremacists now that world opinion has been alerted to the realities in the colony. If Southern Rhodesia were to declare her independence unilaterally, it is certain that few would recognize it—at the most, Portugal and the Republic of

South Africa. It is doubtful if the Republic of South Africa, in the face of world opinion, would be willing to add to her own problems by agreeing to annex the colony with its non-Afrikaner Europeans and its militant Africans.

If the Conservative Government decides to try to solve the problem before it holds its own elections, there seems to be no other course but to play for time by granting the Africans reforms substantial enough to enable them to hold office in company with Europeans for a few more years, with a promise of African control at an early date. This is what the Africans expected at the end of 1960, and they may settle for it now. Whether the settlers would accept it is anyone's guess. It is certain that the Rhodesian Front Government will never itself initiate the necessary constitutional change. So the task will fall on the British to impose a constitution of their choice, with or without further consultation in the colony. Only the future can tell whether they will wait until events in Rhodesia or the dissolution of the Federation gives them an opportunity to intervene, or whether they will take the step on their own initiative. It is the only policy left that has any chance of saving the settlers from the fate of their compatriots in Kenya or the *colons* of Algeria.

Dissolution of the Federation

There remains now only to discuss the Federation itself. The constitution of 1953 required that not less than seven or more than nine years after it had come into force (September, 1953), a conference should be held to review its working, to which delegations should be sent from each of the territories. For many years, the federal government had entertained the hope that the Federation as a whole would become independent within the Commonwealth with all the rights belonging to independence, including control over the amending of the constitution. The British, entertaining the same hope, had always treated the Federation as a state which before long would be independent. It was in this expectation that they and various foreign governments had extended credit to the federal government. Numerous difficulties would arise if each component part were compelled to assume its own share of the debt; and foreign creditors might well object to the transfer of their loans to less prosperous territories such as underdeveloped Nyasaland.

The Africans were not unaware of these difficulties, and if they were the rulers of each of the component territories, they were quite ready to enter into economic agreements with the other parts, or even reconstitute the Federation on a different basis. But they were unwilling to commit themselves to continue the Federation without ironclad assurances that they would soon be permitted to govern it. Hoping to discover some means of reassuring them enough to win their cooperation, the British decided in 1959 to appoint a pre-review advisory commission, under the chairmanship of Lord Monckton, to take evidence in Rhodesia and Nyasaland and make recommendations on possible changes. The Labour Party in Britain, which had always opposed federation, refused to participate in the work because the Commission's terms of reference excluded any recommendations that might lead to its dissolution. In spite of the predominance of Conservatives on the Commission, its recommendations, when issued late in 1960, were remarkably liberal. Although they proposed for the present to retain the qualitative franchise, they recommended that equal numbers of Europeans and Africans sit in the Federal Assembly. Each of the three territories should have identical bills of rights for the protection of minorities, and an African majority should be granted in Northern Rhodesia. With regard to the burning question of secession, they proposed that it be on the agenda of the Review Conference, and that the British Government declare its intention to permit the secession of a territory from the Federation, either after a stated period or on the achievement of responsible government for the territory. Independence for the Federation as a whole should not be considered until after the three territories had each attained responsible government.

Sir Roy Welensky and other European leaders at once condemned the report, finding the right of the territories to secede completely unacceptable. In this frame of mind, they attended the Review Conference, which met on December 5, 1960. Since the African delegates insisted on discussing secession, no progress could be made, and the Conference broke up on December 18, with the understanding that constitutional changes in the territories would be made before it reconvened. By July, 1963, when it was evident that the Federation would be permitted to dissolve, there was no need to reconvene the Review Conference. A five-day meeting of representatives from each territory and the Federation was enough to settle the outstanding questions of liquidation and to divide the assets. Dissolution was to be completed by December 31, 1963.

The liquidation of the Federation in itself provides no permanent solution for the problems of the three territories. However, both Nyasaland and Northern Rhodesia have been promised their independence. Nyasaland, with a Prime Minister and full internal self-government, awaits only the approval of the British Parliament. Northern Rhodesia, with its African-controlled coalition government, must hold new elections before there will be a majority government to carry the country over until independence. But no difficulties were expected in either territory.

Southern Rhodesia continues to present intractable problems. Britain, with the United Nations pressing her for a solution, does not have unlimited time at her disposal. If nothing is done before the end of 1963, Southern Rhodesia will revert to her pre-Federation status, as a self-governing colony with a government dominated by Europeans. Replying to a U.N. subcommittee that visited London in April, 1963, British ministers pointed out that if only 8 per cent of the African population of the colony were to qualify for the vote under the present constitution, the Africans could legally take over the government. If the United Nations and Southern Rhodesian Africans were prepared to wait several more years, then of course everything would work to the advantage of the British. They would not be compelled to use their reserve powers to change the Southern Rhodesian constitution, and normal evolution would take its course. But the Africans are not prepared to wait, nor will U.N. pressure on the British cease until something more acceptable is devised.

Indeed, the British were compelled in September, 1963, to cast a veto in the Security Council—only the third time they had done so in the history of the United Nations. Eight nations, including Norway, a NATO ally, voted for a resolution calling upon Britain to refrain from handing over the former Federal Air Force, manned almost exclusively by white Southern Rhodesians, to the territorial government of Southern Rhodesia after the dissolution of the Federation. France and the United States abstained from voting.

In the months since it won power, the Rhodesian Front Government has busied itself in perfecting the apparatus of repression under law, but it has made no move toward finding any solution of its own that would involve a break with the British, except to extend its railroad system at top speed to complete a link with the South African Railways, thus freeing itself from dependence on Northern Rhodesia for its outlet to the sea. Europeans have been leaving the territory in large numbers, and the economy is in serious disrepair. If Southern Rhodesia again becomes a self-governing colony, the Europeans will continue to rule, and the local Africans can do relatively little by themselves against the preponderant might of the government, armed with the legal apparatus of a police state. A political solution must be reached, sooner or later, agreed to or imposed.

From the point of view of Africa and the world, there clearly ought to be an economic union between Northern and Southern Rhodesia, and economic ties between these two and Nyasaland should be preserved. The Federation was generally considered an economic success while it lasted, although its benefits were distributed unevenly. But economic benefits to the people of the territories could not compensate for the failure of the ruling whites to give any real substance to the ideal of partnership expressed in the preamble to the federal constitution. In 1953, the Africans might have given their full cooperation to the Europeans if they had honestly tried to be partners; in 1963, this is no longer even worth trying. They will settle for nothing less than African majority rule, and though they will cooperate with the Europeans who stay, it will be on their own terms. This is how it has been in the rest of independent Black Africa, and this is how it will be in Rhodesia.

10. The New Africa—French Zone

When France surrendered to the Germans in 1940, most of the French colonial governors at first remained loyal to the Pétain regime. The major exception was Félix Eboué, a French Guianan of African descent, who was Governor of the Equatorial territory of Chad. When General de Gaulle appealed to all Frenchmen to declare for Free France, Eboué declared for him, to be followed soon afterward by the other governors of French Equatorial Africa and by some in French West Africa. The Africans from the beginning preferred De Gaulle, and French Equatorial Africa (F.E.A.) in particular made important contributions to the war effort of the Free French—a service never forgotten by De Gaulle.

As early as January, 1944, at a conference assembled at Brazzaville in F.E.A., the General himself proclaimed that Africans after the war would be permitted to share in the management of their own affairs, in association with France. Although this was a small enough promise, the French were already considering how this association—which in no way implied full self-government by Africans, still less independence—could be put into effect after the war. The result proved to be the French Union (Union Française) of 1946.

The French Union

POLITICAL INSTITUTIONS. The communes of Senegal, inhabited by Africans who had for more than a century been French citizens, sent deputies to Paris to sit in the National Assembly in the interwar years. Under the French Union, all French African territories now sent their representatives to the Assembly and Senate (Conseil de la République) in Paris. The French citizens (both French and African) voted on a different roll from noncitizens, but the noncitizen roll elected more members than the citizens. Africans sent their elected representatives also to an Assembly of the Union that, though it offered advice, had little power.

It had always been French policy to regard their colonies as extensions of the mother country. Colonial legislation was passed by the French Assembly and Senate and put into effect by the governors-general and the territorial governors in each territory, who were responsible to the minister of colonies in France. It was assumed—which was far from true—that all the colonies had reached a similar stage of development and that the same legislation could be applied to all. In practice, the governors-general were given a very free hand with their respective "federations," and modified the legislation as they thought necessary. When a very great step forward was taken in 1956, the French parliament actually passed what it called a "framework" law or enabling act (*loi-cadre*) that was to take effect in each territory only when supplementary decrees were passed applicable to each particular territory. One major result of this centralized system was that the Africans of any particular area could not hope to win special treatment for their own territories. They could apply pressure only in France; and whatever they won through their representatives or by other means would be applied in all the colonies alike.

In 1946, a Grand Council was instituted for each of the two federations, and territorial councils for each of the territories in the federations. The territorial councils were elected by Africans and resident Europeans, who in turn nominated some of their number for the grand councils. The councilors were limited to giving advice, which the governors were not required to accept, though in certain matters they had to consult their councilors before taking action. The French never used the British system of nominating councilors whom they regarded as reliable. The long revolutionary tradition in France prevented the adoption of such an "undemocratic" device. The French officials in the colonies preferred to put pressure on the electors and even interfered with elections in order to ensure the choice of persons they preferred. There were probably no perfectly free elections in any French colony before 1956. Nevertheless, the fact that territorial councils existed, made up of elected councilors, made it possible for the French to convert them into genuine national assemblies in due course. Council members had won experience in them, which could be put to full use when the time came to prepare for independence.

ADVANTAGES OF THE SYSTEM. Although its value may not have been appreciated during the twelve years of the French Union, the system of electing deputies to the French parliament was by no means only a device to enable France to preserve the colonial system. Although it did serve to keep the French Africans tied to France at a time when Africans under the British colonial system were beginning to look forward to full independence, it gave them some benefits not enjoyed by the British Africans. Within the French parliamentary system, in which party alignments were extraordinarily fluid and party discipline lax, Africans interested in a particular policy for Africa could exercise considerable influence. Although they were little interested in much of the French domestic legislation that came before them, their votes were needed to pass it; and they could trade them for votes for their own program. Like other deputies, they served on committees, especially those concerned with African policy. Unlike their British counterparts, they did not have to go hat in hand to the colonial office, put their views forward, be listened to, and then perhaps find a constitution imposed upon them, passed by the British Parliament in which they were not represented. In any changes initiated by the French, the Africans not only were consulted, but played a full part in the legislative process. Dr. Félix Houphouët-Boigny of the Ivory Coast, more than any other man, was responsible for the crucially important legislation of 1956 that set French Africa on the path to independence.

Even more important in the eyes of the French Africans was the simple fact that their deputies in France were given absolutely equal social rights with the French themselves. They sat beside them in the National Assembly, and no discrimination was possible against them because they were Africans. From 1956 onward, there was never a French cabinet in which at least one African was not a member, sometimes more than one. Houphouët-Boigny was even French Minister of Health for a time. The deputies might be only a small group of elite, well-educated Africans, thoroughly at home in the French language, who regarded Paris as their second capital. But the implication was not lost on all Africans that members of their race could be treated as equals by white Frenchmen and that this was not a matter of personal relations with a few Frenchmen, but a part of their system. Westminster might be admired by British Africans, and its forms imitated in their own parliaments; but they could not aspire to it. All they could do was to try to free themselves altogether from their condition of dependency. There can now be little doubt that this long and intimate association of Africans with Frenchmen in France has in large part been responsible for the continued close association between Africans and French that is such a remarkable

feature of the former French colonies in Africa—not even entirely
excepting the two dissidents, Mali and Guinea.

FORMATION OF POLITICAL PARTIES. An important consequence of
the French Union system was the early formation of parties. In
France itself, the earliest tendency was for the African deputy to
associate himself with one or another of the major French parties
and vote and work with it. At least one important African party
was always an affiliate of the French Socialist Party (SFIO). At
times, the French African deputies associated with one another in
a loose party, which would then ally itself with a French party that
supported its policy on Africa. In every African territory, parties
were also formed to fight elections, each autonomous in itself,
and usually confined to the one territory. But this tendency to
particularism was offset by a considerable innovation, unique in
French Africa and with no counterpart in British Africa, the inter-
territorial *rassemblement*, or rally.

The first and always the most powerful of these was the Rassemblement Démocratique Africain (RDA), which was not itself a
party but what its name implied, a union of African parties to
press for the same goals. It encouraged the formation of an
affiliated party in each territory, and at election time the resources
of the whole organization would be placed at the disposal of the
local affiliate. The local leaders formed the directorate of RDA,
and by no means always agreed with the views of Houphouët-
Boigny, who has been the leader of RDA since its founding. For
several years after 1946, RDA took a consistently pro-Communist
line both in France and Africa, and was regarded by the French
Communist Party as its African affiliate. But when it tried to take
over RDA and bend it completely to its will, RDA split.
Houphouët-Boigny took the greater part of the organization along
with him in his new policy of full cooperation with the French, a
policy from which he has never subsequently wavered.

THE LOI-CADRE OF 1956. During the years from 1946 to 1956,
their was very little change in the French Union system. A few
more Africans were elected when the "double college" (two electoral rolls) system was modified. This semistagnation was in
large part due to the weakness of successive French governments
and the fact that their regimes were so short-lived that it was impossible to get any major African legislation passed. When the
Socialist government of Guy Mollet at last managed to survive

long enough to interest itself in the by now seriously overdue reforms needed for Africa, the *loi-cadre* was passed (1956) and came into operation in the territories in 1957. Under the new system, both federations were dissolved, to become "groups of territories," and the various territorial councils were granted semi-responsible government in their territories. Although the French governors still presided over the territorial cabinets (Councils of Ministers) each of them took an African vice-president, the head of the majority party in the territory, who was expected in due course to take over the president's position. The French governors were required to take the advice of their vice-presidents on all matters of importance that came before them. The double college voting system was abolished, and universal adult suffrage granted. Henceforth, if any Europeans remained in the African territorial councils or as representatives of Africans in the French Assembly, it would be only because Africans had freely elected them.

The reception of the *loi-cadre* in Africa was mixed. Those territories that had expected less and where there was only a very small minority of educated men suddenly found themselves called upon to accept responsibilities for which they were very little prepared. But they were delighted to make the effort and were aided by French officials whom they elected to their councils and who as a rule became members of their parties. In the more developed territories, more had been hoped for, and much concern was expressed, especially in Senegal, at what was described as a French attempt to "balkanize" their African territories, thus making them incapable of freeing themselves from French economic domination and gaining a genuine independence as viable states. The opponents of the new system objected to the dissolution of the two federations. They had hoped to see their grand councils granted the status of true federal parliaments and the establishment of a responsible African federal executive, with powers as great as those of the previous governor-general and his advisers. The grand councils at Dakar and Brazzaville were now required to be consulted on the Group budget, and they were expected to coordinate the work of the territories and provide for the continuation of common services. But they had been given no new powers; and the leading politicians, elected as they were by the territorial councilors, would be tempted to exercise the new substantial powers granted in the territories in preference to devoting themselves seriously to the additional work in the Group capitals.

The Franco-African Community

Establishment of the Community

THE BAMAKO CONFERENCE (1957). In a great conference held by RDA at Bamako in Soudan in September, 1957, the Africans clarified their own views on what should be the future of the African colonies, putting forward for the first time the idea of the Franco-African Community, which was brought into existence later by De Gaulle. Such a conference was necessary not only because of differences among Africans but because the successive short-lived French governments, trying without secure majorities to settle both the Algerian war and their usual domestic problems, were unable to devote much of their time and thought to Africa. Few French Africans in 1957, dependent as they were on the continued inflow of French aid and investment, believed in the possibility of complete independence at an early date, but they were envious of Ghana, which had attained her independence six months before the opening of the conference. Was any intermediate stage feasible between absolute independence, which might arrest the flow of French funds, and the semiresponsible government they now enjoyed?

Three points of view were considered at Bamako, two proposed by separate wings of RDA and a third that had already been put forward by Léopold Senghor of Senegal, whose party was not an RDA affiliate and was therefore not officially represented at Bamako. What Senghor desired was first the organization of a federal executive at Dakar and Brazzaville, followed by the independence of both of the former federations. These states, which would be economically viable, would then enter into a federal relationship with the Republic of France, and with such other of the former French colonies, as, for example, the North African Mediterranean states, as might wish to join. This was his version of the Franco-African Community. He was resolutely opposed to a federal relation between France and the smaller territories, which were apparently being groomed for separate independence. The latter, in his view, ought to be integrated at once, though they should retain some degree of autonomy in local affairs.

Houphouët-Boigny and the RDA minority agreed with Senghor on the necessity of a federal relationship with France, and the creation of a Franco-African Community. But he believed that the territories, not the former federations, should be the component parts, each achieving independence as separate states while at the same time having a direct relationship with France through the proposed Community institutions. Houphouët, being from the Ivory Coast, the richest of the French West African territories, deeply distrusted the notion of reconstituting the two federations and giving them power over the territories. In his view, the more numerous poorer territories would be likely to use the resources of the Ivory Coast for their own benefit and discriminate against her if they became responsible for the allocation of French economic aid. In this viewpoint, he was naturally supported by Léon Mba, Vice-President of the council of Gabon, the richest state of French Equatorial Africa. But Houphouët went further. In an eloquent speech, he explained to the Conference that he was himself not greatly interested in independence as such. He regarded it as a somewhat outdated ideal in a world in which all states were now interdependent. A greater ideal was "Community," specifically a Franco-African Community, which would be of value not only for Africans but for France. She would obtain a new lease on life from her association with younger peoples, who in time would have much to contribute to the common whole, even though for the moment it would necessarily be one-sided. In his view, the Community would be a much stronger association than the Commonwealth, since its institutions, unlike those of the Commonwealth, would be truly federal. Thus it was unnecessary to organize a federal executive in Africa, as Senghor had urged. The Community executive, though temporarily in France, could meet wherever it wished, but all its component parts would always have a common say in its common tasks.

The RDA majority, led by Sékou Touré (now President of Guinea, but Vice-President of the Council at the time), unmoved by Houphouët's ideal, did not think of independence as outmoded. Touré agreed with Senghor that the former federations, not the separate territories, should become independent as a whole and they could then enter into a loose association with France, similar to that of the Commonwealth, though he was willing to call it a Community. Modibo Keita, now President of the Republic of Mali, approved of the idea of the Community, but thought there was little chance of obtaining the agreement of the French. Like Senghor, he believed the Federation should be reconstituted and thereafter taken into a federal relation with France.

POLICY OF DE GAULLE. Although Houphouët did not prevail at Bamako, his views received official sanction from France when De

Gaulle took power in May, 1958, and was granted the right to rule by decree pending a new constitution for the Fifth Republic. He became one of De Gaulle's four principal ministers of state, and his ideas found a receptive ear in the General. The latter, with his exalted notions of France in the world, envisaged her as the head of a great Community of African peoples, all freely associated with her by their own will—thus completely solving the problems that had beset the loosely organized Commonwealth of separate, totally independent nations, each with its own foreign policy and free to oppose Britain if they wished. The French African states would be completely self-governing in themselves; but in affairs that concerned them all they would agree to a diminution of sovereignty by sharing it with France. As a preparation for the future, De Gaulle quickly granted full self-government to the territories, by withdrawing the French presidents of the territorial councils, thus permitting all the African vice-presidents to become presidents or prime ministers in their place.

The next step was to set up the Community as an integral part of the new French constitution, to establish its common organs, and submit the whole to a referendum, not only of all metropolitan Frenchmen but of all French citizens throughout the whole of overseas France. Each territory should vote on the question of whether to accept the constitution, and if so what position to hold in it. They could become overseas departments, like Martinique, Réunion, or other small countries, ruled as part of France and participating fully in French institutions; overseas territories, like French Somaliland, with limited self-government; or autonomous republics within the Community, a new status which it was believed would meet the aspirations of the African territories. If the constitution received a No vote in any territory, it could at once become independent and sever its association with France. No territory under the original constitution was permitted to become independent and yet remain within the Community.

REFERENDUM OF 1958—SECESSION OF GUINEA. During most of the referendum campaign, it appeared likely that all the African territories would vote Yes. The only seriously doubtful territory was Guinea, whose leader, Sékou Touré, despite the urgings of all the other RDA leaders, had not yet urged an affirmative vote. When at last he instructed his followers to vote No, he was obeyed. De Gaulle kept his word. The next day, Guinea became independent (September 29, 1958). The display of bad temper by the French at the result of the vote and the ungenerous attitude of local officials, who did their utmost to prevent the new regime from functioning, have embittered Franco-Guinean relations ever since. Only in recent months has there been any significant improvement, in part as the result of increasing disillusionment in Guinea with the results of her flirtations with the Soviet bloc. Behind the treatment of Guinea lies a serious dilemma which faced De Gaulle. If he had treated Guinea in exactly the same way as he treated those who had voted to join the Community, the new Community members would recognize that they, too, would have nothing to lose by demanding independence. When Guinea in fact survived in spite of French displeasure, the autonomous republics decided to follow the same path. But apparently De Gaulle had learned his lesson, and these later efforts were treated with courtesy and sympathy.

In accordance with the mandate received from all other territories, the Community was duly organized, with an Executive Council, a Senate, and other common institutions. But even as they were beginning to function, rifts began to appear. While Sékou Touré's new nation was admitted to the United Nations, other French African leaders had to be content with appointment to the French delegation. No one regarded them as leaders of independent states; the concept of a self-governing republic in a Community led by France was not understood. Africans and Asians who had won their own independence looked upon it as nothing but disguised colonialism, a French device for sidetracking true independence. This lack of international esteem rankled in spite of the outpouring of French money, and many began to wonder if their affirmative votes in the referendum had not robbed them of their chance to play the part in the world outside to which they were entitled.

Community versus International Sovereignty

THE FEDERATION OF MALI. Parallel with the increasing desire for independence was the need of the republics to overcome the weakness resulting from their lack of resources and manpower, which made them so dependent on France. Obviously, the best way to gain strength was to amalgamate with one another. The initiative in West Africa was taken by Senghor of Senegal and Keita of Soudan, who desired nothing less than the reconstitution of the old Federation. Niger, which was geographically closely connected with French Equatorial Africa and would add little strength to the proposed union, could be ignored, as could Muslim Mauritania, which had little in common with Senegal, her neighbor to the south. But agreement in principle was won from Upper Volta and Dahomey. The big stumbling block was the Ivory Coast, which under its President Houphouët was no more inclined toward amalgamation than in 1957. Not only did Houphouët refuse to join, but he put pressure on Dahomey and Upper Volta to withdraw their agreement, in which he was aided by the dependence of Upper Volta on the Ivory Coast for her only outlet to the sea. Overpopulated Dahomey likewise needed the Ivory Coast as employer of her surplus labor.

So Senegal and Soudan were left to amalgamate with one another in the short-lived Federation of Mali, with Keita as federal President and Senghor as President of the federal Assembly. It survived uneasily from January, 1959, to August, 1960, when differences between the two leading personalities came to a head, and Senegal seceded, claiming that Keita was plotting to turn the Federation into a unitary state. Meanwhile, Houphouët had formed a loose league, known as the Conseil de l'Entente, between the Ivory Coast, Upper Volta, Dahomey, and Niger, with a customs union and provisions for mutual consultation. All its leaders belonged to the RDA and were accustomed to accepting the leadership of Houphouët-Boigny.

The formation of the Federation of Mali precipitated a number of changes in the Community. The new Federation first gave notice to the Executive Council of the Community that the two states wished in future to be treated as one. This request was granted, as it presented no difficulty. Then both the Federation of Mali and the autonomous Malagasy Republic (Madagascar), presented De Gaulle with the demand for full independence. They wished to remain associated with France in the Community, but preferred to negotiate treaties for mutual defense and other matters themselves, rather than being bound in the excessively close relationship of the Community. De Gaulle treated these requests with respect, but pointed out that the constitution of the Community did not permit of independence within the Community. He did not like the term independence, he said, since this implied something that could hardly be attained anywhere in the world, least of all in undeveloped Africa. He preferred the term "international sovereignty," and this he was prepared to grant provided the constitution were changed and agreements drawn up with all those states that wished to change their status.

After some hard bargaining, Mali and the Malagasy Republic signed the agreements. Houphouët-Boigny, on behalf of the Conseil de l'Entente, made a similar application, but he regarded it as beneath the dignity of Africans to be faced with a demand that treaties be signed first as a condition for independence. Behind this insistence were two considerations of importance in the African leader's mind. Clearly, the Community he had envisaged, with close and unbreakable ties with France in a federal framework, was not to be. At first, therefore, he had opposed the Mali and Malagasy requests; then, seeing that they were certain to win their independence, he gracefully withdrew his opposition. But, in his view, there was now no need for a Community at all; an ordinary treaty-based association would be ample to take care of the new situation, and he did not care for his ideal to be debased. Less important, but also no doubt of interest to him, was the fact that if the Ivory Coast were already independent, the French would have lost their bargaining counter. He could then sign less onerous agreements with France, thus improving his position at home with his own nationalists.

TRIUMPH OF NATIONALISM. For a while the French, most of whom had never taken the ideal of the Community as seriously as Houphouët, were deeply shocked by the attitude of the man they had thought to be their best friend. But they soon recovered and unconditionally agreed to the independence of Ivory Coast and her associated states. As soon as the constitutional changes permitting independence within the Community had been ratified (July 2, 1960), Houphouët expressed himself as ready to negotiate agreements—and they proved indeed to be the most favorable conceded to any former French colony. Meanwhile, all the African states had petitioned for and been granted full independence (or "international sovereignty"), all achieving their goal before the end of 1960. But neither Ivory Coast nor the other three states of the Entente ever rejoined the Community. On the dissolution of the Mali Federation, Mali likewise refused to rejoin. Thus the Community, usually known as the Franco-African Community, now has only seven members: the four former territories of French Equatorial Africa, Senegal and Mauritania from the old French West Africa, and the Malagasy Republic. The Community, though still legally in existence, is now only a shadow, its

Executive Council meetings replaced by occasional Community conferences and its Senate and Court of Arbitration left with nothing of any significance to do.

In late 1961, twelve former French colonies, including the trust territory of Cameroun and independent Senegal, organized a union known as the African and Malagasy Union, with a number of common institutions, including an airline and travel agency, several economic committees, and a permanent headquarters and secretariat. Other African nations showed an interest in this Union, including some, like Liberia, which are not French-speaking. Even Mali and Guinea made inquiries regarding their possible membership. Then in May, 1963, a Summit Conference of Independent African States met in Addis Ababa to discuss the question of African unity. The conference was attended by every African nation except Morocco, which refused to attend because of the presence of Mauritania, and Togo, whose new government, following the assassination of Sylvanus Olympio, was not yet recognized by most of the states. The conference set up an Organization of African Unity (OAU), with a detailed charter, comparable to that of the Organization of American States, and a permanent secretariat. Former French colonies were active at the conference, and were largely responsible for its moderation. But when it was suggested after the conference that there was no further need for the African and Malagasy Union, its members demurred, preferring to let it "fade away" if it was later shown that the OAU had become a truly functioning organization. The Ghana-Guinea-Mali Union, however, was dissolved at the initiative of Sékou Touré.

Meanwhile the members of both former French African federations have customs unions among themselves, and some of them have customs unions with outside countries—for example, Upper Volta with Ghana. An economic union of most of independent Black Africa might provide these now too often excessively small states with a firm basis for changing for the better the arbitrary boundaries imposed by European imperialists in the nineteenth century.

Despite the absence of strict forms, the feeling of community among "African states of French expression" is far from unreal. Their economies are closely associated with France, which was able to drive a good bargain for all when she brought them as associated states into the European Common Market (EEC), with all its privileges and few of its responsibilities, and France has treaties with almost all. Perhaps even more important are the strong lines of cultural force flowing from France to her former colonies and back again—as there are, indeed, in all former colonies of all the Western powers. French culture is so pervasive and has taken such deep roots in the Africans who have been educated in France, not excepting Guineans and Malians, that it is often extremely difficult for them to meet on common ground with Africans of British expression. Even Togo and Cameroun, trust territories that were never administered in common with either of the French federations, have continued close relations with France after independence and look to her for economic, technical, and educational aid.

A close relationship, much stronger than in the former British colonies, continues to exist between one French-speaking territory and another. Although naturally encouraged by France, it appears to be genuinely desired by the African leaders and results from the fact that, not only were the colonies under a single administration, but their leaders were either educated together, sat together in the French Assembly, or belonged to the same political rally. They do not often vote in a bloc at the United Nations; nevertheless, with the exception of Guinea and Mali, it is possible to discern a general tendency among all the states to vote a little conservatively and adopt few radical positions except when the question of colonialism is at stake.

French African Trust Territories

Togoland

The two trust territories of Togoland and Cameroun require separate treatment from the rest of French Africa, since, unlike the British sectors of these territories, they were not administered in conjunction with their French-speaking neighbors but had their own separate administrations. Indeed, French Togoland was used as a kind of pilot plant for political innovations, and the fact that petitioners from the trust territories were frequently heard by the United Nations Trusteeship Council no doubt played some part in the political initiatives first taken in the trust territories. Although France legislated separately for her trust territories, they were granted the same privileges as her colonies under the French Union, including the same territorial councils and the right to send representatives to the French Assembly and Senate.

In the early years of the French Union, the most important political party in Togoland was the All-Ewe Congress, led by

Sylvanus Olympio, whose aim at the time was to reunite all the Ewe people in one state. Naturally, this aim was of little interest to the non-Ewe; and although Olympio was able to put the Ewe case effectively before the United Nations, his single-minded efforts prevented him from becoming a truly national leader. By the early 1950's, he realized that such a policy played into the hands of the French local officials, who backed quite openly the other parties and were able to keep him from power. By the time that the French decided in 1955 to give the Togolese a foretaste of what the other territories would gain by the *loi-cadre* of 1956, Olympio's party, renamed the Committee for Togolese Unity, with a program of early independence for the whole state, would probably have commanded enough support in the country to have won the first elections under the new statute. But the French were not prepared to grant a truly free election and did not refrain from their customary pre-1956 interference with registration and voting. Olympio and his party thereupon boycotted the election, with the result that the French-supported party, led by Nicholas Grunitsky, won every seat.

This situation did not at all please the United Nations, which could not but be aware of it; nor did the United Nations approve when the French, the following year, proclaimed the establishment of what they called an autonomous Togolese Republic. It considered, quite justly, that this so-called republic was in fact a French puppet regime, tied to the French Union and led by a party that had won power in elections controlled by the French. Nevertheless, the French proposed to the Trusteeship Council that the establishment of the Republic be regarded as fulfillment of the United Nations trust and requested it to send a mission to observe a plebiscite to be held in the territory. Although the other colonial powers loyally supported their ally, no majority could be found to support the proposed mission. Despite this lack of enthusiasm, the French duly held the plebiscite, which presented the choice to the Togolese of either continued trust status or the new status as an autonomous republic, but it did not mention independence as a possible alternative. To no one's surprise, 71 per cent of those voting chose to accept the second alternative, and the Republic of Togoland came into being.

The French then issued another invitation to the United Nations, suggesting that a mission be sent to take note of the genuineness of the independence enjoyed by the republic. This offer was accepted, and the mission reported that the French were indeed interpreting the statute very liberally, but insisted that there must be another election, this time a free one, before independence. The French agreed, and in spite of extensive use by Grunitsky of tactics hitherto used by the French, Olympio, to his own surprise, was the winner. Eighteen months later, on April 27, 1960, Togoland became independent under the title of the Republic of Togo. Sylvanus Olympio remained President and Prime Minister of the new nation until he was assassinated on January 13, 1963, by some disgruntled soldiers, whereupon Grunitsky returned from exile and took his place.

Cameroun

The trust territory of Cameroun presented a far more difficult problem, in part for lack of a leader with the stature of Olympio capable of uniting the whole sprawling country and in larger part because of tribal and religious dissensions. As in Nigeria, much of Northern Cameroun is Muslim, and the peoples in the south are on the whole more prosperous and better educated. In the cities, the strongest political party, the Union des Populations Camerounaises (UPC), had a positive program capable of uniting all the peoples and possessed strong tribal support among the Bassa, one of the most powerful of the tribes. But this party, an original affiliate of the RDA, had refused to follow the RDA leaders when they broke with the French Communist Party in 1950. It remained extreme left-wing, even Communist, in orientation, though far from all its leaders were Communists.

When the French in 1955 were attempting to institute constitutional reforms comparable with those in Togoland, the UPC organized demonstrations in Douala, the chief commercial city and a stronghold of the Bassa, which developed into serious riots in which several Europeans were killed. But their most enduring effect was the revival of tribal antagonisms which carried over into all future elections. The UPC was proscribed, and many of its leaders sent to jail or exiled. Nevertheless, the new constitution was proclaimed, and elections held. The UPC members and sympathizers boycotted the election and engaged in acts of terrorism, including the murder of a couple of candidates. Since the UPC was the only party with a national following, the resulting government was a coalition whose leader, a Catholic named André Mbida, spent much of his energies in continuing to combat the UPC, whose members engaged in local guerrilla warfare against him and his government.

Meanwhile, the independence movement, by no means confined to the UPC and its supporters, was growing in the country. Mbida's coalition began to break up when he refused to support demands made by other parties for an early independence, and he resigned; his place was taken by Ahmadou Ahidjo, a young Muslim from the northern part of the territory. Since he showed himself capable of governing and possessed the backing of the strongest political party, the French, who by this time were anxious to concede independence, gave him their support.

Meanwhile, the UPC was still active, though illegal. If the party, which had not abandoned its sporadic guerrilla warfare, were to be legalized, it might win control of the government in free elections and thus upset the precarious political equilibrium in the territory. This the French were determined not to allow, in spite of the strong possibility that the United Nations would insist on new elections before independence. An amnesty was granted to individual UPC members, most of whom returned to the territory; but the UPC itself remained banned. Its leaders addressed the United Nations but lost their case by refusing to forgo violence. Although it was well known that the last elections, held as long ago as 1956, had been unfree and the result unfair to left-wing electors, the Indian delegate, whom no one could accuse of being colonialist, fought effectively in the United Nations for immediate independence without an election, in preference to granting the UPC the right to participate in an election without having abjured the use of violence. Other members were undoubtedly impressed by the French argument that independence was likely to be indefinitely delayed if there were a new election. Thus, in spite of the solid opposition of the Soviet bloc and most of the independent African states, the French viewpoint was upheld in two successive sessions of the United Nations General Assembly, and the Cameroun Republic was allowed to become independent on January 1, 1960, in exchange for an undertaking by Ahidjo to hold elections as soon as feasible after independence.

The independence celebrations were marred by riots in Douala, the center of UPC strength, and only very slowly has order been established in the territory. When a referendum on the form of the new constitution was submitted to the electorate the following month, seventy-seven more persons were killed. The UPC boycotted the referendum, but there was a 66 per cent turnout, the vote going to the new constitution by a relatively small majority. Both the chief cities voted against it by overwhelming majorities. When the results of the referendum were known, the ban was lifted on the UPC, which was thus able to fight the ensuing election. Ahidjo, strongly backed in the north, won 61 seats out of 100, the UPC winning only 22. Ahidjo then became President of the new republic, a position he continues to hold today. When Nigeria became independent later in the same year, the British trust territory of the Cameroons was required to choose between union with Nigeria or the Cameroun Republic. The southern sector chose to join Cameroun, as noted in the last chapter.

The Malagasy Republic

REBELLION OF 1947. The island of Madagascar, unlike mainland Africa, was regarded by the Allies during World War II as a strategic outpost; and it was believed that the Japanese might well attempt to take it, since naval power after the disasters of 1941 and 1942 was no longer securely in Western hands. The French naval base of Diego Suarez in particular seemed vulnerable to possible Japanese attack. It was also considered possible that the French Governor of Madagascar, who was loyal to Vichy, might be instructed to collaborate with the Japanese and agree to do so. The British, therefore, with the aid of South African troops, took possession by force of the island in 1942 against sporadic but not negligible resistance. They handed over the civil administration to the Free French in the following year.

The Malgache people, who had noted French weakness during the war, expected to be able to extract major reforms from their masters as soon as the war was over, though few wished to be altogether free of France. During their period of rule, the French had, at least since the regime of Galliéni, to a large degree neglected the island, and it had rarely been blessed with good governors. But one thing they had certainly achieved, albeit unintentionally: The memories of the old Merina tyranny had largely disappeared. What remained was a nostalgic memory of the centuries of independence. Moreover, in Madagascar there had been little social mixing between the French and Malgache. The Merina aristocracy in particular held itself aloof, and the two communities lived side by side without much contact, in spite of the interest displayed at all times by French savants in the native Malgache culture.

After the war, Madagascar, like other French colonies, became part of the French Union with the same political institutions as elsewhere. But the size of the island made provincial assemblies necessary in addition to a territorial assembly, which was elected indirectly by provincial assemblies, themselves directly elected but under a restricted franchise and by the usual double electoral college. The nationalist party, Mouvement Démocratique de la Rénovation Malgache (MDRM), though devoted to the restoration of Malgache autonomy, was willing to accept the framework of the French Union, but at least it expected to control the territorial assembly. But the French systematically supported an opposition party, which, combined with the vote of the European electoral college, succeeded in preventing the nationalists from winning control, whereupon an insurrection broke out, directed partly against the French and partly against their collaborators. The nationalists may well have felt that the French would not persist in their policy if they were compelled to fight and that their losses would persuade them that it was not worth fighting to keep an island that had always been an economic drain on metropolitan resources. Nevertheless, the French, as usual in such circumstances, decided to fight. It took them about three years to suppress the rebellion in all parts of the country; it was estimated that more than 80,000 Malgache were killed during the operation. Two of the three chief political leaders of the MDRM were condemned to death, and a third to penal servitude for life. The sentences of the first two were commuted. All were exiled to France.

The part of the country where the rebellion was most prolonged was utterly devastated. The French provided substantial funds for reconstruction (more than $300 million in ten years), but the economy of the island remained depressed, and there were large annual budget deficits. The nationalist movement continued to seethe under the surface, while the French took careful steps to see that only moderate men were elected in future to the French and territorial assemblies.

ACHIEVEMENT OF SELF-GOVERNMENT. In 1956, the *loi-cadre* was passed, giving Madagascar the same reforms as in other French colonies. The provincial assemblies were revived, and each became semiresponsible. But, at the center, there was set up a real federal executive, which possessed powers delegated to it by the provincial assemblies sufficient to enable it to become a true government for the island. A former schoolteacher named Philibert Tsiranana, a non-Merina, who had been a Socialist deputy in France, was strong enough, in the absence of the leading nationalists, to win election as President of one of the provincial assemblies and Vice-President of the central government. Although not himself a member of an extreme nationalist party, he was a very astute politician, and well understood just how much the French were prepared to grant at one time. With a secure electoral base of his own in the provinces, he could afford to disregard the Communist and nationalist opposition in the cities, especially the capital of Tananarive. It is probable also that he used his influence in France to prevent the return of the nationalists "martyred" in 1947, who might well have undermined his electoral support. Instead, he arranged for an amnesty for them, under which they were still kept out of Madagascar itself.

In the Constitutional Referendum of 1958, Tsiranana called for a Yes vote against the continued opposition of the extreme nationalists and Communists, who still believed he would never win independence by his methods. He assured his supporters, however, that independence would not be long delayed once Madagascar was in the Community. As it turned out, he was as good as his word. At the first opportunity he was offered to escape from the last restrictions on independence, he joined with Mali in asking for a new status for his island in exchange for which he was willing to sign a treaty with France. The French agreed and on June 26, 1960, the island became independent under the name of the Malagasy Republic, with a constitution in many respects similar to that of the Fifth French Republic. Malagasy is no longer a federal state, and the provincial councils possess only very limited autonomy. Philibert Tsiranana remains President, an office he has held since May, 1959. The amnestied nationalists returned, and two hold office in his government.

All the French territories in Africa are now independent with the exception of French Somaliland, which by its own choice in the referendum of September 28, 1958, remains an overseas territory with limited self-government. With the achievement of independence by Algeria in July, 1962, France ceased to have an overseas empire beyond the overseas territories and *départements*, small islands, and mainland enclaves, all too small to be interested in or capable of maintaining their "international sovereignty."

11. The Belgian Congo and Ruanda-Urundi

The Belgian Congo

THE CONGO AS A MODEL COLONY. For many years, Belgium was widely believed to have been the most successful of the European colonizers. There were few disturbances in the Congo, and it seemed there was little demand on the part of the Congolese for an increasing share of the government. What the Belgians, unlike other colonial powers, had provided was enough paid employment in the cities to keep the rural Congolese who migrated there reasonably content with their lot. They had not kept Congolese from rising as high in industry as their capacities warranted. They had prevented the rise of a *colon* class by restricting the immigration of Europeans to those who could show they had either a job to do in the country or sufficient means to start a business; they had prevented them from gaining political power by the simple means of never giving either Belgians or Congolese the vote. They had entered into partnership with the large Belgian and international corporations which provided the wealth of the country and compelled them to adopt a relatively enlightened labor policy and to give their employees a modicum of amenities. They had built huge housing projects to provide shelter for urban employees, incidentally helping to civilize them. They had given them more primary education than any other colonial power in Africa, and withal, they had not given them enough education beyond the primary level to make them discontented at the lack of opportunity to use it.

Thus, in their own opinion, which was shared by many foreign powers, the Belgians had succeeded in avoiding the mistakes made by others. The British and French had given "their" Africans too much education, especially higher education. The result was a class of underemployed professional men for whom there was no work in the higher ranks of the civil service, since these positions were reserved for the British and French themselves.

303

In the Congo, there were no hideous shantytowns, such as are to be seen in or outside almost every British city in Africa and in Portuguese Luanda in Angola. Unlike the French, they had not tried to assimilate the Congolese and pretend they could be made into Belgians. But, as human beings, the Congolese could be persuaded to desire material objects; and if they worked hard enough, they might hope to earn enough to buy manufactured products, starting with a bicycle and ending with a Cadillac. There was no question of settlers demanding, much less enjoying, rule over Africans and Africans fighting back, as in Kenya or Southern Rhodesia. No powerful labor unions had grown up in the Congo. The government compelled big business to grant the demands of the Congolese if they were justified. There was no insulting provision for separate facilities, as in Kenya and Rhodesia (at least not officially), still less any such nonsense as that Africans were incapable of working heavy machinery and driving trains, as in the Portuguese territories and Rhodesia. The same train, indeed, that passed through Angola started its run in the Congo with African engineers. Léopold- ville and Elisabethville were clean, beautiful, safe cities, and Cité Leo II in Léopoldville was an attractive if somewhat anti- septic suburb, inhabited entirely by Africans and served by busi- nesses owned and operated by Africans. Why, the Belgians asked, should anything go wrong when everything had been taken care of in such a neat and orderly manner?

Yet, today the very word "Congo" suggests to most people the antithesis of all this. It has become a byword in the history of colonialism, the one colony that was granted independence before there had been any real preparation for it; it has been forgotten, if it was ever known, that the Belgian system was once so greatly admired.

The Belgian attitude to the Congolese may be summed up in one word—"paternalism." The Congolese, to the Belgians, were children who had to be treated kindly but firmly, and grad- ually brought to maturity. When they reached maturity, papa would be around to help them when necessary and would have the right to share in the fruits of a long and honorable career. The trouble with this notion was that, while Africans elsewhere belonging to the same Bantu groups were being given positions of responsibility by their colonial masters, and later while they were fighting for and eventually winning independence, the Belgians stubbornly stuck to the same program which had hitherto worked satisfactorily. They could not imagine that their Congolese were like other Africans, that sooner or later they would begin to demand political changes and that some policy would have to be devised for meeting the new situation.

POLITICAL DEVELOPMENT ACCORDING TO PLAN. Looking back on the postwar period in the Congo, it would now seem that the crucial failure occurred as long ago as 1952. At that time, the Gold Coast had a semiresponsible government with a recently appointed chief minister, but no other Black African territory, British or French, had reached the same degree of political development. Belgian officialdom had come to the decision that municipal elections should be held in the Congo as the first step toward the devolution of governmental powers on the Congolese. But the step was not taken. Postponed from year to year for no good reason, the elections did not take place until January, 1957, by which time, the Gold Coast was due to receive independence in two months and the French colonies were already wrestling with the *loi-cadre* and setting up semiresponsible governments. Almost all the British colonies had by this time overtaken and passed the Congo.

Educational facilities for African secondary and higher education had likewise been proceeding at a snail's pace. The University of Lovanium and the National University at Elisabethville had been operating, respectively, for three years and one year. But there were as yet no Congolese graduates, and education abroad had always been discouraged. The universities had been planned with considerable care and preparations made long in advance. In order to keep the standards equal to those in Belgium so that resident Belgians as well as Congolese could attend them, thus avoiding the all-African colleges favored by the British, a limited number of Congolese were admitted to those high schools which prepared students for the University. A special pre-university year was provided for those Congolese with insufficient preparation, during which they could cram for the entrance examination. Everything had been carefully thought out as if the Belgians had all the time in the world. But, in fact, they had no more time than the other colonial powers; and when they were forced to abandon their timetable, they became rattled, ultimately leaving their valuable colony precipitately with their work of preparation for independence not even half done.

The municipal elections of 1957 were held in three cities

only, and resulted in the election of Joseph Kasavubu, President of the ABAKO Party, as mayor of a Léopoldville suburb. Although Kasavubu was supported in the election mainly by the Bakongo cultural association, as a well-known Congolese nationalist he enjoyed some support also from other tribes in the capital. At this time, Patrice Lumumba was a moderate pro-Belgian, not yet active in politics, who did not stand for any of the positions open for election in 1957. Kasavubu, once he had been elected, decided to use his office as a means for promoting the ABAKO program of early independence; other Congolese, realizing that political reform was on the way, began to form parties, including the Mouvement National Congolais (MNC), led by Patrice Lumumba, which was the only party that tried to win members throughout the entire Congo and adopted a truly national program. All the other parties of consequence were based, like ABAKO, on tribal affiliations.

In January, 1959, a few days before the new reforms were due to be announced, disturbances broke out in Léopoldville. Kasavubu and Lumumba had just returned from the All-African People's Conference held in Accra—where, indeed, they had both spoken in a most moderate manner—and had been booked to speak at a meeting in the capital. At the last moment, the government prohibited the meeting, and the rioting began, apparently without premeditation, causing many casualties. There was much pent-up resentment among the Africans, who were suffering from severe unemployment, for which they blamed the Belgians. The policy of paternalism had not led to good race relations.

The Belgians, frightened by the outbreaks, nevertheless suppressed them quickly and set up a commission to inquire into their causes. ABAKO was banned but soon reorganized under a different name, and Kasavubu was briefly detained. However, the reforms were announced on the appointed date, and King Baudouin paid a visit to the colony, taking the opportunity to announce that it was his government's policy to lead the Congo "without harmful procrastination but also without thoughtless haste toward independence, in prosperity and peace." Then the political leaders, including Kasavubu and Lumumba, with whom the Belgians knew they would have to work, were invited to Belgium and given a tour, at government expense, to enable them to appreciate something of Belgian life and institutions. Included in the reforms was a timetable for the holding of elections in 1959-60 for a hierarchy of governmental bodies. Each superior council would as a rule be elected by the lower councils, and the latter would be chosen by universal suffrage. It was an extremely carefully worked out plan and by March, 1960, would have provided the Congo with a central government, with a Congolese majority, chosen indirectly by the Congolese; some safeguards and reserved powers would be held in Belgian hands until independence, for which no definite date was set.

THE PLAN GOES AWRY. The year 1959 proved to be crucial. The Congolese, knowing that the Belgians were pledged to independence and that there would be elections within the year, feverishly began to build parties able to fight them. Having had little political experience and faced with a totally inexperienced electorate, the nationalists felt that to win the elections—and in this they may well have been right—they had to outbid one another in promises. No political profit could be gained by accepting the Belgian timetable. Although some tribal parties were quite content with the Belgian program, they deprived themselves of an appealing election slogan by admitting the fact, instead of demanding immediate independence like the nationalists. Few, indeed, of the small businessmen and clerks who now led political parties had the least idea of what independence would mean to a people without political experience.

Meanwhile, the Belgians, both in Belgium and the colony, began to have second thoughts as to the wisdom of granting so much so soon. The Belgian Colonial Minister was greeted with contumely by the settlers and European businessmen in the colony, and his position at home was undermined to such a degree that he was compelled to resign. His successor did not change the policy, but exhibited a little less public enthusiasm for it. Throughout the year, minor disturbances were frequent, and it was becoming increasingly difficult for the Belgians to keep order at the numerous political meetings, at which Congolese incessantly demanded the revision of the timetable and the immediate establishment of a central government. Faced with this clamor, the Belgians at last came to the conclusion that the only solution was to discuss all the problems openly with the Congolese leaders at a conference. Before the conference was convened in Brussels, on January 21, 1960, the Belgian Cabinet reached the decision that it was best to concede early independence and take all the risks involved, in preference to trying to maintain law and order during the proposed period of transition from semiresponsible government to independence—a task it seems to have believed was beyond the power of a small nation.

UNPLANNED INDEPENDENCE. The conference began with a statement of their decision by the Belgians, which succeeded in shocking most of the Congolese leaders, who had never expected such a complete capitulation. No political party had as yet established its ascendancy in the Congo, though Lumumba, who had himself just been released from prison to take part in the conference, was probably in the lead on a nationwide basis. With independence only five months away, it was urgent for the leaders to return to the territory to make preparations. Although Belgian technical experts laid their plans before them, it is evident that their minds were elsewhere, in large measure accounting for the most conspicuous failure of the conference, the postponement of the decision on the kind of government to be established at independence. Kasavubu and the Katangan leader, Moise Tshombe, strongly urged the creation of a federal state; Lumumba, the outstanding personality at the conference, opposed them. The Belgians, who had always administered their colony as a unitary state, not wishing to see it disintegrate into its numerous tribal parts, backed Lumumba's viewpoint but did not impose a solution, preferring to leave the decision to the National Assembly, which would call a convention to write the constitution after independence. The "organic laws" under which the Congo was to operate until the new constitution was accepted provided for a strong central government, but assumed it would be headed by a man who could command enough support from the whole Congo to win the necessary agreement for his constitution.

It was evident enough at the time and became more evident later that the Belgians expected to be asked by the Congolese to stay on and help them run the country after independence. They made elaborate provisions for maintaining their administration; though Congolese would set the policy, it would be Belgians who would carry it out and preserve the administrative framework of their own regime. This was a system used by the British in the last years of a colony, during which the Africans enjoyed responsible government but were not yet independent. The Belgians now proposed to grant full independence in exchange for a mere written agreement that the Congolese would retain enough Belgian officials to enable them to run the country. Since it was common practice in newly independent nations to employ expatriate officials and military personnel for a considerable period after independence, there was no reason in theory why the Congolese could not have done the same thing. But the Congolese had not been trained in government, and there was no period of transition during which they could learn their jobs under Belgian tutelage, with the Belgians retaining ultimate control of the country. The Congolese were less, not more, educated and experienced than their counterparts in the British and French colonies. Only very minor administrative positions in the government had been filled previously by Congolese, and the Belgians never put into operation an accelerated program of training, such as other colonial powers, especially Italy in Somalia, had done. When the British were preparing to grant independence to their colonies, they always gave serious thought to the task of "Africanizing" the civil service and set up numerous commissions to recommend and report on progress in this field before taking the final step. In short, the Belgians, after believing for decades that the Congolese were children, suddenly acted as if they were mature and responsible human beings who would realize that the administration would collapse if they ceased to make use of their former masters. It did not occur to the Belgians that most of the Congolese leaders were so inexperienced and ignorant that they did not realize how impossible it would be to run a huge and wealthy country without Belgian assistance, and that in the new-found exhilaration of independence they would grab the opportunity presented to get rid of their masters; nor did they realize how cordially they were disliked by so many, especially by the rank and file of the army.

Lastly, the Belgians did not appreciate fully the difference in status between an independent state and a self-governing colony. An independent state could present its case in the United Nations and win invaluable support from former colonial nations, as well as from nations like the Soviet Union which made a profession of anticolonialism. It could persuade the United Nations to forbid even the colonial power that had just granted independence to keep its troops in the now independent state, on pain of sanctions, in spite of treaties to the contrary. The United Nations could take the position that the independence was not genuine as long as the Belgians were in the country as advisers, that independence was merely the continuation of colonialism in a slightly disguised form. If the Congo had been only a self-governing colony, Belgium would have been under no legal obligation to obey the injunctions of the United Nations. She could have continued to take such steps as she wished to maintain law and order and to see that the Congolese wrote themselves a suitable constitution on pain of seeing their total independence postponed until they did. These errors of judgment have cost not only Belgium but the Congo and the world dearly, and it still does not seem to this writer at least that the situation in February, 1960, had deteriorated so seriously that Belgium was left no choice but to do what she did.

In May, 1960, elections were held for both the provincial and national assemblies. Tshombe's party won by a small margin in Katanga, and he became Premier of that province. Both Lumumba and Kasavubu formed electoral alliances to fight the elections for the National Assembly, but neither group won an over-all majority. According to the organic laws, the King was to choose a prime minister who would then, as under most Continental constitutions, have to win the approval of the Assembly for his investiture. Lumumba, as leader of the largest bloc, was first chosen; when he failed, the choice fell on Kasavubu, who likewise failed. Lumumba then tried again, and this time there was a deal. He was approved as Prime Minister, and a few days later Kasavubu won the apparently less important position of Head of State.

The Republic of the Congo

MUTINY AND ITS AFTERMATH. Independence day passed safely, and power was duly transferred to Congolese hands. A few days afterward, a mutiny broke out in the Congolese Army, known as the Force Publique. Belgian officers were deposed by their men, of whom the top-ranking were only sergeant-majors. A number of atrocities were committed, Belgians were murdered, and a panic followed among the Belgian civilians who tried to cross the Congo to the French Congolese capital of Brazzaville. The Belgian crack parachutists, sent to restore law and order, took some reprisals of their own, but succeeded partially in their task.

On the outbreak of the mutiny, Kasavubu and Lumumba tried to reason with the leaders and persuade them to return to obedience, but the rioting soldiers refused to recognize their authority. To them they were merely African politicians of no particular account who had been nobodies a year ago. They did not recognize the authority of their own noncommissioned officers, and for weeks they were a law to themselves, terrorizing the country by their apparently purposeless looting and atrocities. They had been trained by the Belgians in the use of arms, but having been granted little responsibility by their officers, could not be expected to show it now that they were on their own. Lumumba, finding he could make no headway with the army, decided to join its new leaders in their demand that all Belgian officers must leave the country; but Kasavubu, disapproving of his Prime Minister's decision, retired to his house to sit out the rebellion. In Katanga, Tshombe, with the aid of the Belgians, was able to restore order quickly in his province and on July 11 declared it to be an independent state with himself as President. The following day Lumumba appealed to the United Nations for aid in expelling the Belgians. The Security Council then met, authorized Secretary-General Dag Hammarskjöld to assemble and send a United Nations force to the Congo, and called upon the Belgians to withdraw their troops; but the Secretary was instructed not to interfere in domestic matters.

U.N. PRESENCE AND CONGOLESE CONFLICTS. Such an assignment was in fact impossible, since the local government was never at any time in control of the situation. At first, the United Nations troops, mostly recruited from African countries, began to disarm the Force Publique. If this policy had been consistently carried out and U.N. troops had taken their place—at their maximum there were 18,000 U.N. troops, as compared with 25,000 in the Force Publique—then the constitutional convention could have met under U.N. protection and written a federal constitution, to which Tshombe, who had not yet consolidated his hold on his province, might well have agreed. If he had refused, then the United Nations would have been justified in using force against him and would have been strong enough to prevail. But in preserving the fiction that the Congo was an independent, self-governing state and Lumumba its legitimate Prime Minister whose rapidly changing whims were entitled to full consideration, the United Nations missed its opportunity, which never recurred. Lumumba, with the strong support of the African countries in the United Nations and the Soviet bloc, insisted on the departure of the Belgian troops and administrators, thus leaving the country a prey to anarchy, except for Katanga, whose President, Tshombe, refused to admit either military or civilian representatives of the central government into his province. Under strong U.N. pressure, he at last agreed to let his Belgian troops go, but the United Nations was unable to prevent him from hiring military advisers, some of whom were Belgian, and recruiting mercenary troops wherever he could find them. Having at his disposal the considerable taxes paid by the mining corporations of his province, which he could not yet be compelled to share with the central government, he did not experience any difficulty in finding enough money to pay them.

Meanwhile, Lumumba refused to call a constitutional convention, and the United Nations made no move to compel him to do so. The majority of the nations in the Assembly, including the Soviet Union, assumed with Lumumba that the Congo must be a unitary state. Any attempt to give substantial autonomy to the provinces was believed, for some reason, to serve the interests of the colonial and imperialist powers. When, more than a year later, the United Nations threw its weight behind the idea of a federal state, it proved to be extremely difficult to persuade Tshombe to agree, since by that time he was exercising undisputed power in his own "independent" province.

In September, 1960, it was announced that Lumumba had taken delivery of ten airplanes provided by the Soviet Union, presumably to aid him in suppressing the revolts in Katanga and South Kasai, which had also seceded from the rule of the central government. At this apparent direct intrusion of the Cold War into Africa, President Kasavubu emerged from his semiretirement, declared Lumumba deposed, and nominated Joseph Ileo, a moderate intellectual, in his place. The following day, Lumumba and his cabinet reciprocated by relieving Kasavubu of his duties. Since Kasavubu, as leader of the Bakongo Party, had more strength in the capital than Lumumba, he was able to prevent the latter's escape to his own center of support in Stanleyville; a few days later, Lumumba was arrested by the Force Publique, now under somewhat better discipline and generally obedient to the control of its chief of staff, Colonel Joseph Mobutu. Mobutu himself then declared that he personally was taking control of the government and appointed a commission composed of young educated Congolese to perform the functions of government. These young men were guided throughout by Belgian advisers.

The civil war continued sporadically during the next months. Mobutu, aided to some degree by the wary neutrality of the United Nations forces, was able to exercise some authority over the areas around Léopoldville and some parts of the rest of the country. Kasavubu's position, in spite of some differences with Mobutu, improved accordingly, and his delegation, after a closely contested vote, was accorded recognition by the U.N. General Assembly in preference to a group nominated by the ousted Prime Minister. Meanwhile, Tshombe remained in control of his own province. Lumumba's supporters, led by Vice-Premier Antoine Gizenga, retained Stanleyville and its environs and made occasional raids into Katanga, while Kasavubu, Tshombe, and other provincial leaders declared themselves ready to negotiate with one another on the future form of the state. Although at times it seemed they were ready to accept Lumumba into an eventual government and come to terms with him, no conclusions were reached, and no actual negotiations were undertaken. When he tried to escape, he was recaptured and transferred to Katanga for safer custody.

All this time the Belgians, including military personnel, had been returning to the Congo in ever greater numbers with the purpose of preventing their once prosperous colony from relapsing into chaos, a task which the U.N. experts, dedicated and devoted as most of them were, lacked the experience to do by themselves. Nevertheless, the U.N. chiefs in the Congo bitterly complained of the lack of cooperation of the Belgians and insisted that they were hampering them in their task. Backed by the Russians and their allies in the United Nations, they accused the Belgians of trying to restore the country to its colonial status and refused to take seriously the Belgian claim that "local authorities" had invited them. They, as well as the Belgians, knew well enough how little authority was actually wielded by the Congolese; but far too much of the energies of both groups, which should have been working together for the restoration of the country, was wasted in bickering between themselves on the right of the other to be there. The Belgians were the men with experience of the Congo; but the Security Council consistently demanded their withdrawal, and little attempt was made by anyone of responsibility to persuade them to cooperate in the almost insuperably difficult task that would have taxed their combined abilities to the full.

Early in February, 1961, Kasavubu declared he was restoring

civil government and reappointed Ileo as Prime Minister. Colonel (now Major-General) Mobutu, who had been losing ground in recent weeks owing to military reverses and inability to exercise full control over the Force Publique, retired to devote his full time to his military duties. A few days later, it was announced that Lumumba had escaped from his prison in Katanga and shortly afterward that he had been killed. This murder led to bitter recriminations in the United Nations. The Soviet Union—backed among the African nations by Mali, Ghana, Guinea, and the United Arab Republic—recognized Vice-Premier Gizenga's regime in Stanleyville as the only legitimate government of the Congo, while the U.N. majority continued to recognize Kasavubu's dismissal of Lumumba as legal and the government headed by Ileo as legitimate. This situation came to an end only when a new Prime Minister, Cyril Adoula, was appointed in mid-1961. Gizenga soon afterward lost the support of his local army leaders, and was handed over to the central government, which has kept him in custody ever since. Adoula's Government is now the only internationally recognized Congolese Government.

Early in 1961, Tshombe summoned a conference to be held in Tananarive in the Malagasy Republic, to which went Kasavubu, Ileo—as Prime Minister—and Adoula, at that time Minister of Trade in the central government. Tshombe dominated the conference, from which emerged a plan for a loose confederation of Congolese states, each with virtual autonomy. A further conference at Coquilhatville in Equateur Province was convened to settle the details of the Tananarive constitution, but Tshombe, who believed he had devised an acceptable formula under which the U.N. officials would leave the country, walked out when he found that the central government leaders had no intention of requesting U.N. departure. When he tried to return to Katanga, he was arrested and held for two months, after which he was released by Mobutu in exchange for a verbal agreement that he refused to honor once he was back in Katanga.

RE-ESTABLISHMENT OF CONGOLESE UNITY. After further futile attempts to persuade Tshombe to negotiate seriously, in the course of which Secretary-General Hammarskjöld lost his life in an air crash, the United Nations decided to take military action in Katanga to force Tshombe to accept a federal state that would not leave the federal government powerless. After two failures against the Katangan troops, led by foreign mercenaries paid out of the proceeds of taxes on the mining companies in the province, it was finally successful. Tshombe bowed to the inevitable and went abroad for his health, while Adoula sent Joseph Ileo as the representative of the central government to supervise the reintegration of the rebellious province. In April, 1963, two members of Tshombe's party became ministers in a new all-party cabinet led by Adoula.

Meanwhile, the Congolese Government requested several nations to assist in the retraining of the Force Publique. In the expectation that this would be accomplished by the end of 1963, U.N. Secretary-General U Thant announced his intention to withdraw the last U.N. troops from the country. Despite uncertainty over whether this could be accomplished, U Thant felt it necessary to make the announcement in view of the perilous condition of U.N. finances, and the refusal of several nations, including France, which opposed the actions of the United Nations in the Congo, to contribute to its expenses. However, various nations, including France, have offered increased technical and direct financial aid, which will help to put the country on its feet. But even if the Congo can hold together under a federal or semifederal constitution, which still remains to be written and accepted by Congolese politicians, there can be no doubt at all that the process of nation-building has hardly begun. Potentially, the Republic of the Congo is the richest nation of independent Africa, as it was the richest colony. But to realize this potential her tribesmen must become patriots, her politicians must become statesmen, and her foreign supporters must cooperate for the benefit of the Congo and not their own.

The Congo has already been a test for the United Nations, which has emerged with a measure of success. At the least the U.N. averted chaos and prevented the Congo from becoming a battleground in the Cold War. In the next stage, the Congo will be a test of African capacity for self-rule, and—be it said—self-abnegation. If the Congo, despite the history of the last three years, can become a prosperous modern nation, it will only be because the Congolese and their foreign supporters cooperated to make it so, and put the interests of the country—and the world—before their own.

Rwanda and Burundi

THE TRUST TERRITORY OF RUANDA-URUNDI. After World War I, Belgium was granted a League of Nations mandate over a small sector of the former German East Africa, known thereafter as

Ruanda-Urundi, which was converted into a United Nations trust territory after World War II. It consisted of two separate kingdoms, each ruled by a Mwami who belonged to a conquering African tribe usually known as the Batutsi (or Watutsi), a people of Hamitic stock who often attained to very great physical stature. In each kingdom, the Batutsi were in a minority, but succeeded in dominating and even enslaving the existing Bantu tribes, especially the Bahutu; and the Bami (plural of Mwami) ruled as absolute monarchs wielding political and religious power.

The Belgians maintained these kings in office, but in other respects extended their Congolese centralized bureaucratic system to Ruanda-Urundi. The Bami were expected to conform to Belgian policy and accept the advice of Belgian officials. The country, unlike the Congo, was both poor and overpopulated; it was a drain on Belgian resources, but Congo revenues helped to keep it solvent. Since Ruanda-Urundi was a U.N. trust territory, the Belgians constantly had to listen to criticism of their policy in the United Nations, especially their failure to grant political reforms. For this reason, the first experimental elections for advisory councils took place in Ruanda-Urundi as early as 1956, the Belgians using this experience as a guide for the 1957 elections in the Congo. But thereafter Ruanda-Urundi was not brought ahead as quickly as the Congo. When the latter became independent, the Belgians were still putting the final touches on a new program of reforms in Ruanda-Urundi. The major difficulty in the trust territory was the existence of the Bami and their rulership over the more numerous Bahutu. Obviously, if there were to be an immediate grant of democratic self-government under universal manhood suffrage, the Bahutu parties would win and might be expected in turn to suppress their former masters and might even take revenge upon them, unless the Belgian army stayed to prevent this.

CIVIL WAR. The death of the Mwami of Ruanda in 1959 was the beginning of troubles in that kingdom. The Batutsi chiefs, as was their right, chose a new Mwami from a minor chiefly family, passing over the royal heirs. The young man they chose, who took the name of Kigeli V, at once began to play an active part in politics, backing the activities of the Union National Ruandaise (UNAR), which was calling for early independence. Soon after the accession of Kigeli to the throne of Ruanda, civil war broke out between the Batutsi and the Bahutu. The latter overwhelmed their numerically inferior enemies and drove many of them out of the country. It was in part this civil war—which the Belgians took their time in suppressing—that determined the Mwami to try to win independence quickly before the Bahutu had been able to organize a political party of their own. The UNAR, which was made up primarily of the ruling Batutsi but, like the UPC in the Cameroons, included also nationalists, still had a chance of winning an election if it were held soon enough. But many Belgian officials desired a social revolution that would depose the Batutsi from their ruling position before the first important elections in the territory. They were, therefore, not too displeased with the recent civil war, which had resulted in considerable redistribution of land and a partial breakup of the large Batutsi holdings, regarding this as a first step toward eventual Bahutu rule. When UNAR leaders began to demand immediate independence, some of them were arrested, but the Mwami himself went abroad. The elections which followed in July, 1960, resulted in a victory for the younger Bahutu party (Parmehutu). Shortly afterward, the Belgians formed a provisional coalition government made up of thirty-five Bahutu and twelve Batutsi of their choice. All the new ministers were either Belgians assisted by Africans or Africans assisted by Belgians. The Mwami was then forbidden to return to the country.

In Burundi (Urundi's name since it became an independent state), the Batutsi Mwami preferred to act as a constitutional monarch and had not been active in politics. Perhaps for this reason, the Bahutu did not regard the Batutsi as enemies. Politics in Burundi consisted rather of interfamily rivalries, and political parties were organized by the leading Batutsi feudal families, each with its own Bahutu retainers. Unlike in Rwanda (Ruanda's name since independence), no social revolution had as yet taken place in this territory, nor was one in prospect. But, as in Rwanda, one nationalist independence party known as the UPRONA existed, which the Belgians treated in much the same way as they treated the UNAR in Rwanda. When, therefore, local elections resulted in a victory for the opponents of the UPRONA, the Belgians decided to hold territory-wide elections as soon as possible and then, with the consent of the United Nations, grant an early independence.

But it proved impossible to win the consent of the United Nations. In the Fourth Committee, it was urged that the Belgians had systematically prevented both the nationalist parties from having a fair chance to come to power, that this must have been done because they did not propose to grant genuine independence, that the Mwami of Rwanda had been kept in exile improperly, and that no opportunity had been given to his subjects to express their wishes. Lastly, it was suggested that the Belgians were magnifying the rivalry between the Batutsi and the Bahutu for their own colonial and nefarious purposes, to which the Belgians replied that the number of Batutsi refugees from Rwanda and Burundi spoke for itself. But the General Assembly firmly requested them to postpone the proposed elections in both territories, to which, after long consultation with the political leaders in Burundi and Rwanda, they agreed. All the more moderate leaders asked for a period of autonomy before independence in order to allow the communal rivalries to subside. Following the conference, the provisional government of Rwanda, still dissatisfied, declared the country to be independent and formally deposed the Mwami (January, 1961); but as in Buganda, this had no effect since no one else recognized it.

U.N. INTERVENTION AND INDEPENDENCE. The problem thus fell to the United Nations to solve, and it proved to be probably the most effective and sensible action the United Nations has yet taken in any colonial territory. A commission visited Ruanda-Urundi in mid-1961 and reported that conditions in the territories had changed enough for elections to be held, with a fair chance that the results would truly reflect opinion in the territories. The commission then supervised elections in both Rwanda and Burundi. In Rwanda, a plebiscite was also held on the question of whether the territory should become a republic or whether the Mwami should return as ruler. In Burundi, the elections passed off peacefully. The nationalist UPRONA, with a leadership that was mainly Batutsi, campaigned that it was the party of the popular Mwami and won comfortably. It was the best-organized party; but the noninterference and general benevolence of the Mwami may well have been the deciding factor, even though he gave no overt support to the party which claimed him. In Rwanda, the atmosphere in which the election was held was described later in the Fourth Committee as one of fear and intimidation marked by repeated assassinations. The victory was won by the Bahutu tribal party without difficulty; but the defeated UNAR complained bitterly that both the administering authority and its protégés, the Bahutu party, made it impossible for the people to express their true preferences. The Mwami, who had been overwhelmingly repudiated by the electorate, joined in the protest.

When the commission reported on the results to the United Nations, it was admitted that conditions in Rwanda had been as bad as the opposition claimed. But this did not mean that any other elections in the near future would be any better. Max Dorsinville of Haiti, the chairman of the commission, while criticizing the Belgians for their previous policy that had contributed to the situation, nevertheless made a powerful plea that the election results should be accepted as the only means by which Rwanda could have a stable government and go forward to independence, which was planned for mid-1962. The Committee and the General Assembly agreed with his conclusions, but authorized two more commissions, one to see if UNAR's opposition could be overcome by compromise between the parties and a second to see whether there was any possibility that the two territories, one a monarchy and the other a republic, could be reunited and to supervise the last details prior to independence. The first of these succeeded in persuading the Bahutu majority party to accept two ministers from the UNAR, with which the latter expressed itself as satisfied. The ensuing government would be a national coalition government. The second commission was able to win only an economic union. The leaders of both territories refused to unite before independence, though they expressed a willingness to enter into negotiations afterward.

With these reports before it, the General Assembly dropped the effort to unite the territories and authorized independence for the two separate new nations, the Kingdom of Burundi and the Republic of Rwanda, to become effective July 1, 1962. The debates were marked only by an attempt by the Soviet bloc and others to compel the Belgians to remove their troops by the date of independence and to prevent the two countries from making use of Belgian troops even if they needed them to maintain law and order. The Belgians retorted that, if anarchy followed their withdrawal, they could not be expected to contribute the large amounts of aid they had promised to see the countries through. Eventually, these efforts failed, and the proposals were voted down. Independence for both nations became effective on schedule.

12. The Old Africa—
Portugal's Overseas Provinces

While the other colonial powers were coming to terms, each in its own way, with the rising African nationalism of the postwar period, Portugal preferred to deny that she had any problem in her territories, and thus made no serious attempt to deal with it. This attitude did not conceal any lack of interest in the colonies. On the contrary, the long-lived Salazar dictatorship has spent much effort in trying to make them pay their way and strengthen the feeble Portuguese economy. Without her colonies, Portugal would be merely a small European nation, almost its poorest in money and resources with the highest percentage of illiteracy and the smallest provision for higher education. With them, she remains head of a great nation with a long and glorious history—not a Portuguese empire, but a nation with many provinces, some in Portugal, others separated by great expanses of ocean.

Portugal has been accused of converting her colonies into "overseas provinces" in 1952 because she planned to apply for membership in the United Nations and did not wish to supply information about them as non–self-governing territories. The reason for her step lies deeper than this. It was giving legal expression to her conviction that a nation consists of all its possessions and not only the metropolitan country. Portugal has never at any time recognized the right of a people to exercise sovereignty over a neighboring territory just because of proximity to it. Not even when it was totally surrounded by foreign territory was land under Portuguese sovereignty to be alienated. India might annex Goa by military force, but it was unthinkable that Portugal should ever have *agreed* to cede either Goa or any of her enclaves within India or elsewhere. This, of course, the Indians knew very well; therefore, they had either to let Portugal keep Goa for ever and ever, simply because she insisted that it was hers by right of possession, or to take it by force. Portugal, in her own view, had neither any duty to consult the inhabitants on their wishes nor any obligation to return what she had taken by military force. The cession of a colony was not a fit subject for negotiation.

The Portuguese have not only preserved the fiction that their large colonies of Angola and Mozambique, and the smaller West African colony of Portuguese Guinea, are parts of their home territory and therefore cannot be any concern of the United Nations, they also claim they are self-governing because a few representatives of these colonies, almost always residents of Portugal, sit in the National Assembly at Lisbon, chosen by the limited overseas franchise. Captain Henrique Galvao took his responsibilities as representative of Angola very seriously for the period of his tenure and criticized the colonial administration unmercifully. When his term of office was over, he landed in jail, though he lived to escape and astonish the world with his capture of the Portuguese liner the *Santa Maria.*

The National Assembly has, in fact, little influence on Portuguese administration, either at home or in the colonies. The Portuguese Council of Ministers, dominated by Premier Salazar, is supreme in both. It sets policy and appoints the governors-general who apply that policy in the colonies. The regime is wholly centralized, with authority delegated from the center down to humble native subchiefs who are responsible to the Portuguese regional administrators. The settlers and business interests in the provinces are given special privileges by the government in exchange for their contribution to the colonial economy, though a system of rigorous quotas and high taxation hamper local enterprise. But all control is in the hands of the Portuguese Government, which delegates executive power to the Portuguese governors. To make sure that he behaves himself, the governor is granted an honor guard of secret police (PIDE) who are responsible to the Portuguese Government and not to him. Lest they be contaminated by contact with colonials, these men are almost invariably metropolitan Portuguese.

Portuguese Colonial Theory and Practice

The Portuguese have expended much serious thought on their colonial system, and have developed theories on how colonies should be governed that owe much to Catholic social theory. They believe that all men, including Africans, have the duty to work and that idleness is sinful; ever since the abolition of the Portuguese-dominated slave trade, the African has been compelled to work at least six months in the year for wages. Numerous Africans in both Angola and Mozambique are rounded up annually by local officials and sent to the South African mines, where the Portuguese African is highly regarded for his docility. The government draws a sizable income for this service, both from the paypacket of the working Africans and from the cooperating foreign government. The African must show respect, as a child respects his elders; if he does not, corporal punishment is regarded as a suitable means to enforce respect. Only the *assimilado*, who has managed to surmount the innumerable roadblocks and become both educated and self-supporting, is exempted from these liabilities. He knows Portuguese, is probably a Catholic, and, if he applies for the status and is accepted, he is no longer treated as a native, or *indigenato*, but supposedly as an equal of the civilized Portuguese. Some positions in the government become open to him, and he has the right to go to Portugal and live and work there, in full possession of all the rights held by Portuguese. Indeed, it is probably better for him if he does go to Portugal. If he returns to Africa, he is likely to be regarded as a potential danger to the social and political fabric of his homeland, unless he shows a high degree of cooperation with the Portuguese. If he does cooperate, he is treated as an outcast by his fellow Africans.

It is the proud boast of the Portuguese that this policy of nonracialism is the real solution to the problem of the Europeans in Africa. Yet, only a very small percentage of those who have the qualifications to become *assimilados* have ever done so, which suggests that Portuguese citizenship may not be highly regarded by the Africans, in spite of its material advantages. Official social discrimination may be absent; at all events it is totally unlike the system in Kenya, Southern Rhodesia, or the American South. But the "uncivilized" African, though in theory he can become civilized, in practice has very great difficulty in rising out of his class. The great majority of the existing *assimilados* are mulattoes who have been born into an educated environment, and not "bush" Africans. In the cities, both *assimilados* and "natives" have considerable difficulty competing with the large numbers of lower-class and frequently illiterate Portuguese who, unlike in other colonies, occupy most of the lower-grade jobs. Bus drivers, for example, almost everywhere else are Africans; in Portuguese territories, most are Portuguese, as are railroad employees. Employers almost invariably tend to favor the immigrant Portuguese over the African; with the great increase in immigration in recent years, this tendency has become accentuated. In the large-scale land settlement schemes inaugurated by the Portuguese, the Portuguese peasant again seems to be systematically favored over the African, though there are a few settlements where Portuguese and Africans have worked together in some harmony. For a long time, the Portuguese pointed to the absence of a nationalist movement as evidence of the general contentment of the Africans in their colonies. It is much more probable that they were kept in check by the presence of far more permanent troops than any other colonial power saw fit to maintain in its colonies.

Angola

LIBERAL SETTLER OPINION. It was, of course, impossible that Portuguese Africans could be insulated against the independence movements that have swept through Africa in recent years. In fact, there is widespread discontent in the colonies which has in the last two years erupted into open rebellion in several parts of Angola, especially in the north, and in Portuguese Guinea. Discontent is not confined to the Africans; Portuguese residents complain of the authoritarianism of the Salazar regime and wish to replace it with a democratic form of government. These men should be the natural allies of the educated Africans who are fighting for self-government, but few think they are as yet ready for it. They favor instead the progressive and systematic promotion of Africans to positions of importance, and their inclusion in Portuguese councils, more or less as the British did in their colonies a decade or two ago. They look toward a multiracial government and the fulfillment of the Portuguese promise of genuine equality between Africans and Portuguese. Such men are Captain Henrique Galvao and his superior officer, General Humberto Delgado, a former candidate for the presidency likewise in exile in Brazil today. If their program were to be realized, it would probably mean the virtual separation of Mozambique and Angola from Portugal and the replacement of the present one-sided union by at most a loose confederation of autonomous states. Other settlers wish only to be rid of the dead hand of Portuguese authoritarian control, which they find irksome. They also resent the domination of the metropolitan Portuguese in the colonial government. The goal of these men is the separation of the overseas provinces from Portugal, but this would be followed by a settler government such as that in Southern Rhodesia or the Republic of South Africa, which would continue to keep the Africans in their place and exploit their labor. It is unlikely that the government would be multiracial.

NATIONALIST RIVALRY. Most African groups do not wish to get rid of the Portuguese altogether. The more realistic among them recognize that they will continue to need them for some time to come. But they wish to retain only those who would be willing to work for them as employees and subordinate advisers. These Africans are working for an immediate African majority government, followed after a transitional period by full independence. All African political groups have complete independence as their goal, though they vary in their antipathy to the Portuguese and their willingness to cooperate with them before and after independence.

When the Belgian Congo became independent in June, 1960, Léopoldville, which was not many miles from the border of Angola, naturally became a haven for nationalist Angolese politicians. Political parties, though not forbidden in Portuguese territory, were kept under strict control and were therefore useless as spearheads for the independence movement. The exiles were bitterly divided among themselves, especially on the question of the means to be used against the Portuguese. The more moderate groups thought it was useless to fight all by themselves against the superior might of the Portuguese and preferred the policy of trying to interest outside powers like the United Nations, although they were prepared to use force as a last resort. Others, who knew the stubbornness of the Portuguese, believed that only an armed insurrection could succeed. The Angolans, like the Congolese, were also plagued by tribal enmities and dissensions. The Bakongo, who were strong in Léopoldville and Brazzaville, were the leading tribe in the Angola districts nearest to the Congo. It was easy for the Angolan Bakongo party to win the support of fellow tribesmen in the Congo who had recently won their independence; it was far less easy to win the support of other tribes elsewhere in Angola. Nevertheless, the Union of Angolese Peoples (UPA), which was originally only a Bakongo party, in recent times has made impressive gains, and succeeded in attracting other groups, in part because of its sponsorship of the great rebellion in northern Angola in early 1961. Its leader, the forceful and single-minded Roberto Alvaro Holden, a native Angolan who left his country as a child and who worked as a civil servant in the Belgian Congolese Administration, has always refused to join with other parties unless they accepted his undisputed leadership.

The other party of significance, which has shown itself more ready to cooperate with rival groups, is the Peoples Movement for the Liberation of Angola (MPLA), founded in 1956, which has no particular area of support, appealing mostly to intellectuals and city-dwellers. It is led by Africans and mulattoes, mostly *assimilados* who, until they were forced into exile to escape government persecution, had spent all their lives in the country. The MPLA does not claim, and probably does not have, as many members as the UPA. But it maintains close contact with anti-Salazar Portuguese, and would probably cooperate in forming a multiracial government, perhaps for a time even one dominated by liberal Portuguese, so long as Africans were granted equal rights and could look forward to eventual majority rule and independence. This party is led by a famous Angolan poet and medical doctor, Agostinho Neto, who recently escaped from a Portuguese prison. During his imprisonment, his position was taken by Mario de Andrade.

In July, 1963, the UPA received a decisive boost in prestige when the government in exile it had formed some months before in Léopoldville was recognized as the legitimate government of Angola by the Congolese Government of Adoula. Tunisia followed with recognition shortly thereafter. Then in May, 1963, the Summit Conference of Independent African States appointed a committee to look into the question of recognition of the government in exile, and to enter into discussions with both the UPA and the MPLA. The committee came to the conclusion that the UPA was the party most likely to command country-wide support —perhaps because its leadership was wholly African and unprepared for any accomodation with the Portuguese. The committee reported its findings to the meeting of thirty-two foreign ministers of OAU, held in Dakar in August, 1963, which accepted the recommendation and urged all its member states to recognize Roberto Holden and his government in exile.

BEGINNING OF ARMED CONFLICT. In March, 1959, the Portuguese struck at the MPLA, which at that time was merely agitating for reforms, and arrested many of its leaders. The remainder escaped and carried on their movement from Conakry, the capital of independent Guinea. In February, 1961, a concerted attempt was made, mainly under MPLA leadership, to free nationalists who were held in prison in Luanda, the Angolan capital. This attempt coincided in time with the successful hijacking of the *Santa Maria* by Captain Galvao. The Portuguese were able to bring these first disturbances in Luanda under control, though at the cost of a considerable number of lives.

A few weeks later, northern Angola was invaded from the Congo by Angolan Africans under the direction of the UPA, with the purpose of inciting a general rebellion against the Portuguese. This attack was marked by numerous acts of terrorism against Portuguese settlers and officials and the intimidation of those Africans who would not join. The Portuguese rushed as many troops as they could spare to northern Angola and called for reinforcements from Portugal. When these arrived, they retaliated, killing upward of 50,000 Africans. About 200,000 were reliably reported to have fled to the Congo, where they created great difficulties for the United Nations and the local government. Armed bands of Portuguese settlers played an important part in the suppression and most of the numerous counteratrocities committed by Portuguese against the Africans have been attributed to them. Even today, over two years later, much of northern Angola remains devastated, and some areas are still in rebel hands. Considerable numbers of Portuguese troops, which the country can ill afford to maintain, are tied up in the area in the attempt to keep the rebellion from spreading into central Angola.

BELATED EFFORTS AT REFORM. The Portuguese Government recognized that some long-overdue reforms ought to accompany the military operations. Forced labor was brought to an end, and the *indigenato* statute was abolished, thus at least in theory establishing equality of treatment for all Africans. Some economic and educational reforms were promised. But conspicuously absent was any measure that could encourage the Africans to look toward eventual independence. On the contrary, the major program of the Salazar regime consisted of a campaign to settle more Portuguese immigrants in the country. Although the Overseas Minister publicly urged the Portuguese peasants to intermarry with Africans, and thus help create a "new Brazil," the Africans, far from welcoming the newcomers, were inclined to regard them as potential reinforcements for the Portuguese colonial army, ready to aid in crushing any future revolt.

Recently, so far as can be ascertained from the meager information that trickles out of the country, even these few reforms are being slowed down, and Dr. Adriano Moreira, who, as Minister for Overseas Provinces, introduced the early reforms, has been dropped from the Portuguese cabinet and replaced by the former Governor of Portuguese Guinea, Antonio Augusto Peixoto Correia, a military man. Prime Minister Salazar has reiterated his refusal to consider independence even as a remote possibility, since the overseas provinces are an integral part of Portugal.

PROSPECTS FOR INDEPENDENCE. The remaining rebels in northern Angola cannot win an outright decision without outside help, which President Ben Bella of Algeria, among African leaders, has promised, if the occasion arises when it can be useful. What are the prospects for such outside help? The United Nations, particularly its Special Committee on Colonialism, has made persistent efforts to persuade the Security Council to take action against Portugal. But difficulty has arisen over the question of which article of the U.N. Charter authorizes legal action against a country that does not ask for its assistance. The General Assembly has no coercive power; it can only recommend action to its members and to the Security Council. Efforts have been made to force the Portuguese to submit information on its colonies under Article 73, on the ground that the Portuguese overseas provinces are "Non-Self-Governing Territories." The Portuguese retort that the provinces *are* self-governing, since their representatives sit in the Portuguese parliament. When the rebellion broke out, the anticolonial nations insisted that the situation threatened international peace and thus fell within the jurisdiction of the Security Council. But the threat has at no time been immediate enough for a majority of the members of the Security Council to feel it necessary to take action, not even the imposition of economic sanctions on Portugal, a course favored by the anticolonial nations and the Soviet Union. However many resolutions are passed by the General Assembly, Portugal cannot be compelled to obey them. She can be expelled from the United Nations, but this need not deter her. She is a fairly recent member, and has gained little from the association. Those nations that wish to obey the recommendations of the General Assembly are, of course, free to do so, but they are not the powers on which Portugal is dependent for survival.

Yet, Portugal is a small nation with limited resources. She cannot keep large armies indefinitely in her three African colonies, in two of which the armies are already engaged in trying to suppress rebellions. Portuguese Guinea, hemmed in by Senegal and Guinea, both hostile to her and both evidently supporting the rebellion in that territory, could be lost by military action, and Portugal can hardly expect to win U.N. support if she claims that international peace is being endangered in her province, as indeed it is. If the drain on her resources becomes too heavy, it is possible that even the docile army officers who owe their position to the dictator may decide that the price of retaining Salazar in office is too high. Without military support, no group of dissident liberals in Portugal is in a position to overthrow him.

As a NATO member, Portugal has had the use of the NATO arms she possessed at the beginning of the Angolan outbreak. However, all her NATO allies have since placed curbs on their arms exports to Portugal. Nevertheless, as long as Portugal is a member of NATO they cannot be cut off altogether, and there is no way to prevent these arms from being sent on to Africa. (A similar situation prevailed in Algeria, where France used NATO arms and supplies to suppress the rebels.) Portugal has placed the United States in a difficult position in the Azores, where there is an important American base, the lease for which has expired. Portugal has tried to make the U.S. pay for the base, which was formerly leased without charge. Up to the present no agreement has been reached, since the United States hesitates to pay money to Portugal which would be used against Africans.

The situation in Angola therefore remains extremely fluid. The anticolonial nations are pressing hard. The United States is sympathetic to the aspirations of the Angolan nationalists, but she is not as yet prepared either to abandon Portugal as an ally or to use the U.N. Security Council for purposes for which she does not believe it was intended, and which are of doubtful legality. Nevertheless, it is far from impossible that the rebellion might receive military support from other African countries that would bring it within the unquestioned province of the U.N. Security Council. The United States would then be faced with a decision she could no longer avoid.

Mozambique and Portuguese Guinea

In Mozambique, where the Portuguese maintain considerable forces, there are stirrings of political activity and signs of serious restiveness. The two leading Mozambique nationalist parties, which cooperate with one another, have set up headquarters in

Dar es Salaam, the capital of Tanganyika, which gives them an opportunity to organize. No parties are permitted to function in Mozambique itself, and there is no free press. Africans are also forbidden to listen to foreign radio broadcasts.

Mozambique nationalists are no more ready to postpone their independence than are Africans in the other Portuguese provinces. But the Portuguese military position is stronger there, and the precautions taken against rebellion have hitherto been effective. There can be little doubt, however, that once the Portuguese position, for whatever reason, begins to crumble in Angola, it will crumble as quickly in Mozambique. It is certain that it will not be possible for Portugal to retain Mozambique as an overseas province if Angola wins her independence.

The Portuguese Guinea nationalists in Dar es Salaam are currently engaged in maneuvering for position, and quarreling with each other. The OAU has refused to recognize any of these parties as the nucleus for a government in exile, and it is clear that none has achieved a commanding political position. If the rebels in Portuguese Guinea show signs of being able to win a decisive victory, it is possible that Senegal and Guinea will take a more active hand in trying to resolve the quarrels.

13. The Far East and the Pacific

The Federation of Malaya

ATTITUDE TOWARD BRITISH RETURN. When the British returned to Malaya in 1945, they were greeted with rejoicing, a reception very different from the customary hostile acquiescence which greeted the returning colonial powers. The Japanese occupation in Malaya had seriously damaged the previous prosperity of the peninsula, and the Malays had not received even nominal independence from the hands of their conquerors. Nor did they as yet desire it. The sultans were still the nominal and in some states the actual rulers; and the Malays, though they were a majority, were only one of the three major peoples in the Federated Malay States. In Singapore and the other Straits Settlements, they were not even a majority, nor were they a majority of the whole peninsula if Penang and Singapore were included. Accustomed to being ruled by the sultans and protected by the British, they had been dismayed by the complete failure of the British to perform their function in 1942. But even so, they had as yet no thought of forgoing this protection in the future and learning to fend for themselves.

Nor had they shown any interest in politics. Temperamentally the Malays were not self-assertive, and as good Muslims they respected existing legitimate authority and had no wish to assume it themselves. The Chinese and the Indians (mostly Tamils) had come to Malaya as workers and businessmen to perform the tasks the Malays preferred to avoid. Many had been born in Malaya but retained their loyalty to the governments in the countries from which they hailed rather than to a vague entity called Malaya. This was particularly true of the Chinese, many of whom would return to their homeland before they died. What these immigrant peoples wished from Malaya was a chance to earn a better living than they had at home. They might criticize the existing government, but they did not as yet desire to run it, even in their own interests. The majority of all the peoples in Malaya were therefore prepared to see the British return and re-establish their old form of government. It had met their needs in the past and had prevented any single people from being dominated by the others.

But the British themselves, under their new Labour Government, had no intention of returning to the good old ways, especially not the Federation, which to them seemed inefficient and old fashioned. On the one hand, the country had deteriorated so badly during the Japanese occupation that they believed they would need much stronger powers to cope with the work of reconstruction than those they had hitherto possessed; on the other hand, they were anxious to associate the Malayan peoples in the work of government. For the Labour Party, this did not mean self-government of the old kind under nine different sultans but modern, democratic self-government with a central parliament, leaving only minor functions to be performed by the separate states. Obviously, the country was too small for such a proliferation of government as had existed before the war.

"MALAYAN UNION." Soon after the war, a British emissary was sent out to call upon the sultans to relinquish their powers voluntarily. The sultans, most of whom had to some degree collaborated with the Japanese, believed this was intended as a punishment and hastened to agree to the proposal as a means of at least keeping their thrones. From the Malay point of view, a second British proposal to grant citizenship freely to all permanent residents of the country was far more disturbing. If all Chinese and Indians had the vote, the Malays would soon cease to control the government, which would fall into the hands of the more populous Chinese.

The so-called Malayan Union drew an outraged protest from the educated Malays, who for the first time formed a political party, the United Malay National Organization (UMNO), led by the Chief Minister of the unfederated state of Johore. Supported by the dispossessed sultans, the UMNO demanded the cancellation of the recent treaties and criticized the proposals for citizenship on the ground that it was unfair to give even quite recent immigrants as much say in the new government as the Malays themselves, who had no other homeland. The Chinese and Tamils, the beneficiaries of the new system, showed little interest in it and remained no more concerned with politics than before. The British, thus faced with the wrath of all articulate Malays and with no support from any quarter, withdrew their proposals and reverted to their usual colonial practices, which included the

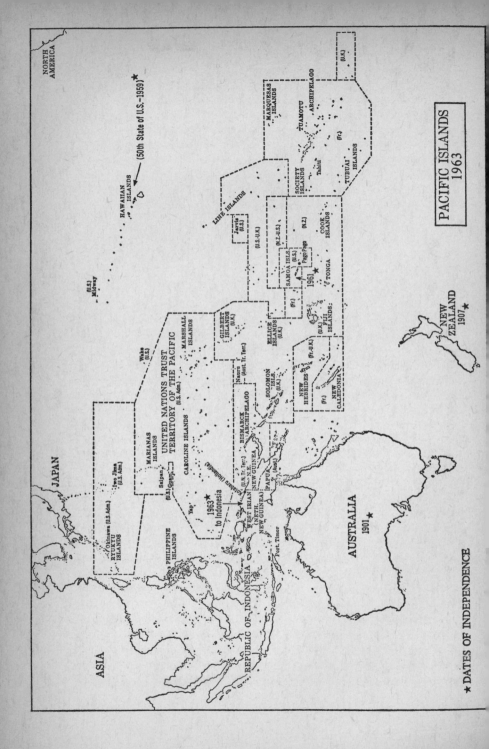

PACIFIC ISLANDS
1963

★ DATES OF INDEPENDENCE

establishment of an Executive Council dominated by officials and a Legislative Council in which all members except a few persons elected by commercial interests in Penang and Malacca were nominated by the High Commissioner. The majority of these nominees were Malays, and the non-Malays were substantial persons who could be relied upon to support the government. The sultans were given back the substantial powers in the affairs of their states they had possessed before the war. The High Commissioner for Malaya (still Governor of Singapore, as before the war) was granted ample powers in reserve in case the Legislative Council did not cooperate.

COMMUNIST UPRISING AND POLITICAL REFORMS. In June, 1948, a serious Communist outbreak occurred, which soon developed into a full-scale guerrilla war. The leaders of the movement were Chinese Communists, who had judged the time ripe to take over Malaya by force and control its considerable resources of wealth in rubber and tin. The estate owners and managers, who by this time had returned to the country, were the first victims of the Communists; for a long time, they and their employees lived in constant danger of their lives. The British sent in reinforcements and considerable air power; but though the Communists were few in number, probably never more than 10,000, it was years before they were able to gain control of the situation. General Sir Gerald Templer at last adopted the policy of resettling the Chinese peasant farmers in fortified villages, thereby both protecting them and preventing them from giving voluntary or compulsory aid to the Communists. Neither the Tamils nor Malays aided the Communists voluntarily. But the Chinese peasants in Malaya could not be sure that their compatriots might not win the war, especially after the victory of the Chinese Communists in China, and they dared not refuse help to the guerrillas until it was certain that the British and their Malay allies would win. Eventually, the menace was reduced to bearable proportions, and the British, who had instituted no political reforms during the "emergency," decided that it was time to devolve some of their powers on the loyal Malays.

However, it still remained difficult to decide what kind of reforms could be granted without disturbing the delicate balance between Chinese and Malays. The great city of Singapore was the best port in Malaya, and by far its greatest commercial and industrial center. But Singapore was virtually a Chinese city, with only a small minority of Malays. If the Singapore Chinese received the vote in the Federation, they would be able to tip the balance against the Malays in the whole peninsula. Singapore had had its separate government since the war, and unlike the rest of the former Straits Settlements, it had not been incorporated in the Federation. The Malay majority in the Federation preferred to keep it separate, in spite of the economic loss involved. Singapore therefore continued to have its own government, and it began to make some political progress, as will be discussed later.

FORMATION OF THE ALLIANCE PARTY. Many of the Malay leaders in the Federation nevertheless recognized that they could never form a stable government, much less win actual independence, without the cooperation of the other peoples in their own territory. An attempt to bring Chinese into the UMNO failed when the Malay particularists, still hoping to maintain their privileged political position in spite of their economic inferiority, refused to consider granting them full political rights. The effort split the party, whose new President, Tunku Abdul Rahman, decided to try to make a deal with a separate Chinese political and cultural organization, the Malayan Chinese Association, rather than invite them into the party. This effort was successful, and the new alliance had no difficulty in winning the elections they contested. They were now ready to play a part on the national scene.

The leaders of both these communal parties were conservatives, the Malay leaders mainly aristocrats and government officials and the Chinese men of wealth and position in their community. What they lacked was a popular program that could win them votes under a liberal franchise. The only such program on which both could agree was independence, for which the Malays would have to pay the price they had hitherto refused. After long discussions, they agreed to liberalize the requirements for citizenship, thus enabling most permanent residents of the Federation, Chinese and Tamils included, to vote in future elections.

The leaders then began to put pressure on the British for constitutional reform and an elected majority in the federal parliament, to be followed by independence within three years. Although the British refused to commit themselves on independence, they granted the elected majority and universal suffrage for all citizens under the liberalized formula for citizenship. By this time, the Malay and Chinese communal parties had reached agreement with the leading Indian communal party, and together they fought the elections under the banner of the new Alliance Party formed for the purpose. The coalition won fifty-one of fifty-two seats available for election. The British, who had provided for no fewer than forty-six nominated members in the Legislative Council, expecting that their votes would be used to give one party a precarious majority, now found themselves faced with a party that commanded a secure majority of its own (for a comparison with the Gold Coast in 1951, see Chapter 9). They therefore had no option but to allow Tunku Abdul Rahman to form the government. Shortly afterward, he became Prime Minister of the Federation.

ACHIEVEMENT OF INDEPENDENCE. At once the demands for early independence were renewed. But before this could be granted, it was necessary to reach a satisfactory compromise on a number of important questions, especially the requirements for citizenship. The Alliance Party, as representative of all three communities, took it upon itself to work out the solutions, which it then presented to the British. The British, for their part, had to consider whether the Alliance would hold together after its immediate aims had been gained. Moreover, the independent Federation would still have to bring to a conclusion the struggle against the Communists who were still fighting in the Malayan jungles. From the British point of view, Abdul Rahman was obviously a near-perfect Chief Minister, and he deserved their support. If his demands were refused, he might lose the confidence of the people and a more radical party would replace the Alliance. They decided to give their consent to all the Alliance proposals, including the plan to have one of the sultans as head of state on a rotating basis. Although the Queen would not be head of state, the new Federation of Malaya proposed to remain in the Commonwealth.

Merdeka, or independence, was achieved on August 31, 1957, Malaya becoming the second British colony to win that status in the 1950's, nearly six months after the Gold Coast had become the independent state of Ghana. In spite of doubts that the Alliance would hold together once independence had been won, it held together for the next election, which went in its favor by almost as large a margin as the first. An Alliance Government, headed by the Tunku, is still in office today.

The State of Singapore

POLITICAL ADVANCES. Although the citizens of Singapore had long been entitled to vote, less than 10 per cent of those eligible had troubled to exercise the privilege before 1955. In that year, a new and more democratic constitution came into effect, with automatic registration. Now that they could vote with a minimum of trouble, the percentage of voters rose to 53. Since that time, the Chinese, especially those too young to vote, have become almost passionately interested in the politics of Singapore.

In the years following the war, while Britain was pouring millions into reconstruction of the great port and her military, naval, and air bases, she did not think it wise to allow much constitutional advance to the island. When the "emergency" began in Malaya, the time was obviously inopportune, although the terrorists did not operate in Singapore island, which lacked jungle for their concealment. There were plenty of Communists in Singapore, and numerous fellow travelers; but they used the more usual Communist methods of infiltrating into labor unions and agitating, rather than direct military action. But the British deemed it wise to be careful since the terrorists, like three-quarters of the population of Singapore, were Chinese; they were far from sure that even native-born Singapore Chinese would be loyal to Malaya in preference to the land of their ancestors, especially after 1949 when China herself became Communist. However, since other colonies were being prepared for self-government, Singapore should not be left behind, even though a single city could not become independent on its own.

The Rendel Constitution of 1955 was filled with safeguards, including the right of the governor to nominate four members of the Legislative Council, which might be enough to give the chief minister a workable majority even if he had not won a majority in the elections. Certain subjects were wholly reserved for the British, including defense and internal security. The election was won by the Labor Front, led by an Iraqi-Jewish lawyer named David Marshall; but its majority was so small that it needed the votes of both the British officials and the nominated members to rule. A left-wing party, the People's Action Party (PAP), which included at this time known Communists and had a broad working-class appeal, under the leadership of Lee Kuan Yew, the present Prime Minister, won only three seats in the 1955 elections. But this party was only just beginning to be organized seriously and was not anxious to be placed in a position of responsibility under a semiresponsible coalition government. Since the British were certain to hold the balance of power, it was better for a radical party like the PAP to work for the future and to organize itself in order to win the next elections, under a more workable form of government.

INTERNAL SECURITY AND DEFENSE. David Marshall, too, was not satisfied with the constitution. What he wanted was full control of at least internal security, though he was prepared to concede to the British control over external affairs and defense. But the British argued that if internal security broke down, this would affect their defense capabilities in a strategic area like Singapore. They proposed a defense and security council to be composed of three British nominees, three nominees of the Singapore Government, and the British High Commissioner, as chairman. Marshall refused this offer, together with the otherwise fully responsible government that went with it, and resigned. All constitutional changes were then postponed; Marshall's second in command, a Singapore Chinese named Lim Yew Hock, became Chief Minister in his place and governed the country for the next three years, until 1959. Marshall retired from the Labor Front, to organize in due course another party of his own (Workers' Party).

The Lim regime frequently found itself compelled to take active steps against the Communists, especially the Communist-dominated unions, which often resorted to political strikes. Several members of Lee Kuan Yew's party were detained and were not freed until after the next elections. Meanwhile, the Federation of Malaya had become independent, and some solution had to be found for Singapore. Tunku Abdul Rahman was still unwilling to admit it as a member of the Federation, especially since it was probable that the next government in Singapore would be left-wing, if not Communist. But the British were still ready to grant the responsible government to which they had agreed in 1956, even if the PAP were to win the election, as long as they could safeguard their strategic interests. To meet Marshall's former complaint that the defense and security council had a built-in British majority through the casting vote of the High Commissioner, they now suggested that the chairman be a nominee of the Federation Government—one of the very compromise proposals put forward by Marshall himself, in 1956, that the British had been unwilling to grant at that time. This was acceptable to Lim Yew Hock and his government, and the constitutional changes duly went into effect. However, Lim's moderate government evidently had not pleased the electors, and his reorganized party lost overwhelmingly to Lee Kuan Yew's PAP, which won forty-three of the fifty-one seats available for election. Lee became Prime Minister of the newly proclaimed State of Singapore.

REGIME OF LEE KUAN YEW. Once he was in office, Lee, who was a Cambridge graduate and far more moderate himself than the party he had organized and led, gradually moved further to the right, thereby winning the confidence of a large part of the business community, which had expected the worst after the election. He also maintained increasingly friendly relations with Abdul Rahman, Prime Minister of the Federation, with whom he played golf. He did not neglect social reform, but showed himself well aware of the fact that Singapore had been built upon business and that, without the support of the business community, there would be a flight of capital and thus no means of providing employment for the huge number of young people who were constantly entering the labor market. Nevertheless, the left wing of the party has become increasingly dissatisfied, which has led to serious splits in the party. Even Marshall has made a comeback with his new party, which has won some by-elections. Lee therefore no longer has an assured majority in the Assembly. But he was able to bring negotiations with the Federation to a successful conclusion in 1962, and his policy of including Singapore in a larger Federation of Malaysia was ratified both in the Assembly and in a referendum. Under the new Federation, Singapore has full local self-government, but a smaller number of seats in the new federal Parliament (15 out of 159) than the population of Singapore would justify. Lee was willing to pay this price for union with Malaya, since he did not believe the federal government would interfere very much in Singapore's local affairs, which would continue to be managed by the Chinese, and he was not interested in running the affairs of the Federation outside Singapore.

The Federation of Malaysia

BRITISH AND MALAYAN PLANS FOR FEDERATION. The Federation of Malaysia, which came into existence on September 16, 1963, was the brainchild of Prime Minister Tunku Abdul Rahman of Malaya, who proposed it in 1961. His formula called for the union of the smaller British possessions on the island of Borneo—North Borneo, Sarawak, and Brunei—with Singapore and his own Federation of Malaya. The smaller territories would have a large measure of self-government within the new Federation, and could make political progress at their own pace after joining it. This proposal had the merit that defense and internal security would become the responsibility of the Federation of Malaysia as a whole, and thus prevent the Singapore base from falling under the control of a left-wing Singapore Government. The additional territories would bring more Malays than Chinese into the Federation, thus helping the Tunku to keep his population in balance. Although the Chinese own most of the commercial enterprises in the colonies, they are not numerically strong. There are several primitive groups, especially in North Borneo—including the Dyaks, who are scattered throughout the whole island of Borneo. Ethnically, the Dyaks are not Malays, though they are more closely related to the Malays than to the Chinese.

Between 1946 and 1961, constitutional development was slow in the colonies of North Borneo and Sarawak. In the oil-rich protected state of Brunei, the Sultan remained an absolute ruler, and long delayed his repeated promises to grant his state a constitution. After 1961, the two colonies received several political concessions, but until June, 1963, neither had a directly elected Legislative Council. Sarawak held elections in June and July, 1963, under universal adult suffrage, but the decision to unite with Malaya was taken earlier by an indirectly elected Legislative Council chosen under a restricted franchise. North Borneo elections held in March, 1963, were indirect, and only about one-third of the population voted. Before these last elections, there was no fully representative body in either colony entitled to take such an important decision as union with Malaya.

When the Sultan of Brunei at last granted a constitution, in 1962, the Brunei Peoples' Party, which won the elections by an overwhelming majority, opposed union with Malaya. Soon after the election in Brunei, which was only for members of a council to give advice to the still absolute Sultan, a rebellion broke out, sponsored by Sheik Azahari, leader of the winning party. The rebellion was suppressed by British troops. Azahari directed it from the safe refuge of Manila, but later went to Jakarta, where he was welcomed by the Indonesians, who had given some slight support to the rebellion. The rebellion no doubt had some effect on the Sultan's later decision to abstain from joining the Federation. After first giving his consent, he withdrew it at the last moment, giving as his reason the failure to reach agreement on financial matters. Britain then abandoned all further pressure on him, leaving the Malayans to exercise the necessary persuasion after federation.

Since it was far from clear in 1961 and 1962 whether the peoples of North Borneo and Sarawak approved of the plans being made for them, the British Government appointed a commission (Cobbold Commission) to sound out their views. Four thousand interviews later, the Commission concluded that opinion was overwhelmingly in favor of the merger, and the British appointed an intergovernmental committee (Lansdowne Committee) to arrange the details with Malaya and Singapore and draw up an agreement. It was this agreement that was finally signed on July 3, 1963, by all the governments concerned. Meanwhile, the 1963 elections in both North Borneo and Sarawak were won by pro-Malaysia parties.

OPPOSITION OF THE PHILIPPINES AND INDONESIA. Nevertheless, the governments of the Philippines and of Indonesia were dissatisfied. The Philippine Government has a long-standing claim to part of Borneo, based on the question of whether the disputed territory was leased or ceded outright by the Sultan of Sulu to Baron Overbeck and Sir Alfred Dent, in 1878. The British have never wavered in their contention that it was ceded outright, but the copy of the treaty available in the Philippines differed on this point from the copy held by the British. For a long time, the British paid no attention at all to the Philippine claim, and even refused to let the Filipinos see the British copy. When they invited the Filipinos to London in 1963, the latter remained unconvinced. They were not to remain without support. In mid-1963, President Sukarno of Indonesia, whose country had recently acquired West Irian without a fight, decided to make serious trouble for the new Federation by putting in his own claim for North Borneo and Sarawak, saying that the colonies ought to be permitted a plebiscite to demonstrate their own preference. Sukarno and President Macapagal of the Philippines, therefore, put pressure on Tunku Abdul Rahman to meet with them in Manila for an airing of the whole question. The meeting took place in early August, 1963, only a few weeks before the date the new Federation was scheduled to come into being (August 31, 1963).

At this meeting, the Tunku set his signature to a document providing for mutual consultation between the three nations, and greatly displeased the British by publicly admitting that the Singapore base and the British military presence in the Far East were only "temporary in nature." With regard to the disputed question of Malaysia, all three parties agreed to request the services of U.N. Secretary-General U Thant to determine whether or not the peoples of North Borneo and Sarawak actually desired to enter the Federation. The U.N. observer team that was sent to the colonies determined that a majority did favor federation, and the Federation thereupon came into being on September 16, 1963.

If President Sukarno really wished to prevent the Federation from being formed, he left it until very late to declare himself. He may merely have used this opportunity to proclaim the general hegemony of Indonesia in this area, and to let the world know that she expects to be consulted when major changes are made. If so, he made his point at minimum cost and risk, while extracting an implied agreement from the Tunku that when the time is ripe Britain will be expected to withdraw her armed forces from Southeast Asia. Thus the Dutch, in 1962, and the British, in 1963, formerly two of the greatest of the colonial powers, were both administered diplomatic defeats by a former colony—a pleasant-tasting triumph for Sukarno, who was in a Dutch prison until he was freed by the Japanese in early 1942, and who in 1945 and 1946 had to fight both the Dutch and the British for the independence of his country.

Minor Pacific Territories

Fiji

Of the other Far Eastern and Pacific colonial territories, the trust territory of Samoa under New Zealand administration has become independent, and West New Guinea has just recently changed masters. No major changes have taken place elsewhere. The British have long been anxious to devolve greater powers on the inhabitants of Fiji, but without much success. If majority rule were conceded in the islands, then the immigrant Fiji Indians, who now constitute an actual majority of the inhabitants, would presumably win the majority of seats and take over the government, unless the voters chose to disregard the racial issue. Rather than allow this to happen, a system of communal electorates has been in operation ever since 1937. The Legislative Council has been composed of fifteen elected members—five Europeans, five native Fijians, and five Indians—plus sixteen British officials; the Executive Council also has had a majority of officials. The local inhabitants have obtained no increase in self-government since the war; and whenever the question has been discussed, the majority of the unofficials in the Legislative Council has voted to maintain the existing system.

However, the British introduced some changes for the 1963 elections, which took place in April and May. There are now 12 constituencies, electing 4 Fijians, 4 Indians, and 4 Europeans; an additional 6 members, two from each race, are nominated by the Governor. The Governor also appoints a Speaker, and not more than 19 officials. The British still keep a majority of officials in the Executive Council, but in the event that the unofficial members get together and accept "collective responsibility" for decisions, that is, if they form a cabinet, the British are prepared to reduce the number of officials in both councils, giving the unofficials a majority. Obviously, this can be done only if at least two of the three races, and preferably all three, form a biracial or triracial party. The constitution has therefore been devised in such a way as to make it worth while for politicians to form such a party. Only if they do so can they look forward to independence. Even so, a biracial party that excludes either Indians or Fijians will probably continue to meet British opposition. The British can thus retain control of the colony indefinitely, through the right of the Governor to nominate officials, until a party of unofficials arises that meets their approval.

Hong Kong

Hong Kong has not as yet reached even this degree of political responsibility. When the British returned after the war, there was a tremendous task of reconstruction to be accomplished. Almost as soon as this was on the way to completion, the small colony had to take care of refugees from Communist China, who have been coming to the colony ever since 1949. There have always been some refugees to be looked after, but at certain times their numbers have approached flood proportions. When the last great wave in early 1962 attempted to enter, the British had to put a stop to it. Almost all the Chinese in Hong Kong have relatives in China, for whom indeed they now prepare numerous food packages to relieve the famine conditions on the mainland.

This has meant that Hong Kong has had an enormously difficult and important task to perform, which has often been done superbly. Tremendous housing projects have been completed; the money to pay for it has come almost exclusively from the extremely enterprising business interests in the colony. Hong Kong was a commercial city before the war; most of its wealth is now drawn from manufacturing industry. But the Chinese, who form almost the entire population, have shown little interest in taking part in the government. All they have demanded is that it be efficient and provide a suitable framework within which they can pursue their economic ends. This the British have provided, and they continue to control the Legislative and Executive councils of the colony, though there are nominated Chinese and European members in each. There is no visible desire for a change, and much apparent objection to any change which would give even a modicum of power to elected members chosen by the majority of the inhabitants of the colony.

United States Pacific Possessions

The United States has a number of outright possessions in the Pacific and some other territories, taken from Japan, which are under provisional U.S. administration. Under the provisions of the Japanese-American treaty of 1951, Japan retains residual sovereignty over some territories which may at a future date be returned to her. Of these, the most important is Okinawa, an island with a population of close to 700,000. Responsibility for the administration of this island rests with the United States Department of Defense, and its high commissioner is appointed by the Department with the consent of the President and the Secretary of State. The island is internally self-governing, with its own elected legislature, and a chief executive who has to be approved by the high commissioner.

American Samoa, with a population of 20,000, administered for the first half of the century by the Department of the Navy, is now under the Department of the Interior, which appoints its governor with the consent of the President. Samoa has an elected legislature and an upper house of chiefs. Guam, with its great naval base, has a governor appointed by the President and an elected unicameral legislature, which passes laws on local matters. Such laws may be annulled by United States Congress within one year of their enactment. The other islands are under direct U.S. administration. None of the above is being prepared for independence, though at least Okinawa will presumably be returned one day to Japan.

Pacific Trust Territories

It will be recalled that all U.S. trust territories are expected to be granted independence in due course and are to be prepared for it by the administering authority. Oddly enough, the U.S. Trust Territory of the Pacific, which comes under the authority of the Security Council rather than the General Assembly and unlike other trust territories may be fortified, may look forward to independence only because the United States accepted a Soviet proposal to this effect at the time the trust agreements were being drawn up. The original draft had called only for self-government, not independence. It is difficult to imagine how these islands, more than two thousand in number, with a total population of under 80,000, scattered over 3 million square miles, could possibly be brought together under one local independent administration. Yet, the attempt is being made, to the accompaniment of some prodding by the United Nations.

A high commissioner, appointed by the President, is the supreme authority in the islands, which now all come under the jurisdiction of the Department of the Interior, though Saipan was under the Navy until 1962. In August, 1961, a Council of Micronesia was brought into being, with a Micronesian chairman, to replace a former Inter-District Advisory Committee, and elections have been held under universal adult suffrage. Saipan has been designated as the capital, and a territorial flag has been adopted. It is now expected that at the latest by 1965 there will be a regular Territorial Legislative Council. Meanwhile, local and municipal councils in the different islands have been functioning for many years, empowered to pass local legislation, supervised by district commissioners responsible to the high commissioner. So the islands are moving toward regular territorial status, and it is evident that the United States is doing her best to prepare them for eventual independence as a single governmental unit. Presumably, the final decision will be taken only when the administering power decides that they are no longer strategic territory or that present defense arrangements can be replaced by treaties. Other colonial powers, notably France, have accepted treaties as a suitable substitute for sovereignty, but their experience has not perhaps been such as to encourage others to follow their example.

Western Samoa, under New Zealand administration, became independent on December 31, 1961. The social system in Western Samoa, whose inhabitants are Polynesian, has always been based on the recognition of the authority of heads of families, known as *matai*, who are chosen by members of the family but are not necessarily hereditary chiefs. Despite the customary demand of the United Nations for the institution of universal suffrage, New Zealand was reluctant to force it upon the territory, since the Samoans already had an electoral system of a kind to which they were attached. They regarded it as most improper for anyone other than a *matai* to sit in the legislative councils or hold high office. Two constitutional conventions held in Samoa have endorsed the principle of *matai* rule. The second convention, held in 1960, recommended the establishment of fully responsible cabinet government, to be followed, after a period of trial, by independence. New Zealand had no objections and therefore requested the United Nations to consent to independence when Samoa itself asked for it. The United Nations, still unwilling to abandon universal suffrage without the explicit consent of the people involved, then held a plebiscite under universal suffrage. When this resulted in a very large majority for the constitution, the United Nations gave its approval. Since the constitution does not make it mandatory for the *matai* vote to be used exclusively in all future elections, it remains possible to change the system if Samoan opinion ever turns against it; no change in the constitution would be necessary. After independence, Samoa signed a treaty of friendship with New Zealand under which the latter will undertake some of the tasks customarily performed by modern nations, and the Prime Minister of the new country informed the United Nations that it was not his present intention to ask for admission.

Nauru

This island in the remote Pacific is a trust territory under the administration of Australia. It has one industry, and one way of making a living—the mining of phosphates. A British company which owns the concession employs every able-bodied person on the island who wishes to work and pays for all the expenses of government. This has resulted in a small and prosperous welfare state with universal education for the 2,000-odd inhabitants. But there is a fly in the ointment, which has given much concern both to Australia and to the United Nations. At the present rate of extraction, the phosphate deposits will be exhausted in about thirty years, and the island can never again be used for agriculture. Before the Germans took the island in the early part of the century, a population of about 1,000 were able to make a meager living from cultivating the small amount of arable land. The present population could not be supported from that strip of land even if new topsoil were to be brought in, and most of the rest of the island is rock.

Australia has agreed to do everything possible to relocate the islanders when the time comes. A visiting commission suggested that they might be given a special suburb close to one of Australia's bigger cities, where they could remain together as they wish to do. Australia herself has suggested they become Australian citizens and live wherever they wish. What the islanders desire is to remain together, preferably on another island, slightly larger and even more paradisiacal. But island paradises are apparently scarce, and none has yet been found which fulfills the minimum requirements of the Nauruans. It is also claimed that they have become too much accustomed to free movies, school bus service and the like to be capable of living an ordinary life! The Soviet Union has not too helpfully suggested that, if the British were to turn over their phosphate plant to the islanders themselves, they could dole out the phosphate more slowly and thus live on the proceeds over a 100 years, in which case the problem could be suitably shelved for a future generation to decide. Meanwhile the islanders, who have their own local councils but do not share much in the government of the whole island, have made no decision and as yet have accepted no offers; the United Nations is faced with the distinct possibility that it will have no trust territory besides Nauru on its hands and a whole Trusteeship Council to look after it.

New Guinea

The great island of New Guinea is made up of three separate territories: Western New Guinea, until 1962 a Dutch colony; Southeastern New Guinea, an Australian colony usually known as Papua; and Northeastern New Guinea, a U.N. trust territory under the administration of Australia. Ever since the achievement of independence by Indonesia, a dispute has been in progress between Indonesia and the Netherlands over the possession of Western New Guinea, which the Indonesians call West Irian. Although the people of the whole island are among the most primitive in the world, in recent times both the Australian and Netherlands administrations have given ever-increasing numbers of them some education, training, and contact with the outside world. Many now live in the larger towns where they have had constant contact with Europeans and have been introduced to Western civilization.

The Dutch, especially since 1949, when their territory became their last undeveloped colonial possession, engaged in a crash program of considerable proportions to bring their charges to the point where they could take some part in the government. But they were unable to bring their work to fruition in the face of Indonesian threats, followed by actual armed attacks by commando bands. Rather than have the colony fall prey to civil war and have their work go for nothing, in 1962 they agreed to an arrangement worked out by U.S. Ambassador Ellsworth Bunker and U.N. Acting Secretary-General U Thant. This called for a direct administration by the United Nations until May 1, 1963, at which time the Indonesians assumed control, though under the general supervision of the United Nations. In 1969, when Indonesia should have educated the people to the stage where they can express their own opinions, a plebiscite is to be held under which they may choose to remain an integral part of Indonesia or to become an independent state.

The Australian Government, which administers its two territories together, has been required to accept some supervision from the United Nations in its trust territory, but only supplies information regarding the non–self-governing territory of Papua. Both areas were of considerable strategic importance to Australia during the war, when she had to fight hard to prevent the Japanese from using them as a staging ground for attacks on the mainland. She had therefore been somewhat slow in granting them any measure of self-government. The last U.N. visiting mission, headed by Sir Hugh Foot, an experienced British colonial administrator, while conceding that Australia had done a good job in opening up the difficult country and providing it with an effective administration, suggested she now try a "more imaginative" approach. Specifically, she might attempt some new institutions stronger and more representative than the existing local councils and the Legislative Council for the two territories, which is dominated by officials. The mission proposed that Australia set up a central parliament with a majority of members elected by the Papuans. Although much of the Australian press ridiculed the proposals, it was not possible to disregard them as blithely as previous proposals put forward by the United Nations in earlier years, when missions had been headed by men without colonial experience. The government therefore promised to give them careful attention.

The result of these efforts was a new bill, passed by the Australian Parliament in mid-1963, providing for some changes in the Australian half of the island. The bill established a new House of Assembly, with a Speaker and more native members, although they do not constitute a majority. At the same time, Prime Minister Menzies warned Indonesia that Australia was prepared to defend New Guinea and Papua "as if they were part of the mainland."

There the matter now rests. It is difficult to say which of the Pacific trust territories, the only three remaining trust territories in the world, each with its very different problems, will be the first to achieve independence, the goal of all trust territories. All that can be said now is that none of them look as if they would be following Western Samoa in the near future. But if Western Samoa succeeds in managing its own affairs creditably, at least one question will have been answered—whether it is possible for a nation of a bare 100,000 people to be independent in the nationalist world of today.

14. Residual British Colonies

The Caribbean

The Federation of the West Indies

There have been few changes in the Caribbean in the years since World War II, with the single exception of the efforts by the British to form a federation of their West Indian islands. The Federation formed in January, 1958, was composed of two large islands, now independent, Jamaica and Trinidad, with its dependency of Tobago; the Leeward Islands (Antigua, Montserrat, St. Kitts-Nevis-Anguilla); the Windward Islands (Dominica, St. Lucia, St. Vincent, Grenada, and the Grenadines); and the larger and more populous separate island of Barbados. Jamaica, Trinidad and Tobago, and Barbados have been able to pay for their own costs of administration, whereas none of the other islands have been able consistently to do so—although in more prosperous years prior to Hurricane Janet in 1955, Grenada was usually able to join the larger islands in solvency. The smaller islands have been able to keep their financial heads above water only with the aid of grants from the British treasury.

The main reason for the insolvency of the smaller islands has been the excessive cost of government, including the payment of salaries from local sources to British officials. The cost of government has been due to the fact that historically each island has always had its own separate government and greatly dislikes the idea of losing it. The British have attempted economies by such devices as forming two separate "federations" of the Leeward and Windward islands and sharing common services and some higher officials; but these worked badly and effected negligible savings. Obviously, this was no solution to the problem, nor did it appear likely that any increase in income would be sufficient to pay for all the governments. Lastly, there was no chance that the separate smaller islands could ever become independent on their own, and thus they would remain forever a charge on the British taxpayer.

The preferred solution was an obvious one, to persuade the

larger islands that had viable economies to undertake to make up the deficiencies of the smaller ones and then let all become independent together as a single state. This would appeal to the nationalist spirit of the islanders if they had or could be induced to acquire one, and would at the same time relieve the British taxpayer of his burden. The budgetary deficits of the insolvent islands were not, in absolute terms, very great. There was no reason why the more prosperous islands should not be able to make them up; if they could also institute some economies in the administration by disposing of some of the expatriate officials through abolishing their jobs, this too would be all to the good. After the war, therefore, the British sounded out some of the local politicians to see whether the scheme sounded as good to them as to themselves. The islanders obliged by setting up a Standing Closer Association Committee (SCAC) to explore the problem.

There followed years of negotiations between the islanders, and between SCAC and the British government. Trinidad objected to unlimited immigration from the other islands, which would upset its standard of living; none of the islands could see how they could pay their way without customs duties, which were currently imposed by each island on a different scale and against each other's products. Jamaica, in particular, did not want a federal income tax because she had already promised to refrain from taxing for some years any foreign corporations wishing to set up business in Jamaica. A federal income tax would offend these corporations and could even be considered a breach of contract; new capital on the same terms would be discouraged. Also, Jamaica, containing more than half the population of the whole Federation, wished to have seats in the federal parliament commensurate with her numbers—a notion that outraged the other islands, which had no wish to be ruled by a permanent Jamaican majority. Lastly, none of the islands was at all anxious to abandon its existing form of government, and all were extremely loath to relinquish any of their powers to the center.

FAILURE OF THE FEDERATION. Nevertheless, the political attractions of an independent federation were manifest, and no politician wished to reject them. The difficulties were great, but they did not seem insurmountable. The mistake was that the islanders did not try to surmount them before putting the Federation into operation; they merely tabled them, hoping that the Federa-

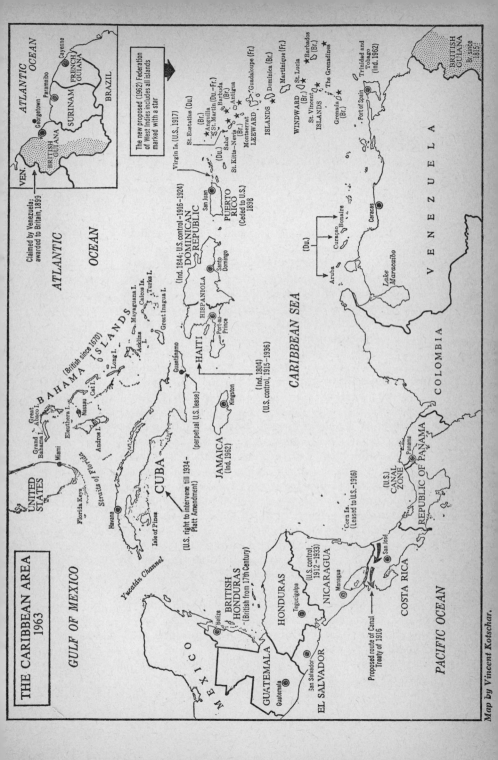

THE CARIBBEAN AREA
1963

GULF OF MEXICO

UNITED STATES

Florida Keys
Straits of Florida

Miami

BAHAMA (British since 1670) ISLANDS

Grand
Bahama I. Great
Abaco I.
Eleuthera I.
Nassau Cat. I.
Andros I. Long I.
Mayaguana I.
Acklins
I.
Caicos Is.
Turks I.
Great Inagua I.

ATLANTIC
OCEAN

Claimed by Venezuela;
awarded to Britain, 1899

ATLANTIC
OCEAN

VEN.

BRITISH
GUIANA
Georgetown
Paramaribo
Cayenne
SURINAM
FRENCH
GUIANA

BRAZIL

The new proposed (1962) Federation
of West Indies includes all islands
marked with a star

Yucatán Channel

CUBA

Havana
Isle of Pines

(U.S. right to intervene till 1934—
Platt Amendment)

Guantánamo
(perpetual U.S. lease)

JAMAICA
(Ind. 1962)
Kingston

HAITI
(Ind. 1804)
(U.S. control, 1915–1936)

HISPANIOLA
Port-au-
Prince

DOMINICAN
REPUBLIC
(Ind. 1844; U.S. control–1916–1924)
Santo
Domingo

PUERTO
RICO
(Ceded to U.S.)
1898
San Juan

Virgin Is. (U.S., 1917)
St. Eustatius (Du.)
★Anguilla
(Br.) ★St. Martin (Du.–Fr.)
(Du.) ★Saba★Barbuda
(Br.)
St. Kitts–Nevis
(Br.)
Montserrat
LEEWARD ★Antigua
(Br.)
ISLANDS ★Dominica (Br.)
★Martinique (Fr.)
WINDWARD ★St. Lucia
(Br.) ★St. Vincent
ISLANDS
Grenada
(Br.) The Grenadines
★Barbados
(Br.)
★
(Fr.)
Trinidad and
Tobago
(Ind. 1962)
★Port of Spain

Guadeloupe (Fr.)

BRITISH GUIANA
Br. since 1815

M E X I C O

Belize
BRITISH HONDURAS
(British from 17th Century)

GUATEMALA
Guatemala

HONDURAS
Tegucigalpa

NICARAGUA
(U.S. control,
1912–1933)
Managua

EL SALVADOR
San Salvador

Corn Is.
(Leased to U.S.–1916)

CARIBBEAN SEA

COSTA RICA
San José

Proposed route of Canal
Treaty of 1916

PACIFIC OCEAN

REPUBLIC OF PANAMA

(U.S.)
CANAL
ZONE
Panama

COLOMBIA

Aruba
Curaçao
Bonaire
(Du.)

VENEZUELA
Caracas

Lake
Maracaibo

Map by Vincent Kotschar.

tion would solve the problems. The federal government they set up was too weak and possessed so few worth-while powers that it could neither coerce nor lead its component islands, which wanted the Federation as a matter of pride but did not wish to pay the price for it. The federal government that came into being in January, 1958, did not have the right to impose an income tax; there was no customs union, only a commission studying it; and even free interisland migration, though agreed to in principle, was to come into effect at a later date. Worst of all, the income of the Federation was limited to a fixed monetary amount contributed by the different islands according to an agreed formula. Except for what profit it could make from issuing a West Indian currency, it had no means of enlarging its income, however efficient it proved to be; and since it had no sure source of increased income, it could hardly expect to be able to contract debts, even though it could receive outright grants if any were offered. As a result, it is not surprising that the federal government lived a somewhat shadowy existence for the four years it was in operation, though it was able to set up a considerable number of common services that would have proved helpful if the Federation had survived. To compensate him for what he had given up at home, the federal Prime Minister, formerly Chief Minister of Barbados, was given a knighthood. The premiers of Jamaica and Trinidad cannily stayed home and made no move into the federal arena.

Meanwhile, the British were gradually devolving more power on the existing local governments of the islands. Jamaica had been granted semiresponsible government in 1953, but she did not receive full internal self-government until 1959. Trinidad, where there is a racial problem owing to the presence of almost as many Indians as Negroes, received semiresponsible government in 1956 and internal responsible self-government as late as 1961. Barbados had semiresponsible government at the time of entering the Federation; she is not fully self-governing yet. The other islands all received some constitutional advances in 1959, but are not yet fully self-governing. In most of the smaller islands, the officials still have the largest share of governmental responsibility; and it was they who decided that their islands should enter the Federation in 1958. Now every island has an elected majority in its Legislative Council and future decisions can be made by the elected representatives.

As Prime Minister of the Federation, Sir Grantley Adams

showed himself to be an accomplished tactician and did the best he could with the means at his disposal. But he continued to be greatly concerned with the efforts of Jamaica and Trinidad to attract capital and industry into their territories on the basis of a promise to forgo income tax. Although he did not yet have the power to impose it, before the Federation had been in operation for a year, he warned that the federal government would soon have an income tax itself, which would be made retroactive. In 1959, a conference was called to see if any of the outstanding problems could be solved. The delegates could only agree to disagree, and set up committees for further study. Jamaica wanted either a still weaker federation or Jamaican control of the federal government; Norman Manley, her Chief Minister, was anxious for the Federation to survive, but pushed by his opposition—led by his predecessor in office, Sir Alexander Bustamante—even he demanded more federal seats for Jamaica than had been allotted to her by the constitution of 1957. Trinidad, on the contrary, led by Dr. Eric Williams, formerly a professor of history, called for a much stronger federation, free from control by any single island.

Independence of Jamaica and Trinidad

In mid-1960, Norman Manley promised the Jamaicans to let them vote in a referendum on whether or not Jamaica should secede from the Federation. The following year, the British held a further conference in midsummer in which all the island governments put forward their views; a decision was made, and accepted by Manley as the Jamaican Premier, that the Federation should become independent on May 31, 1962. But, though this was entirely satisfactory to the other islands, Bustamante now insisted on holding the Jamaican referendum promised the previous year, to which Manley agreed. The referendum was held in September, 1961, and by a majority of 256,261 to 217,319, the electorate voted for secession. Since Premier Manley and the British Government had agreed to accept the results of the referendum, steps were then taken to allow Jamaica to become independent in her own right. Sir Alexander Bustamante and his Jamaica Labour Party won the pre-independence elections held in April, 1962, and he took office as Prime Minister under a new constitution that came into effect on independence day, August 6, 1962.

There remained to clear up the debris left by the dissolution and to see whether the other islands, led by Trinidad, could perhaps form a federation of their own. Dr. Williams, who was himself facing an election, entered into discussions, but would not commit himself before the verdict of the electorate was known. When he was returned to power with an absolute majority in December, 1961, he at once summoned a conference of his victorious party, which decided, like Jamaica, for independence, to which the British Government agreed. Thus Trinidad and Tobago became independent only a few weeks after Jamaica, on August 31, 1962. Both Jamaica and Trinidad agreed to maintain such common services of the Federation as were compatible with their new status.

EFFORTS TO FORM A NEW FEDERATION. Efforts to reconstitute the rump of the Federation into a new and smaller one have so far collapsed against the incurable particularism of the separate islands. Although they have agreed to a federal income tax and customs union, their present aim is to reconstitute another weak federation, not dissimilar to the last. This time, however, there has been a much louder outcry from business and other interests, who are convinced that the weakness of the central government led to the previous collapse. Barbados, the most important of the remaining territories, is filling the role formerly played by Trinidad and demanding a stronger central structure. The British, who continue to insist that each separate unit legislature must agree to the new structure, may once more fail to find a consensus except for a weak federation, and in spite of several conferences no agreement has yet been obtained. The recently elected government of Grenada has requested annexation by the independent state of Trinidad, a solution the British hesitate to endorse, since it would leave the proposed new Federation without its second most important unit.

Meanwhile, the islands continue to possess their precious governments, including Montserrat, with a population of about 12,000 and a Legislative and Executive Council complete with ministers. It may yet be that the British will be forced to use their reserve powers, of which they have plenty, and push this new Federation into being with a stronger central executive than the smaller islands have hitherto been willing to accept; and then, however reluctantly, give it another push to independence.

British Guiana

ECONOMIC DIFFICULTIES. British Guiana is a large country in comparison with the British West Indian islands, but apart from the coastal area it is lightly populated. Its slightly more than half a million population is less than half that of Jamaica. Its checkered postwar political history is in large measure due to its condition of permanent economic depression, unemployment, and underemployment, which has made moderate political parties in the country rarities and unlikely to win many votes.

Upcountry British Guiana is hardly developed at all. There is a wide expanse of savannah with an attractive climate; but the soil is seriously eroded, and the cattle that graze there need an immense acreage for their sustenance. They have to be butchered close to their range since there is no method of shipping them to the coast except by air; use of the ancient cattle track from the savannahs to the coast took so much weight off the cattle that they had to be fattened again when they reached it. Between the savannahs and the coast is a rain forest with immense stands of timber, mostly hardwood. But not much of this is valuable, costs of transportation are formidable, and nature has not provided for pure stands of any marketable tree. Logging roads from the trees to the river are prohibitive in cost since they are so little used. The rivers themselves are navigable for only a short distance on account of rapids; there is one short railroad whose sole function is to carry traffic from one river to the next, which is parallel to it. Bauxite is mined under concession to a Canadian corporation, which has solved the transportation problem for its particular product. Diamonds are found and mined, but not in great quantities together, and also a little gold. Oil is widely believed to be available, but so far no prospecting has been successful in obtaining it in commercial quantities.

Thus the country, once thought of as an El Dorado, is still extremely poor though it looks as if it ought to be rich; and the vast majority of its inhabitants live in the steaming coastal area, growing rice and sugar, dependent, as always, on the vagaries of the market. The population, a majority of whom is East Indian, though Negroes of African descent form a very substantial minority, is thus dependent for employment on estate owners, who are themselves dependent on the prices obtained for their products. There is relatively little subsistence farming; even if the large sugar estates were subdivided, it is very doubtful whether they could make ends meet without at least strong cooperatives, community marketing, and common use of machinery.

These economic facts are of the utmost importance in understanding the political situation in British Guiana, which has been promised independence at as early a date as feasible. The capital investment needed for the development of communications, on which depends the possible exploitation of the hinterland, is extremely substantial; and it is not at all sure that there would be any worth-while returns for the expenditure. The maintenance of roads through the rainforest is expensive and difficult even if the initial costs of construction were met. The question remains, therefore, as to how any government of any political complexion can solve the economic problems presented to it. The British, who ordinarily would be delighted to leave British Guiana on her own under the government of her choice, still hesitate to hand her over to Dr. Cheddi Jagan and his People's Progressive Party (PPP), who, if not a Communist, is at the very least strongly oriented toward Marxism and is a fervent admirer of Fidel Castro. An independent Guiana under his rule would without doubt turn to the Soviet bloc for capital, and the Soviets might provide it in the hope of gaining some political, if not economic, dividends. British and American and other Western private capital expects to see dividends earned on its investments; there seems to be little chance of this in the short run. Private capital is also very wary indeed of lending money to a man who might turn out to be another Castro. American Government investment or substantial aid is hardly any more likely to be drawn, in present circumstances, to a left-winger of the type of Cheddi Jagan. Britain's will to help may be there, but her purse is limited, and the demands from other Commonwealth countries are great. Now that the Federation of the West Indies has dissolved, there is no hope from this source, and the new and smaller Federation based on Barbados will have no capital to spare.

It had always been hoped that British Guiana would join the Federation and thus the extremist left-wing government would find itself compelled to deal with more moderate governments in the West Indies. When her representatives showed little interest and Dr. Jagan insisted that his country must first be self-governing and then hold a referendum on the subject, the British were content to wait, believing that she would find it in her interest to join, as the main opposition party wished.

But now the Federation has dissolved, and British Guiana is still not quite fully self-governing, though she is close to it.

SUSPENSION OF THE 1953 CONSTITUTION. Before the war, the Legislative Council of British Guiana already contained a majority of partly elected unofficial members. Dr. Jagan, a dentist of East Indian ancestry, was first elected a member in 1947. In 1950, a British constitutional commission (Waddington Commission) recommended changes that were on a very liberal scale in view of the economic and political conditions in the country. Indeed, the new constitution amounted to virtual semi-responsible government, without the usual intermediate stage of representative government. An elected majority was granted for both the Legislative and Executive councils, with a Council of Ministers, the majority of whom were appointed on the advice of the elected members. To guard against impulsive legislation, a State Council, most of whose members were chosen by the governor at his discretion, was given a suspensory veto. A joint session of the two houses could override the veto, but this had to be convened by the governor, who also retained his usual reserve powers.

Although this constitution gave a great deal of power to the elected members, it attempted at the same time to prevent them from abusing it. A party that wished to make it work could have done so, and similar constitutions have worked elsewhere. But it was so close to responsible government that it was tempting for a radical party to use it only to win more concessions, in preference to using constructively what had been granted. (David Marshall, Chief Minister in Singapore under the Rendel Constitution of 1955, likewise attempted to win more concessions in preference to governing under a similar constitution.) Dr. Jagan, after winning a majority in the elections under the Waddington Constitution, was himself of two minds whether he ought to accept office at all or to force the British hand by boycotting the Council. Even if he had gained nothing at the time, this might have proved better for him and his program in the long run. At least his government would not have been publicly branded as under Communist control.

It is quite possible that the Waddington Commission, which contained no Guianese members, was unaware of the crucial fact that a radical Marxist oriented party had grown up in British Guiana in the early 1950's pledged to a thoroughgoing social reform along Marxist lines. It was an inter-racial party with an East Indian President and a Secretary, American-born Janet Jagan, who was at least as Marxist as her husband, and a large Negro membership led by a young lawyer named Forbes Burnham. No other party in the colony was of any importance; and as long as the alliance between the Jagans and Burnham held together, it was certain to win the first elections under the new constitution. The People's Political Party was also strongly supported by the sugar workers and other unions, in which most of the party leaders were active. But the PPP could do little to implement its Marxist program unless it had more power than it had been granted under the constitution. Officials still controlled finance and internal security, and the State Council had a suspensory veto on legislation. Such obstacles to what it thought of as progress were intolerable to a party in a hurry.

So when the PPP won eighteen seats of twenty-four in the Legislative Council and appointed its six ministers to the Executive Council, the stage was set for a serious struggle between the ministers and the colonial establishment. The PPP and its leaders did more agitating than governing; they undoubtedly failed in their responsibility to introduce and pass laws that could have been passed and were much needed; they probably fomented strikes for political purposes; and they were extremely disrespectful to the Governor, officials, and members of the State Council. They also permitted unlimited importation of Communist literature by party members.

It is debatable whether these misdeeds in total amounted to enough of a breakdown in government to justify the Governor's suspension of the constitution, after only a few months' trial. It has never been proved, nor indeed has any substantial evidence ever been cited in support of the thesis, that the PPP was planning a Communist takeover of the government, as the British alleged in their subsequent defensive White Paper. The warships and troops sent to the colony to suppress the demonstrations certainly found nothing whatever to do. Later, the police were to have a field day in searching private homes and confiscating books that contained even footnotes referring to Marxist literature. But the constitution remained suspended. Security regulations were issued, which the Jagans disregarded, thereby earning short prison sentences. Following the report of the inevitable British commission of enquiry, a new constitution was promulgated under which the Governor ruled entirely with the aid of officials and such nominated unofficials as were willing to deny themselves any chance of a political career thereafter. This government, with economic aid from the British in more substantial quantities than had ever been given to British Guiana before, did some good work; but it was certain that it could not last forever and that the government would soon have to return to the electors. The British in preparation for that day provided the Governor with a new constitution, which he was authorized to proclaim when he judged the time to be ripe.

Meanwhile, after much political maneuvering, Burnham decided to part company with the Jagans and formed another party which he called the People's National Congress. His program was not noticeably different from theirs; he differed mostly on the question of tactics, preferring to move more slowly and pass at least some of the necessary laws. Unfortunately, this split, which has continued to the present time, has led to the increase of racial feeling in the colony; Negroes tend to follow Burnham and Indians Jagan, although the PPP still has a following of Negroes and a few Negro leaders. There have even been sporadic demands for communal electorates.

RESTORATION OF CONSTITUTIONAL GOVERNMENT (1957). When Governor Sir Patrick Renison decided to proclaim the new constitution, it still seemed evident that Jagan had not lost his popularity, at least not among the Indians. But there was no point in waiting any longer; someday the nettle had to be grasped. The British had done their best to make it difficult for the PPP to repeat its former tactics. Not only were there to be the customary three civil servants in the Legislative and Executive councils, but the Governor was to have the power of nominating to the Legislative Council as many members as he wished up to the full number of the elected members. In elections held in August, 1957, the PPP won nine of fourteen elected seats, while Burnham's PNC won three, the other two being independents. As the British had foreseen, the PPP commanded a reliable majority in neither the Legislative nor Executive Council and could govern only with the aid of officials. Nevertheless, Jagan decided to take office, cooperated with the officials, and showed some aptitude for government. But he also made it clear that his political views had not changed, though he did admit that British Guiana was not necessarily ripe for a full Marxist program. Indeed, as Minister of Trade and Development, he was well aware of the need for foreign capital, and he promised not to nationalize the sugar industry, even if he came to full power at a later time. Insisting that there were too many foreign companies already in British Guiana, he proposed to offer no tax concessions to them, but to organize government-owned and -operated companies for developing the country.

In 1960, British Guiana achieved responsible government, modified only by continued British control of defense and external affairs and by the reserve powers of the Governor, which are more comprehensive than usual at this stage of constitutional development. The government has full control of finance. In August, 1961, Dr. Jagan, after winning an over-all majority (twenty of thirty-five seats) in the elections, became Premier. The first PPP budget, which called for an austerity program, including heavier taxation on a pay as you go basis, caused an uproar in the Assembly and disturbances outside, which had to be suppressed with the aid of the British military requested by the unfortunate Premier. A long strike, brought on in mid-1963 by the attempt of the government to take control of the labor unions, led to increased racial strife, especially in the capital of Georgetown, where Negroes are strongest. Dr. Jagan has gone abroad several times in search of more capital, but has met with indifferent success—in July, 1963, a written request to President Kennedy was once more turned down. Nor has Britain been willing to set a date for independence. The best hope is still for a coalition government led by Burnham and Jagan. But as yet there are few signs of such a compromise, and none is feasible until racial strife has had a chance to subside.

There the situation rests: with independence promised but the date undecided; with the economic future as murky as ever; with a Premier who is unwilling to abandon his expressed principles and is thus unable to speak the words that might give him some recognition in the West for his more moderate deeds in the years since 1953. Recent events have tended to show that he cannot command support from both races in his country. But it is difficult to determine how much of this opposition is due to the hardly concealed pressure of the United States, which is preventing him from gaining any foreign aid, thus making him appear as a man who will lead his country to destruction if he is allowed to become its first independent Prime Minister.

British Guiana no longer has any future to move toward except independence; but it is difficult indeed to see how this can be granted unless the British (and the Americans) are willing to see a South American country (even one with little strategic value) in extreme left-wing hands, either accepting aid from the Soviet bloc or floundering along as best it can without any aid until its government changes.

British Honduras

British Honduras has problems of a different kind. With a population of fewer than 100,000, it may not be too small to become an independent state. Western Samoa does not have many more. If one accepts the notion that a state can be independent or, in De Gaulle's phrase, have international sovereignty, without necessarily having to be represented directly in the United Nations or keeping a national army or possessing any other of the trappings of a sovereign state, then British Honduras could become independent. Nevertheless, she cannot support from her own resources a governmental establishment even on the scale she has hitherto known; in the past, Britain has had to make up the annual budgetary deficits. Now that she has to build a new capital city to replace low-lying Belize destroyed by Hurricane Hattie in 1961, British Honduras can hardly hope to be economically on her own for many years to come.

As if this were not enough, the small, independent state of Guatemala claims the whole country by right of inheritance on the ground that she fell heir to Spanish possessions in the area; she broke off diplomatic relations with Britain in July, 1963. Mexico has acquiesced in British rulership of the colony; but if Britain were to relinquish it, she too would put in her claims, which are neither better nor worse than those of Guatemala. Political leaders of the colony at different times have flirted with Guatemala; some of them have been convicted for "seditious utterances" and served time in jail. George Price, the present First Minister, had some personal contacts with the Guatemalan embassy in London during a constitutional conference, whereupon the British indignantly broke off the talks, expelled Price from the Executive Council, and tried to have him convicted of "seditious intent toward the Queen." More fortunate than others, he was acquitted. When the British in February, 1960, at last granted substantial reforms, the party leaders, including George Price, pledged loyalty to the Queen and promised to exclude the Guatemalan issue from the next elections, going out of their way to proclaim that the claim of Guatemala was "unfounded" and a "grave affront to the people of British Honduras." In spite of the proximity of the two countries, there have never been any significant numbers of Guatemalans in British Honduras, and Spanish is virtually an unknown language. Like British Guiana, it is one of the most English of colonies; and today no one surely would talk, as they did in the early 1950's, of the contrast between "colonial" Honduras and "free" Guatemala.

British Honduras has no shortage of land, even cultivable land; in this respect, it is better off than British Guiana, though, like the latter, her economic interests were for a long time neglected by the British. The infrastructure is weak, the transportation system primitive, and most of the population is concentrated in Belize and the few other towns. However, the resources are there, and in recent years Mennonites have shown that it is possible to make a living in the empty countryside. Despite the small population and the backward economy, political advance in the colony has in recent years been fairly steady. In 1954, under a new constitution, George Price's People's United Party (PUP) won all the elected seats in the Legislative Council (9 of 15), but officials controlled the Executive Council. Reforms would have been granted earlier if the British had not harbored doubts of Price's loyalty. For some time after his expulsion from the Executive Council at the end of 1957, his position seemed to be weakening, and several members of his party ceased to vote with him in the Legislative Council. But he made a triumphant comeback in the 1961 elections under the new constitution, which gave the elected members majorities in both Councils. His PUP won all eighteen seats available for election, and he himself became First Minister. Internal self-government was promised for January 1, 1964.

It had always been hoped that British Honduras would join the Federation of the West Indies, but there was never any substantial opinion in favor of it in the colony. PUP's opposition, the National Independence Party, looked only for independence. Both parties might have been willing to join after independence, but they feared the predominance of Jamaica, which might have tried to unload her surplus population in British Honduras. If the Federation had been reconstituted under the leadership of Trinidad and without Jamaica, British Honduras might well have agreed to enter. But there is not much likelihood of her joining the rump, led by Barbados. Although her greatest need is for immigrants, whom the PUP has undertaken to encourage, Hurricane Hattie quickly turned the government's attention to even more pressing needs.

British Honduras will probably continue for a year or two more under her present constitution and government, build her new capital, and try to attract immigrants and new industry. Then once again there will be constitutional talks, and Britain will agree to independence. For Britain, the time for shedding this small, long-neglected Central American foothold can hardly come too soon. But for British Hondurans, who know they can have independence when they are ready, the time has now come for making the most of the British connection before they are fully on their own.

Other British Colonies

Britain still possesses many small colonies scattered around the world, but few of them can hope for more than a limited self-government. Such small islands as the Solomon Islands, Ascension, St. Helena, the Falkland Islands, the Seychelles, Tristan da Cunha, Pitcairn Island, and the protected state of Tonga under its colorful Queen need no attention here. Even Gibraltar, the rock fortress on the Spanish mainland held by the British since 1704, cannot achieve a separate independence and already has as complete a self-government as is compatible with its circumstances.

Mauritius in the Indian Ocean and Malta in the Mediterranean both have populations many times greater than does West Samoa or British Honduras. The sugar island of Mauritius, ceded by France to Britain in 1814, with its East Indian majority, is close to responsible government and may soon attain it. But it has not yet been decided whether she is strong enough to stand on her own. Quite possibly her constitutional advance, by agreement with the British, may stop at the last stage before independence.

Malta

Malta's problems are different. The island was given semi-responsible government after World War I, but the constitution was suspended in 1933, largely because of Italian intrigues backed by a section of the population and the powerful Catholic Church.

After World War II, she was given full internal self-government, but this constitution was suspended in 1958 when the Prime Minister made unacceptable demands on Britain, and his opponent was unable to form a government. Although nothing had been settled, the constitution was restored in late 1961; the former opposition leader, Dr. Borg Olivier, won the subsequent elections, and it seems now that he will succeed where his truculent predecessor, Dom Mintoff, failed.

The basic problem is economic, not political. A huge naval dockyard formerly provided the bulk of the employment in the island, and its payroll filtered through the economy, enabling it, with the aid of special grants from Britain, to pay its way. When the navy found no further use for the dockyard, it was sold to a British company that employs almost as many men as the former naval base. But this employment, in spite of British governmental guarantees, remains less certain. The company has experienced many difficulties, blamed by the British on bad management, and the island is hopelessly vulnerable to economic depression. It cannot feed itself, its light industries supply few salable exports, its water supply is inadequate. Only its tourist industry shows promise. Yet, the people of Malta thirst for independence, and both major parties have promised it. The British dared not concede it to a firebrand like Mintoff, who insisted he would nationalize the dockyard and sell it to the highest bidder, nor do they wish to make up its budgetary deficits forever. It is doubtful if the island in any circumstances could pay its way when it has to import so much of its food. Its only chance is to develop some line of merchandise that will have appeal in foreign markets, and it is difficult to see what this could be, even if the island had access to substantial foreign capital.

Extended discussions took place between the Maltese and the British in July, 1963, with all parties represented. Numerous difficulties arose when attempts were made to devise a constitution acceptable to all. The Maltese delegates agreed on almost no point. They disputed the question of the status of the Catholic Church, whether the state should be a republic or accept Queen Elizabeth as sovereign, whether elections should be held before or after independence, and so on. After sixteen days of this, Mr. Duncan Sandys, the British Colonial Secretary, gave Malta until May, 1964, to write her own constitution. Britain, he said, would grant independence then, whether or not they had come to an agreement.

A similar ultimatum worked in India in 1947. It remains to be seen whether it will work in Malta. The British must have taken the decision with regret, for during World War II the Maltese people were awarded the George Cross for their heroism under fire, and British sentiment in favor of the islanders has always been strong. But the disputatiousness of the Maltese is notorious, and on this occasion the British do not seem to have had any alternative.

15. *The Evolution of Anticolonialism Since World War II*

At the end of World War I, no colonial power seriously considered the possibility of granting independence to any of its colonies. But the former German colonies and Turkish provinces were not granted to the victorious powers as outright colonies, as had happened after previous wars. Under the mandate system, the administering powers undertook to regard their new acquisitions as "a sacred trust of civilization," and those who administered the former Turkish provinces were instructed to prepare them for independence. Thus, for the first time, two principles were accepted: that colonial powers bore some responsibility for the welfare of their colonial subjects, and that independence was a goal to which non-European dependent territories, with the approval of international opinion, could aspire.

Between the two world wars, anticolonial opinion continued to grow. When Mussolini took steps to extend his African empire, world opinion as expressed in the League of Nations strongly condemned him. The attempt of the British and French foreign ministers to give Italy a part of what she desired, while preserving the rest of Ethiopia intact, would have seemed entirely reasonable in the nineteenth century. But it was foiled by public opinion, and Sir Samuel Hoare, the British Foreign Minister, was compelled to resign. Although the sanctions imposed by the League of Nations did not prevent the Italians from gaining a temporary victory, notice had nevertheless been served that any nation attempting to follow a similar course in the future would have to brave not only public opinion but possibly more effective sanctions.

The independence movement in India led by Gandhi drew the attention of the world to the means by which a colonial power could be coerced into giving a greater measure of self-government than it wished. Public opinion throughout the world was sympathetic to Indian aspirations, as were considerable numbers of

366

the British themselves. Although the British might have been able to keep India for many years more, it could only have been by force. They did not wish to be regarded as tyrants, remaining in India only because they had the power to enforce their rule, and it was possible that they might eventually lose more by making enemies of the Indians than if they retired gracefully before it was too late. Even though they did not name a date, their promise to Indians in 1929 that Dominion status would ultimately be granted changed the whole course of colonial history. It was then conceded that a valuable colony could leave an empire by permission of its masters. From this moment, other colonies could hope to achieve the same goal; even if the British were not prepared to agree, similar means could be used against them elsewhere with the same hope of success as in India.

By the outbreak of World War II, the major British colonies in Asia, as well as the Philippine Islands, fully expected an early independence, but none of the less-developed and politically inexperienced territories of any colonial power had as yet received the encouragement to believe in the possibility of independence for themselves. The Japanese victories during the war, however, suggested to all dependent peoples that the colonial powers were no longer invulnerable. Several of the Far Eastern colonies that had been given a nominal independence by the Japanese were no longer prepared to accept with resignation the return of their prewar masters. The African colonies, however, could not hope for a similar military intervention on their behalf. The sub-Saharan French colonies that had voluntarily aided the Free French hoped to be rewarded with a greater share in their own government, but as yet had no serious thought of independence. French North Africa, parts of which had been fought over during the war and had witnessed the defeat of their masters by the Germans, was unwilling to accept less than was to be granted to formerly Italian Libya, the least developed of all North African territories, and was already preparing to demand as a minimum the replacement of direct French rule by a free partnership.

By no means all the colonial powers were reconciled to relinquishing their empires. France, smarting from her recent defeat, which had in her eyes been far from compensated by her ultimate victory, wished to recover some of her lost prestige, whatever the cost. Belgium and the Netherlands believed they needed the resources of their colonies to restore their economic fortunes. Only Britain, under her Labour Government, was doubtful whether it was worth while trying to recover her empire. India, Burma, and Ceylon were on the point of independence, and she was ready to accept the general thesis that her colonies could look forward to independence when they were ready for it. In order to set in motion the process of releasing them from her rule, she began at once to associate some of her colonial subjects in the work of their governments. At the same time, she gave them to understand that, once they had shown themselves capable of exercising their limited powers responsibly, they would be given more.

By 1950, India, Burma, Ceylon, and the Philippines had been peaceably granted their independence, and Indonesia had won it after a long, drawn-out struggle with the Dutch. The promises made to the Class A mandates after World War I had now been fulfilled, and all were independent members of the United Nations. These former mandated territories and colonies, together with Egypt, Iraq, and others, formed an important anticolonial bloc in that body, ready to exercise such influence as they could to help in the destruction of the entire colonial system. In this aim, they found powerful allies in the Soviet bloc, and particularly the Soviet Union herself.

It is ironical indeed that the Soviet Union, who, alone of the great powers, had incorporated under her direct or indirect rule so many new territories after the war, should have been able to voice the hopes of the dependent peoples as effectively as she did. But it is only necessary to read a few of the thousands of speeches made by her representatives in the Trusteeship Council and in the Fourth Committee to recognize how effective her skeptical pinpricks could be. Time after time, the special representative of some trust territory would present a detailed report explaining the advances being made in his territory, only to be met by a barrage of remarks from the Soviet delegate drawing attention to what he considered to be the true facts of the case, as seen through Marxist and Leninist spectacles. The Soviet delegate rarely neglected his homework and was thoroughly well grounded in the knowledge of all facts that could be used to torment the colonial representative. The less well prepared delegates of the nonadministering powers in the Council would then usually pick up the cue and hammer away at the same points. Any petitioner with a grievance against the administering power knew he would always receive a sympathetic hearing from the Soviet delegate, whether it was in the Trusteeship Council, the Fourth Committee, the General Assembly, or even the Security Council, in all of which the Soviet Union as a great power had a seat. The petitioner neither knew nor cared what the motives of the Soviet delegate were—still less that the Soviet Union herself was one of the few remaining imperialists in the world.

When the Soviet Union taunted them as "imperialists," it was difficult for the colonial powers to defend themselves by throwing the same charge back on the Russians. Although they might win some praise from the neutrals when they granted independence to a colony, there were always other colonies which had not yet received it and where they could be accused of moving too slowly. Until very recent times, even the United States, which had long ago granted independence to the Philippines, could not come out as strongly as the Soviet Union for the immediate abandonment of colonialism. The colonial powers were her allies, and she owed them some loyalty. Moreover, she was aware that they could not simply withdraw and leave the colonies to themselves, in spite of her belief that independence as a general principle was morally justified. The Soviet Union, on the other hand, might care not at all whether or not the colonies won their independence. Since her only purpose was to embarrass the colonial powers and the United States, their ally, she need have no scruples in making completely irresponsible demands. As ever more ex-colonies entered the United Nations, she became ever more successful in winning the support of the whole body for resounding anticolonial resolutions and was the undisputed champion of and one of the most effective spokesmen for the remaining colonies, and the aspirations of their peoples.

Under this type of pressure, the various colonial powers reacted differently. Portugal to this day has resisted, to the limits of her ability, any kind of pressure. Britain has resented being pushed and has frequently complained that her critics do not understand the problems involved in granting independence. She prefers to take her own time, and it is difficult to point to a single instance in which she has speeded up her timetable in response to anticolonial speeches and resolutions. It was not pressure from the United Nations that persuaded France to grant independence to her African colonies, though the frequent U.N. debates on Algeria may have had some effect. The United Nations had little influence on the Belgian decision to grant independence to the Congo, though it intervened afterward to prevent the new nation from relapsing into chaos. The importance of anticolonial ideology in the United Nations lies in the manner in which moral pressure has consistently been used to mobilize and give expression to anti-colonial sentiment. The result has been that the granting of independence has come to be regarded as a virtue of which the colonial power has the right to feel proud, whereas all delays and refusals have put it on the defensive, forcing it to make excuses for its dilatoriness.

The winning of independence by the former colonies has therefore been in very large measure the work of the nationalists in the colonies themselves. Their "positive action" and agitation, including in some instances armed insurrection, have gradually made it clear to the colonial powers that, in the existing state of world opinion, it was not worth their while to attempt to hold the colony by force and that it was better to retreat with the best face possible, salvaging what they could and trying to retain as much good will as possible for the postindependence era. Except for the Portuguese colonies, this process is now almost complete.

The British salvage operation was greatly facilitated by the existence of a ready-made system in which all their former colonies could find their place if they wished. The British Commonwealth of Nations, renamed simply "the" Commonwealth, had neither rules nor regulations. It was an organic structure with no specific rights or obligations binding on its members. No former colony that joined the Commonwealth would feel itself to be alone in the world once it had won its independence. If it entered, it would have the economic benefit of tariff preferences, the first refusal of any economic aid that might be available, and it would be an obvious choice for investments by any of the more developed Commonwealth nations that had surplus funds. The Commonwealth was an association to which any newly independent nation could belong without loss of dignity. For the British, it enabled them to retain ties with their former colonies and at the same time it enhanced their own dignity as leaders of a free association that had grown organically out of the empire for which there was no longer a place in a world of self-governing nations.

The French, having been badly defeated by the Germans in the war, could not adapt themselves so easily to the changed world in which they had to live. With a military tradition far stronger than that of the British, for them the possession of an empire meant that they were once more a militarily significant people. It also meant that they could continue to spread their culture, which they regarded as the highest expression of Western civilization, among the backward peoples. The long struggle in Indochina was fought more for the sake of the military ideal; quite simply, they did not wish to be worsted in battle. In Algeria, they believed, rightly, that the material changes they had wrought in a difficult land were achievements of which they had reason to be proud; but they also believed it was degrading to be deprived of this by force. In sub-Saharan Africa, where they could probably have held their empire for many years more by force, the civilizing mission eventually came to take precedence over material interests. The price to be paid was continued association with France. If this price was paid, then the former colony could look forward to far more technical and financial aid than colonies of other powers, even though such aid and investments can never be economically profitable to the French people. Although the Community has fallen by the wayside, the aid continues; and the new nations remain closely associated with France, even while enjoying "international sovereignty."

Both Belgium and the Netherlands had colonies that were of great economic value to them—far more valuable proportionately than the French or British colonies. Influential commercial interests in these small countries wished to keep them as long as possible, even though, for the Netherlands, it meant the reconquest of her former colony. Even today, many thousands of Dutchmen continue to resent the manner in which the Indonesians backed by international opinion forced them out of the Indies, which they had held so long and had converted into a paying venture. When they withdrew from Indonesia, they still insisted on retaining New Guinea, and allowed the Indonesians to expropriate much of their remaining investment in the country rather than yield on New Guinea. They gained nothing from New Guinea comparable to this material loss, but they wished to show the world they were as good colonizers as anyone, and in the last years of their tenure, they made a prolonged and expensive effort to bring the New Guinean natives to the point where they could stand on their own feet and govern themselves.

The Belgians also were proud of their material achievements in the Congo and of their work in converting the natives to Christianity. They believed they were teaching the Congolese to appreciate the benefits of Western civilization, in which they were gradually acquiring a share. But they did not read the signs of the times quickly enough. Unused to opposition in the colony and unaccustomed to dealing with it, they suddenly found themselves faced with problems different from any they had experienced before and could not adjust themselves. The Belgians conceived a plan assuming they would have thirty years to put it into effect, and they could not modify it to fit a five-year schedule. They took the chance that the Congolese would be so grateful for self-government that they would willingly cooperate for an indefinite future with their benefactors. They did not foresee that the inexperienced Congolese would be unable to govern at all and that their primary desire was to get rid of their former masters, irrespective of the cost to themselves, which their very inexperience caused them to underestimate.

It is now abundantly clear that colonialism, at least of the kind described in this book, is rapidly nearing its end. Some problems remain to be solved, notably in the colonies that have been dominated by white settlers. But it is unlikely that the remaining colonies, perhaps not even the Portuguese overseas provinces, will survive this decade. Perhaps the most extraordinary feature of the retreat from colonialism has been the small part that naked force has played in the process. Words, not arms, have been used as weapons; actual military power has seldom been brought to bear, not even the threat of military action. The new nations of sub-Saharan Africa among them can hardly muster a division of effective troops, or the hardware to equip them. Even today, if all other powers left them alone, it is doubtful whether they could defeat the white troops of the Federation of Rhodesia and Nyasaland, let alone those of the Republic of South Africa. But they *can* speak in the world's forum at the United Nations and win overwhelming majorities for their resolutions; though the resolutions themselves have no power of coercion, the colonial powers have preferred to obey them—even if not at the speed demanded by their proponents.

Through the machinery of the United Nations, it has become possible to address the world's conscience in a manner unknown before. Moreover, that conscience itself has developed, so that colonialism now appears to the great majority of nations to be morally wrong, whereas self-government, however feeble, even tyrannical, it may be, seems morally right. Now that this moral insight is being translated into practice and all colonies capable of independence are receiving it, it remains the responsibility of mankind to give equal attention to the truth that no nation is fully independent in all things, but that all nations are *interdependent*—a truth too often neglected while the heady wine of nationalism continues to intoxicate new and old nations alike.

SELECTED
BIBLIOGRAPHY

Selected Bibliography

Since the main purpose of this book is to present in necessarily brief outline a history of colonialism covering all parts of the world, it is natural that specialists interested in a particular region will be fully familiar with that region, but may lack more than a passing knowledge of others. This bibliography will therefore list outstanding books in every major area covered, and these books in most cases contain further bibliographies which can lead the student deeper into his study. To make this bibliography as useful as possible to those institutions which may be planning to introduce the subject of colonialism into their curriculum, the writer has given preference to books currently in print when a choice of useful books has been available. Only books in the English language are included.

Though the author himself has had to draw upon newspapers and official publications such as those of the British Information Services and the Service de Presse of the Ambassade de France, and other periodical literature, for the most recent information contained in this book, such sources are not listed here. The few articles from periodicals mentioned in this bibliography include important information that has not yet appeared, as far as the author is aware, in book form. Nevertheless, for the benefit of students and libraries who may not be familiar with it, a special mention should be made of the invaluable *Africa Digest*, which has been appearing five times a year since 1953 (Africa Publications Trust, 65 Denison House, Vauxhall Bridge Road, London, S.W.1). This Digest is nonpartisan and gives both official information and extracts from speeches and other comments published in the periodical press.

The bibliography is divided into four parts: A. General books on imperialism and colonialism, including textbooks, which cover mainly the period up to 1939, though they may cover later material also; B. More specialized studies covering the same period; C. General books covering the retreat from colonialism after 1939; D. More specialized regional studies. Since more books are listed for Africa than for all the others combined, Section D is divided into two parts, the first for Africa and the second for the other areas.

A. General Works Covering the Period to 1939

BODELSEN, C. A. *Studies in Mid-Victorian Imperialism.* New York: W. S. Heinman, 1924.

376 Bibliography

BURT, A. P. *The Evolution of the British Empire and Commonwealth*. Boston: D. C. Heath & Company, 1956. Standard text.

Cambridge History of the British Empire. New York: The Macmillan Company, 1929–40. Especially Vol. V on the Indian Empire.

Cambridge History of the British Empire. Vol. III. New York: Cambridge University Press, 1959.

CARRINGTON, C. E. *The British Overseas*. New York: Cambridge University Press, 1950. A detailed text, occasionally critical but usually strongly pro-British.

CLARK, GROVER. *The Balance Sheets of Imperialism: Facts and Figures on Colonies*. New York: Columbia University Press, 1936. Argues that expenses exceeded returns.

EDWARDES, MICHAEL. *Asia in the European Age, 1498–1955*. New York: Frederick A. Praeger, 1962. A general survey.

FEIS, HERBERT. *Europe, the World's Banker*. New York: Augustus M. Kelley, 1930.

GARVIN, J. L. *Life of Joseph Chamberlain*. 4 vols. New York: St Martin's Press, 1932–34. Vols. III and IV cover the career of Chamberlain at the Colonial Office.

HEUSSLER, RORERT. *Yesterday's Rulers: The Making of the British Colonial Service*. Syracuse, N.Y.: Syracuse University Press, 1963.

HOBSON, J. A. *Imperialism*. New York: The Macmillan Company, 1933. This classic attack on imperialism, which first appeared in 1902, has never been allowed to go out of print.

KNAPLUND, PAUL. *The British Empire, 1815–1939*. New York: Harper and Brothers, 1941. Standard earlier text.

LANGER, WILLIAM L. *The Diplomacy of Imperialism, 1890–1902*. New York: Alfred A. Knopf, 1935.

LENIN, V. I. *Imperialism: the Highest Stage of Capitalism*. New York: International Publishers, 1939. Influential Marxist critique.

MOON, PARKER T. *Imperialism and World Politics*. New York: The Macmillan Company, 1926.

MUIR, RAMSEY. *The Expansion of Europe*. London: Constable and Co., 1926.

ROBINSON, R. *Africa and the Victorians*. New York: St Martin's Press, 1961.

SEELEY, J. R. *The Expansion of England*. New York: The Macmillan Company, 1902. Influential lectures first given in 1883, at the beginning of the new age of expansion.

SNYDER, LOUIS L. *The Imperialism Reader*. Princeton, N.J.: D. Van Nostrand Co., 1962. Valuable collection of documents and comments from various writers on different aspects of imperialism.

STRAUSS, WILLIAM L. *Joseph Chamberlain and the Theory of Imperialism*. Washington, D.C.: Public Affairs Press, 1942.

THORNTON, A. P. *The Imperial Idea and Its Enemies*. New York: St Martin's Press, 1959.

TOWNSEND, MARY E. *European Colonial Expansion Since 1871.* Philadelphia: J. B. Lippincott Co., 1941.

WALTERS, F. P. *History of the League of Nations.* 2 vols. New York: Oxford University Press, 1952.

WILLIAMSON, JAMES A. *A Short History of British Expansion: The Modern Empire and Commonwealth.* 4th ed. New York: St Martin's Press, 1953. Standard British text.

WINSLOW, E. M. *The Pattern of Imperialism.* New York: Columbia University Press, 1948.

WRIGHT, HARRISON M. *The New Imperialism.* Boston: D. C. Heath & Company, 1961. (Available only in paperback.) Contains extracts from the works of various writers with opinions on the nature and value of imperialism.

B. Specialized Studies Covering the Period to 1939

ANTONIUS, G. *The Arab Awakening.* Philadelphia: J. B. Lippincott Co., 1939. A pioneer work on the Arab attitude to the postwar settlements.

BAUER, LUDWIG. *Leopold the Unloved.* Boston: Little, Brown & Co., 1935. Critical account of the beginnings of the Congo Independent State.

BUELL, RAYMOND V. *The Native Problem in Africa.* 2 vols. New York: The Macmillan Company, 1928. This standard work on the subject in its time is still useful.

BURNS, ALAN C. *A History of the British West Indies.* New York: The Macmillan Company, 1954.

CADY, J. F. *The Roots of French Imperialism in Eastern Asia.* Ithaca, N.Y.: Cornell University Press, 1954.

COUPLAND, R. *East Africa and Its Invaders.* Oxford: The Clarendon Press, 1938.

———. *The Exploitation of East Africa.* London: Faber and Faber, 1939.

———. *India: A Restatement.* New York: Oxford University Press, 1946.

EVANS, I. L. *The British in Tropical Africa.* New York: The Macmillan Company, 1929.

FISHER, S. N. *The Middle East: A History.* New York: Alfred A. Knopf, 1959. Contains useful material on the nineteenth and twentieth centuries.

FLINT, J. E. *Sir George Goldie and the Making of Nigeria.* New York: Oxford University Press, 1960.

FORBES, WILLIAM C. *The Philippine Islands.* 2 vols. Boston: Houghton Mifflin Company, 1928.

FRIEDEL, FRANK. *The Splendid Little War.* Boston: Little, Brown & Co., 1958. The war of 1898.

FURNIVALL, J. S. *Colonial Policy and Practice: A Comparative Study of Burma and Netherlands India.* New York: New York University Press, 1956.

―――. *Netherlands India: A Study of a Plural Economy.* Cambridge, England: Cambridge University Press, 1939. Two pioneer studies, still the best in the field.

GROSS, F. A. *Rhodes of Africa.* New York: Frederick A. Praeger, 1957.

GRUNDER, GAREL, and LIVEZEY, WILLIAM E., *The Philippines and the United States.* Norman, Okla.: University of Oklahoma Press, 1951.

HAILEY, LORD. *African Survey.* 2d ed. Revised by Margery Perham. New York: Oxford University Press, 1956. An enormous work, full of important material.

HAYDEN, J. R. *The Philippines: A Study in National Development.* New York: The Macmillan Company, 1942. The author is a former Governor of the Philippines.

HEADLAM, CECIL (ed.). *The Milner Papers, South Africa, 1897–1899.* London: Cassell & Co., 1931. A work by the British High Commissioner who held office in the crucial years preceding the South African War.

LUCAS, CHARLES. *The Partition and Colonization of Africa.* Oxford: The Clarendon Press, 1922.

LUDOWYK, E. F. C. *The Story of Ceylon.* New York: Roy Publishers, 1962. The last third of this informative history is on the present century.

LUGARD, F. D. *Diaries,* ed. Margery Perham. Evanston, Ill.: Northwestern University Press, 1960–63. An invaluable firsthand account by the greatest of British administrators in Africa.

―――. *The Dual Mandate in British Tropical Africa.* 5th ed. Edinburgh and London: William Blackwood and Sons, 1963. Explains the Lugard system of "indirect rule."

―――. *The Rise of Our East African Empire.* Edinburgh and London: William Blackwood and Sons, 1893.

MACNAIR, J. *Livingstone the Liberator.* London: William Collins and Sons, 1940.

MAGNUS, PHILIP. *Gladstone.* New York: E. P. Dutton & Co., 1954.

―――. *Kitchener: Portrait of an Imperialist.* New York: E. P. Dutton & Co., 1959.

MANSERGH, NICHOLAS. *South Africa, 1906–1961: The Price of Magnanimity.* New York: Frederick A. Praeger, 1962. Brief but informative lectures.

MARLOWE, JOHN. *Anglo-Egyptian Relations, 1800–1953.* Chester Springs, Pa.: Dufour Publications, 1954.

MILLIAN, G. S. *Cecil Rhodes.* New York: Harper & Brothers, 1933.

NEHRU, JAWARHARLAL. *The Discovery of India.* New York: Peter Smith, 1960. (Also available in Anchor paperback.) The Indian

Prime Minister's severe critique of British policy, written while he was in jail.

OLIVER, ROLAND. *The Missionary Factor in East Africa.* London: Longmans, Green & Co., 1952.

————. *Sir Harry Johnston and the Scramble for Africa.* New York: St Martin's Press, 1957.

PARRY, J. H., and SHERLOCK, P. M. *A Short History of the West Indies.* New York: St Martin's Press, 1956.

PERKINS, D. *Hands Off: A History of the Monroe Doctrine.* Boston: Little, Brown & Co., 1941.

PRATT, JULIUS W. *America's Colonial Experiment.* Englewood Cliffs, N.J.: Prentice-Hall, 1950.

————. *Expansionists of 1898: The Acquisition of Hawaii and the Spanish Islands.* New York: Peter Smith, 1936.

PRIESTLEY, HERBERT I. *France Overseas: A Study of Modern Imperialism.* New York: Appleton-Century Company, 1938.

ROBERTS, S. H. *A History of French Colonial Policy, 1870–1925.* Chicago: King Co., 1929.

RUDIN, HARRY R. *The Germans in the Cameroons, 1884–1914: A Case Study in Modern Imperialism.* New Haven, Conn.: Yale University Press, 1938.

RUNCIMAN, STEVEN. *The White Rajahs, A History of Sarawak from 1841 to 1946.* New York: Cambridge University Press, 1960.

SANDERSON, GORHAM D. *India and British Imperialism.* New York: Bookman Associates, 1951. Well documented but furiously anti-British attack on the British Raj. Valuable contrast to the customary self-praise of British writers.

SCHNEE, HEINRICH. *German Colonization: Past and Future.* London: George Allen and Unwin, 1926. An apologia by a former Governor of German East Africa.

SHEEAN, VINCENT. *Mahatma Gandhi.* New York, Alfred A. Knopf, 1955. A sympathetic biography.

SHUSTER, W. MORGAN. *The Strangling of Persia.* New York: The Century Company, 1920.

SINGLETON-GATES, PETER, and GIRODIAS, MAURICE (eds.). *The Black Diaries of Roger Casement.* New York: Grove Press, 1959. Contains the famous exposé of Leopold's regime in the Congo.

SLADE, RUTH. *King Leopold's Congo.* New York: Oxford University Press, 1962.

SMITH, V. H. *The Oxford History of India.* 3d ed. New York: Oxford University Press, 1958.

SPEAR, PERCIVAL. *India: A Modern History.* Ann Arbor: University of Michigan Press, 1961. About one-fifth of this book covers the years since 1914.

STANLEY, HENRY MORTON. *The Congo and the Founding of Its Free State.* 2 vols. London: Sampson, Low, 1885.

STANLEY, HENRY MORTON. *In Darkest Africa.* London: Sampson, Low, 1890.

———. *Through the Dark Continent.* London: Sampson, Low, 1878. These three books duplicate each other to some degree, but among them contain the journalist-explorer's own accounts of his voyages.

STANLEY, RICHARD, and NEAME, ALAN (eds.). *The Exploration Diaries of H. M. Stanley.* New York: Vanguard Press, 1963. Recently discovered and hitherto unpublished diaries of the explorer, written on his second and most important journey. Valuable to read in conjunction with his books, which unlike the diaries were tailored for publication.

TOWNSEND, MARY E. *The Rise and Fall of Germany's Colonial Empire, 1884–1918.* New York: The Macmillan Company, 1930.

WALKER, E. A. *A History of South Africa.* 2d ed. London: Longmans, Green & Co., 1940.

WARHURST, P. R. *Anglo-Portuguese Relations in South Central Africa, 1890–1900.* New York: Longmans, Green & Co., 1962.

WEINBERG, A. K. *Manifest Destiny: A Study of Nationalist Expansion in American History.* New York: Peter Smith, 1958.

WIESCHOFF, H. A. *Colonial Policies in Africa.* Philadelphia: University of Pennsylvania Press, 1944.

WILLIAMS, BASIL. *Botha, Smuts and South Africa.* New York: The Macmillan Company, 1948.

———. *Cecil Rhodes.* London: Constable & Co., 1921.

C. General Works on the Modern Period

BRADLEY, KENNETH (ed.). *The Living Commonwealth.* London: Hutchinson & Co., 1961. Various writers attempt to explain the Commonwealth.

BURNS, ALAN C. *In Defence of Colonies: British Colonial Territories in International Affairs.* New York: The Macmillan Company, 1957. A spirited defense by a former British colonial governor.

CARRINGTON, C. E. *The Liquidation of the British Empire.* London: Harrap, 1961. Lectures on what Carrington calls "the new partition of Africa."

EASTON, STEWART C. *The Twilight of European Colonialism: A Political Analysis.* New York: Holt, Rinehart & Winston, 1960. Primarily a study of the political forms under which the steps toward independence were taken.

EMERSON, RUPERT. *From Empire to Nation.* Cambridge, Mass.: Harvard University Press, 1960. (Also available in Beacon paperback.)

GOLDBERG, HARVEY. *French Colonialism: Progress or Poverty?* Holt, Rinehart & Winston, 1959. (Available only in paperback.)

INGRAM, DEREK. *The Commonwealth Challenge.* London: George Allen and Unwin, 1962. The contemporary operations of the Commonwealth.

JENNINGS, W. I. *The Approach to Self-Government.* New York: Cambridge University Press, 1956. Broadcast lectures by a British constitutional expert.

MANSERGH, NICHOLAS, et al. *Commonwealth Perspectives.* Durham, N.C.: Duke University Press, 1958. Brief studies by several scholars.

MANSUR, FATMA. *The Process of Independence.* New York: Humanities Press, 1962. Study by a Turkish sociologist of the stages by which independence was reached, using India, Pakistan, Indonesia, Ghana, and Nigeria as examples.

MILLER, J. D. B. *The Commonwealth in the World.* Cambridge, Mass.: Harvard University Press, 1959.

MOSELY, LEONARD. *The Last Days of the British Raj.* New York: Harcourt, Brace and World, 1962.

MURRAY, JAMES N., JR. *The United Nations Trusteeship System.* Urbana, Ill.: University of Illinois Press, 1957. An indispensable study.

PERHAM, MARGERY. *The Colonial Reckoning.* New York: Alfred A. Knopf, 1962.

PLAMENATZ, JOHN. *On Alien Rule and Self-Government.* New York: Longmans, Green & Co., 1960.

STRACHEY, JOHN. *The End of Empire.* New York: Random House, 1960.

STRAUSZ-HUPÉ, ROBERT, and HAZARD, HENRY W. (eds.). *The Idea of Colonialism.* New York: Frederick A. Praeger, 1958. Collection of writings on the meaning of imperialism and colonialism.

UNDERHILL, FRANK H. *The British Commonwealth: An Experiment in Cooperation Among Nations.* Durham, N.C.: Duke University Press, 1956. Three useful lectures.

WIGHT, MARTIN. *British Colonial Constitutions, 1947.* New York: Oxford University Press, 1952. Indispensable reference book on the various types of constitutions in the colonies before serious steps had been taken toward independence.

WISEMAN, H. V. *The Cabinet in the Commonwealth.* London: Stevens & Sons, 1958. Contains much detailed information on the functioning of colonial governments.

D. Regional Studies of the Modern Period

1. Africa

ADAM, THOMAS R. *Government and Politics in Africa South of the Sahara.* Rev. ed. New York: Random House, 1962. (Available only in paperback.)

ANDERSON, R. EARLE. *Liberia: America's African Friend.* Chapel Hill, N.C.: University of North Carolina Press, 1952.

APTER, DAVID. *The Gold Coast in Transition.* Princeton, N.J.: Princeton University Press, 1955.

APTER, DAVID. *The Political Kingdom in Uganda*. Princeton, N.J.: Princeton University Press, 1961.

ASHFORD, D. E. *Political Change in Morocco*. Princeton, N.J.: Princeton University Press, 1961.

AZIKIWE, NNAMDI. *Zik: A Selection from the Speeches of Nnamdi Azikiwe*. New York: Cambridge University Press, 1961. The author is the leading Nigerian nationalist.

BARBOUR, NEVILL (ed.). *A Survey of North West Africa*. New York: Oxford University Press, 1959. Includes Spanish Morocco.

BEHR, EDWARD. *The Algerian Problem*. New York: W. W. Norton & Company, 1962. A well-informed review of events from the beginning of the rebellion.

BELLO, AHMADU. *My Life*. New York: Oxford University Press, 1962. Autobiography of the Premier of Northern Nigeria and leader of the Northern People's Congress. Extremely informative on the struggle for independence and its difficulties.

BOURRET, F. *Ghana: the Road to Independence, 1919–1957*. Stanford, Calif.: Stanford University Press, 1960.

BURNS, ALAN C. *A History of Nigeria*. 5th ed. New York: The Macmillan Company, 1955.

CARTER, GWENDOLEN. *Independence for Africa*. New York: Frederick A. Praeger, 1960. (Also available in Praeger paperback.)

CHIDZERO, B. T. G. *Tanganyika and International Trusteeship*. New York: Oxford University Press, 1961.

CLARK, MICHAEL S. *Algeria in Turmoil*. New York: Frederick A. Praeger, 1959. (Also available in Universal paperback.) Well-informed, but strongly antinationalist.

COHEN, ANDREW. *British Policy in Changing Africa*. Evanston, Ill.: Northwestern University Press, 1959. The author is a former Governor of Uganda.

COLEMAN, JAMES S. *Nigeria: Background to Nationalism*. Berkeley, Calif.: University of California Press, 1958.

COWAN, L. GRAY. *Local Government in West Africa*. New York: Columbia University Press, 1958. Although concerned with local government, this book is especially useful as one of the few to deal comparatively with French and British institutions.

CREIGHTON, T. R. M. *Southern Rhodesia and the Central African Federation: the Anatomy of Partnership*. New York: Frederick A. Praeger, 1961.

CROWDER, MICHAEL. *A Short History of Nigeria*. New York: Frederick A. Praeger, 1962. A first-rate general survey from the earliest records to 1960.

DELAVIGNETTE, ROBERT. *Freedom and Authority in French West Africa*. New York: Oxford University Press, 1950.

———. *French Equatorial Africa*. New York: Hastings House, 1958.

DELF, GEORGE. *Jomo Kenyatta*. Garden City, N.Y.: Doubleday &

Company, 1961. A study fully exculpating Kenyatta from complicity in Mau Mau. See Majdalany, Fred.

DIA, MAMADOU. *The African Nations and World Solidarity*. New York: Frederick A. Praeger, 1961. (Also available in Praeger paperback.) Thoughts on the emerging nations of Africa by the former Prime Minister of Senegal, now serving a sentence in jail for conspiracy.

DUFFY, JAMES. *Portugal in Africa*. Cambridge, Mass.: Harvard University Press, 1962. A shorter version of *Portuguese Africa*, brought up to date to 1962.

————. *Portuguese Africa*. Cambridge, Mass.: Harvard University Press, 1959. An indispensable study.

DUNN, CYRIL. *Central African Witness*. London: Victor Gollancz, 1959. A firsthand report by a Rhodesian journalist.

EZERA, KALU. *Constitutional Developments in Nigeria*. New York: Cambridge University Press, 1960.

FABUNMI, L. A. *The Sudan in Anglo-Egyptian Relations*. New York: Longmans, Green & Co., 1960.

FAGE, J. D. *Ghana: A Historical Interpretation*. Madison, Wisc.: University of Wisconsin Press, 1959.

————. *A History of West Africa*. 2d ed. New York: Cambridge University Press, 1960. A short survey. (Also available in Cambridge paperback under the title *Introduction to the History of West Africa*.)

FITZGERALD, WALTER. *Africa: A Social, Economic, and Political Geography*. 9th ed. New York: E. P. Dutton & Co., 1961.

GANN, L. H. and DUIGNAN, P., *White Settlers in Tropical Africa*. Baltimore; Penguin Books, 1962. (Available only in paperback.)

GORDON, KING. *The United Nations in the Congo*. New York: Carnegie Endowment for International Peace, 1962.

HANNA, A. J. *The Story of the Rhodesias and Nyasaland*. New York: Humanities Press, 1961. A single-volume survey of the history of the three territories that formed the Federation.

HENNESSEY, MAURICE N. *The Congo: A Brief History and Appraisal*. New York: Frederick A. Praeger, 1961. A useful, compact introduction.

HODGKIN, THOMAS. *Nationalism in Colonial Africa*. New York: New York University Press, 1957.

HUXLEY, ELSPETH, and PERHAM, MARGERY. *Race and Politics in Kenya*. Hollywood, Fla.: Transatlantic Arts, 1956. The correspondence of the two authors with each other before the war, revised for publication. Mrs. Huxley, a long time resident of Kenya, proved a worse prophet than the colonial specialist.

INGHAM, KENNETH. *A History of East Africa*. New York: Frederick A. Praeger, 1962.

INGHAM, KENNETH. *The Making of Modern Uganda.* New York: The Macmillan Company, 1958.

JUNOD, V. I., and RESNICK, I. N. *The Handbook of Africa.* New York: New York University Press, 1963. A country-by-country handbook of reference information.

KARIUKI, JOSIAH M. *Mau Mau Detainee.* New York: Oxford University Press, 1963. This firsthand account by one of the men imprisoned for his part in the Mau Mau rebellion is remarkably lacking in bitterness. Nevertheless it is a damning picture of British rule during the "emergency," and is important to set beside the official histories of the period. The author is now an elected member of the Kenya National Assembly. Margery Perham has written an introduction.

KAUNDA, KENNETH. *Zambia Shall be Free.* New York: Frederick A. Praeger, 1963. Autobiography of the present leader of Northern Rhodesia, likely to be its first Prime Minister after independence.

KEATLEY, PATRICK. *The Politics of Partnership.* Baltimore: Penguin Books, 1963. (Available only in paperback.) Sad and indignant summary of the Federation of Rhodesia and Nyasaland.

KENT, RAYMOND K. *From Madagascar to the Malagasy Republic.* New York: Frederick A. Praeger, 1962. Political, economic, and social background of the Republic; the only available study in English.

LEGUM, COLIN. *Congo Disaster.* Baltimore: Penguin Books, 1961. Informative survey of the background to the Congo crisis. (Available only in paperback.)

———— (ed.). *Africa: A Handbook to the Continent.* New York: Frederick A. Praeger, 1962. Country-by-country survey, including general essays on art, culture, religion, etc.

LEYS, COLIN. *European Politics in Southern Rhodesia.* New York: Oxford University Press, 1959.

MAJDALANY, FRED. *State of Emergency: The Full Story of Mau Mau.* Boston: Houghton Mifflin Company, 1963. The author is a British journalist.

MAQUET, JACQUES J. *The Premise of Inequality in Ruanda.* New York: Oxford University Press, 1961. Study of the means by which the Batutsi dominated the Bahutu.

MARTELLI, GEORGE. *Leopold to Lumumba.* London: Chapman and Hall, 1962. Pro-Belgian account; the author thinks a great injustice was done to the Belgians.

MASON, PHILIP. *The Birth of a Dilemma.* New York: Oxford University Press, 1958. Detailed study of Rhodesia and the background to the Federation.

————. *Year of Decision: Rhodesia and Nyasaland in 1960.* New York: Oxford University Press, 1960. (Also available in Oxford paperback.)

MASON, PHILIP, et al. *Angola: A Symposium. Views of a Revolt.* New

York: Oxford University Press, 1962. Views, both pro- and anti-Portuguese, of Angola at the outbreak of the 1961 rebellion.

MERRIAM, ALAN P. *Congo: Background of Conflict.* Evanston, Ill.: Northwestern University Press, 1961. The most comprehensive study available.

MUKHERJEE, RAMKRISHNA. *The Problem of Uganda: A Study in Acculturation.* Berlin: Akademie-Verlag, 1956. Interesting and well-documented Marxist study.

NASSER, GAMAL. *Egypt's Liberation.* Washington, D.C.: Public Affairs Press, 1955.

————. *The Philosophy of the Revolution.* Washington, D.C.: Public Affairs Press, 1955. (Also available in Economica paperback.) By the principal actor in the drama.

NKRUMAH, KWAME. *Ghana: the Autobiography of Kwame Nkrumah.* Camden, N.J.: Thomas Nelson & Sons, 1957. In detailing the steps by which his country became independent, the President of Ghana provides much useful information, although it is naturally colored by his own opinions and desire for self-justification.

O'BRIEN, CONOR CRUISE. *To Katanga and Back.* New York: Simon and Schuster, 1963. This account of the efforts by the United Nations to restore Katanga to the Congolese Central Government, written by the chief United Nations representative, is an extremely one-sided picture and should be used with caution.

OKUMA, THOMAS. *Angola in Ferment.* Boston: Beacon Press, 1962. Discusses the growing nationalist movement and the nationalist parties.

PICKLES, DOROTHY. *Algeria and France: From Colonialism to Cooperation.* New York: Frederick A. Praeger, 1963. Concentrates on the impact of Algeria on France.

PORTER, ARTHUR T. *Creoledom.* London: Oxford University Press, 1963. Useful account of the differences in Sierra Leone between the Protectorate Africans and the descendants of freed slaves.

SHEPHERD, G. W., JR. *The Politics of African Nationalism.* New York: Frederick A. Praeger, 1962. A survey of various patterns of African nationalism: pro-Western, ultra-African, white racist, and others.

SILBERMAN, LEO. "Change and Conflict in the Horn of Africa," *Foreign Affairs,* July, 1959. One of the few accounts in English of the rise of Somali nationalism, written just prior to the independence of Somalia.

SLADE, RUTH. *The Belgian Congo.* New York: Oxford University Press, 1960. (Available only in paperback.) A brief survey.

SOUTHORN, LADY. *The Gambia.* New York: The Macmillan Company, 1952.

STILLMAN, CALVIN, et al. *Africa in the Modern World.* Chicago: University of Chicago Press, 1955. See especially the article in this collection by Kenneth Robinson, "Political Development in French

West Africa," which is one of the clearest accounts of the political structure under the *Union Française* before the passing of the *loi-cadre* in 1956.

TAYLOR, J. CLAGETT. *The Political Development of Tanganyika.* Stanford, Calif.: Stanford University Press, 1963. Brief political history from 1880 to 1961.

THOMPSON, VIRGINIA, and ADLOFF, RICHARD. *The Emerging States of French Equatorial Africa.* Stanford, Calif.: Stanford University Press, 1960.

————. *French West Africa.* Stanford, Calif.: Stanford University Press, 1958. Two of the solidest accounts in English. Especially useful for reference.

TILLION, GERMAINE. *Algeria: the Realities.* New York: Alfred A. Knopf, 1958.

————. *France and Algeria: Complementary Enemies.* New York: Alfred A. Knopf, 1961. Two fair and compassionate studies.

TOUVAL, SAADIA. *Somali Nationalism.* Cambridge, Mass.: Harvard University Press, 1963.

WALLERSTEIN, IMMANUEL. *Africa: the Politics of Independence.* Random House, 1961. (Vintage book original.) Interpretative essay on modern political developments concentrating on the African social structure.

WARD, W. E. F. *A History of Ghana.* New York: Frederick A. Praeger, 1963.

WIEDNER, DONALD L. *A History of Africa South of the Sahara.* New York: Random House, 1962. A convenient one-volume history with emphasis on recent developments.

WODDIS, JACK. *Africa: The Roots of Revolt.* New York: Citadel Press, 1961. (Available also in Citadel paperback.)

YANCY, ERNEST J. *The Republic of Liberia.* London: George Allen and Unwin, 1959. Simple but informative account of a semiofficial nature by a Liberian.

2. *Other Areas*

AYEARST, MORLEY. *The British West Indies.* New York: New York University Press, 1960.

BRAMELD, THEODORE. *Remaking of a Culture: Life and Education in Puerto Rico.* New York: Harper & Brothers, 1959.

BRECHER, M. *Nehru: A Political Biography.* New York: Oxford University Press, 1959.

————. *The Struggle for Kashmir.* New York: Oxford University Press, 1953.

BURNS, ALAN C. *Fiji.* The Corona Library. London: Her Majesty's Stationery Office, 1963.

CADY, JOHN F. *A History of Modern Burma.* Ithaca, N.Y.: Cornell University Press, 1958.

COLE, ALLAN B. *Conflict in Indochina and Its International Repercussions.* Ithaca, N.Y.: Cornell University Press, 1956.

COULTER, JOHN WESLEY. *The Pacific Dependencies of the United States.* New York: The Macmillan Company, 1958.

ENDACOTT, G. B. *A History of Hong Kong.* New York: Oxford University Press, 1958.

ESSAI, BRIAN. *Papua and New Guinea.* New York: Oxford University Press, 1962. A survey of the territory, its peoples, government, and economy.

HAIM, SYLVIA (ed.). *Arab Nationalism.* Berkeley, Calif.: University of California Press, 1962. A collection of writings by various authors.

HICKINBOTHAM, TOM. *Aden.* London: Constable and Co., 1958. The author is a former Governor who had previously been an unofficial in the Legislative Council. The book gives a valuable account of the activities of unofficials in British colonies.

HUREWITZ, J. C. *The Struggle for Palestine.* New York: W. W. Norton & Company, 1950.

JAGAN, CHEDDI. *Forbidden Freedom: The Story of British Guiana.* New York: International Publishers, 1954. The story of the suspension of the Guianan constitution in 1953, by the leading participant.

JEFFRIES, CHARLES. *Ceylon: the Path to Independence.* New York: Frederick A. Praeger, 1963.

JOSEPH, BERNARD. *British Rule in Palestine.* Washington, D.C.: Public Affairs Press, 1948.

KENNEDY, J. *A History of Malaya.* New York: St Martin's Press, 1962. Concise history, including nationalist developments and independence.

KAHIN, GEORGE McT. *Nationalism and Revolution in Indonesia.* Ithaca, N.Y.: Cornell University Press, 1957. Indispensable study.

LANCASTER, DONALD. *The Emancipation of French Indochina.* New York: Oxford University Press, 1961.

LEGGE, J. D. *Australian Colonial Policy.* Sydney, Australia: Angus Robertson, 1956.

LENCZOWSKI, G. *The Middle East in World Affairs.* 2d ed. Ithaca, N.Y.: Cornell University Press, 1956. Informative survey of the years since World War I.

LOWENTHAL, DAVID. *The West Indies Federation.* New York: Columbia University Press, 1961. Four essays on the political and social perspectives of the West Indies.

LONGRIGG, STEPHEN H. *Syria and Lebanon under French Mandate.* New York: Oxford University Press, 1958.

MAIR, LUCY P. *Australia in New Guinea.* London: Christophers, 1948.

MAUNG MAUNG. *Burma in the Family of Nations.* Amsterdam: Djanbatan, Ltd., 1956. Interesting observations on the independence struggle by a Burmese scholar.

MEADOWS, MARTIN. "The Philippine Claim to North Borneo," *Politi-*

cal Science Quarterly, September, 1962. The most comprehensive and clear account available.

MILLS, LENNOX. *Malaya: A Political and Economic Appraisal*. Minneapolis, Minn.: University of Minnesota Press, 1958. Covers the postwar period, but not independence.

PALMIER, LESLIE H. *Indonesia and the Dutch*. New York: Oxford University Press, 1962.

PERKINS, WHITNEY T. *Denial of Empire*. Leyden, Holland: Sijthoff, 1962. A study of the American experience in governing colonies and dependencies, including material on Alaska, Puerto Rico, Hawaii, the Virgin Islands, the Philippines, and the Pacific islands.

PHILIPS, C. H., *et al. The Evolution of India and Pakistan, 1858–1947.* New York: Oxford University Press, 1962. Documentary materials.

ROBEQUAIN, CHARLES. *Malaya, Indonesia, Borneo and the Philippines.* 2d ed. New York: Longmans, Green & Co., 1958.

ROSE, SAUL. *Britain and South East Asia*. Baltimore: The Johns Hopkins Press, 1962. Britain's role since the Japanese invasion.

SMITH, RAYMOND T. *British Guiana*. New York: Oxford University Press, 1962.

SPEAR, PERCIVAL. *India, Pakistan and the West*. 3d ed. New York: Oxford University Press, 1958.

TAYLOR, ALASTAIR. *Indonesian Independence and the United Nations*. Ithaca, N.Y.: Cornell University Press, 1960.

TOMASEK, ROBERT D. "British Guiana: A Case Study of British Colonial Policy," *Political Science Quarterly*, September, 1959. Excellent short study.

VLEKKE, B. H. M. *Nusantara—A History of Indonesia*. Chicago: Quadrangle Books, 1960.

WADDELL, D. A. G. *British Honduras: A Historical and Contemporary Survey*. New York: Oxford University Press, 1961.

WEST, FRANCIS. *Political Advancement in the South Pacific*. London: Oxford University Press, 1962. A comparative study of Fiji, French Polynesia, and American Samoa.

WILLIAMS, ERIC. *A History of the People of Trinidad and Tobago*. Port of Spain, Trinidad: P.N.M. Publishing Co., 1962. This study by the Prime Minister of the newly independent country, who is also a professional historian, is both informative and, under the circumstances, extremely objective.

WOODMAN, DOROTHY. *The Making of Burma to 1948*. London: Cresset Press, 1962.

Index